Theory of General Economic Equilibrium

£20·10

I

THEORY OF GENERAL ECONOMIC EQUILIBRIUM

TROUT RADER

Washington University
St. Louis, Missouri

1972

ACADEMIC PRESS   New York and London

ACADEMIC PRESS, INC.
111 Fifth Avenue, New York, New York 10003

United Kingdom Edition published by
ACADEMIC PRESS, INC. (LONDON) LTD.
24/28 Oval Road, London NW1

LIBRARY OF CONGRESS CATALOG CARD NUMBER: 70-182622

PRINTED IN THE UNITED STATES OF AMERICA

To my beautiful wife, Deanna

Contents

PART I

WELFARE

Chapter 1. **Efficiency**

Chapter 2. Optimality

PART II

STATICS

Chapter 3. Bargaining

Chapter 4. General Equilibrium

Chapter 5. Macrostatics

PART III

DYNAMICS

Chapter 6. **Classical Dynamics**

Chapter 7. **Adjustment Dynamics**

Chapter 8. **Stabilization**

References   343

Preface

This book is a survey of general economic equilibrium theory, written for professional economists and advanced graduate students in economics. It could serve as a main text for an advanced course in mathematical economics or general equilibrium theory or as a supporting text for the real theory of international trade. [For trade theory, the most important parts are Chapters 1 (Section 7), 2 (Sections 11 and 12), 5 (Sections 2–4), 6 (Section 1), and 8 (Problem G).]

The presentation reflects the author's special interests in several respects. Welfare economics is given first place in keeping with the view that economics must be a prescriptive science. Also, considerable time is devoted to dynamics even though it is likely that the dynamical theory has not reached its final form.

Prerequisites are first-year graduate theory and familiarity with economic applications of matrix algebra, advanced calculus, and elementary set theory and topology. All these can be obtained from study of my book, *Theory of Microeconomics*, Academic Press, which hereafter will be referred to as the companion volume. It is not a prerequisite for this volume, but at least the reader should have mastered some elements of modern mathematical economic theory before serious study of general equilibrium. Possible alternative sources would be Koopman's *Three Essays on the State of the Economic Science*, Lancaster's *Mathematical Economics*, and Quirk and Saposnik's *Introduction to General Equilibrium Theory and Welfare Economics*, or even specialized books like Katzner's *Static Demand Theory*. A somewhat more difficult beginning could be made with Debreu's *Theory of Value*.

Material published here for the first time includes several results on welfare economics (Chapter 2), theory of bargaining (Chapter 3), an asset–price adjustment model (Chapter 7), and a theory of stabilization (Chapter 8). It is hoped that the professional economist will find these chapters of special interest.

In the figure below the interrelationships between the various chapters is indicated. Solid arrows show when one chapter or section is a prerequisite for another. Dotted arrows indicate cases where one section or chapter may help in understanding another, although there is no necessary order of study.

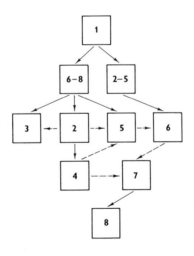

Acknowledgments

I am indebted to lectures and/or conversations with T. Bergstrom (Chapters 2, 4–6), G. Debreu (Chapters 2, 4–6), L. McKenzie (Chapters 1, 2, 4–7), T. C. Koopmans (Chapters 1, 2, 4–6), L. Hurwicz (Chapters 2, 6), J. Chipman (Chapters 2, 5), and H. Scarf (Chapters 3, 4, 7). I am also indebted to J. Ochs (Chapters 5, 6), J. Moore (Chapter 2), W. Hildenbrand (Chapters 2, 4), H. Sonnenschein (Chapter 5), R. Clower (Chapters 6, 7), J. Quirk (Chapters 5, 7), L. Shapley (Chapters 2, 3), R. Aumann (Chapter 3), J. Tobin (Chapter 7), H. Minsky (Chapter 7), R. Cornwall (Chapter 2), R. Starr (Chapter 4), A. Kermin (Chapter 3), J. Green (Chapter 3), J. Harsanyi (Chapter 3), and R. Utz (Chapter 6).

The book would not have been completed without my wife's encouragement. For typing, I am indebted to her and to Mrs. Vicki Ibera, Mrs. Pat Denault, Mrs. Bess Erlich, Miss Bonnie Moore, Miss Barbara Silverman, Miss Cathy Todd, Mrs. Helen Reed, and Mrs. Margerie Adams.

List of Special Definitions[1]

A definition of $x^n \to x$ defines a topology. $\mathscr{A} \subset \mathscr{X}$ is closed in $\mathscr{X}$ if $x^n \in \mathscr{A}$, $x^n \to x$, $x \in \mathscr{X}$ imply $x \in \mathscr{A}$. The closure of $\mathscr{A}$ is the smallest closed set containing $\mathscr{A}$. A set $\mathscr{B} \subset \mathscr{X}$ is open if $\mathscr{A} \sim \mathscr{B}$ is closed. If the closure of a set contains no open sets, the set is nowhere dense. The set is first category if it is the countable union of nowhere dense sets. A topology requires that the union of open sets is open and the intersection of closed sets is closed. Also the finite intersection of open sets is open and the finite union of closed sets is closed. Finally, the universe and the empty sets are both open and closed. A space is connected if it is not the union of two open subsets whose intersection is empty. A space is separable if it has a countable subset whose closure is the space. A space is completely separable if there are a countable number of open sets from which any other open set may be constructed by unions and/or finite intersections.

A function $f : \mathscr{X} \to \mathscr{Y}$ is continuous if the inverse image of open sets is open. f is concave if $f(tx + (1 - t)y) \geqslant tf(x) + (1 - t) f(y)$ for $1 \geqslant t \geqslant 0$. It is strictly concave if $f(tx + (1 - t)y) > tf(x) + (1 - t) f(y)$ for $1 > t > 0$. It is quasiconcave if $f(tx + (1 - t)y) \geqslant \min(f(x), f(y))$ for $1 \geqslant t \geqslant 0$. It is

---

[1] See also the companion volume.

strictly quasi concave if $f(tx + (1-t)y) > \min(f(x), f(y))$ for $1 > t > 0$.
f is differentiable if there is a matrix, $\partial f / \partial x$, such that

$$\lim_{y \to x} \left(\frac{f(y) - f(x)}{|x - y|} - \frac{\partial f}{\partial x} \frac{y - x}{|y - x|} \right) = 0.$$

f is a homeomorphism if f^{-1} is a function and both f and f^{-1} are continuous.
f is homogeneous of degree n if $f(tx) = t^n f(x)$, $t \geqslant 0$. It is linear homogeneous
if $f(tx) = tf(x)$, $t \geqslant 0$.

A relation $\mathscr{R}$ is a subset of $\mathscr{X} \times \mathscr{X}$, ordinarily written as $x \mathscr{R} y$ equivalent to
$(x, y) \in \mathscr{R}$. $\mathscr{R}$ is reflexive if $x \mathscr{R} x$. It is complete if either $x \mathscr{R} y$ or $y \mathscr{R} x$. It is
transitive if $x \mathscr{R} y$, $y \mathscr{R} z$ implies $x \mathscr{R} z$. $\mathscr{R}$ is a partial ordering if it is reflexive
and transitive. $\mathscr{R}$ is an ordering if it is reflexive, complete, and transitive. $\mathscr{R}$ is
lexicographic if there are relations $\mathscr{R}_1$, $\mathscr{R}_2$ such that

(a) $\mathscr{R}_i \neq \mathscr{X} \times \mathscr{X}, \mathscr{R}_i \neq \bigcup_{x \in \mathscr{X}} (x, x)$, $i = 1, 2$.

(b) $x \mathscr{R} y$ if $x \mathscr{R}_1 y$, unless also $y \mathscr{R}_1 x$ whereupon $x \mathscr{R} y$ if also $x \mathscr{R}_2 y$.

In $\mathscr{E}^n$ the measure of a hyper-rectangle with sides of length l_i is $\prod_{i=1}^{n} l_i$. A set
in $\mathscr{E}^n$ has measure zero if it can be covered with rectangles having arbitrarily
small summed measure.

A Metzler–Mosak matrix, A, is one which has positive off-diagonals and
negative diagonals.

Let $2^{\mathscr{X}} = \{\mathscr{X}' \mid \mathscr{X}' \subset \mathscr{X}\}$.

Axiom of Choice.   There exists a function

$$c : 2^{\mathscr{X}} \to \mathscr{X}$$

such that $c(\mathscr{X}') \in \mathscr{X}'$ for all $\mathscr{X}' \in 2^{\mathscr{X}}$.

Let $\vartheta, n \subset 2^{\mathscr{X}}$. Then n is a nest in ϑ if

(i) $\vartheta \supset n$ and

(ii)   for $\mathscr{Y}, \mathscr{Z} \in n$, either

$$\mathscr{Y} \subset \mathscr{Z} \quad \text{or} \quad \mathscr{Z} \subset \mathscr{Y}.$$

The nest n is maximal in ϑ if also

(iii)   If $\{\mathscr{W}\} \cup n$ is a nest in ϑ, then $\mathscr{W} \in n$.

Maximal Principle (Equivalent to the Axiom of Choice)   For every nest n in
$\vartheta \subset 2^{\mathscr{X}}$, there is a maximal nest $n' \supset n$. The word maximal is often used with
the meaning, largest possible collection of subsets satisfying certain properties,
whether or not it is applied to a nest.

A set is X convex if $tx + (1 - t)y \in X$ whenever $x, y \in X$ and $0 \leqslant t \leqslant 1$. A set is strictly convex if $tx + (1 - t)y \in \text{Int } X$ whenever $x, y \in X$ and $0 < t < 1$. A set is strongly convex if it is convex and $tx + (1 - t)y \in \text{Int } X$ whenever $x, y \in X$, $0 < t < 1$, and $x \neq ky$ for $k \in E^1$.

Minkowski's Theorem. If X is a convex subset of E^n, $x \in \text{Bnd } X$, then there exists a $p \neq 0$ such that $py \geqslant px$ for all $y \in X$.

List of Notational Conventions and Basic Symbols

Capital script letters	Sets, e.g., $\mathscr{A}$
Lower case script letters	Traditional economic notations, e.g., mc
Capital Latin letters	Matrices
Lower case Latin letters	Points, vectors, and numbers
Lower case Greek letters	Numbers

$x \in \mathscr{A}$	x is a member of $\mathscr{A}$
$x \notin \mathscr{A}$	x is not a member of $\mathscr{A}$
$\mathscr{A} \subset \mathscr{B}$	$\mathscr{A}$ is contained in $\mathscr{B}$
$\{x \mid P\}$	The set of x satisfying proposition P
$\mathscr{A} \cup \mathscr{B}$	The set union of $\mathscr{A}$ and $\mathscr{B}$
$\mathscr{A} \cap \mathscr{B}$	The set intersection of $\mathscr{A}$ and $\mathscr{B}$
$\mathscr{B} \sim \mathscr{A}$	The set of points in $\mathscr{B}$ but not in $\mathscr{A}$
$\sim \mathscr{A}$	The set of points not in $\mathscr{A}$
$\varnothing$	The empty set
$\{x\}$	The singleton set of x
$\mathscr{A} \times \mathscr{B}$	The cartesian product of $\mathscr{A}$ and $\mathscr{B}$
$P_{\mathscr{S}}(\mathscr{A})$	The projection of $\mathscr{A}$ on $\mathscr{S}$
$\bigcup\limits_{\alpha \in \mathscr{A}} \mathscr{B}_{\alpha}$	The set union of $\mathscr{R}_{\alpha}$, α in $\mathscr{A}$
$\bigcap\limits_{\alpha \in \mathscr{A}} \mathscr{B}_{\alpha}$	The set intersection of $\mathscr{B}_{\alpha}$, α in $\mathscr{A}$

$\underset{\alpha \in \mathscr{A}}{\times} \mathscr{B}_\alpha$	The cartesian product of $\mathscr{B}_\alpha$, α in $\mathscr{A}$
$\mathscr{R}$	A reflexive, binary relation
$\mathscr{P}$	An irreflexive binary relation
$\mathscr{I}$	An equivalence relation
$2^{\mathscr{S}}$	The set of subsets of $\mathscr{S}$
$\mathscr{R}(x)$	$\{y \mid y \, \mathscr{R} \, x\}$
$\lim x_n$	The limit of x_n
$x_n \to x$	The limit of x_n is x
$\overline{\mathscr{A}}$	The closure of $\mathscr{A}$
Bnd $\mathscr{A}$	The boundary of $\mathscr{A}$
Int $\mathscr{A}$	The set of internal points of $\mathscr{A}$
$f(x)$	The function f evaluated at x
f^{-1}	The inverse correspondence for the function f
$\| x \|$	The norm of x
$N_\epsilon(x)$	The ϵ neighborhood of x
$x = (x_1, ..., x_n)$	A row vector
x'	A column vector
$x \geqslant y$	$x_i \geqslant y_i$ for all i
$x > y$	$x_i \geqslant y_i$ for all i and for some j, $x_j > y_j$
$x \gg y$	$x_i > y_i$ for all i
(x, y)	The set of points between x and y according to the (partial) ordering $\gg$
$\langle x, y \rangle$	The line segment between and including x and y
Ω	The nonnegative orthant
$(x_\alpha, \alpha \in \mathscr{A})$	The abstract vector with coordinate index set, $\mathscr{A}$
$x_{\mathscr{I}}$	The vector with coordinates only in $\mathscr{I}$
$\underset{\alpha \in \mathscr{A}}{\Sigma} x_\alpha$	The sum of vectors in $\mathscr{A}$
$\| x \|$	$(\Sigma x_i^2)^{1/2}$
$\mathscr{A} + \mathscr{B}$	The set of all sums of pairs of elements, one in $\mathscr{A}$ and one in $\mathscr{B}$
$-\mathscr{B}$	The set of elements whose negatives are in $\mathscr{B}$
$a\mathscr{B}$	The set of elements which when divided by a are in $\mathscr{B}$
Δx	The change in x
(a_{ij})	The matrix with typical elements, a_{ij}
$\int f(x) \, dx$	The integral of f over linear measure
df/dx	The derivative of f with respect to x
f'	The derivative of f with respect to x
$\partial f/\partial x_i$	The partial derivative of f with respect to x_i
$(\partial f/\partial x_i)$	The vector of partial derivatives of f
$\lim \inf$	The greatest lower bound
$\lim \sup$	The least upper bound
$E(x)$	The expected value of x

I

Welfare

1

Efficiency

. . . largely the same fund of technical knowledge and experience is utilized under an amazing variety of institutional arrangements, ranging all the way from American corporate and individual enterprise to Soviet communism. Within Western "capitalism," governmental and private enterprise operate side by side in different or even in the same industries. Within the private "Sector," the problems of explaining how production tasks are distributed as between different firms, and of recommending how they could best be distributed, belong to one of the most challenging and least clarified areas of economics. There is therefore a need for the evaluation of institutional arrangements as well as for the prediction of production capabilities in any particular institutional setting. To make progress in these various directions, it may help to start from models that formalize nothing but the range of technological alternatives open to a producing organization, ... In this way the character and range of the possible decisions are clarified before the decision makers, their functions and their incentives enter upon the stage of the analysis.

Tjalling Koopmans

in THREE ESSAYS ON THE STATE
OF THE ECONOMIC SCIENCE, 1957, page 71[1]

---

[1] Quoted by permission, McGraw-Hill Book Company, New York.

3

1. Existence of Efficient Paths

The theory of efficient production and growth is a vestigial form of general equilibrium theory, where consumer preferences play a subordinate role. For the case where preferences satisfy appropriate conditions, efficiency theory is superseded as normative analysis by optimality theory (Chapters 2, 4, 6). For cases where markets are well organized, efficiency theory is superseded as positive analysis by the general theory of markets (Chapters 3–5, 7, 8). However, efficiency is crucial whenever consumer preferences are not known—as in a Soviet-type economy—or when criteria for development other than consumer sovereignty are being applied—as in many noncapitalist economies. Furthermore, from a welfare viewpoint, optimization of preferences may not be desirable. For example, over infinite time, optimization of consumer preferences leads to the decline of many families (Chapter 6). Therefore alternative schemes of social choice should be found. Sometimes the simplest way to find them is to abstract from consumer preferences and consider various technical possibilities. Among these there may appear "natural" social choices.

Points described by an industry production function relating outputs to inputs have the property that, given inputs, no greater outputs can be obtained. Nevertheless, more output might be obtainable by the redistribution of inputs among industries. This leads to the notion of efficient input–outputs, whereby a maximal output is obtained from a minimal capital stock. This notion is easily extended to all industries where production factors are distributed so as to obtain a maximal output from the given factor supplies. Notice that the terms maximal and minimal have been used rather than maximum and minimum, the reason being that several commodities (factors) may be produced (used) with emphasis on one or another, depending on preference and factor supplies.

In view of the emphasis here on time, the problem of choice over time will be of special interest. In this context, when we pass from the mere existence of efficient paths to their various properties and characterizations, the assumptions of convexity and closedness of the production sets are of great help. The convexity assumption excludes increasing return to scale, and the use of the assumption therefore limits application. Hence, we put off the convexity assumption as long as possible (Section 2). Unfortunately, the theory of dynamic efficiency under increasing returns has not yet been developed along lines comparable to that of static efficiency. When a theory of dynamic efficiency without convexity is fully developed, it should start with the concepts of efficiency that have been studied in a world of convex production. Such a new theory will also benefit from the example of the theory prevailing now.

In this section, several kinds of efficiency are considered and the existence of efficient production paths is proved. As a prerequisite, the mathematics of optimization is explained in the context of economic efficiency.

One particular concept is final state efficiency, whereby the economy seeks to accomplish a certain target capital stock at some future date. Various types of final state efficiency are studied in Sections 2–5. The general concept of efficiency is treated more fully in Sections 6–8, which do not require preparation beyond this section. However, the sections on final state efficiency give a detailed study of systems that are less general than those in Sections 6–8. Therefore, Sections 2–5 may provide some insight into possible applications of the results in the later sections.

Normally, the analysis of efficiency is fairly straightforward. This was the case in Chapter 4 on production in the companion volume. However, such a simple theory is possible only in finite-dimensional space. With an infinite time horizon, it is necessary to proceed with more caution and in more detail. Even the definition of efficiency allows more variety.

There are two main notions of efficiency in the literature on production economics. The first is so-called *Malinvaud efficiency* (Malinvaud [1953]), whereby we seek maximal consumption paths over time. This can be characterized by the artifice of distinguishing goods according to whether they are only consumer goods or are used for production purposes. Pure consumer goods do not grow without the presence of producer goods, and consumer nondurables (which are the kinds of consumer goods normally analyzed in this framework) have very rapid decay; that is, in the absence of producer goods, only a decrease in total commodities is possible, and with a preponderance of consumer nondurables this decrease is rapid. Hence, Malinvaud efficient paths are those which exphasize consumer goods and include producer goods only to the extent that they are necessary for production of future consumer goods.

The second notion of efficiency, due to Dorfman, Samuelson, and Solow [1958], is efficiency with respect to final state of capital goods. Here producer goods are emphasized to the exclusion of any unproductive consumer goods.

Let $_t\mathscr{Y}_{t+1}(y)$ be the set of outputs in time $t + 1$ that can be attained from a capital stock of y in time t. Let $_0\mathscr{Y}_\infty(y(0))$ be the set of (infinite vectors of) outputs in times $t = 1, 2,...$ attainable from $y(0)$ in time zero.

A path of capital stocks

$$(y(t), \quad t = 1, 2,...) \in {}_0\mathcal{Y}_\infty(y(0))$$

is *efficient* if there does not exist in ${}_0\mathcal{Y}_\infty(y(0))$ a path

$$\bar{y}(t) \geqslant y(t)$$

but

$$\bar{y}(t) \neq y(t)$$

(that is, $\bar{y}_k(t) > y_k(t)$ for some t and some k) for some $\bar{y}(t)$ in ${}_0\mathcal{Y}_\infty(y(0))$. We consider subsets of commodity types $\mathcal{I}_t$, $t = 0, 1,...$. The path

$$(y(t), \quad t = 0, 1, 2,...) \in {}_0\mathcal{Y}_\infty(y(0))$$

is $\mathcal{I}_t$-*efficient* if there does not exist a ($\bar{y}(t)$, $t = 0, 1, 2,...$) such that

$$\bar{y}_i(t) \geqslant y_i(t)$$

for all i in $\mathcal{I}_t$, for all t, and

$$\bar{y}_{i_0}(t_0) < y_{i_0}(t_0)$$

for some i_0 in $\mathcal{I}_t$. If $\mathcal{I}_t$ is exactly the set of consumer goods, the concept of $\mathcal{I}_t$-efficiency is that of Malinvaud efficiency. If $\mathcal{I}_t$ is empty except for period t, $\mathcal{I}_t$-efficiency is *final state efficiency* for the time period $[0, t]$. More generally, infinite paths are considered and referred to as *t-state efficient* paths.

A particular version of efficiency that does not fit into the foregoing definition is that of the *intertemporally efficient* (I.E.) *path* (first analyzed by Furuya and Inada [1962]). This is the path that is final state efficient for all t. Since it has a "large" capital stock for each period, it is of some interest. Actually, in certain circumstances, the I.E. path eventually gives larger quantities of each good than any other path (Section 4). Each generation will prefer that path which obtains for it a high proportion of consumer goods. Normally, consumer goods are less productive than other goods, and excessive production of consumer goods today will cut down on that which is available for later generations. Therefore, in comparison with another path, the (unique) I.E. path will be preferred by an infinite number of generations and the other will receive only a finite number of votes. Oddly enough, for any given generation t, there is always one path that it prefers, which is t-state efficient but which also has a large percentage of consumer goods in time t. Hence, the I.E. path is never best for any generation, but it might be regarded as a golden rule compromise between generations, analogous to that defined by Robinson [1956] and Phelps [1961] in another context (Section 6).

The I.E. path represents the extreme instance of the Protestant ethic, where each generation, future or present, is weighted equally. Several justifications could be imagined for adopting the I.E. path; either for society or the family, it might be regarded as the method for maximizing the probability of the existence of future generations. To ensure against future contingencies, we might wish to maximize available physical resources. The survival of the society would be the justifying judgment.

In order to show the existence of efficient paths, some analytical techniques are developed. In the companion volume, it was shown that regular partial orderings take optima on compact sets (Section 3 of Chapter 5). This is the basic result for efficiency, since the relation optimized by efficient paths is regular in a topology in which the production possibilities are compact. In this way, optimization theory is based on preferences and on the set on which choice is made. Furthermore, it can be shown that this independence is the best available procedure. In the demonstration, we study compactness in a deeper way than in Chapter 2 of the companion volume. Then it is shown that $_0\mathscr{Y}_\infty$ is compact, and therefore efficient points exist. Finally, the case of I.E. paths requires a special consideration.

From a mathematical viewpoint, optimization proceeds as follows. Let $>$ be transitive and reflexive, and let it be *directed*, that is, if α, $\alpha' \in \mathscr{A}$, there exists $\alpha'' \in \mathscr{A}$ such that $\alpha'' > \alpha$, $\alpha'' > \alpha'$. Consider a *net* of points in $\mathscr{X}$,

$$x_\alpha , \qquad \alpha \in \mathscr{A},$$

$\mathscr{A}$ ordered by a directed partial ordering $>$,[1]

$$x_\alpha > x_{\alpha'} , \qquad x_\alpha \neq x_{\alpha'} ,$$

whenever

$$\alpha > \alpha', \qquad \alpha \neq \alpha'.$$

Note that a net is a generalized sequence in that it differs only insofar as the index set $\mathscr{A}$ need not be the set of positive integers. Construct a net as follows. So long as there exists an $x \in \mathscr{X}$ not equal to but at least as great as x_α, for all $\alpha \in \mathscr{A}$, expand $\mathscr{A}$ to still larger elements. Take a largest possible $\mathscr{A}$. If $>$ is a partial ordering, then it is a directed

---

[1] For our partial ordering $>$, we require $x > y$, $y > z$ implies $x > z$, not $x > x$; however, x and y may not be comparable under $>$.

partial ordering on $\{x_\alpha \mid \alpha \in \mathscr{A}\}$, which is therefore a net. Also, if there exists a maximal α in $\mathscr{A}$ with x_α that cannot be exceeded, then x_α is the maximal element in $\mathscr{A}$. What is required is that there be some x in $\mathscr{X}$ for which

$$x \geqslant x_\alpha, \qquad \alpha \in \mathscr{A}.$$

Whether such an x exists depends upon $\mathscr{X}$. Clearly, if

$$\mathscr{X} = (0, 1) \quad \text{or} \quad \mathscr{X} = (0, \infty),$$

there is no largest element in $\mathscr{X}$. Such cases can be excluded by making assumptions about closedness under appropriate kinds of convergence.

First, we define convergence and related concepts. A net $(x_\alpha, \alpha \in \mathscr{A})$ is *frequently* in $\mathscr{X}$ if for every $\alpha \in \mathscr{A}$, there is an $\alpha' \in \mathscr{A}$, $\alpha' > \alpha$, such that $x_{\alpha'} \in \mathscr{X}$. The net is *eventually* in $\mathscr{X}$ if there is an $\alpha \in \mathscr{A}$ such that for all $\alpha' > \alpha$, $x_{\alpha'} \in \mathscr{X}$. If for every open set $\mathcal{O}$ containing x, a net is frequently in $\mathcal{O}$, x is a *cluster (limit) point* of the net. If for every open set $\mathcal{O}$ containing x, a net is eventually in $\mathcal{O}$, the net *converges* to x.

Second, we consider nets in the context of the partial ordering to be optimized. A net is *monotone* if $x_{\alpha'} \geqslant x_\alpha$ whenever $\alpha > \alpha'$ or if $x_{\alpha'} \leqslant x_\alpha$ whenever $\alpha > \alpha'$. Let $x \geqslant x_\alpha$ for all $\alpha \in \mathscr{A}$ and there is no $y < x$ such that $y \geqslant x_\alpha$ for all $\alpha \in \mathscr{A}$. Then x is the monotone limit of the net $\{x_\alpha \mid \alpha \in \mathscr{A}\}$. It might be assumed that $\mathscr{X}$ is closed under monotone convergence, whereupon the limit of a maximal, monotone net would be the $\geqslant$ optimizer x. Of course, not all maximal nets have monotone limits. An example would be $\mathscr{E}^1$ under the relation $\geqslant$. (The maximal net is $\mathscr{E}^1$ itself.) At the very least, the maximal net must have a cluster point. More specifically, if every net has a cluster point, the set is *compact*. This definition is different from but implies the one in the companion volume (Exercise 8).

1 Remark An optimizer for a partial ordering $\mathscr{R}$ on $\mathscr{X}$ exists if $\mathscr{X}$ is compact in monotone convergence (defined in terms of $\mathscr{R}$).

Although the remark appears very powerful, in practice it is difficult to show compactness in the topology of monotone convergence. In some cases the maximal net will have no limit in a natural sense even though it has a monotone limit. For example, let $x \in \mathscr{E}^2$ be compared by

$$x \, \mathscr{R} \, x' \quad \text{if and only if} \quad x_2 \leqslant x_{2'}.$$

Then, the following is a sequence increasing under $\mathscr{R}$ that has no natural limit, even though it has a limiting level of preference under $\mathscr{R}$. Let $x = (0, 1)$.

$$x_i = \left(i, 1 - \frac{1}{i}\right), \qquad x_i \to (\infty, 1)$$

If

$$\mathscr{X} = \bigcup_{i=1}^{\infty} \{x_i\} \cup \{x\},$$

then clearly $\mathscr{X}$ has an optimum under $\mathscr{R}$, but the procedure above does not work unless we already know that x is the optimum. By considering the topology of the domain independently of the partial ordering, exactly these difficulties can be avoided, without going into a long discourse on the nature of a particular $\mathscr{R}$. Therefore, it is useful to consider certain cases where, for *every* net $(x_\alpha, \alpha \in \mathscr{A})$, there is a *convergent subnet* $(y_\beta, \beta \in \mathscr{B})$ defined as a net that has the property that $\mathscr{B} \subset \mathscr{A}$, and for any $\alpha \in \mathscr{A}$ there is a $\beta \in \mathscr{B}$ such that $\beta \geqslant \alpha$ and y_β converges to y. If $\mathscr{X}$ has the property that every net has a convergent subnet, it is said to be *compact*.

The conditions used that assure optimization are that the relation be regular and the domain compact in a natural topology, since then the domain will be compact in monotone convergence (Theorem 4 of Chapter 5 of the companion volume).

2 Lemma (Bolzano–Weierstrass)   *A set in Euclidean n-space is compact if, and only if, it is both bounded and closed.*

So long as we are in a finite-dimensional Euclidean space, Lemma 2 is a sufficient criterion for compactness. In infinite space, however, some ambiguity arises as to the meaning of convergence. Consider the case of sequences. Does $(x^n(i), i = 0, 1, 2,...)$ converge to x whenever $x^n(i)$ converges to $x(i)$, or must the convergence be more rapid? The answer depends on the context of the problem. Therefore, it is said that x^n converges *pointwise* to x if each $x^n(i)$ converges to $x(i)$. It is said that x^n converges *uniformly to x*, according to the metric d,[2] if

$$\sup_i d(x^n(i), x(i))$$

tends to zero. Alternatively, x^n converges uniformly to x if for $\varepsilon > 0$, there is an $N(\varepsilon)$ such that for all i

$$d(x^n(i), x(i)) < \varepsilon$$

---

[2] A metric satisfies the three requirements, $d(x, y) \geqslant 0$; $d(x, y) = 0$ only if $x = y$; $d(x, y) \leqslant d(x, z) + d(z, y)$.

whenever $n \geqslant N(\varepsilon)$. Evidently, it is harder for a sequence to converge uniformly than pointwise. Therefore, it is easier for a set to contain its limit points and there are more sets closed and open in uniform convergence than in pointwise convergence. For example, for

$$e_i = (0,...,0, \overset{i\text{th}}{1}, 0,...),$$

$\bigcup_{i=1}^{\infty} e_i$ is closed in the uniform convergence limit; since it does not include zero, it is not closed in pointwise convergence. Therefore, it is harder for a function to be continuous in pointwise convergence. For example, in $[0, 1]^{\infty}$, $f(x) = \sup x_i$ is continuous in uniform convergence but not in pointwise convergence.

The topology derived from pointwise convergence is usually referred to as the product topology, since the Tychonoff theorem applies:

3 Lemma   *The Cartesian product of compact sets is compact in pointwise convergence* (Kelley [1955], p. 143).

This is the basic result whenever we make use of the notion of pointwise convergence.

The following theorem shows compactness of the paths beginning from the initial stock of factors $y(0)$.

4 Theorem   *Suppose* $_i\mathscr{Y}_{t+1}(y(t))$ *is closed and bounded by* $k(t) \mid y(t)\mid$. *Then* $_0\mathscr{Y}_{\infty}(y(0))$ *is compact in the product topology and bounded by the metric*

$$\| _0y_{\infty} \| \equiv \sum_{t=0}^{\infty} \mid y(t)\mid \prod_{s=0}^{t-1} \frac{1}{(k(s))(2)^t} .$$

Proof

$$\mid y(t+1)\mid \leqslant k(t) \mid y(t)\mid, \qquad \mid y(t)\mid \leqslant \prod_{0}^{t-1} k(s) \mid y(0)\mid$$

and

$$\| _0y_{\infty} \| \leqslant \sum_{t=0}^{\infty} \frac{(\prod_0^{t-1} k(s))}{\prod_0^{t-1}(k(s))} \, 1/2^t \mid y(0)\mid$$

$$= \sum_{t=0}^{\infty} 1/2^t \mid y(0)\mid = \mid y(0)\mid.$$

Closedness follows from the closedness of $_i\mathscr{Y}_{t+1}$. Apply the Bolzano–Weierstrass and Tychonoff theorems (Lemmata 2 and 3).   q.e.d.

It is now easy to verify that an $\mathscr{I}_t$-efficient path exists, since we can take a net of ever greater paths.

5 Corollary *If $_t\mathscr{Y}_{t+1}$ is closed and $_t\mathscr{Y}_{t+1}(y(t))$ is bounded by $k(t) \mid y(t)\mid$, then there is an $\mathscr{I}_t$-efficient path $(y(t), t = 0, 1, 2,...)$ in $_0\mathscr{Y}_\infty(y)$ greater than or equal (in all components i in $\mathscr{I}$) to $(y(t), t = 0, 1, 2,...)$ in $_0\mathscr{Y}_\infty(y)$.*

It remains to derive conditions for the existence of intertemporally efficient paths. All that is necessary is to add the assumption that commodities are *(not negatively) productive*; that is, if

$$(y(t), t = 0, 1, 2,...) \in {}_0\mathscr{Y}_\infty(y(0)), \qquad \bar{y}(T) < y(T),$$

then there is a path $(\bar{y}(t), t = 0, 1,...) \in \mathscr{Y}(\bar{y}(0))$ such that $\bar{y}(t) > (\geqslant) y(t)$ for all $t > T$. In effect, the extra commodities in $\bar{y}(t)$ over $y(>t)$, once they appear, can cause an increase in production. Then we can extend final state efficient paths in time s to final state efficient paths in time t, obtaining a gradually decreasing set of paths which, as it turns out, must have a limit.

6 Theorem *Suppose $_t\mathscr{Y}_{t+1}(y)$ is bounded and closed and goods are productive. Then a time τ-final state efficient path is time σ-final state efficient for $\sigma < \tau$ and there is an intertemporally efficient path $(y(t), t = 0, 1, 2,...)$ in $_0\mathscr{Y}_\infty(y)$ (which is for each time $t > 0$ efficient in final state). The set of such intertemporally efficient paths is compact.*

If negatively productive goods have negative intrinsic (utility or market) value, then they can be regarded as having negative quantities and the foregoing theorem still applies, except that efficiency requires the minimization of the negatively productive goods.

The strategy of the proof of Theorem 6 is to proceed by induction; namely, by showing that a time t–final state efficient path can be made final state efficient for each earlier path. We then obtain a decreasing sequence of sets of final state efficient paths as $t \to \infty$. This decreasing sequence has a nonempty intersection, namely, the set for largest t. Applying the finite intersection property of compact sets (Exercise 9), we find that the intersection of the compact sets is nonempty; that is, there are limit paths. These limit paths are final state efficient for each t and are I.E. paths.

Proof Suppose $(y(t), t = 0, 1, 2,...)$ is τ_0-state efficient. Then for any time $\sigma \leqslant \tau_0$, there is a $(\bar{y}(t), t \in [0, \infty])$ that is σ-state efficient and for which

$$\bar{y}(\sigma) \geqslant y(\sigma).$$

If $\bar{y}(\sigma) \neq y(\sigma)$, then by virtue of the productivity of commodities, there is a path $\bar{y}$ such that

$$\bar{y}(t) = \bar{y}(t), \qquad 0 \leqslant t \leqslant \sigma,$$
$$\bar{y}(t) > y(t), \qquad t \geqslant \sigma.$$

In particular,

$$\bar{y}(\tau) \geqslant y(\tau),$$

whereupon by the time τ–final state efficiency of y,

$$\bar{y}(\tau) \geqslant y(\tau).$$

But then we have that

$$\bar{y}(\sigma) = y(\sigma)$$

or that $(y(t), t = 0, 1, 2,...,)$ is σ-efficient.

It is clear that the compact set of time t–final state efficient paths $t \leqslant \tau$, which will be denoted $\mathscr{V}_\tau$, is contained in the set of the t-efficient, time s–final state efficient paths $s \leqslant \sigma$, $\mathscr{V}_\sigma$ for $\sigma \leqslant \tau$. Therefore,

$$\bigcap_{\tau \in [0,\infty]} \mathscr{V}_\tau$$

is the compact intersection of decreasing compact sets.

For any finite intersection of the sets, the intersection is nonempty and, in particular, equal to $\mathscr{V}_\sigma$ for the largest σ in the finite set of time points that are the subscripts for the $\mathscr{V}_\tau$. Therefore, the finite intersection property for compact sets gives that the intersection is nonempty.

Consider x^n time t efficient, $x^n \to x$. There cannot exist y such that $y(t-1) > x(t-1)$, for then the extra goods could be utilized to obtain $y(t) \gg x(t)$ and therefore $y(t) \gg x^n(t)$ for large n, which is impossible. Therefore, $x(t)$ is time $t-1$ efficient. A path in the intersection is final state efficient for all time periods in $\bigcup_{t=0}^{\infty} \{t\}$ and is therefore an I.E. path.   q.e.d.

Exercise 1 Show that every bounded subset $\mathscr{X}$ of real numbers has a sequence $(x_i, i = 1,..., n)$, $x_i \in \mathscr{X}$, tending to its least upper bound (greatest lower bound).

Exercise 2 Show that every bounded sequence of real numbers $(x_i, i = 1,..., n)$ has a convergent subsequence.

Exercise 3 Show that every sequence of points in a bounded subset of $\mathscr{E}^n$ has a convergent subsequence.

Exercise 4 Let $\mathcal{X}$ be a metric space, that is to say, we define convergence in x with respect to a particular metric. Show that every cluster point for the net $(x_\alpha , \alpha \in \mathcal{A})$, $x_\alpha \in \mathcal{X}$, is the limit of a subnet that is also a sequence.

Exercise 5 Prove the Bolzano–Weierstrass theorem. (Hint: Use the fact that $\mathcal{E}^n$ is separable.)

Exercise 6 Why is there necessarily a maximal, $\mathcal{R}$-monotone net?

Exercise 7 A *cover* of $\mathcal{X}$ is a collection of sets $(\mathcal{X}_\alpha , \alpha \in \mathcal{A})$ such that $\mathcal{X} = \bigcup_{\alpha \in \mathcal{A}} \mathcal{X}_\alpha$. An *open cover* is a cover all of whose members are open. A *subcover* is a cover $(\mathcal{X}_\beta , \beta \in \mathcal{B})$ such that $\mathcal{B} \subset \mathcal{A}$. Show that every open cover of a compact set $\mathcal{X}$ has a subcover with a finite number of members.

Exercise 8 Show that if every intersection of a finite number of compact sets $\mathcal{X}_\alpha , \alpha \in \mathcal{A}$, is nonempty, then

$$\varnothing \neq \bigcap_{\alpha \in \mathcal{A}} \mathcal{X}_\alpha .$$

Exercise 9 Show that continuous functions take compact sets into compact sets.

Exercise 10 Show that if $\mathcal{F}(x)$ is an upper semicontinuous correspondence and a function and $\mathcal{F}(x) \cap \mathcal{X}$, is compact, then $\mathcal{F}$ is a continuous function.

2. von Neumann Growth

For obvious reasons, economists are concerned with finding out whether a system can be expanded. The simplest kind of expansion is proportional growth of all commodity stocks. Under constant returns to scale and where the time horizon is long, this balanced growth will be seen to be characteristic (Sections 3–5). Therefore, it is well to begin with a study of balanced growth. First we show the existence of a most rapid balanced growth path system. Special effort is made to show when all goods are expanding. Then we find a price system with respect to which balanced growth is profit maximizing. This is used to show bounds on the nonnegative production paths starting from a given $y(0)$. The compactness of $_0\mathcal{Y}_\infty(y)$ and therefore the existence of efficient paths is shown under conditions alternative to those of Theorem 4. Special emphasis is placed on the Leontief system.

A theorem due to von Neumann [1937] gives the existence of maximal growth path. Generalizations are due to Loomis [1948], Kemeny, Morgenstern, and Thompson [1956], and Gale [1956].

7 Theorem *If $_t\mathscr{Y}_{t+1}$ (contained in $\mathscr{E}^n$, n finite) is closed and if there is no free production in the limit, then there is a maximum λ with associated y such that*

   (i) $|y| = k$,
   (ii) $y > 0$,
   (iii) $\lambda y \in {}_t\mathscr{Y}_{t+1}(y)$.

If there is no technical change and constant returns to scale, we can set

$$y(t + 1) = \lambda y(t)$$

and obtain the path $y(t) = \lambda^t y(0)$. This is the famous *von Neumann growth path*, which represents the fastest possible *balanced* growth path, that is, the fastest possible growth whenever all sectors are required to develop at the same rate. Normally, the von Neumann path is of interest only when y is strictly greater than zero in every component (and when $\lambda(y)$ is not zero). Otherwise, there might be growth only of a single fast-reproducing good (say, rabbits), with no stocks of any other commodities. To prove the theorem, we need two mathematical results. It is said that a function f is *upper semicontinuous* or *regular* if the inverse image of a half-closed line $[x, \infty)$ is closed. Alternatively, f is regular if $x^n \to x$ implies

$$f(x) \geqslant \lim f(x^n).$$

On the other hand, a correspondence $\mathscr{F}$ is *upper semicontinuous* if $x_n \to x$, $y^n \in \mathscr{F}(x^n)$, $y^n \to y$ implies $y \in \mathscr{F}(x)$.

8 Lemma *If f is a regular function, $\mathscr{F}$ is an upper semicontinuous correspondence, and $\mathscr{F}(x) \subset \mathscr{X}$, $\mathscr{X}$ compact, then the maximum of f on $\mathscr{F}(x)$, ϕ, is a regular function of x.*

Proof Let $\phi(x) = f(y)$, $y \in \mathscr{F}(x)$, $\phi(x^n) = f(y^n)$, $y^n \in \mathscr{F}(x^n)$. Compactness of $\mathscr{X}$ gives a subsequence $y^{n_k} \to \bar{y}$, $k = 1,...,f(y^n k) \to c \leqslant f(\bar{y})$ (regularity of f). For $x^n \to x$, $\bar{y} \in \mathscr{F}(x)$ (upper semicontinuity). Hence, $\phi(x) \geqslant c$.   q.e.d.

9 Lemma *Regular functions have maxima on compact sets.*

For example, if $\mathscr{F}$ varies over compact $\mathscr{X}$, ϕ has a maximum.

Proof Evidently, if f is not bounded from above, $f(x^n) \to \infty$, but for some subsequence x^{n_k} converges to (some) x and $f(x) \geqslant \lim f(x^n) = \infty$, which is impossible. Therefore, $f(x) \leqslant c$ determines a unique maximizer $\bar{x} \in f^{-1}(f(x))$ (Axiom of Choice). Then $\bar{x}(f(x))$ is a net with index set $f(\mathscr{X})$, $\mathscr{X}$ compact. The index converges to c and has a convergent subnet for the index set $\mathscr{Z} \subset f(\mathscr{X})$ such that

$$\bar{x}(f(x)), \quad f(x) \in \mathscr{Z},$$

converges to $\bar{x}$.

Evidently, $c = \lim f(\bar{x}(f(x))) \leqslant f(\bar{x})$, and since $f(\bar{x}) \leqslant c$,

$$f(\bar{x}) = c. \qquad \text{q.e.d.}$$

Proof (of Theorem 7) It is necessary to consider only those elements of ${}_t\mathscr{Y}_{t+1}(y)$ which are proportional to y, that is,

$${}_t\mathscr{Y}_{t+1}(y) \cap \{(y, y') \mid y' = sy \quad \text{for} \quad s \in \mathscr{E}^1\}.$$

By the hypothesis of no free production in the limit, this set is bounded from above for $y \geqslant 0$. The set is also closed. Therefore, it has a maximum. Call this maximum for each y, $\lambda = \lambda(y)$. (See Figure 1.)

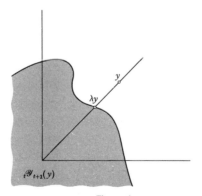

Figure 1

Elementary derivations verify that ${}_t\mathscr{Y}_{t+1}(y) \cap \{(y, y') \mid y' = sy$ for $s \in \mathscr{E}^1\}$ is upper semicontinuous in y. Therefore, λ is a regular function as the maximum of a continuous function (the identity function) on an upper semicontinuous correspondence (Lemma 8).

Now consider $\{y \mid |y| = k\}$, which is a closed, bounded subset of $\mathscr{E}^n$ and therefore a compact set (Lemma 2). $\lambda(y)$ takes a maximum on this set (Lemma 9).　q.e.d.

Note that in Theorem 9, it was necessary to assume the number of commodities n to be finite. Unfortunately, the unit sphere

$$\left\{ \frac{y}{|y|} \,\middle|\, y \neq 0 \right\}$$

is not compact in infinite-dimensional spaces.

Sometimes, those vectors in $\mathscr{V}$ of norm one are isolated and are called the *von Neumann facet*. The set $\mathscr{A}$ is *convex* if $t\mathscr{A} + (1 - t)\mathscr{A} \subset \mathscr{A}$ for all $0 \leqslant t \leqslant 1$. $\mathscr{A}$ is a *cone* if $a\mathscr{A} \subset \mathscr{A}$ for all $a \geqslant 0$.

10 Remark　If ${}_t\mathscr{Y}_{t+1}$ is convex, the set of von Neumann vectors $\mathscr{V}$ is a convex cone.

Proof　If $\lambda y \in {}_t\mathscr{Y}_{t+1}(y)$ and $\lambda \bar{y} \in {}_t\mathscr{Y}_{t+1}(\bar{y})$, then $t(\lambda y) + (1 - t)\lambda\bar{y} = \lambda(ty + (1 - t)\bar{y}) \in {}_t\mathscr{Y}_{t+1}(ty + (1 - t)\bar{y})$.　q.e.d.

Often there may be several balanced growth paths, of which the maximal one is simply one example. The associated y may not include all goods in positive quantities, so that all goods may not be growing simultaneously. The question of discovering paths with all goods can be resolved in the case of *Leontief systems* where

$$\Delta y \leqslant (I - A)x \qquad \text{(raw materials requirements)},$$
$$Bx \leqslant y \qquad \text{(capital requirements)},$$

or

$$B(I - A)^{-1}\,\Delta y \leqslant y.$$

Normally,

$$B \geqslant 0, \qquad (I - A)^{-1} \geqslant 0,$$

and the balanced growth is obtained by solving

$$(\lambda - 1)y = B(I - A)^{-1}y.$$

According to the Frobenius theory of matrices (Problem J of Chapter 10 of the companion volume), the maximum λ is greater than one if $(I - A)\,B^{-1}$ is nonsingular; that is, if B^{-1} exists. Also, if $(I - A)^{-1}$ is indecomposable, then λ is greater than one and unique, and y is strictly positive in every component. Otherwise, this will not necessarily be so, and balanced growth may exclude certain goods.

Suppose

$$B(I - A)^{-1} = \begin{pmatrix} C_1 & & 0 \\ & \cdot & \\ & & \cdot \\ X & & C_m \end{pmatrix}.$$

There is, for each indecomposable C_i, a maximum balanced growth path solving as

$$\begin{pmatrix} C_1 & & 0 \\ & \cdot & \\ & & \cdot \\ X & & C_m \end{pmatrix} y = (\lambda_i^{-1}) y^i$$

where the λ_i^{-1}'s are the maximum (real part of) roots of C_i. Some of the y^i's may well be strictly positive. If not, but if there is convexity with zero output (inaction), then we can alter each $\lambda_i y^i$ (inefficiently) to the level

$$\frac{\min_i \lambda_i}{\lambda_i} \lambda_i y^i = \delta_i \lambda_i y^i \quad \text{where} \quad 0 \leqslant \delta_i = \frac{\min \lambda_i}{\lambda_i} \leqslant 1.$$

This gives that the minimum λ_i can be obtained in balanced growth *and* with a positive amount of any good. In general, if for any subset of subscripts $\mathscr{I}$, $\sum_{i \in \mathscr{I}}^{y^i} y^i$ is strictly positive, then we can grow at $\min_{i \in \mathscr{I}} \lambda_i$.

11 Theorem *If there is a Leontief system, B^{-1} exists, or else $B(I - A)^{-1}$ is indecomposable, then there is a maximum rate $\lambda > 0$, associated with $\bar{y}/|\bar{y}|$ strictly positive in coordinate in $\mathscr{I}$ such that*

$$\lambda y \in {}_t \mathscr{Y}_{t+1}(y).$$

Proof Simply take the maximum of $\min_{i \in \mathscr{I}} \lambda_i$ over all $\mathscr{I}$ for which $\sum_{i \in \mathscr{I}} y^i$ is strictly positive for coordinates in $\mathscr{I}$. q.e.d.

The efficacy of balanced growth depends on rather special behavior of production technology over time. For example, if one capital good were to become relatively more productive, it might pay to accumulate that good at an ever increasing rate. To avoid this, we make special assumptions about technology over time.

The set ${}_t \mathscr{Y}_{t+1}$ is *homogeneous* in time if ${}_t \mathscr{Y}_{t+1}(y) = h(t) \, {}_0 \mathscr{Y}_1(y)$. If

$$h(t) \geqslant h(s) \quad \text{for} \quad t > s,$$

there is *no technical regress.* If

$$h(t) \leqslant h(s) \qquad \text{for} \quad t > s,$$

there is *no technical progress.*

If ${}_t\mathscr{Y}_{t+1}$ is homogeneous, a change of the units of measurement over time gives ${}_t\mathscr{Y}_{t+1}(y) = {}_0\mathscr{Y}_1(y) \equiv \mathscr{Y}(y)$ (divide ${}_t\mathscr{Y}_{t+1}(y)$ by $h(t)$). Hence, there is no need for an independent consideration of $h(t)$. All results in the homogeneous case are to be understood to apply only after the appropriate change, and reference is made to $\mathscr{Y}(y)$.

It is said that a good k is a *universal capital good* if for a nonnegative, nonzero capital stock y an increase in the kth component of $y(t)$ can lead to an increase in any component of $y(t + 1)$ in ${}_t\mathscr{Y}_{t+1}(y(t))$. An example of a universal capital good is the labor good, if it is treated as a stock. A good is *substitutable in production* if a decrease in its production can, for any other good, lead to an increase in its production.

In the Leontief system, if the input–output matrix A is indecomposable, then every good is jointly produced; $y = (1 - A)^{-1}x$ is strictly positive whenever x is nonnegative. If the capital matrix B is indecomposable, every good not in oversupply is a universal capital good.

A set $\mathscr{A}$ is *convex* if $ta + (1 - t)b \in \mathscr{A}$ whenever $a, b \in \mathscr{A}, 0 \leqslant t \leqslant 1$. It is *strictly convex* if $ta + (1 - t)b$ is in the interior of $\mathscr{A}$ whenever $a, b \in \mathscr{A}, 0 < t < 1$. It is *strongly convex* if $ta + (1 - t)b$ is in the interior of $\mathscr{A}$ for $0 < t < 1$ and $a \neq kb$ for any $k \geqslant 0$. $\mathscr{Y}(y)$ is *(strictly, strongly) convex* if the graph $\{(z, y) \mid z \in \mathscr{Y}(y)\}$ is a (strictly, strongly) convex set.

The theorem following shows that there is a price system in which the von Neumann vectors are at least as profitable as others. Hence, the value accruing under balanced growth will be at least as great as that under any other growth path.

12 Theorem   *Suppose* ${}_t\mathscr{Y}_{t+1} \subset \mathscr{E}^{2n}$ *is closed,* $\bar{y}/|\bar{y}|$ *maximizes*

$$\lambda(y) = \max\{\lambda \mid \lambda \in \mathscr{Y}(y), \ |y| = 1\},$$

${}_t\mathscr{Y}_{t+1}(y)$ *is convex with constant returns in* y *and homogeneous in* t, *and there is free disposal. Let*

$$\bar{y}(0) = y(0), \qquad \bar{y}(0) = s\frac{\bar{y}}{|\bar{y}|}$$

for some $s > 0$. *Then there is a* $p > 0$ *such that*

$$p(\bar{y}(t) - \lambda\bar{y}(t)) \geqslant p(\bar{y}(t) - y(t))$$
$$\geqslant p(\bar{y}(0) - y(0))\lambda^t, \quad \text{where} \quad \bar{y}(t) = \bar{y}(0)\,\lambda^t.$$

If every good is either a universal capital good or substitutable in production, then p *is strictly positive. Consequently,* $y(t)$ *remains bounded and*

$$_0\mathcal{Y}_\infty(y(0)) = \{(y(t), \quad t = 0, 1, 2,...,) \mid y(t+1) \in \mathcal{Y}(y(t))\}$$

has no free production in the limit. If $\mathcal{Y}(y(t))$ *is also superadditive in* $y(t)$, *then* $_0\mathcal{Y}_\infty(y(0))$ *is irreversible in the limit.*

13 Corollary *Under the hypothesis of Theorem* 12,

$$\lim \sup \frac{1}{t} \log p(\bar{y}(t) - y(t)) = \lambda_0(y).$$

Theorem 12 is a simple consequence of the following lemma.

14 Lemma *If* $\mathcal{Y}(y) \subset \mathcal{E}^n$ *is convex in* y *and has constant returns to scale in* y, *there is free disposal, and* $\bar{y}$ *maximizes* $\lambda(y)$ *for* $y > 0$, *then there exists a* $p \neq 0$, $p > 0$, *such that*

$$0 = p(\lambda\bar{y} - \lambda\bar{y}) \leqslant p(\lambda y(t) - y(t+1))$$

for all $y(t+1)$ *in* $\mathcal{Y}(y(t))$. *Consequently,*

$$py(t) \leqslant py(0)\,\lambda^t.$$

If a commodity k *is either a universal capital good or substitutable in production, then* p_k *is positive.*

Proof Consider the convex set

$$\mathcal{C} = \{y(t+1) - \lambda y(t) \mid y(t+1) \in \mathcal{Y}(y(t))\}.$$

Then there does not exist a member of $\mathcal{C}$ that is also an interior point of the convex set

$$\Omega = \{w \mid w \geqslant 0\}.$$

Otherwise, there would be some $y(t+1)$, $y(t)$ for which

$$-\lambda y(t) + y(t+1)$$

is strictly greater than zero and, by an appropriate disposal of $y(t + 1)$, for some $\mu > 0$,

$$-\lambda y(t) + y'(t + 1) = \mu y(t) \qquad \text{or} \qquad y'(t + 1) = (\lambda + \mu) y(t),$$

contradicting the maximality of λ.

By Minkowski's theorem there exists a vector p such that

$$pw \geqslant 0 \geqslant p(y(t + 1) - \lambda y(t)),$$

for w in Ω, for all $y(t + 1)$ in $\mathscr{Y}(y(t))$, $y(t) > 0$. Clearly, p has no negative components, for then there would be a w in Ω such that

$$pw < 0.$$

If a good k is a universal capital good, its price p_k cannot be zero, for then

$$\lambda \bar{y} - \lambda y$$

may be changed to

$$y(t + 1) - \lambda(\bar{y} + e_k) \qquad \text{where} \quad e_k = (0,..., 0, \underset{k\text{th}}{1}, 0,..., 0).$$

Consequently, there is a $y(t + 1)$ in $\mathscr{Y}(\bar{y} + e_k)$ such that $y(t + 1)$ is strictly greater than $\lambda \bar{y}$ in a component i, for which $p_i > 0$. Therefore, by $p_i > 0$, $p > 0$,

$$py(t + 1) - p\lambda(\bar{y} + e_k) < 0 \qquad \text{for} \quad p_k = 0,$$

which contradicts the construction of p. Alternatively, if j is substitutable in production, p_j cannot be zero. For then we could decrease $y_j(t + 1)$ and increase $y_k(t + 1)$ for any other k without changing the capital stock $\bar{y}$. This would increase

$$y(t + 1) - p\lambda \bar{y}$$

from

$$0 = p\lambda \bar{y} - p\lambda \bar{y}$$

for $y(t + 1)$ in $\mathscr{Y}(\bar{y})$ to obtain a positive value. Again, this contradicts the construction of p.   q.e.d.

Proof of Theorem 12

$$p(\lambda \bar{y}(t) - \lambda \bar{y}(t)) \leqslant p(\lambda y(t) - y(t + 1))$$

or

$$0 \geqslant p\lambda[\bar{y}(t) - y(t)] - p[\lambda \bar{y}(t) - y(t + 1)]$$

or

$$p\lambda[\bar{y}(t) - y(t)] \leqslant p[\bar{y}(t + 1) - y(t + 1)]$$

or

$$p\lambda^{t+1}[\bar{y}(0) - y(0)] \leqslant p[\bar{y}(t + 1) - y(t + 1)]. \qquad \text{q.e.d.}$$

It is easy to verify that for p strictly positive,

$$K|x| \geqslant px \geqslant k|x|.$$

From Lemma 14, if $y(0) \geqslant \bar{y}(0)$, then

$$\left(\frac{K}{k}\right)^2 (\bar{y}(t))^2 \leqslant (\lambda^t)^2 (\bar{y}(0) - y(0))^2$$

or

$$|\bar{y}(t) - y(t)| \leqslant \lambda^t |\bar{y}(0) - y(0)| \frac{K}{k}.$$

Therefore, at any time period, deviations of outputs from the von Neumann path are bounded. Since at any time period the von Neumann path is bounded, we can deduce the compactness of the set of possible paths from $y(0)$.

15 Theorem *Suppose $_t\mathscr{Y}_{t+1}(y)$ is convex, there is no free production in the limit, there is free disposal, there are not increasing returns in y, and $_t\mathscr{Y}_{t+1}$ is closed. Suppose further that there is an $h(t)$ such that $_t\mathscr{Y}_{t+1}(y) \subset h(t)_0\mathscr{Y}_1(y)$ (technical progress is limited) and every good is either a universal capital good or substitutable in production. Then $y(t)$ can be continued over $0, 1, 2,\ldots$ and remains bounded from above by some path $x(t) > 0$, $t = 0$, $1, 2,\ldots$, and $_0\mathscr{Y}_\infty(y(0))$ has no free production in the limit; that is, $_0\mathscr{Y}_\infty(y(0))$ is compact in pointwise convergence.*

Application is to the induced preferences in Chapter 9 of the companion volume.

Exercise 11 Prove that regular functions take maxima on compact sets using only sequences.

Exercise 12 For factor connected, interindustry production as defined in the companion volume, show that all goods are substitutable in production. Show that all factors are universal capital goods.

Exercise 13 In the Leontief case, where $B(I - A)^{-1}$ is decomposable, is $_0\mathscr{Y}_\infty(y(0)$ compact in pointwise convergence ?

Exercise 14   In the Leontief system, how is the price system related to the balanced growth path? (See Chapter 7, Sections 5 and 6, for an analysis of characteristic vectors.)

PROBLEM

A. Balanced Growth I

Show that the von Neumann path is intertemporally efficient from $y(0) = \bar{y}$ whenever production is convex, there is free disposal and constant returns to scale, and every commodity is either a universal capital good or substitutable in production. (Hint: Use Lemma 14 and Corollary 13.)

UNSOLVED PROBLEM

B. Compactness of $_0\mathcal{Y}_\infty(y(0))$

Generalize Theorem 14 (and subsequent theorems) to cover the case of a Leontief system with decomposable $B(I - A)^{-1}$.

3. *t*-State Efficient Paths and von Neumann's Path

In order to show that the I.E. path eventually dominates all other paths, it is shown that it is asymptotic to the von Neumann path. This will be accomplished by showing first that *t*-state efficient paths are near to von Neumann's path, a result interesting in its own right. As a consequence, economic development with a long-run target capital stock should be nearly balanced and in the von Neumann facet.

In this section constant returns to scale are assumed throughout. Also, we consider the case where growth in excess of zero requires matter beyond that already embodied in the commodities. While allowing the possibilities of positive growth, we are especially concerned with the case of only zero growth.

To begin, Radner's lemma gives a price system in which the von Neumann vectors are the only most profitable productions.

16 Lemma   *Suppose that in addition to the hypothesis of Lemma 14, $\mathcal{Y}(y(t))$ is upper semicontinuous and strongly convex. If $\varepsilon > 0$, then there is a $\delta(\varepsilon) > 0$ such that*

$$py(t + 1) - (\lambda - \delta(\varepsilon))\, py(t) \leqslant 0$$

for $y(t + 1)$ in $\mathscr{Y}(y)$, $y/|y|$ at least ε from $\mathscr{V}$. If good k is either a universal capital good or substitutable in production, then $p_k > 0$.

Proof 1. If $p(y(t + 1) - \lambda y(t)) = 0$, $y(t) \neq k\bar{y}$, then $\frac{1}{2}\bar{y} + \frac{1}{2}y(t)$ can yield $\bar{y}(t + 1) \gg \frac{1}{2}y(t + 1) + \frac{1}{2}\lambda\bar{y}$. Hence,

$$p(\bar{y}(t + 1) - \lambda(\tfrac{1}{2}\bar{y} + \tfrac{1}{2}y(t)))$$
$$> p(\tfrac{1}{2}\bar{y}(t + 1) + \tfrac{1}{2}\lambda y(t) - \lambda(\tfrac{1}{2}\bar{y} + \tfrac{1}{2}(y(t))) = 0,$$

contrary to the definition of p.

2. Observe that in Lemma 14, $p(y(t + 1) - \lambda y(t))$ is continuous in $y(t)$ and $y(t + 1)$. Therefore, if $y(t)$ remains a distance $\varepsilon > 0$ from $\mathscr{V}$, $|y(t)| = 1$, there is an η such that

$$p(y(t + 1) - \lambda y(t))$$

is of distance η from $(\lambda\bar{y} - \lambda\bar{y}) = 0$ for all $\bar{y}$ in $\mathscr{V}$. Otherwise,

$$p(y(t + 1) - \lambda y(t))$$

tends to zero for $y(t)$ of distance ε from $\mathscr{V}$. There is a subsequence of $(y(t + 1), y(t))$ convergent to $(\hat{y}(t + 1), \hat{y}(t))$, $\hat{y}(t)$ of distance ε from $\mathscr{V}$. Since $\mathscr{Y}(y)$ is upper semicontinuous,

$$\hat{y}(t + 1) - \lambda\hat{y}(t) \in \mathscr{Y}(y) \qquad \text{and} \qquad p(\hat{y}(t + 1) - \lambda\hat{y}(t)) = 0$$

contrary to $\hat{y}(t)$ of ε distance from $\mathscr{V}$. Therefore,

$$p(y(t + 1) - \lambda y(t)) \leqslant -\eta \qquad \text{or} \qquad p(y(t + 1) - (\lambda - \delta)y(t)) \leqslant 0$$

for $\delta > 0$ sufficiently small, $y(t)$ bounded, and

$$\delta p y(t) \leqslant \eta \qquad \text{or} \qquad \delta \leqslant \frac{\eta}{py(t)}. \qquad \text{q.e.d.}$$

To obtain the main result (Theorem 17), we need to assume that all commodities can be sustained. If there are a finite number of commodities, and if the mass of the system is fixed, then generally there must be a way to obtain a zero growth rate, possibly by holding a bundle containing that least complex commodity to which other commodities can only deteriorate and therefore from which no deterioration can take place. The question naturally arises whether there is some way that all commodities can be preserved at a zero growth rate. If so, this would correspond to a von Newmann growth path

$$y(t) = y(0), \qquad t = 0, 1, 2,\ldots,$$

with $y(0)$ strictly positive. If such were not possible, we would conclude that once a particular set of commodities were preserved, all other commodities must necessarily deteriorate indefinitely. In effect, some commodity bundles would always be unstable. Whether this is so or not is an empirical question, but it would be surprising if it proved to be the case that no strictly positive commodity bundle could be sustained.

In general, if the total mass in the system were changing at an exponential rate, as in von Neumann growth, within the constraints of this growth rate, we might hope that all commodities would preserve their relative growth. Formally, the system is *indecomposable* or the commodity classification is *stable* if there is a von Neumann growth path with a positive amount of each commodity. For example, a very stringent assumption assuring indecomposability is that every good be necessary for production of any good.

The following characterizes final state efficient paths.

17 Theorem *Suppose $y(0)$ is strictly positive, commodities are not negatively productive, the production system $\mathcal{Y}(y)$ is indecomposable and strongly convex, $\mathcal{Y}(y)$ is upper semicontinuous (and homogeneous in t), there are constant returns in y, and every good is either a universal capital good or substitutable in production. Then a τ-period–final state efficient path $(y^\tau(t), t = 0, 1, 2,...)$ is such that*

$$\frac{y^\tau(t)}{|y^\tau(t)|}, \qquad 0 \leqslant t \leqslant \tau,$$

is within ε of the set of von Neumann vectors $\mathcal{V}$ except for time periods of number $N(\varepsilon)$. Consequently, for large τ,

$$(y^\tau(t), \quad t = 0, 1, 2,...)$$

is near the set of von Neumann vectors most of the time. Hence, an I.E. path is near the set of von Neumann vectors for all except a period of time $N(\varepsilon)$.

Theorem 17 is a version of the "turnpike" theorem, first suggested by Dorfman, Samuelson, and Solow [1958]. The first rigorous versions of a turnpike theorem were due to Radner [1961] and Morishima [1961]. (The latter analyzed the Leontief case.) Various aspects of the foregoing generalized theorem are due to Furuya and Inada [1962] and McKenzie [1963, 1963a]. Essentially, final state efficiency is obtained by moving to the von Neumann ray and then growing along the von Neumann path until toward the end of the time period, at which time we move toward the desired capital proportions.

A generalization of Theorem 17, whereby product averaged over time tends to the von Neumann rate, allows us to drop the requirement of indecomposability of $\mathcal{Y}(y)$ (Morishima [1964]).

The idea of the proof is illustrated schematically in Figure 2, where

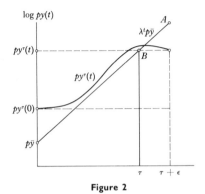

Figure 2

the capital stock is measured in value terms py. Beginning at $y(0)$, we have $py(0)$ as the value of the capital stock. Gradually reducing the capital stock to the von Neumann stock $\bar{y}$, we can obtain the exponential growth $py\lambda^t$, as illustrated. For large t, some commodity must have at least this growth rate, and therefore eventually $py(t)$ must grow at least at rate x. The value py can grow no faster, by virtue of the Radner lemma (Lemma 16). Therefore, if the path $py^\tau(t)$, whose growth is necessarily not greater than that of the von Neumann path, is to be at least as efficient as $y(t)$, its growth must for large t be between $py^\tau(t)$ and $p\bar{y}\lambda^t$. Therefore, it must be approximately the von Neumann path except at the beginning and at the end. The reader can convince himself of this by examining Figure 2 and observing that the optimal path must be between $apy^\tau(0)$ and $bpy^\tau(0)$. For large t, the direct path $py^\tau(t)$ becomes very nearly $p\bar{y}\lambda^t$ except at the beginning and the end. Hence, proportional growth of $py^\tau(t)$ per period becomes nearly $\lambda - 1$, which by Radner's lemma is possible only if $y^\tau(t)/|\, y^\tau(y)\, |$ is nearly a von Neumann path.

The foregoing explanation is very rough and the reader is invited to examine the proof.

Proof 1. Suppose $(y^\tau(t), t = 0, 1, \ldots)$ is of distance ε from $\mathscr{V}$ for times in $\mathscr{N} \subset \bigcup_{i=1}^{\infty} \{i\}$. Since there are constant returns to scale, production sets at $|\, y\, | \neq 1$ are merely multiples of those for $y/|\, y\, |$.

Therefore, the relationships of the Radner lemma 16 hold in general:

$$p(y(t+1) - \lambda y(t)) \leqslant 0 \qquad \text{for} \quad t \text{ in} \bigcup_{s=0}^{\tau} \{s\} \sim \mathcal{N}$$

and

$$p\,y(t+1) - (\lambda - \delta(\varepsilon))\,y(t)) \leqslant 0 \qquad \text{for} \quad t \text{ in } \mathcal{N}.$$

Therefore,

$$py(t) \leqslant py(0) \prod_{\substack{s \in \sim\mathcal{N} \\ s<t}} \lambda \prod_{\substack{s \in \mathcal{N} \\ s<t}} (\lambda - \delta(\varepsilon)) = py(0)\,\lambda^{t-u}(\lambda - \delta(\varepsilon))^u$$

where u is the number of elements of $\mathcal{N}$ less than t.

2. On the other hand, a possible path is to take $y(0)$ and consider $k\bar{y}(0) \leqslant y(0)$ for a strictly positive $\bar{y}(0)$ maximizing $\lambda_0(y)$, that is, for a strictly positive von Neumann vector in $\mathcal{V}$. If goods are not negatively productive, then there is a path from $y(0)$ and a $k > 0$ such that

$$y(t) < k\bar{y}(0)\lambda.$$

Furthermore, $y^\tau(\tau)$ is greater than or equal to $y(\tau)$ in at least one component, so that there is an i such that

$$y_i^\tau(\tau) \geqslant y_i(\tau) \geqslant k\bar{y}(0)\,\lambda^\tau \qquad \text{or} \qquad p_i y_i^\tau(\tau) \geqslant k(py(0))\,\lambda^\tau.$$

Therefore,

$$p_i y^\tau(\tau) \geqslant k \min_j(p_j\bar{y}_j(0))\,\lambda^\tau.$$

Also, since p and $y^\tau(\tau)$ are nonnegative,

$$py^\tau(\tau) \geqslant p_i y_i^\tau(\tau) \geqslant k \min_j(p_j\bar{y}_j(0))\,\lambda^\tau.$$

3. Putting 1 and 2 together, we get

$$py(0)\,\lambda^{\tau-u}(\lambda - \delta(\varepsilon))^u \geqslant py^\tau(\tau) \geqslant k \min_j p_j\bar{y}_j(0)\,\lambda^\tau.$$

Therefore,

$$py(0) \geqslant k(\min_j(p_j\bar{y}_j(0))\left(\frac{\lambda}{\lambda - \delta(\varepsilon)}\right)^u.$$

4. Taking natural logarithms, we obtain

$$u = N(\varepsilon) \leqslant \frac{\log \dfrac{py(0)}{k \min_j p_j\bar{y}_j(0)}}{-\log \dfrac{\lambda - \delta(\varepsilon)}{\lambda}},$$

which proves that $\mathcal{N}$ has an upper bound, given ε. Time τ–final state efficient paths are within ε of $\mathscr{V}$ except for $N(\varepsilon)$ times.

5. Since the I.E. path is time τ–final state efficient for all $\tau \geqslant 0$, the I.E. path is within ε of $\mathscr{V}$ except for time of distance $N(\varepsilon)$.   q.e.d.

The strong convexity assumption is sufficiently stringent to exclude the interindustry case (Remark 8 of Chapter 4 of the companion volume). However, if industries have strongly convex input–output sets, then Radner's lemma can be modified so as to apply to industries. In such a case, industry factor utilizations that differ from the balanced growth ones will have a smaller value. Hence, unbalanced growth can take place without a loss in value, but only if the industries are producing according to the von Neumann technology. Let $y_j{}^i$ be the utilization of factor j in industry i under the von Neumann system. Then, $Yv = \bar{y}$ for $v = (1,..., 1)$. Also, $Y\xi = y$ is a possible input for $\xi > 0$ with net output $X\xi$. Let y deteriorate to Ay. Then,

$$y^t = Ay^{t-1} + X\xi$$
$$= Ay^{t-1} + XY^{-1}y^{t-1}$$
$$= (A + XY^{-1})^{t-s} y^s.$$

Evidently,

$$\lambda^t Yv = (A + XY^{-1})^t Yv.$$

Otherwise, in many cases, $\xi^t = Y^{-1}(A + XY^{-1})^{t-s}y^s$ may violate $\xi^t > 0$ for large $t - s$. Hence, production cannot continue along von Neumann lines and must switch to a less "valuable" method of production. Only modified turnpike theorems can be proved for such cases. For example, if $(A + XY^{-1})$ has a unique largest positive root with positive characteristic vector, then it can be shown that only vectors that were initially on the von Neumann facet can be sustained indefinitely (see Morishima [1961]).

For example, if there are no intermediate products, $A = I$, then $(I + Y^{-1})$ can be shown to have a largest positive characteristic root equal to one plus the root of Y^{-1} equal to one over the root of $Y > 0$. The "characteristic vector" is that of Y. (See Problem J of Chapter 10 of the companion volume.) Difficulties will arise if there are several von Neumann vectors with different Y.

Exercise 15   In order for a Leontief system to be indecomposable, is it required that $(I - A)^{-1} B$ be indecomposable?

Exercise 16   In a Leontief system, when is every good either a universal capital good or else substitutable in production? What alternative hypothesis would give the turnpike theorem?

PROBLEM

C. Optimal Development I

Show that if the von Neumann path is unique, and the hypothesis of Theorem 17 holds, then for large t, a t–final state efficient path is within ε of the von Neumann path for an "interval"

$$[t_1, t_2] \subset [0, t]$$

such that

$$[0, t] \sim [t_1, t_2]$$

is bounded by $M(\varepsilon, y(0))$. (Hint: Use Lemma 14 and Lemma 16 to show that if $\varepsilon > 0$, there is a large t and $\delta > 0$ such that the path $y(t)$ for which

$$|y(t)/|y(t)| - \bar{y}| < \delta, \qquad t = 0, t,$$

is τ-efficient only if $|y(t)/|y(t)| - \bar{y}| < \varepsilon, 0 \leqslant t \leqslant \tau$.)

This is the so-called catenary property whereby the path goes to the von Neumann path and stays there most of the time.

Different versions are due to Samuelson [1965], McKenzie [1963], Nikaido [1964], Inada [1964], and Winter [1967].

4. Dominance and the I.E. Path

Here the characterization in Theorem 16 is used to show that the I.E. path is the one and only path efficient in the very long run. For this result, uniqueness of the von Neumann vector is required.

Consider the set of I.E. paths. Even though they are the only paths that are final state efficient for all time periods, it is still possible that other paths may give a larger quantity, ultimately, of some particular commodity. In that case, a sequence of time τ–final state efficient paths, $\tau \to \infty$, with still larger ultimate quantities of that output could be found, but the limiting I.E. path would not be final state efficient. There is nothing in the mathematics of vectors to prevent this possibility. For example,

$$y^\tau(t) = (2, 1,), \qquad 0 \leqslant t \leqslant \tau - 1,$$
$$y^\tau(t) = (2, e^{t(t-\tau)}), \qquad t \geqslant \tau - 1,$$

has the property that the second component eventually exceeds the second component of

$$y^*(t) = (2, 1)\, e^t,$$

but $y^\tau(t)$ tends to

$$y(t) = (2, 1), \qquad t \geqslant 0,$$

$$y(t) < y^*(t), \qquad t > 0.$$

A property that will help in avoiding such a possibility is that of *primitivity*, whereby if y is a nonnegative nonzero capital stock, then it can be utilized in such a way as to produce positive amounts of each commodity, eventually. If goods are not negatively productive, this positive amount can then be sustained indefinitely.

As an example, consider the Leontief system,

$$\mathcal{Y}(y) = \{y + z \mid B(I - A)^{-1} z \leqslant y\}.$$

If $(I - A)^{-1}$ is indecomposable, then $(I - A)^{-1}$ is strictly positive. Therefore, let z_i be positive whenever y_i is zero. This is possible if there is some good that exists in positive quantity and that can be depleted to obtain positive z. In particular, if B is positive in every component, then z_j can be set negative for some good j, for which y_j is positive, and for all other i, z_i can be made positive, z_i sufficiently small. Then, over a short time period j will be decreasing in quantity and other commodities will increase in quantity. Therefore, at the end of this short time period in which j is not completely depleted, all commodities will exist in positive quantities. More generally, if B is indecomposable, it can be shown that the system is primitive.

18 Theorem *Suppose that in that addition to the hypothesis of Theorem 17, the von Neumann path is unique and $\mathcal{Y}(y)$ is primitive. Then any path other than the I.E. path eventually gives less of every good than the I.E. path.*

Theorem 18 was stated in a less general form by Rader [1965]. Related results appear in Section 5.

Under the hypothesis of Theorem 18, by a method similar to that in parts 4, 5, and 9 of the proof of the theorem, it can be shown that the I.E. path is unique (Problem G). Hence, under these rather stringent conditions, the I.E. path represents the extreme case where future generations are never sacrificed to the present ones. To some people, this seems reasonable on the grounds that an infinite number of generations should always outweigh a finite number. In retrospect, those who follow the ethic of favoring the future over the present appear as the great benefactors or as the misers of society, depending on the observer.

Let labor be one of the commodities under consideration. In order for the I.E. path to have welfare significance, it is necessary that some commodity be desirable in ever larger quantities and that no commodity be undesirable in larger quantities. In particular, the expansion of the economy must be desirable even at the cost of a lower per capita income or more labor hours. This may not seem an especially useful welfare concept, except possibly on the frontier. One way out is to specify the amount of labor available in each period, not allowing it to be determined by the production decisions. Then there would normally be strictly decreasing returns to scale as the factors other than labor increase. The analysis in this case is given in Chapter 6.

In any case, Theorem 18 is the analog of Phelps–Robinson analysis of the one-commodity Solow model, the so-called neoneoclassical theorem, where the highest sustainable consumption is associated with a path tending to the balanced growth path.

The strategy of proof for Theorem 18 is to show that any path $y(t)$ giving more of commodity i than an I.E. path must eventually grow in value, $py(t)$, by the proportional rate λ. Therefore, it must approach the von Neumann vector, which is unique. Furthermore, it must approach this level at least as high as does the I.E. path $y^*(t)$. Finally, since $y(t)$ is eventually final state inefficient, for a time τ superior path ($y^\tau(t)$, $t \in [0, \infty]$), the surplus of $y^\tau(t)$ over $y(t)$ at time τ can be used to get a still higher exponential growth of output toward the von Neumann path, which will therefore be at a strictly higher level than that of $y^*(t)$. Since each commodity in the von Neumann vector has positive quantity, this proportional growth at a higher level necessarily leads to more of every good than $y^*(t)$. Of course, this contradicts the intertemporal efficiency of $y^*(t)$.

Up to now, the von Neumann path has not been assumed unique. It can be seen that uniqueness is necessary for Theorem 18. Let $\bar{y}$ and $\bar{\bar{y}}$ be two von Neumann vectors for which $\bar{y}_i < \bar{\bar{y}}_i$. Let

$$y(0) = \bar{y} + \varepsilon e_i, \qquad e = (0, \ldots, \underset{i\text{th}}{1}, \ldots, 0).$$

Then, let $y(1) = \bar{y}^{\lambda_0}(y)$, disposing of εe_i. Let $y(t) = y\lambda^t$. Normally, $y(t)$ is not efficient. Nevertheless, if i is relatively unproductive, an efficient path tending to $\bar{y}\lambda^t$ cannot catch $y(t)$ in the ith component.

With strong convexity, it is easy to prove the uniqueness of the von Neumann vector. If production is a dynamical Leontief system, then indecomposability does the same job (Problem E). It can also be shown that with strong convexity the I.E. path is unique (Problem G).

19 Theorem *Suppose that $\mathscr{Y}(y)$ is strongly convex in y. Then the von Neumann vector $\bar{y}$ is unique.*

Proof   If

$$\lambda \bar{y} \in \mathscr{Y}(\bar{y}) \qquad \text{and} \qquad \lambda \bar{\bar{y}} \in \mathscr{Y}(\bar{\bar{y}}), \qquad \frac{\bar{y}}{|\bar{y}|} \neq \frac{\bar{\bar{y}}}{|\bar{\bar{y}}|},$$

then

$$s\bar{y} + (1-s)\bar{\bar{y}}, \qquad \lambda(s\bar{y} + (1-s)\bar{\bar{y}})$$

is the interior of $\mathscr{Y}$, so that we can go out in the direction of

$$s\bar{y} + (1-s)\bar{\bar{y}}$$

to obtain

$$\lambda(s\bar{y} + (1-s)\bar{\bar{y}}) + \delta(s\bar{y} + (1-s)\bar{\bar{y}}), \qquad \delta < 0,$$

in $\mathscr{Y}(s\bar{y} + (1-s)\bar{\bar{y}})$. Therefore, $s\bar{y} + (1-s)\bar{\bar{y}}$ gives a still higher growth rate than $\bar{y}$ or $\bar{\bar{y}}$.   q.e.d.

Proof of Theorem 18   1. Let $(y(t), t = 0, 1, 2,...)$ be any path, and let $y^*(t)$ be an I.E. path. Eventually, $y^*(t)$ is greater than or equal to $c\bar{y}(t)$ for some $c > 0$, $\bar{y}(t)$ the von Neumann balanced growth path. Applying the Radner lemma gives

$$py(t) \leqslant \lambda^{t-u}(\lambda - \delta(\varepsilon))^u \, py(0)$$

where u is the number of $s \leqslant t$ for which $y(s)/|y(s)|$ is ε from $\bar{y}$, and of course,

$$py^*(t) \geqslant c p\bar{y}(t) = cp\bar{y}\lambda^t.$$

Then,

$$\frac{py(t)}{py(t)} \geqslant \left(\frac{\lambda}{\lambda - \delta(\varepsilon)}\right)^u \frac{cp\bar{y}}{py(0)},$$

since

$$p_i y_i \leqslant py(t) \qquad \text{or} \qquad \frac{1}{p_i y_i} \geqslant \frac{1}{py(t)}$$

and

$$py^*(t) \leqslant K p_i y_i^*(t),$$

$$\frac{cp\bar{y}}{py(0)} \left(\frac{\lambda}{\lambda - \delta(\varepsilon)}\right)^u \leqslant K \frac{p_i y_i^*(t)}{p_i y_i(t)} = K \frac{y_i^*(t)}{y_i(t)}.$$

When u is not bounded,

$$\left(\frac{\lambda}{\lambda - \delta(\varepsilon)}\right)^u \to \infty,$$

as does $y_i^*(t)$. Evidently, $y_i^*(t)$ is eventually greater than $y_i(t)$ unless $y(t)/|y(t)|$ tends to $\bar{y}$. If $y_i(t)$ is frequently greater than $y_i^*(t)$ and frequently $y(t)/|y(t)| \to y^*(t)/|y^*(t)| \to \bar{y}$, then $|y(t)|/|y^*(t)|$ is frequently almost 1, or else more than 1.

Let τ be the largest t for which $y(t)$ is t efficient. Let $\alpha(t)$ be $\tau + 1$ efficient and $\hat{y}(\tau + 1) \geqslant y(\tau + 1)$, $\hat{y}(\tau + 1) \neq y(\tau + 1)$. Use $\hat{y}(\tau + 1) - y(\tau + 1)$ to produce a strictly positive quantity in time $\tau_1 > \tau + 1$ (primitivity). Then obtain at least $\delta y(t)$ extra output (superadditivity). Denote the path from $\tau + 1$ to ∞ by $\delta(t)$.

Derive

$$\bar{y}(t) \geqslant \begin{cases} y(t) & t \leqslant \tau + 1 \\ y(t) + \delta(t), & t > \tau + 1. \end{cases}$$

Then $y(t)$ is at least equal to $y(t)(1 + \delta)$ for $t > \tau$. Since $|y(t)|/|y^*(t)|$ is frequently nearly 1, $|\bar{y}(t)|/|y^*(t)|$ is frequently nearly $1 + \delta$ and at the same time $\bar{y}(t)/|\bar{y}(t)|$ is near $\bar{y}(1)$. This implies that $\bar{y}(t)$ frequently dominates the I.E. path in all commodities, which is impossible.   q.e.d.

Exercise 17   Modify Theorem 18 so as to apply to the dynamical Leontief system.

PROBLEMS

D. Optimal Development II

Suppose we are maximizing a linear homogeneous utility $u(y(\tau))$ that is continuous and monotonically nondecreasing in each y_i. Suppose the hypothesis of Theorem 17 and show that the utility maximizing path is near the I.E. path except for a period of time bounded in total length for a large t. (Hint: In part 2 of the proof of Theorem 17, show that

$$k_0 py \leqslant u(y) \leqslant k_1 py$$

and therefore that

$$k_1 py^t(t) \geqslant u(y(t)) \geqslant k_0 py(t) \geqslant k_0 kp\bar{y}(t)$$

where $\bar{y}(t)$ is the von Neumann path at time t.)

This problem was first solved by Radner [1961] and was the first turnpike theorem established.

E. Leontief Production I

Consider the dynamical Leontief system

$$B (I - A)^{-1} \frac{dy}{dt} \leqslant y, \qquad y \geqslant 0.$$

Show that if B is strictly positive and the system is productive, then it is primitive.

F. Leontief Production II

Show that for B strictly positive, there is a unique von Neumann vector.

G. Optimal Development III

Suppose the hypothesis of Theorem 18. Show that the I.E. path is unique if all I.E. paths tend to the unique von Neumann path. (Hint: Consider convex combinations of two I.E. paths that give an exponentially (at rate λ) growing path converging to both I.E. paths, which converge to each other. Then construct a path still better with regard to ${}_{0}\mathscr{Y}_{\infty}(y)$ than the convex combination, and use the extra commodities to obtain an additional bundle of commodities growing exponentially at rate λ, which is possible by primitivity. Then show that the new path converges to a von Neumann path greater than the von Neumann rate to which the others converge, which gives a greater output in all commodities.)

This problem was first solved by Furuya and Inada [1962].

H. Optimal Development IV

Show that in comparison with any other path, the I.E. path eventually has a value of $u(y(t))$ (in C) higher than that of any other path, where u is either homogeneous or monotonic.

This problem is a special case of the analysis in Section 5.

I. Balanced Growth II

Consider interindustry production with capital distributed per unit output by the matrix Y. Suppose no derioration so that

$$y^{t+1} = \xi^t + y^t, \qquad \xi^t = Y^t y^t.$$

(i) Without assuming Y nonsingular, show that there is a unique von Neumann vector, provided production functions are strictly quasi concave. (Hint: Show that maximum balanced growth implies one particular Y and solve

$$y^{t+1} = (Y + I) y^t$$

for the balanced growth vector using Frobenius' theorem (Problem J of Chapter 10 in the companion volume). What conditions must be imposed upon Y?)

(ii) Prove the analogs of Theorems 17 and 18.

J. The von Neumann Model

In the von Neumann model, m activities $x(\in \mathscr{E}^m)$ require n commodities as inputs and yield n commodities as outputs. The outputs do not exceed Bx, B an n-by-n matrix, and the inputs must not be less than Ax. Therefore,

$$\Delta y \leqslant Ax \quad \left(\text{or} \ \ \frac{dy}{dt} \leqslant Ax\right), \qquad y \geqslant Bx, \quad y \geqslant 0.$$

1. Show that the Leontief model in Problem E is a special case of the von Neumann model.
2. Show that the von Neumann model has ${}_t\mathscr{Y}_{t+1}(y)$ that are convex and upper semicontinuous in y.
3. Show that there is free disposal, inaction is possible, and commodities are not negatively productive.
4. Let $A \geqslant 0$, $B \geqslant 0$. Show that if B is strictly positive or A strictly positive in the ith row and if the relevant constraint holds with equality, then the ith commodity is a universal capital good or jointly produced, respectively.
5. Let $A \geqslant 0$, $B \geqslant 0$. Show that the maximal growth path is given by a nonnegative activity for which

$$(A - \lambda B)x = 0.$$

This problem was first solved by von Neumann [1937]. Another method is presented by Karlin [1959].

K. Leontief Production III

In Problem I, suppose there is but one constraining factor. Show that the system reduces to a Leontief production system.

The solution is due to Samuelson and to Georgescu–Roegen [1951], among others.

UNSOLVED PROBLEM

L. I.E. Path Dominates

Generalize Theorem 19 to the case where there are several possible von Neumann vectors. (Information: Part 1 of the proof applies to this case, and some reconstruction of Radner's lemma is necessary.)

5. Overtaking and Golden Ages

In very general technologies, a weak version of intertemporal efficiency can be defined. Efficient paths are those ultimately maximizing a utility function over time. It is shown that such an efficiency requirement is attainable and that it requires per capita production to tend to points of zero growth. Indeed, output must tend to the best possible point of zero growth, which is called the golden age. There results a parable: society should seek to attain the golden age. Application to an efficient per capita capital stock appears at the end of the section.

The theory in this section is exceptional because it defines the goals of society explicitly in terms of utility, although no effort is made to study the way such a utility function can be constructed from that of many individual consumers. Therefore, like so much of the theory of efficiency, and in contradiction to many-consumer welfare economics, the theory is more a preview of what will hopefully be a future many-person theory. For this reason and because the balanced growth theorems recur here, we consider the overtaking theory in this chapter rather than later, when consumer preferences are integrated more elaborately into welfare economics.

Let there be a preference relation $\mathscr{R}$ that is defined for each $2\tau + 1$ time period. Hence, $\mathscr{R}$ ranks vector of the form

$$x^t = {}^{t-\tau}y^{t+\tau} = (y^{t-\tau}, ..., y^{t+\tau}).$$

It will be assumed that the x^t from x^{t-1} are limited by a *possibility transformation* $\mathscr{T}$, $x^t \in \mathscr{T}(x^{t-1})$. Normally, $\mathscr{T}$ requires that the time s components of x^t be equal to the time $s + 1$ component of x^{t-1} except for $s = t + \tau$ and $s = t - \tau - 1$. Then $\mathscr{T}(x^{t-1}) = ({}^{t-\tau+1}y^{t+\tau}, \mathscr{Y}(y^{t+\tau}))$. One *path* $(x^0, x^1, ...)$ *overtakes* another $(\bar{x}^0, \bar{x}^1, ...)$ if there is a T such that

$$\frac{1}{t}\sum_{i=0}^{t-1} x^i \mathscr{R} \frac{1}{t}\sum_{i=0}^{t-1} x^i \qquad \text{for all} \quad t > T.$$

In effect, the average consumption of one is better than that of the other. For example, $\mathscr{R}$ might evaluate only quantities of a utility produced by a consumer good. Then, $(x^0, x^1,...)$ overtakes $(\bar{x}^0, \bar{x}^1,...)$, if there is a T such that

$$\frac{1}{t} \sum_{i=0}^{t-1} u^i > \frac{1}{t} \sum_{i=0}^{t-1} \bar{u}^i$$

or, what amounts to the same thing,

$$\sum_{i=0}^{t-1} u^i < \sum_{i=0}^{t-1} \bar{u}^i \qquad \text{for all} \quad t > T.$$

This is the overtaking criterion presented by von Weizsäcker [1965] and treated by Koopmans [1965], Gale [1967], McFadden [1967], Atsumi [1965], and McKenzie [1968], among others. The source idea is due to Ramsey [1928].

A path $(x^0, x^1,...)$ *strongly overtakes* $(\bar{x}^0, \bar{x}^1,...)$ if there exist a y and a T such that

$$\frac{1}{t} \sum_{i=0}^{t-1} x^i \mathscr{P} y, \qquad y \mathscr{P} \frac{1}{t} \sum_{t=0}^{t-1} \bar{x}^i \qquad \text{for all} \quad t < T.$$

In the *von Weizsäcker case*, there is a t and a T such that

$$\sum_{i=0}^{t} u^i < \sum_{i=0} \bar{u}^i + \varepsilon t \qquad \text{for} \quad t < T.$$

We show that there is a path that is not strongly overtaken. The output y is *stationary* if $y \in \mathscr{T}(y)$.

A stationary point is *attainable* if, starting from x_0, there is an $(x_0, x_1,...)$, $x^t \in \mathscr{T}(x^{t-1})$, $x^t \to y$. If production is separate from consumption and if rates of depreciation are not too fast with regard to the growth of population, every stationary point is attainable. Simply have no consumption until the necessary capital stock for a stationary point has accumulated, at time T. Thereafter, the average consumption is

$$\frac{1}{n}(n - T)y \xrightarrow[n \to \infty]{} y.$$

20 Theorem *If*

(i) $\mathscr{T}$ *is upper semicontinuous, as it would be if production were closed,*

(ii) *there is a b such that $x^t \in \mathscr{T}(x^{t-1})$ is eventually bounded by b,* as in the case of a fixed limiting factor or that of x^t a per capita capital stock and a labor supply growing sufficiently fast to make infinite per capita capital stocks unattainable,

(iii) $\mathscr{R}(x)$ is closed (or $\mathscr{P}^{-1}(x)$ is open) for all x.

(iv) $\mathscr{T}$ is convex, as in the case of convex production,

(v) all stationary points are attainable.

Then there is a path $(x^0, x^1,...)$, $x^t \in \mathscr{T}(x^{t-1})$ that is not strongly overtaken by any other.

Proof If the x^t eventually fall within certain bounds, then

$$\frac{1}{n} \sum_{i=0}^{n-1} x^i$$

has limit points. Let

$$\mathscr{L} = \left\{ y \;\middle|\; \frac{1}{n_j} \sum_{i=0}^{n_j-1} x^i \xrightarrow[n_j\to\infty]{} y \quad \text{for some path } (x^0, x^1,...) \text{ from } x^0 \right\}.$$

The theorem will be proved if $\mathscr{R}$ takes an optimum on $\mathscr{L}$, for the path for which the foregoing average frequently tends to y will not be strongly overtaken by any other. If the optimum is unique, the path will not be overtaken by any other.

To show that $\mathscr{L}$ is bounded, observe that for every path $(x^0, x^1,...)$, there are b and T such that

$$|x^t| < b \qquad \text{for} \quad t > T.$$

Hence,

$$\left| \frac{1}{n} \sum_{i=0}^{n-1} x^i \right| \leqslant \frac{1}{n} \sum_{i=0}^{n-1} |x^i|$$

$$= \frac{1}{n} \left(\sum_{i=0}^{T} |x^i| + \sum_{i=T}^{n-1} |x^i| \right)$$

$$\leqslant \frac{1}{n} \sum_{i=0}^{T} |x^i| + b \frac{n-1-T}{n}$$

Hence,

$$\limsup \left| \frac{1}{n} \sum_{i=0}^{n-1} x^i \right| \leqslant \limsup \frac{1}{n} \sum_{i=0}^{T} |x^i| + \limsup \frac{n-1-T}{n} b$$

$$= b.$$

By (i), the set $\mathscr{S}$ of stationary points is closed, and by (v), $\mathscr{L} \supset \mathscr{S}$. From the lemma following, we have $\mathscr{L} = \mathscr{S}$, so that $\mathscr{L}$ is closed

Therefore, $\mathscr{L}$ is compact and $\mathscr{R}$ takes a maximum on $\mathscr{L}$ (Theorem 4, of Chapter 5 of the companion volume). It remains to show $\mathscr{L} \subset \mathscr{S}$.

q.e.d.

21 Lemma   *Under the hypothesis of Theorem* 20, *for any path* $(x_0 , x_1 ,...)$,

$$\lim \frac{1}{n} \sum_{i=0}^{n-1} x^t$$

contains only stationary points.

Proof   If $\mathscr{T}$ is convex and

$$\frac{1}{n_i} \sum_{t=m}^{n_i-1} x^t \to x^m$$

then $x^m \in \mathscr{T}(x^{m-1})$ (upper semicontinuity). Also,

$$x^m = x^{m-1} + \lim \frac{1}{n_i} (x^{m+n_i-1} - x^{m-1})$$

$$= x^{m-1} \qquad \text{by boundedness of} \quad x^{m+n_i-1}.$$

Hence, all limits of sums are stationary.   q.e.d.

Let y be stationary. From y, at say, T, return to no consumption for one period, splurge the next, and return to y for $2T$ periods; save, splurge, and return to y for $3T$ periods; etc. The resulting path has

$$\frac{1}{n} \sum_{t=0}^{n-1} x^t \to y$$

but $x_t \to y$ only for "most time periods." Let y be the sum $\frac{1}{2}(x + z)$, x, z stationary points. Then suppose it takes T periods to move x to z. Stay at x for $2T$ periods, move to z in T periods. Stay at z for $2T$ periods, move to x for $3T$ periods, etc. Again, the path cannot be overtaken, but x^t is never even near y.

Existence of a path not overtaken by another is doubtful. If consumer goods are durable, any path can be overtaken by delaying consumption and spreading it out over all time periods. If consumer goods are not durable, then the same effect can be obtained by accumulating more capital for nonsustainable consumptions. These are examples of cake eating, where one can eat say $u_t = 1/2^t$ in time $t > 0$ or $u_t^T = 1/2^{t-T}$ for time $t > T$. Always, u_t^T will overtake u_t for $S < T$. In the limit, $u_t = 0$, which is also overtaken. Hence, there is no path that is not overtaken, and we must be satisfied with one that is not strongly overtaken.

The set of *golden ages* is the set of vectors $\mathscr{G}$ optimizing preferences among those which are stationary. Let $T(\varepsilon, t)$ be the number of x^s within ε of the golden age set $\mathscr{G}$, but s less than t. In a certain sense, consumption tends to the golden age. The function n is (*strictly*) *concave* if $u(tx + (1 - t)y)\ (>) \geqslant tu(x) + (1 - t)\,u/y)$ for all $0 < t < 1$.

22 Theorem *Suppose the hypothesis of Theorem* 20 *and also*

(vi) *there is a single utility "good" "produced" from the others by a continuous, strictly concave function.*

Then, for a path not strongly overtaken, the path tends to the set of golden ages for most periods: for any $\varepsilon > 0$,

$$\lim \frac{T(\varepsilon, n)}{n} \to 1.$$

The following theorem shows that not only average or accumulated utilities are good, but so are the limiting one-period consumptions. More cannot be hoped for because we can always delay consumption in period τ, 3τ, 6τ,..., to increase it in the next, but the total effect gradually disappears in the averages.

Proof The set of stationary points $\mathscr{S}$ is convex and closed. Since all points in $\mathscr{S}$ are attainable, $\mathscr{S}$ is bounded. Hence, $\mathscr{R}$ is optimized at a convex set of points $\mathscr{G} \subset \mathscr{S}$ that have the same utility u_l. For any path that cannot be strongly overtaken,

$$\frac{1}{n_i} \sum_{t=0}^{n_i - 1} x^t \to y,$$

since otherwise the path to y would strongly overtake $(x^0, x^1,...)$.

A property of continuous, strictly concave functions defined on a compact set is that, for any $t > \tau$ and some $\delta > 0$ such that

$$u\left(\frac{1}{n} \sum_{t=0}^{n-1} x^t\right) > \frac{1}{n} \sum_{t=0}^{n-1} u(x^t) + \delta$$

whenever the number of x more than ε away from

$$\frac{1}{n} \sum_{t=0}^{n-1} x^t$$

does not tend to zero relative to n.

To see this, let the ε-neighborhood of

$$y = \frac{1}{n} \sum_{t=0}^{n-1} x^t$$

be enclosed in a small hypercube $\mathscr{C}_0$. Then, consider other hypercubes $\mathscr{C}_i$, which together cover the space of possible x, but have no points in common with the ε-neighborhood of y. There will be a finite number of these, numbered $i = 1,\ldots, m$, and

$$\frac{1}{n} \sum_{t=0}^{n-1} x^t = \frac{1}{n} \sum_i \sum_{<n, x_t \in \mathscr{C}_i t} x^t$$

$$= \sum_i \frac{m_i(n)}{n} \sum_{\substack{x_t \in \mathscr{C}_i \\ t < n}} \frac{x^t}{m_i(n)}$$

where $m_i(n)$ are the number of x^t in C_i but less than n. Since $\mathscr{C}_i$ is convex,

$$\frac{1}{n} \sum_{t=0}^{n-1} x^t = \sum_i \frac{m_i(n)}{n} y^i \qquad \text{where} \quad y^i \in \mathscr{C}_i.$$

A straightforward limit argument shows that changing the x^t,

$$\frac{1}{n} \sum_{t=0}^{n-1} u(x^t),$$

cannot tend to

$$u\left(\frac{1}{n} \sum_{t=0}^{n-1} x^t\right)$$

unless

$$\sum_{i \geqslant 1} \frac{m_i(n)}{n} \to 0.$$

Let the utility good be good k. For the particular case in point, construct a cube around the limiting golden age path:

$$\frac{1}{n_i} \sum_{t=0}^{n_i-1} x^t = \sum \frac{m_j(n_i)}{n_i} \sum y_{ij} \to y.$$

Without loss of generality,

$$y_{\sim k} = \sum_i t_i y_{\sim k}^i \qquad \text{where} \quad y_{\sim k}^i \in \mathscr{C}_i,$$

$\sum t_i = 1$, $t_i > 0$, and $t_i = \lim[m(n_i)/n_i]$ (compactness). Evidently

$t_i = 0$ for all $i > 0$. Otherwise the path attaining $y_{\sim k}$ into the indefinite future strongly dominates by giving δ more utility. Therefore,

$$\sum_{j>1} \frac{m_j(n_i)}{n_i} \to 0$$

or

$$1 \leftarrow \frac{n_i - \sum_{j>1}[m_j(n_i)/n_i]}{n_i} \leqslant \frac{T(\varepsilon, n_i)}{n_i} \leqslant 1 \qquad (y \text{ is in } \mathscr{G}).$$

For every subsequence, there will be a convergent subsequence with this property. Hence,

$$\frac{T(t, n)}{n} \to 1.$$

Evidently, the utility good also converges to its golden age value (continuity of u).   q.e.d.

23 Remark   If, in addition to the hypothesis of Theorem 20, $\mathscr{T}$ is strictly convex, as in the case of per capita capital subject to convexity of production, then there is a single golden age vector of capital stocks and consumptions. It is the limit for most periods of any path not strongly overtaken.

In the model analyzed by Ramsey [1928], Solow [1956], Phelps [1961], Robinson [1956], and von Weizsäcker [1965], there is a single good, which may be consumed or accumulated in capital. It is produced from capital K and labor L, which grows at the natural rate n, by a continuous, concave, and linear homogeneous production function f. The stationary points in par capita terms are given by the equations

$$\frac{K_t}{L_t} = k, \qquad c = \frac{C_t}{L_t} = f(k, 1) - nk;$$

c is per capita consumption, which is less than income, since investment per capita must be equal to nk. The golden age is the unique solution of

$$\frac{\partial f}{\partial k} - n = 0, \qquad k < 0.$$

Clearly, c is a strictly concave function of k. Hence, the paths that are not strongly overtaken in consumer goods tend to the golden age, which is a form of the neoneoclassical theorem.

In Figure 3a, unbounded per capita outputs are possible. In Figure 3b, there is a unique, positive golden age per capita capital stock $\bar{k}$. In

Figure 3c, the labor force grows too fast for a nonzero golden age. The question of the existence of nonzero consumption in the golden age is deferred until Chapter 7.

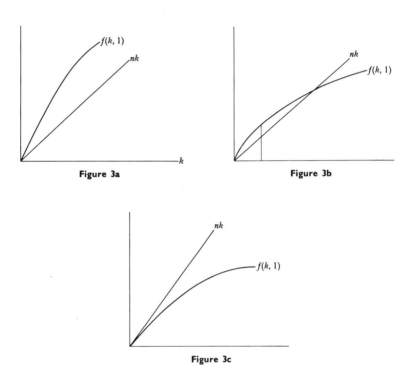

Figure 3a

Figure 3b

Figure 3c

Exercise 18 Show that in the golden age, investment equals the competitive share of capital, consumption, and competitive share of labor (Phelps [1961]).

Exercise 19 Use the proof of Theorem 22 to prove a "utility turnpike" theorem for an economy where all points $\mathscr{S}$ are reachable (McKenzie [1968]). (Hint: Observe that for large fixed n, $\max(1/n) \sum_{t=1}^{n-1} u(x^t)$ is nearly a (reachable) stationary point and dominates a path tending to that point. Then show that most x^t are near the stationary point and therefore near the golden age.)

6. Minkowski's Theorem in ∞-Space

Minowski's theorem has already been invoked to obtain production prices. The derivation of prices is important both as an analytical tool for the theorist and for use in the control of production. Applications appear in Sections 7 and 8 and in Chapter 2. In all cases, the basic result needed is the Minkowski theorem which shows when two convex sets can be separated by a hyperplane. Both because of the importance of Minkowski's theorem to welfare economics and because it is a rather deep mathematical proposition, we devote a section to its exposition.

It is possible to use Minkowski's theorem to develop necessary and sufficient conditions for an optimum in quite general spaces, as in Section 8. However, some restrictions must be made on both the function that is being maximized and the particular subset over which the maximization takes place. The analysis depends on algebraic as well as analytical ideas.

A *real linear space* or a real vector space $\mathscr{L}$ is a set with the operations $+$ (algebraic addition) and $\circ$ (scalar multiplication), for which

(i) $x + y = y + x$, $y \in \mathscr{L}$ (commutativity),

(ii) $x + (y + z) = (x + y) + z$, $x, y, z, \in \mathscr{L}$ (associativity);

(iii) there is a unique $0 \in x$ for which $x + 0 = x$ for all $x \in \mathscr{L}$ (the origin),

(iv) for every $x \in \mathscr{L}$ there is a unique $-x \in \mathscr{L}$ for which $(-x) + x = 0$ (additive inverse),

(v) $t \circ (x + y) = (t \circ x) + (t \circ y)$ for all $t \in \mathscr{E}^1$,

(vi) $(t + s) \circ x = (t \circ x) + (s \circ x)$ for all $x \in \mathscr{L}$, $t, s \in \mathscr{E}^1$ (distributivity),

(vii) $t \circ (s \circ x) = (ts) \circ x$ for all $x \in \mathscr{L}$, $s \in \mathscr{E}^1$ (associativity), and

(viii) $1 \circ x = x$ for $x \in \mathscr{L}$ (the unit).

Examples of linear spaces are Euclidean space, both finite and infinite dimensional. Such an example is a commodity space, where commodity bundles (not necessarily with only a finite number of commodities) can be added by adding the quantities of each separate commodity and multiplied by multiplying the quantities of each separate commodity. In a linear commodity space, commodities can be divided into arbitrarily small parts. Attention is often restricted to convex subset $\mathscr{X}$ of the linear space $\mathscr{L}$. From the opposite point of view, the essential property of $\mathscr{X}$ is that it can be imbedded in a linear space as a convex set (by a 1–1 function). For example, the set of nonnegative commodity bundles may be imbedded in a linear space where negative quantities are allowed.

A linear space is a *linear topological space* if

(i) $t_n x_n \to tx$ whenever $t_n \to t$, $x_n \to x$, and

(ii) $x_n + y_n \to x + y$ whenever $x_n \to x$, $y_n \to y$.

A *linear function* from a linear space $\mathscr{L}_1$ to a linear space $\mathscr{L}_2$ is a function f for which

$$f(t \circ x + (1-t) \circ y) = (t \circ f(x)) + ((1-t) \circ f(y)).$$

A *linear functional* is a linear function from $\mathscr{L}$ into $\mathscr{E}^1$.

An *internal point* x of $\mathscr{A}$ is a point such that for every $y \in \mathscr{L}$, there exists an $\varepsilon > 0$ such that $tx + (1-t)y \in \mathscr{A} > 0 \leqslant t \leqslant \varepsilon$. If A and B are convex and have disjoint, nonempty interiors, then they are separated by a hyperplane.

24 Lemma *Let $\mathscr{A}$ and $\mathscr{B}$ be convex subsets of a linear topological space, and let $\mathscr{A}$ have an internal (interior) point. Then there is a nonzero (continuous) linear functional p "separating" $\mathscr{A}$ and $\mathscr{B}$, that is, such that $p(x) \geqslant p(y)$ for all $x \in \mathscr{A}$, $y \in \mathscr{B}$, if and only if $\mathscr{B}$ is disjoint from the internal (interior) points of $\mathscr{A}$* (Kelley and Namioka [1963, Theorem 14.2]).

In Figure 4, $\mathscr{A}$ and $\mathscr{B}$ are separated by the linear functional given by $p(x) = p_1 x_1 + p_2 x_2$. For all y on $\mathscr{H}(p)$, $z \in \mathscr{A}$, $x \in \mathscr{B}$,

$$p(x) \geqslant p(y) \geqslant p(z) \qquad \text{or} \qquad p(x) \geqslant p(z).$$

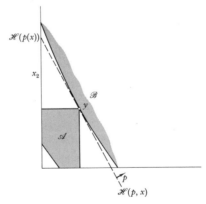

Figure 4

Exercise 20 A *Hamel base* is a collection of vectors $(x_\alpha, \alpha \in \mathscr{A})$ such that for any $x \in \mathscr{L}$, $x = \sum_{i=1}^{n} c_i x_{\alpha_i}$ is a unique representation of x. Show that x_α are linearly independent in that $\sum_{i=1}^{n} c_i x_{\alpha_i} = 0$ implies $c_i = 0$ for different x_{α_i}.

Exercise 21 Show that every linear space has a maximal linear subspace with a Hamel base.

Exercise 22 Show that for every linear subspace $\mathscr{L}'$ without an internal point there is a nonzero linear functional $f(x) = 0$ if $x \in \mathscr{L}'$. (Hint: Construct a Hamel base for $\mathscr{L}'$ and from that, one for $\mathscr{L}$.)

Exercise 23 Let $\mathscr{A}$ be a convex set with an internal point x, and let y be a point not internal to $\mathscr{A}$. Show that there is a linear space $\mathscr{L}'$ such that

   (i) $\mathscr{L}' + \{y\}$ has no points in common with the internal point of $\mathscr{A}$, and
   (ii) the Hamel base of $\mathscr{L}'$ together with any vector in $\sim\mathscr{L}'$ forms a Hamel base for $\mathscr{L}$. (Hint: Translate y to the origin and consider the smallest cone containing $\mathscr{A} - \{y\}$. Show that 0 is not internal to the cone and that the cone is contained in a cone $\mathscr{P}$ that has the properties that

   (a) $\mathscr{P} - \mathscr{P} = \mathscr{L}$,
   (b) no internal points of $\mathscr{P}$ are contained in $-\mathscr{P}$.

Then show that $\mathscr{P} - \mathscr{P}$ is the desired $\mathscr{L}'$.)

Exercise 24 In Exercise 23, show that there is a separating linear functional at y.

Exercise 25 Prove Lemma 24 for the case of "internal" points, and without continuity of p.

7. Short-Run Prices

Price systems characterize efficient points. Which price system is used depends on the technology and the particular concept of efficiency. Much of this book is concerned with further specifying the price system. However, its very existence suggests the possibility of the invisible hand. Decentralized agents can maximize profits with respect to the socially determined price system and thereby contribute to social optimization.

Here we consider prices for production in a single period. In certain circumstances prices not only exist but are unique. The results are especially important in the analysis of statics of short-run supply in Chapter 5. In the next section, prices are derived to guide production over time. Also, decentralization is treated there with regard to all price systems, short run or long run.

For the input–output set $_t\mathscr{Y}_{t+1}$, an efficient point $(y(t), y(t + 1))$ is one for which

$$(y(t), \bar{y}(t + 1)) \geqslant (y(t), y(t + 1))$$

implies

$$\bar{y}(t+1) = y(t+1).$$

For simplicity of notation, let y denote $y(t)$ and x denote $y(t+1)$. In order to decentralize production between units for which

$$_t\mathscr{Y}_{t+1} = \sum_{i=1}^{n} {}_t\mathscr{Y}^i_{t+1},$$

we must make sure that each subunit is led to choose capital inputs $y_i(t)$ consistent with the community requirements $\sum y^i = y$. Therefore, there must be (current) goods prices p and capital rents r, whereby short-run profit maximization leads to the choice of

$$(y, x) = \sum (y^i, x^i), \qquad (y^i, x^i) \in {}_t\mathscr{Y}^i_{t+1}.$$

First, we have the additivity theorem:

25 Theorem *Let p be additive on*

$$\mathscr{Y} = \sum_{i=1}^{n} \mathscr{Y}_i.$$

Then p is maximized at

$$y = \sum_{i=1}^{n} y_i$$

in $\mathscr{Y}$ if, and only if, py is maximized at y_i in $\mathscr{Y}_i$. Hence, it is necessary only to derive a price system for $_t\mathscr{Y}_{t+1}$, which is the reason for adopting a profit maximization scheme for purposes of decentralizing economic decisions. Incidentally, *both produced and unproduced capital goods are considered, so that the number of outputs may well be less than the number of capital goods.*

That which follows contains the elements of distribution theory, as discussed in Section 3 of Chapter 10 of the companion volume. First we show a price–wage system yielding zero profit.

26 Theorem *Let $_t\mathscr{Y}_{t+1}$ be closed and convex. Suppose (y, x) is in the boundary of $_t\mathscr{Y}_{t+1}$. Then there exists a pair $(-w, p)$ such that (y, x) maximizes $px - wy$. The set of all such price–wage pairs is a convex cone. Under constant returns, profits are zero. If there is some degree of free disposal, $px > 0$. If also factors are not negatively productive, then $w \geqslant 0$.*

Proof By virtue of Minkowski's theorem, there exists $(-w, p)$ such that

$$(-w, p)(y, x) \geqslant (-w, p)(\bar{y}, \bar{x}) \qquad \text{for all} \quad (\bar{y}, \bar{x}) \in {}_t\mathscr{Y}_{t+1}.$$

If

$$px - wy \geqslant p\tilde{x} - w\tilde{y} \qquad \text{and} \qquad \bar{p}x - \bar{w}y \geqslant \bar{p}\tilde{x} - \bar{w}\tilde{y},$$

then

$$(ap + b\bar{p})x - (aw - b\bar{w})y \geqslant (ap + b\bar{p})\tilde{x} - (aw + b\bar{w})\tilde{y}$$

for $a > 0, b > 0$.

Under constant returns, $k(px - wy)$ are possible profits, $k > 0$. Therefore, $px - wy \leqslant 0$ for profit maximizing (y, x). In fact, profits are zero since $(0, 0) \in {}_t\mathscr{Y}_{t+1}$. q.e.d.

27 Remark If ${}_t\mathscr{Y}_{t+1}$ is strongly convex, then the set of (y, x) maximizing profits $px - wy$ is unique up to a multiplicative constant. If ${}_t\mathscr{Y}_{t+1}$ is convex, then the set of (y, x) maximizing profits is a convex cone.

Proof If (y, x) and $(\bar{y}, \bar{x})$ are not proportional and have the same profit, then so do their convex combinations $s(y, x) + (1 - s)(\bar{y}, \bar{x}), 1 > s > 0$. Move from $s(y, x) + (1 - s)(\bar{y}, \bar{x})$ in a profit-improving direction. This gives a greater profit than (y, x) and $(\bar{y}, \bar{x})$. q.e.d.

In certain circumstances, p and w may be unique. In this case, it is said that ${}_t\mathscr{Y}_{t+1}$ is *directional dense* at (y, x) for the simple reason that (w, p) is unique up to a multiplicative constant if, and only if, there is a set of vectors dense in $\mathscr{E}^{n+m}$, whose every vector (δ, ε) has properties that $(y, x) + t(\delta, \varepsilon)$ is in ${}_t\mathscr{Y}_{t+1}$ for some $t \neq 0$ (possibly negative).

Technology is said to be *Leontief* if the raw materials requirements are like those in a Leontief system, that is, the intensity of industry (equals gross output) is equal to $(I - A)^{-1} x$ where x is net output.

The theorem following shows that wages are determined entirely by goods prices and factor endowments.

28 Theorem *Let f^i be differentiable and let there be constant returns for all industries, $i = 1,..., k$. Then all industry input–output combinations are equally profitable for all (w, p) leading to profit maximization at (y, x). If y is strictly positive, w is uniquely determined by (y, x) and p.*

If the technology is Leontief, and if all industries are profitable, p is uniquely determined by w.

The idea of the proof is that the marginal product must equal the wage for all factors used. Also, if for a given output price p, there are two input prices w and $\bar{w}$, with industry inputs $\xi_i y^i$, $\xi_i \bar{y}^i$, respectively, and if also the outputs in both cases sum to y, then $\xi_i y^i$ and $\xi_i \bar{y}^i$ are interchangeable, and therefore, the marginal products of y_j must equal tha wage rate of $\bar{w}_j$, as well as w_j.

Proof Different ways of producing z from y are equally profitable:

$$x = \sum \xi_i x^i, \qquad y = \sum \xi_i y^i$$
$$px - wy = 0, \qquad px^i - wy^i \leqslant 0$$

implies that

$$px^i - wy^i = 0 \qquad \text{whenever} \quad \xi_i > 0.$$

Therefore, (y^i, x^i) is profit maximizing, $\xi_i > 0$, whenever (y, x) is profit maximizing.

If $y \gg 0$, each capital good is used in some industry, so that the first-order condition of maximization is that

$$w_j = \frac{\partial px^i}{\partial y_j^i} = \frac{p \partial f^i}{\partial y_j^i}.$$

If there is a different w possible with p and producing (y, x), all ways of producing (y, x) are profitable at $(\bar{w}, p)$ as well. Hence, $p \, \partial f^i / \partial y_j$ is still determined by the preceding equation, that is,

$$w = p \frac{\partial f^i}{\partial y}.$$

Therefore, given p, w is determined.

Also, since $(w, \bar{p})$ does as well as $(\bar{w}, \bar{p})$,

$$w^j = \bar{p} \frac{\partial f^i}{\partial y^i}$$

for y^i profit maximizing. Therefore, *the dimension of variation of* (p, w) *is at most equal to* $m + n$ *minus the number of linearly independent* $(\partial f^i / \partial y^i \mid - I)$, *which equals* $m + n$ *minus the number of linearly independent* $\partial f^i / \partial y^i$. Let $Y = (y_i^j)$ be the distribution of capital among industries, and let $X = (x_k^j)$ be the distribution of output. If the technology is Leontief and if all industries are profitable,

$$pX = wY \qquad \text{and} \qquad p = wyX^{-1}. \qquad \text{q.e.d.}$$

Exercise 26 Suppose there is a single (original) factor of production, labor. What is the distribution of income between laborers and the owners of firms?

8. Long-Run Prices

In considering output over time, we will show that efficiency is roughly equivalent to maximizing an infinite sum of properly discounted gross national products (*gnp*). The theory is in two parts. First, efficiency implies prices and maximization of the sum of *gnp*'s implied by the prices. Second, maximization of a sum of *gnp*'s in terms of given prices leads to an efficient path. We will see that the maximization of summed *gnp* can be decentralized among firms by trading capital goods.

In moving to the long run, a generalization of the notion of efficiency is desirable. We wish to account for a commodity, such as labor, which it may be preferable to minimize, rather than to maximize both output per unit of labor and the amount of labor input. Consider a production path $(y(t), t = 0, 1, 2,...)$ that is maximal in either direction; that is, there does not exist in ${}_0\mathscr{Y}_\infty(y(0))$ a $(y^t(t), t = 0, ., 2,...) \neq (y(t), t = 0, 1, 2,...)$ such that

$$y_i'(t) \geqslant y_i(t)$$

for commodities preferred in larger quantities, and

$$y_i(t) \geqslant y_i'(t)$$

for those preferred in smaller quantities. Efficiency is the special case of maximality where no goods are preferred in smaller quantities. Of course, time t–final state efficiency is a still more restricted case.

A maximal path can be obtained by maximizing a long-run profit function on ${}_0\mathscr{Y}_\infty(y(0))$. Note that a maximal path is in the boundary of ${}_0\mathscr{Y}_\infty(y(0))$. Normally, we would expect to be able to apply Minkowski's theorem directly to a convex ${}_0\mathscr{Y}_\infty(y(0))$ to obtain a linear functional p, such that $p(y'(t), t = 0, 1, 2,...)$ is maximized on ${}_0\mathscr{Y}_\infty(y(0))$ at $y(t)$. This is illustrated schematically in Figure 5 for one commodity and for times t_1 and t_2 after time 0. The larger $y(t_1)$, the larger $y(t_2)$. The largest possible $y(t_1)$ is located at $\bar{y}$. In this case, $\bar{y}$ maximizes profits for the value system $\sum p(t)y(t)$. (Also, $\bar{y}$ maximizes profits for any price system with positive elements.) The point of the example is that ${}_0\mathscr{Y}_\infty$ is convex and there is a separating linear functional. In general, however, t refers to an infinite number of periods, and therefore it is required that

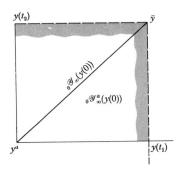

Figure 5

$_0\mathscr{Y}_\infty(y(0))$ have an interior point; that is, we must satisfy the hypothesis of Lemma 24. Clearly, in Figure 5, $_0\mathscr{Y}_\infty(y(0))$ does not have interior points. This is the general case. For example, consider a reduction of $y(t)$ at time t, say, by free disposal. This normally implies that $y(s)$ is reduced for $s > t$. We cannot arbitrarily go out in the direction of lesser amounts in a single component, whereupon $_0\mathscr{Y}_\infty(y(0))$ cannot have any interior points. Hence, $_0\mathscr{Y}_\infty(y(0))$ must be augmented with other points in order to obtain the desired result.

We first show that maximality implies a price system.

29 Theorem *Suppose $_0\mathscr{Y}_\infty(y(0))$ is convex. Let components of $_0\mathscr{Y}_\infty(y(0))$ be bounded by $k(t)$. If $(y(t), t = 0, 1, 2,...)$ is maximal in $_0\mathscr{Y}_\infty(y(0))$, then there is a nonzero linear functional p, continuous in the metric $\| y \|$ $\sup_s |y(s)|/k(s)\, 2^s$, such that $(y(t), t = 0, 1, 2,...)$ maximizes $\cdot$ for z in $_0\mathscr{Y}_\infty(y(0))$. Furthermore, p can be represented as*

$$p(y(t), t = 0, 1, 2,...) = \sum_{t=0}^{\infty} p(t)\, y(t)$$

where $p(t)$ has a consistent sign positive in all components except those which are preferred in smaller quantities and negative in others.

$p(t)$ is referred to as the *time t price system*.

Proof Attention is restricted to those points in $\mathscr{E}^\infty$ for which $\| \|$ is a *norm*. Note that

(i) $\| ay \| = | a |\, \| y \|$ for a constant a,
(ii) $\| x + y \| \leqslant \| x \| + \| y \|$,
(iii) $\| x \| = 0$ if $x = 0$,
     $\| x \| > 0$ otherwise.

It is easy to verify that convergence in the norm defines $\mathscr{L}$ as a linear topological space.

For $(y(t),\ t = 0, 1, 2,...)$ maximal in $_0\mathscr{Y}_\infty(y(0))$, augment $_0\mathscr{Y}_\infty(y(0))$ by adding those points in $\mathscr{L}$ that have no greater coordinates except for commodities preferred in smaller quantities and no less otherwise than some $(y(t),\ t = 0, 1, 2,...)$ in $_0\mathscr{Y}_\infty(y(0))$; that is,

$$_0\mathscr{Y}_\infty^a(y(0)) = \{y'(t),\ t = 0, 1, 2,... \mid y_i'(t) < y_i(t)\}$$

if i is preferred in smaller quantities and $y_i'(t) \leqslant y_i(t)$ otherwise, for some $(y(t),\ t = 0, 1, 2,...) \in {}_0\mathscr{Y}_\infty(y(0)),\ y^t \in \mathscr{L}\}$.

Clearly, $(y(t),\ t = 0, 1, 2,...)$ is maximal in $_0\mathscr{Y}_\infty^a(y(0))$ and is not an interior point. If $y^a(t) = -2^t(k(t), k(t),..., k(t))$, then for $\| x - y^a \| < 1$, $| x(t) - y^a(t) | < k(t)2^t$ for all t and therefore $x(t) \leqslant 0$, so that x is in $_0\mathscr{Y}_\infty^a(y(0))$. Hence, y so defined is an interior point of $_0\mathscr{Y}_\infty^a(y(0))$.

This construction is illustrated in Figure 5, where $_0\mathscr{Y}_\infty^a(y(0))$ is the set of all points $y \leqslant \bar{y}$ also having a zeroth coordinate $y^a(0) \leqslant y(0)$. There is an interior point y^a, augmented from $\bar{y}$, which together with $y_{(0)}^a < y(0)$ forms a point $(y^a(0), y^a)$ in $_0\mathscr{Y}_\infty^a(y(0))$ that is the interior to $_0\mathscr{Y}_\infty^a(y(0))$.

Next, $_0\mathscr{Y}_\infty^a(y(0))$ is convex whenever $_0\mathscr{Y}_\infty(y(0))$ is convex. Therefore, $_0\mathscr{Y}_\infty^a(y(0))$ is a convex set with a nonempty interior and with $(y(t),\ t \in [0, \infty])$ in its boundary. By Lemma 24, there is a separating continuous (in a uniform topology) linear functional p such that $(y(t),\ t = 0, 1, 2,...)$ maximizes $p(z)$ for z in $_0\mathscr{Y}_\infty(y(0))$. Evidently, if $y(t)$ and $\bar{y}(t)$ differ only in a finite number of periods, then clearly $p_i(t)$ must have the desired sign; otherwise, a z in $_0\mathscr{Y}_\infty(y(0))$ augmented from $y(t)$ could be found with a higher value for the sum.

Since $y(t)/k(t)\,2^t \to 0$ for all $y \in {}_0\mathscr{Y}_\infty(y)$, pointwise convergence implies convergence in the metric. Therefore, p is continuous in pointwise convergence.

Letting $p_i = (1/x_i)\,p(0,..., 0, x_i, 0,...)$ for $x_i \neq 0$, it is easy to show that $\sum p_i x_i$ converges for all x in $\mathscr{L}$. First multiply coordinates by minus one whenever they indicate quantities of commodities that are undesirable. Then, $p(x) \geqslant p(y)$ whenever $x \geqslant y$. Also, $\sum p_i x_i$ is defined whenever $\sum p_i \mid x_i \mid$ is defined, which is the case whenever $\sum p_i \mid x_i \mid$ is bounded. Boundedness follows from

(i) $\|(x_1, x_2,...)\|$ is defined implies $\|(\mid x_1 \mid, \mid x_2 \mid,...)\|$ is defined, and
(ii) $p(\mid x_1 \mid, \mid x_2 \mid,...) \geqslant \sum_{i=1}^m p_i x_i$ for all m.

Multiplication by minus one again brings p_i to its value on $\mathscr{L}$.

Let $y \in {}_0\mathscr{Y}_\infty(y)$, $\|(0, 0,..., 0, y_i, y_{i+1},...)\| \to 0$ whenever $i \to \infty$.

Therefore, $(y_1, y_2, ..., y_i, 0, ...)$ tends to y in the metric and $\sum_{i=1}^{m} p_i x_i$ tends to $p(y)$.   q.e.d.

Theorem 29 says that for any convex, pointwise compact subset, $\mathscr{B} \subset \mathscr{E}^\infty$, and for any maximal point in $\mathscr{B}$, there is a linear functional attaining its maximum on $\mathscr{B}$ and continuous in pointwise convergence.

The converse of Theorem 29 is more general; namely, the maximum of a continuous linear functional $\sum_{t=0}^{\infty} p(t) y(t)$ over $_0\mathscr{Y}_\infty(y(0))$, $p_i(t)$ nonzero and with consistent signs over time, gives a maximal point.

30 Theorem   *Suppose* $(y(t), t = 0, 1, 2, ...)$ *maximizes*

$$\sum_{t=0}^{\infty} p_i(t) y(t)$$

on $_0\mathscr{Y}_\infty(y(0))$, $p_i(t) \neq 0$ *of identical and consistent sign. Then* $(y(t), t = 0, 1, 2, ...)$ *is maximal.*

Proof   If not, there is a $(y'(t), t = 0, 1, 2, ...)$ in $_0\mathscr{Y}_\infty(y(0))$ that is actually superior to $(y(t), t = 0, 1, 2, ...)$. Therefore,

$$\sum_{t=0}^{\infty} p_i(t)(y'(t) - y(t)) < 0,$$

$$\sum_{0}^{\infty} p(t) y'(t) \, dt < \sum_{0}^{\infty} p(t) y(t) \, dt,$$

contrary to hypothesis.   q.e.d.

The price systems derived in Theorems 29 and 30 are key for applications to economic control. Unfortunately, there does not appear to be a strict equivalence between maximality and maximization of a linear functional, since a positive price system leads to an efficient (and hence maximal) production path, but a maximal production path might require a zero price for some i. This is the case in Figure 6, in which the efficient point $(0, \bar{y}(1))$ is attainable by maximizing a linear functional only with a zero price for the time one commodity, since $_0\mathscr{Y}_\infty(y(0))$ is bounded by a curve tangent to the vertical line through $(0, \bar{y}(1))$. Furthermore, there is no price system for which profit maximization yields $(0, \bar{y}(1))$ over, say, $(0, 0)$. Perhaps this is a small matter, since some maximizer will be appropriate, but in any case, there is not a one-to-one relationship between maximal paths and nonzero price systems.

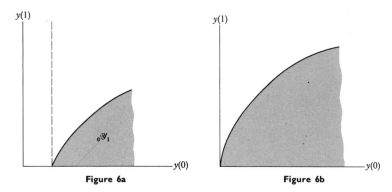

Figure 6a **Figure 6b**

A particular case that allows some degree of decentralization of operation is that for which $(y(t), t = 0, 1, 2,...)$ is efficient, $y(0)$ is distributed among agents in quantities $y_j(0), j = 1,..., n$,

$$_t\mathscr{Y}_{t+1}(y(t)) = \sum_{j=1}^{n} {}_t\mathscr{Y}^j_{t+1}((y^j(t))) \quad \text{and} \quad y(t) = \sum y^j(t).$$

In effect $_t\mathscr{Y}_{t+1}(y(0))$, consists of the collected outputs of the subsystems.

In general, it is impossible to decentralize decisions by using only the capital price system that has been derived. Exchange of capital between units must be allowed. The difficulty is that normally the subparts should specialize in those functions in which they have a comparative advantage and should make contractual arrangements with others for materials that they do not manufacture. Hence, the capital possibility set $_0\mathscr{Y}_\infty(y(0))$ is not the sum of each individual set, disregarding trade between the parts.

As in pure competition with exchange between consumer-producers, the solution consists in allowing each unit to use any desired quantities of capital, but requiring each unit to pay for any changes in capital stock that do not result from its productive activities. Let $z^i(t) \in {}_t\mathscr{Y}^i_{t+1}(y^i(t))$. In effect, the unit maximizes

$$\sum_{t=0}^{\infty} p(t)\, z^i(t) - \sum_{t=0}^{\infty} p(t)\, x^i(t)$$

where it is required that

$$\sum_{t=0}^{\infty} p(t)\, x^i(t) = 0.$$

Application of the additivity theorem gives

$$\sum_{t=0}^{\infty} p(t)\, y^i(t) = \sum_{t=0}^{\infty} p(t)\, z^i(t) - \sum_{i} \sum_{t=0}^{\infty} p(t)\, x^i(t)$$

maximized for each i if, and only if,

$$\sum_{i} \sum_{t=0}^{\infty} p(t)\, z^i(t) - \sum_{i} \sum_{t=0}^{\infty} p(t)\, x^i(t) = \sum_{t=0}^{\infty} p(t) \sum y^i(t)$$

$$= \sum_{t=0}^{\infty} p(t)\, y(t)$$

is maximized. The following corollaries show how allocation decisions can be decentralized.

31 Corollary *Suppose $_0\mathscr{Y}_\infty(y(0))$ is convex, as it would be if $_t\mathscr{Y}_{t+1}(y)$ were convex in y. If*

$$(y(t), \quad t = 0, 1, 2,...) = \sum_{i} (y^i(t), \quad t = 0, 1, 2,...)$$

is maximal in $_0\mathscr{Y}_\infty(y(0))$, then there is a linear functional p, continuous in the metric $\| \ \|$, such that $(y^i - x^i(t), t = 0, 1, 2,...)$ and $(x^i(t), t = 0, 1, 2,...)$ together maximize

$$\sum_{t=0}^{\infty} p(t)\, y^i(t) - \sum_{t=0}^{\infty} p(t)\, x^i(t),$$

subject to

$$\sum p(t)\, x^i(t) = 0.$$

32 Corollary *Suppose $(z^i(t), t = 0, 1, 2,...)$ and $(x^i(t), t = 0, 1, 2,...)$ together maximize*

$$\sum_{t=0}^{\infty} p(t)\, z^i(t) - \sum_{t=0}^{\infty} p(t)\, x^i(t)$$

subject to

$$\sum_{t=0}^{\infty} p(t)\, x^i(t) = 0$$

on $_0\mathscr{Y}_\infty(y(0))$, $p_i(t) \neq 0$ of identical and consistent sign. Then $\sum z^i = (y(t), t = 0, 1, 2,...)$ is maximal.

Exercise 27 What is the relationship between the short-run and the long-run price systems?

UNSOLVED PROBLEM

M. Malinvaud Efficiency

Suppose for every producer good there is a consumer good produced in exactly the same way and under constant returns to scale. Which of the price systems giving efficient outputs gives only Malinvaud efficient outputs? (Hint: The set of possible consumptions is convex.)

2

Optimality

Economic logic prevails over the technological . . . . The economic best
and the technologically perfect need not, yet very often do, diverge, not
only because of ignorance and indolence but because methods which are
technologically inferior may still best fit the given economic conditions.

Joseph Schumpeter
in THEORY OF ECONOMIC DEVELOPMENT, 1934

1. Economic Systems Analysis

The theme of welfare economics is to characterize the various best
points of possible productions, trades, and consumptions in terms of the
individual preferences and various methods of economic organization.
This is a special case of systems analysis.

A management or organizational system is often regarded as a
mechanism by which certain goals are obtained. This mechanism may
be represented sequentially, as either a differential equation system or a
difference equation system. It is often convenient to judge it by three
criteria. First, are the goals it attains "desirable"? Second, does it

attain these goals quickly? Third, what is the cost of maintaining the system? Usually this last query reduces to the question how expensive is the information that is required in order that the system operate effectively?

The goals attained by the system depend on answers to the questions

(1)   Are there equilibria for the system?
(2)   Does the dynamic system tend to the equilibria?
(3)   What "good" do the equilibria attain?

A system that has an equilibrium under a wide range of individual preferences is said to be *complete*, since no further (coercive) restriction on such elements as preferences, production, or wealth is needed to make the system work. The speed with which the system attains its goals is a question of the speed of equilibration of the dynamic system. As it happens, it is analytically related to (2) above. The cost of maintenance is related to the amount of information needed for the system to operate over time.

The argument here proceeds on a plane that holds topics (1) and (2) in abeyance. Existence is the subject of Chapter 4. Chapter 7 discusses how the equilibrium states of the economic system are actually effected. In Chapter 8 there is an analysis of the speed with which equilibrium can be realized. The question of the goals attained by a system, (3) above, decomposes into subquestions:

(3a)   Does the system attain a situation that is judged "best"?

(3b)   Are all "best" situations attainable by the system (perhaps after adjusting certain "policy" parameters)?

For example, a system might attain a Pareto optimal trade, but one that favored only people with green eyes.

A system that attains an optimum under a social (partial) ordering $\mathcal{R}$ is said to be $\mathcal{R}$ *efficient*. A system that attains all optima under $\mathcal{R}$ (after an appropriate adjustment in policy parameters) is said to be *unbiased*.[1] In Sections 2–4, we present versions of the good to be attained by economic systems and some simple results about how to obtain these goods. The balance of the chapter is devoted to showing properties that, if satisfied by an economic system, ensure that it is complete, efficient, and/or unbiased for various social partial orderings. In Sections 5–9 we discuss the equivalence between consumer efficiency and various forms of competition. In Section 10, competitive equilibrium is shown to yield a proper distribution of benefits, presuming the initial

---

[1] The terminology is due to Hurwicz [1960].

wealth to be just. Applications to international trade appear in Sections 10 and 11.

In succeeding sections, we will try to show how society can be organized with different kinds of information relayed to individuals. The kind of information required is implicit in the system used, but it is not clear exactly how much information is really required until the dynamic aspects of the system are specified. For example, knowledge of prices might superficially appear to be sufficient. In fact, individuals might not wish to look only at prices. This is one of the major problems of welfare economics. In this context, certain especially able (and especially rich) traders may try to second guess the mechanism. For example, if there is a competitive price equilibrium, it will be shown that there is Pareto optimality (Section 8). The problem is that some traders are so powerful that they believe that they can influence the price ratios so that it will pay them to subvert the system by behaving in a noncompetitive manner. The only way to make them act in the correct way is to use some form of coercion, that is, to commit the system to a more expensive method of transmission of information.

The reader will recognize that we have restated the incentive problem. The happy economic system is one that can equate the interest of a society with the interest of the individual. Only then can an invisible hand operate effectively. However, if the individual has an incentive to second guess the authority, namely, the price system, then the authority must in turn second guess the individual. This may lead to infinite regression, which although solvable, is likely to involve a solution that is expensive to enforce. These problems are treated only super-ficially in Chapter 3. To a large extent they compose a caveat against welfare economics that is not yet fully understood.

The discussion in Sections 2–4 is on a very general plane. In order to give that discussion a concrete basis, we conclude this section with an outline of the special economic system that is henceforth our primary concern in this book. As explained in Chapter 9 of the companion volume, it has two forms: one is in terms of production and consumption; another is in terms of trade only.

If production is independent between different individuals i, the community output set

$$_0\mathcal{Y}_\infty = \sum_i {}_0\mathcal{Y}_\infty^i$$

is given by the law

$$y(t+1) \in \sum_i {}_i\mathcal{Y}_{t+1}^i(y^i(t)), \qquad \sum y^i(t) = y(t).$$

Let $\mathscr{R}_i$ be individual preferences and $\mathscr{C}_i$ individual consumption sets. Society can be regarded as

$$(\mathscr{R}_1, \mathscr{R}_2, ..., \mathscr{C}_1, \mathscr{C}_2, ... \mathscr{L}) \qquad \text{where} \quad (y^1, y^2, ...) \in \mathscr{L}$$

if and only if

(i) $y^i(t+1) \in {}_t\mathscr{Y}^i_{t+1}(y^i(t))$,
(ii) $y = \sum y^i$.

$\mathscr{L}$ is the *community production set* with the additional information of who produced what. Later, when social partial orderings are specified (Section 3), Theorem 1 will help ensure the existence of an optimum.

1 Theorem *If* ${}_0\mathscr{Y}_\infty(y(0))$ *is compact in pointwise convergence, then* $\mathscr{L}$ *is compact in pointwise convergence.*

Proof Evidently, $\mathscr{L}$ contains only nonnegative elements. Therefore,

$$y = \sum y^i \geqslant y^i \geqslant 0.$$

Since y is bounded, each component of $(y^1, y^2, ...)$ is bounded. This proves compactness in pointwise convergence.   q.e.d.

There are few further references to the production economy until Section 12 of this chapter, and this is one of the few cases where it appears to be more convenient to analyze production directly. Hereafter, the analysis concerns the alternative society

$$(\mathscr{R}_1^*, \mathscr{R}_2^*, ..., \mathscr{X}_1, \mathscr{X}_2, ..., \mathscr{X} \cap \mathscr{H})$$

where $\mathscr{R}_i^*$ is the induced preference relation on trades, $\mathscr{X}_i$ is the set of possible trades, $\mathscr{X} = \mathsf{X}_i \mathscr{X}_i$ and

$$\mathscr{H} = \left\{ (g_1, g_2, ...) \,\middle|\, \sum g_i = 0 \right\}$$

where the g_i are vectors in the linear spaces containing the $\mathscr{X}_i$. This exchange economy is a representation of the original economy and the theorems following are applied to it directly. For simplicity's sake, the $*$ is dropped, whereupon society is

$$(\mathscr{R}_1, \mathscr{R}_2, ..., \mathscr{X}_1, \mathscr{X}_2, ..., \mathscr{X} \cap \mathscr{H}).$$

2. Social Orderings and Welfare Functions

We consider possible specifications of a social ordering of productions, consumptions, etc. By definition this requires that all social states be comparable as socially better, worse, or indifferent. In view of contradictory interests between differing individuals, this is no mean task. In their present form, social welfare functions will be seen to be indeterminate and hence not the most effective tool for welfare economics. Nevertheless, the very possibility of social welfare functions would be an important justification of welfare economics, since at some future date the welfare function could possibly be further specified. In the meantime, the implications of its known properties could be set forth.

Arrow's celebrated impossibility theorem (Problem A of Chapter 3 of the companion volume) states that it is impossible to have an ordering on social alternatives that is determined by individual orderings and that satisfies certain "reasonable" requirements on social welfare. As in Coleman [1966], but for a different reason, it is argued that one of the requirements, namely, the independence of irrelevant alternatives, is unreasonable as applied to the notion of social welfare. Hence, there are many preference relations possible (Hildreth [1953]). In any case, it is important to discuss Arrow's theorem, since his negative conclusion would diminish the usefulness of this chapter. We then show one way to derive a social welfare function.

Given the impossibility theorem, there are two possible approaches. One is to drop the idea of a social welfare function comparing all alternatives and instead adopt ethics, which can give a small finite number of solutions that are then ordered among themselves. In effect, there is defined a social optimum, a suboptimum, a subsuboptimum, etc., according to a certain hierarchy of ethics. This procedure was suggested by Kant [1788, 1797] and is adopted in this chapter. Several ethical judgments will be made and the implication for social policy outlined. We will define, among others, the judgments Pareto optimality, group conservation, equity and divisibility. In particular, it will be shown that under a "convex environment" the social optima defined are related in an intimate way with the classical theory of pure competition.

A second approach is to reestablish the social welfare function by arguing that a particular assumption used to derive the impossibility theorem, namely, the independence of irrelevant alternatives, is too restrictive. This would allow us to speak of the social welfare function as the basis of ethical judgment, and theorems proved with various ethical judgments would be theorems about social welfare.

Marginal utility is arbitrary; therefore, we ought not merely to sum utility between different individuals and set social marginal utility equal to zero. Even in the most restrictive cases on preferences, we can always multiply utility (and marginal utility) by a positive constant, so that one person can be favored by increasing his weight in the social utility function. This leads to the correct view that direct interpersonal utility comparisons cannot be made. On the other hand, it is incorrectly said that interpersonal preference comparisons cannot be made. The assumption that such comparisons cannot be made leads to the impossibility of a reasonable social utility function. This would seem to be a *reductio ad absurdum* of the view that does not allow such preference comparisons. Alternatively, the result could be regarded as a repudiation of welfare economics.

Let $\mathscr{R} \subset \mathscr{X} \times \mathscr{X}$; we write $x\mathscr{R}y$ for $(x, y) \in \mathscr{R}$. The *relation* $\mathscr{R}$ is *reflexive* if $x\mathscr{R}x$. $\mathscr{R}$ is *complete* if for any $(x, y) \in \mathscr{X}$, either $x\mathscr{R}y$ or $y\mathscr{R}x$. $\mathscr{R}$ is *transitive* if $x\mathscr{R}y$, $y\mathscr{R}z$ implies $x\mathscr{R}z$. $\mathscr{R}$ is *ordering* if $\mathscr{R}$ is a reflexive, complete transitive relation.

It is the axiom of the independence of irrelevant alternatives that seems to be crucial. Let $\mathscr{R}$ be the social ordering and $\mathscr{R}_i$ the individual ordering ($x\mathscr{P}_i y$ stands for $x\,\mathscr{R}_i\,y$ but not $y\,\mathscr{R}_i\,x$; $x\,\mathscr{I}_i\,y$ stands for $x\,\mathscr{R}_i\,y$ and $y\,\mathscr{P}_i\,x$.) The independence of irrelevant alternatives amounts to: $\mathscr{R}$ is a function of the pairwise orders by $\mathscr{R}_i$; that is, if

$x\,\mathscr{P}_i\,y \qquad$ for $\quad i \in \mathscr{I}$,

$y\,\mathscr{P}_j\,x \qquad$ for $\quad j \in \mathscr{J}$,

$x\,\mathscr{I}_k\,y \qquad$ for $\quad i \in \sim\mathscr{I} \sim \mathscr{J} \qquad$ implies $\quad x\,\mathscr{R}\,y$,

then for some other set of orders $\mathscr{R}'_i$

$x\,\mathscr{P}'_i\,y \qquad$ for $\quad i \in \mathscr{I}$,

$y\,\mathscr{P}'_j\,x \qquad$ for $\quad j \in \mathscr{J}$,

$y\,\mathscr{I}'_k\,x \qquad$ for $\quad k \in \sim\mathscr{I} \sim \mathscr{J} \qquad$ implies $\quad x\,\mathscr{R}\,'y \qquad$ for $\quad \mathscr{R}'_i, \quad i = 1,..., n.$

That is to say, in two situations, identical patterns of ordering by different people lead to the same choice by society. To see this, consider Arrow's independence of irrelevant alternatives axiom:

> Let $\mathscr{R}_1 ,..., \mathscr{R}_n$ and $\mathscr{R}'_1 ,..., \mathscr{R}'_n$ be two sets of individual orderings and let $c(\mathscr{S})$ and $c(\mathscr{S}')$ be the corresponding social choice function. If for all individuals i and all x and y in a given environment, $\mathscr{S}$, $x\,\mathscr{R}_i\,y$ if and only if $x\,\mathscr{R}_i\,y$, then $c(\mathscr{S})$ and $c(\mathscr{S}')$ are the same (Arrow [1951, p. 27].)

We restrict attention to those environments $\mathscr{S}$ upon which $(\mathscr{R}_1, \mathscr{R}_2, ..., \mathscr{R}_3)$ and $(\mathscr{R}'_1, \mathscr{R}'_2, ..., \mathscr{R}'_3)$ agree. Then it is presumed that social choices as given by $c(\mathscr{S})$ and $c'(\mathscr{S})$, respectively, are identical. In effect, any information about preferences on other "irrelevant" alternatives is ignored.

This procedure seems unreasonable. Admittedly, for an ordering, the idea of intensity of feeling has no immediate application. However, this does not imply that certain vestigial forms of intensity are to be discarded. For example, consider three individuals making a choice among x, y, and z. The orderings are

$$x \, \mathscr{P}_1 \, y \, \mathscr{P}_1 \, z,$$
$$x \, \mathscr{P}_2 \, y \, \mathscr{P}_2 \, z,$$
$$z \, \mathscr{P}_3 \, x \, \mathscr{P}_3 \, y.$$

On the basis of this information, y seems relatively abhorrent to 3, whereas z is relatively valuable. For 1 and 2, y and z are less intensely differentiated. Imagine an egalitarian society. We would think it possible that in comparing z and y the other two would defer to 3, who shows great preference for z. On the other hand, x would undoubtedly be preferred to z, since both 1 and 2 show a strong preference for x, whereas 3 does not seem to greatly dislike x vis-à-vis z. Therefore, for society, $x \, \mathscr{P} \, z \, \mathscr{P} \, y$, which perhaps seems reasonable. If instead

$$x \, \mathscr{P}'_1 \, y \, \mathscr{P}'_1 \, z,$$
$$x \, \mathscr{P}'_2 \, y \, \mathscr{P}'_2 \, z,$$
$$x \, \mathscr{P}'_3 \, z \, \mathscr{P}'_3 \, y,$$

then 3 no longer has the very strong preference for z over y that he formerly had. Therefore, it is possible that the majority will dominate, giving
$$x \, \mathscr{P}' \, y \, \mathscr{P}' \, z.$$
However,

$$y \, \mathscr{P}_1 \, z, \qquad y \, \mathscr{P}'_1 \, z,$$
$$y \, \mathscr{P}_2 \, z, \qquad y \, \mathscr{P}'_2 \, z,$$
$$z \, \mathscr{P}_3 \, y, \qquad z \, \mathscr{P}'_3 \, y,$$

so that the independence of irrelevant alternatives requires that in both cases

$$y \, \mathscr{P} \, z, \qquad y \, \mathscr{P}' \, z.$$

In effect, the independence of irrelevant alternatives forces us to ignore information about preferences beyond the information derived from pairs of alternatives being directly compared. This is a strict requirement. (It is not contended that the suggested outcome would be appropriate in all circumstances. That would also depend on preferences between other "irrelevant" alternatives.)

To consider the general case, let the social preference relation $\mathscr{R}$ be defined. It depends on preferences and the level of preference. $\mathscr{R}$ is a function of the whole set

$$\mathscr{R}_i \subset \mathscr{X} \times \mathscr{X}$$

where $\mathscr{X}$ is the set of all possible alternatives. If the set of possible $\mathscr{R}_i$, which is a set of sets, can be given a completely separable topology, and if $\mathscr{R}$ satisfies the preference continuity conditions of Chapter 5 of the companion volume, there is a continuous social utility function

$$u(\mathscr{R}_1,...,\mathscr{R}_n, x), \qquad x \in \mathscr{X}.$$

For example, if $\mathscr{R}_i$ is represented by a utility function u, continuous on $\mathscr{X}$, then u may be considered as a continuous functional on the Cartesian product of $\mathscr{X}$ with the set of continuous functions on $\mathscr{X}$. The independence of irrelevant alternatives axiom requires that the ranking under u depends only on the comparisons

$$(u_i(x), u_i(y), \quad i = 1,..., n).$$

Therefore, u is a function of the utility values on $\mathscr{X}$:

$$u(u_1(x),..., u_n(x)).$$

This is a considerable restriction on u, since a change in u_i does not change anything other than the number on which u operates. In effect, social utility is no longer essentially an operator on function space but only on a finite-dimensional space. The size of its domain is radically reduced by the axiom of independence of irrelevant alternatives. Not surprisingly, the possible variety in the function u is greatly restricted. Indeed, u must be constant on all except possibly one coordinate if the requirements are made that it be monotonic in the coordinates u_i (Pareto superiority) and that the utility representation is not essential:

$$u(t_1 u_1,..., t_n u_n) \geqslant u(t_1 \bar{u}_1,..., t_n \bar{u}_n)$$

if and only if

$$u(u_1,..., u_n) \geqslant (\bar{u}_1,..., \bar{u}_n),$$

whenever t_i is an increasing transformation (Problem A of Chapter 3 of the companion volume). More generally, if social preference is not regular, social preference must be a lexicographic ordering of individual preferences.

A particular case is one in which the preferences of society are *decomposable* into individuals, namely, $\mathcal{R}_i$ varies only on $\mathcal{X}_i$ and is independent of $\mathcal{R}_j$ on $\mathcal{X}_j$, $j \neq i$,

$$\mathcal{X} = \underset{j=1}{\overset{n}{\times}} \mathcal{X}_j .$$

For example, in classical economic theory, $\mathcal{X}_i$ is the set of trades and/or consumptions on which preferences are independent of the trades of others. There is a *social independence* for all individuals provided that $\mathcal{R}$ is independent in the different pairs $\mathcal{R}_i$, x_i. Social preference is independent if for any $\mathcal{I}$, then given

$$\underset{i \in \mathcal{I}}{\times} \mathcal{R}_i \times \underset{i \in \sim\mathcal{I}}{\times} \mathcal{R}_i$$

preference by $\mathcal{I}$ between $(x_{\mathcal{I}}, x_{\sim\mathcal{I}})$ is not dependent on the values of $x_{\sim\mathcal{I}}$. This is a very strong assumption, but it is nevertheless interesting to see its implications.

If there are three or more individuals, given $\mathcal{R}_i, ..., \mathcal{R}_n$, the additive utility theorem (Theorem 8 of Chapter 6 of the companion volume) applies to give the representation: $u(x_1, ..., x_n) = \sum_{i=1}^{n} u_i(x_i)$, since between different $\mathcal{R}_i$, the linear form of $\sum_{j \neq i} u_j$ remains unchanged (uniqueness of additive utility). Therefore, at least between any finite number of different x_i, $\mathcal{R}_i$,

$$u(\mathcal{R}_1, ..., \mathcal{R}_n, x_1, ..., x_n) = \sum_{i=1}^{n} u_i(\mathcal{R}_i, x_i),$$

which is something of a simplification. If $\mathcal{R}_i$ is representable by a continuous utility function, then u_i is an *operator* on such utility functions. Notice that u_i does depend on $\mathcal{R}_i$, but in the case in which $\mathcal{R}_i$ is fixed, setting

$$v_i(x) = u_i(\mathcal{R}_1, ..., \mathcal{R}_n, x), \qquad v(x) = u(\mathcal{R}_1, ..., \mathcal{R}_n, x)$$

gives

$$v(x_1, ..., x_n) = \sum_{i=1}^{n} v_i(x_i)$$

which is classical social utility function, as used by Bergson [1938]. These results are worth listing.

2 Theorem *Let the $\mathscr{R}_i$ be sampled from a finite space $\mathfrak{s}_i$. Let the set of social possibilities $\mathscr{X}$ be contained in a linear space. Let $\mathscr{R} = \mathscr{R}(\mathscr{R}_1,..., \mathscr{R}_n, \mathscr{X})$ be a social welfare relation under decomposable preferences, with $\mathscr{R}_i$ continuous on $\mathscr{X}_i$ and $\mathscr{R}$ continuous on $\mathscr{R}_i$ and $\mathscr{X}_i$, $\mathscr{X}_i$ completely separable (or connected and separable). If there is social independence, then $\mathscr{R}$ is representable by a sum of continuous utility functions representing $\mathscr{R}_i$, that is,*

$$u = \sum_{i=1}^{n} u_i, \qquad u_i : \mathfrak{s}_i \times \mathscr{X}_i \to \mathscr{E}^1.$$

3 Corollary *If there is also independence of irrelevant alternatives, under the hypothesis of Theorem 2, then*

$$u(\mathscr{R}_1,..., \mathscr{R}_n, x) = \sum_{i=1}^{n} u_i(x_i).$$

If social preferences on uncertain events are simultaneously independent between events and individuals, the foregoing social utility functions are additive in probabilities (Harsanyi [1955]). Therefore the u_i are determined up to increasing linear transformations and, ignoring the constant, the only additive social utility functions are of the form

$$\sum c_i u_i(x_i).$$

Until some principles are found to determine the weights c_i, the social utility function remains only a possibility.

Exercise 1 Use Corollary 3 to show directly a lexicographic ordering under Arrow's postulates (Problem D of Chapter 4 of the companion volume).

PROBLEMS

A. Bergson Welfare Theory

Let the community and individual utility functions be continuously differentiable.

(i) What are the first-order conditions for utility maximization?
(ii) Suppose the exact form of the social utility function is unknown. What are the first-order conditions independent of the social utility function?

This problem was first solved by Bergson [1938].

B. Theory of the Second Best I

Let only one of the conditions for consumers i and j from Problem A be violated by a certain proportion.

   (i)   What are the Kuhn–Tucker–Lagrange conditions for optimization?

   (ii)   How do the conditions for k, not i or j, change from the case in Problem A?

Part (i) of this problem was solved by Lipsey and Lancaster [1956] and part (ii) by Davis and Whinston [1965].

C. Theory of the Second Best II

Suppose preferences are interrelated between individuals i and j. How does this change the answer in Problems A and B for the other consumers?

D. Theory of the Second Best III

Suppose social utility is not additive. Are the first-order conditions in Problem A(ii) as modified in Problems B and C thereby changed? (Hint: Linear functions serve as approximations for concave functions.)

3. Partial Social Orderings

A relation $\mathscr{R}$ is a *partial ordering* if it is reflexive and transitive but not necessarily complete.

Throughout this chapter, unless otherwise stated, it is never assumed that preferences are orderings, but only that they are partial orderings. This gain in generality is at small cost since only in proving the existence of competitive equilibrium has the argument "either $x \mathscr{R} y$ or $y \mathscr{R} x$" ever played a significant role. It might also happen that there is no social ordering, but only a partial social ordering. Also, the assumption of a finite number of individuals is dropped, but it is always assumed that only a finite number of individuals deal (consume or produce) in any one commodity, so that all summations of productions or consumption are well defined.

If a social ordering is not defined, there may be some interest in weak restraints on social choice. For example, it may be desirable that production be operated in an efficient manner. Even if there is allowed the possibility of a social ordering, it does not follow that it is easily determined. Presumably, it will be a refinement of the more evident partial orderings. Here, we define and list simple properties.

The *Pareto social ordering* is the partial ordering

$$x \, \mathcal{R} \, y \qquad (\text{read:} \quad x \text{ not Pareto inferior to } y)$$

if and only if

$$x \, \mathcal{R}_i \, y \qquad \text{for all } i,$$

and

$$x \, \mathcal{P} \, y \qquad (\text{read:} \quad x \text{ Pareto superior to } y \text{ or } x \text{ consumer superior to } y)$$

if and only if $x \, \mathcal{R} \, y$ but not $y \, \mathcal{R} \, x$ (that is, $x \, \mathcal{R} \, y$ and $x \, \mathcal{P}_i \, y$ for some i). Let $\mathcal{Y} \subset \mathcal{X}$ be the set of *feasible* alternatives, productions, or capital stocks. An x in $\mathcal{Y}$ optimizing $\mathcal{R}$ is said to be *Pareto optimal* or *consumer efficient*. In words, x is Pareto optimal if and only if there does not exist a y in $\mathcal{Y}$ that makes one person better off and no one worse off. Pareto optimality is implicit in Kant [1788, 1797] and Bentham [1789]. Indeed, it forms one of the major blocks of their theories of ethics.

The *contour sets* are

$$\mathcal{R}(x) \equiv \{y \mid y \, \mathcal{R} \, x\}, \qquad \mathcal{R}^{-1}(x) = \{y \mid x \, \mathcal{R} \, y\},$$
$$\mathcal{P}(x) \equiv \{y \mid y \, \mathcal{P} \, x\}, \qquad \mathcal{P}^{-1}(x) = \{y \mid x \, \mathcal{P} \, y\},$$
$$\mathcal{I}(x) = \{y \mid y \, \mathcal{I} \, x\}.$$

$\mathcal{R}$ is *regular* if for all x, $\mathcal{R}(x)$ is closed.

The following theorem shows the existence of Pareto optimal points.

4 Theorem *If $\mathcal{Y}$ is compact and the $\mathcal{R}_i$ are regular, then for any $x \in \mathcal{Y}$ there is a Pareto optimal $y \in \mathcal{Y}$ such that $y \, \mathcal{R} \, x$.*

Proof

$$\mathcal{R}(x) = \bigcap_i \mathcal{R}_i(x)$$

is closed. Apply Theorem 4 of Chapter 5 of the companion volume.

$$\text{q.e.d.}$$

The overtaking criterion is not regular. If an individual choosing according to it is in an economy with another valuing more over less, it will always be possible to transfer goods to the other without hurting the one. However, in the limit, the one is in a deteriorated position. There is no optimal distribution between the two except for the one that gives nothing to the one with the overtaking criterion.

Let i and j be permuted in $(\mathcal{Y}, \mathcal{R}_1, \mathcal{R}_2, ...)$ to obtain $(\bar{\mathcal{Y}}, \bar{\mathcal{R}}_1, \bar{\mathcal{R}}_2, ...)$ Then i and j are identical if

$$(\mathcal{Y}, \mathcal{R}_1, \mathcal{R}_2, ...) = (\bar{\mathcal{Y}}, \bar{\mathcal{R}}_1, \bar{\mathcal{R}}_2, ...).$$

Let $\bar{y}$ be y with i and j permuted and let

$$y \, \mathcal{R}_i \, \bar{y}(\bar{y} \, \mathcal{R}_j \, y).$$

Define

$$x \, \mathcal{R}_{ij} \, y \qquad \text{(read: } x \text{ is } i\text{--}j \text{ as equitable as } y\text{)}$$

whenever $y \, \mathcal{R}_j \, x \, \mathcal{R}_j \, \bar{y}$ and $y \, \mathcal{R}_i \, x \, \mathcal{R}_i \, \bar{y}$. In words, x is as equitable as y if it treats equals as equally as y. If it treats equals equally, then x is said to be *absolutely equitable*. Pursuing this line of thought, let $\mathcal{I}$ and $\mathcal{J}$ be subsets of $\bigcup_{i=1}^{n} \{i\}$ and let their subscripts be permuted in $(\mathcal{Y}, \mathcal{R}_1, ..., \mathcal{R}_n)$ according to some rule attaching $f(i) \in \mathcal{J}$, $i \in \mathcal{I}$, f one to one, to obtain $(\bar{\mathcal{Y}}, \bar{\mathcal{R}}_1, ..., \bar{\mathcal{R}}_n)$. Then $\mathcal{I}$ and $\mathcal{J}$ are *identical* if for some such f,

$$(\mathcal{Y}, \mathcal{R}_1, \mathcal{R}_2, ...) = (\bar{\mathcal{Y}}, \bar{\mathcal{R}}_1, \bar{\mathcal{R}}_2, ...).$$

Let $\bar{y}$ be the y with $\mathcal{I}$ and $\mathcal{J}$ permuted, and suppose $y \, \mathcal{R}_i \, \bar{y}$ for all $i \in \mathcal{I}$ ($\bar{y} \, \mathcal{R}_j \, y$ for all $j \in \mathcal{J}$). Define

$$x \, \mathcal{R}_{\mathcal{I}\mathcal{J}} \, y \qquad \text{(read: } x \text{ is } \mathcal{I} \; \mathcal{J} \text{ as equitable as } y\text{)}$$

whenever $\mathcal{I}$ and $\mathcal{J}$ are identical and

$$y \, \mathcal{R}_i \, x \, \mathcal{R}_i \, \bar{y} \qquad \text{for all } \quad i \in \mathcal{I},$$

whereupon

$$\bar{y} \, \mathcal{R}_j \, x \, \mathcal{R}_j \, y \qquad \text{for all } \quad j \in \mathcal{J}.$$

Theorem 5 shows that there are points as equitable as possible.

5 Theorem *If $\mathcal{Y}$ is compact, $\mathcal{R}$ and $\mathcal{R}^{-1}$ are regular, $\mathcal{I}$ and $\mathcal{J}$ identical, then for any $y \in \mathcal{Y}$ there is an x optimal for the ordering $\mathcal{R}_{\mathcal{I}\mathcal{J}}$ such that $x \, \mathcal{R}_{\mathcal{I}\mathcal{J}} \, y$.*

Proof Restrict $\mathcal{R}_i$ to $\mathcal{Y}_i$ for all i; without loss of generality, it can be assumed that $y \, \mathcal{R}_i \, y$, $i \in \mathcal{I}$:

$$\mathcal{R}_{\mathcal{I}\mathcal{J}} = \left\{ \bigcap_{i \in \mathcal{I}} \mathcal{R}_i(\bar{y}) \right\} \cap \left\{ \bigcap_{i \in \mathcal{I}} \mathcal{R}_i^{-}(y) \right\} \cap \left\{ \bigcap_{j \in \mathcal{J}} \mathcal{R}_j(y) \right\} \cap \left\{ \bigcap_{j \in \mathcal{J}} \mathcal{R}_j^{-1}(\bar{y}) \right\},$$

which is closed. Apply Theorem 4 of Chapter 5 of the companion volume: regular orderings take optima on compact sets.   q.e.d.

We can apply Theorem 5 to the output set of Section 1.

6 Corollary   *Suppose the conditions of Theorems* 1 *and* 5; *then for any* $(y^1, y^2,...) \in \mathscr{Z}$ *there is a Pareto superior (or not less* $\mathscr{I} - \mathscr{J}$ *equitable) distribution of output that is Pareto optimal (or* $\mathscr{I} - \mathscr{J}$ *equitable).*

When using these two partial orders, it would seem that the Pareto order has precedence; that is, inequity is justified only if both parties can be made better off than under some more equitable arrangement. Preferences are quasi transferable between $\mathscr{I}$ and $\mathscr{J}$ if, for $x \in \mathscr{Y}$,

$$x \, \mathscr{P}_{\mathscr{J}} \, y,$$

there is a $z \in \mathscr{Y}$ for which

$$z \, \mathscr{P}_{\mathscr{J}} \, x, \quad z \, \mathscr{P}_{\mathscr{J}} \, y, \quad z \, \mathscr{R} \, y.$$

Preferences are *quasi transferable* from $\mathscr{I}$ to $\mathscr{J}$ if a margin favorable to $\mathscr{I}$ can be turned into one favorable to $\mathscr{J}$ with a small effect on $\mathscr{I}$. Preferences are *quasi transferable* if they are quasi transferable from all subsets $\mathscr{I}$ to $\sim\mathscr{I}$. A related notion was originally introduced by McKenzie [1959] under the name of "irreducibility." Quasi transferability will be studied in more detail in Section 6.

It is interesting to see that quasi transferability assures the existence of trades that are both Pareto optimal and absolutely equitable.

7 Theorem   *If preferences are quasi transferable and regular, society is decomposable into individuals, and* $\mathscr{Y}$ *is compact, then the set of Pareto optimal points is compact. If preferences are also continuous, then there are* $y \in \mathscr{Y}$ *both Pareto optimal and absolutely equitable.*

Proof   Applying Theorem 4, we find that the set of Pareto optimal points $\mathscr{Y}$ is non empty, to show that $\mathscr{Y}$ is closed, let $x^n \to x$, x^n Pareto optimal, and suppose $z \in \mathscr{Y}$ Pareto superior to x. Then for some $\mathscr{I}$, $z \, \mathscr{P}_{\mathscr{J}} \, x$ and $y \, \mathscr{R}_{\sim\mathscr{J}} \, x$. By quasi transformability, there exists $z \in \mathscr{Y}$, $z \, \mathscr{P} \, x$ and by regularity, for x^n large, $z \, \mathscr{P} \, x^n$ contrary to x^n Pareto optimal. Applying Theorem 5 to $\mathscr{Y}$, we find that there are equitable trades that are Pareto optimal. Consider such a trade, x. Let

$$x \, \mathscr{P}_{\mathscr{J}} \, \bar{x}$$

where $\mathscr{I}$ and $\mathscr{J}$ are permuted in $\bar{x}$, $\mathscr{I}$ and $\mathscr{J}$ are identical. By quasi transferability, $\mathscr{J}$ can be made better off; that is, there is a y such that

$$y \, \mathscr{P}_{\mathscr{J}} \, \bar{x},$$

$$y \, \mathscr{P}_{\mathscr{J}} \, \bar{x},$$

$$y \, \mathscr{I}_{\mathscr{K}} \, x \qquad \text{for all} \quad \mathscr{K} \cap \mathscr{I} = \mathscr{K} \cap \mathscr{J} = \varnothing.$$

Applying Theorem 4 again, we find that there is a Pareto optimal

$$x \, \mathscr{R}_{\mathscr{K}} \, y, \qquad \text{for all} \quad \mathscr{K}.$$

Evidently,

$$x \, \mathscr{P}_{\mathscr{J}} \, z \, \mathscr{P}_{\mathscr{J}} \, \bar{x} \qquad \text{(Pareto optimality of } \bar{x}),$$

$$\bar{x} \, \mathscr{P}_{\mathscr{J}} \, z \, \mathscr{P}_{\mathscr{J}} \, x,$$

which gives that z is more equitable than x, a contradiction.   q.e.d.

Exercise 2   Suppose $\mathscr{P}^{-1}(x)$ is open. Construct analogs of Theorems 4 and 5. What improvements result when we assume quasi transferability?

4. Social Choice for a Decomposable Environment

Here we consider an economy that can be decomposed among groups. In the context of such an economy, there are ethical principles that are not described by partial orderings. One such principle is that of group conservation. Within the context of a decomposable environment, relationships are specified between different ethical concepts defined here and in the previous section. Then a very simple mechanism is presented that will put the economy in a Pareto optimal state. This mechanism requires much information, and in many cases, it will be superseded by other mechanisms (Sections 6 and 8).

Society can be increased or decreased by adding or subtracting individuals. Let $\mathscr{X}$ be the *social possibilities*. Then a *society* is given by

$$(\mathscr{R}_1, \mathscr{R}_2, ..., \mathscr{X}, \mathscr{Y}).$$

A society is decomposable if

$$(\mathscr{R}_1, \mathscr{R}_2, ..., \mathscr{X}, \mathscr{Y}) = (\mathscr{R}_1, ..., \mathscr{R}_n, \mathscr{R}_{n+1}, ..., \mathscr{X}_1 \times \mathscr{X}_2, \mathscr{Y}_1 \times \mathscr{Y}_2)$$

where

$$(\mathscr{R}_1, \mathscr{R}_2, ..., \mathscr{R}_n) \subset \mathscr{X}_1, \qquad (\mathscr{R}_{n+1}, ..., \mathscr{R}_n) \subset \mathscr{X}_2.$$

In effect, the society can be broken into two independent parts.
 A *k-replica* of a society

$$(\mathscr{R}_1 ,..., \mathscr{R}_n , \mathscr{X}, \mathscr{Y})$$

is the society

$$(\mathscr{R}_1 ,..., \mathscr{R}_n ,..., \mathscr{R}_1 , \underbrace{\quad...\quad}_{k\text{times}}, \mathscr{R}_n , \mathscr{X} \times \underbrace{\cdots}_{k\text{times}} \times \mathscr{X}, \mathscr{Y} \times \underbrace{\cdots}_{k\text{times}} \times \mathscr{Y}).$$

In effect, the society is exactly reproduced k times. Thus, a k-replica is
decomposable into the original identical subsocieties. Note that the social
possibilities are simply the k-replication of the original alternatives,
$x \in \mathscr{X}$. It would seem reasonable to assume that social choice would be
invariant to k-replication, that is, under replication, x^j would not change
in (individual) preference level. For example, invariance would result
from the maximization of an additive social welfare function.

8 Remark Invariance implies $\mathscr{I}-\mathscr{J}$ equity in the k-replication,
$k > 1$.

Proof Clearly, if $\mathscr{I}$ and $\mathscr{J}$ are groups of like consumers, any identical
pair i, j, $i \in \mathscr{I}$ and $j \in \mathscr{J}$, can be assigned to two different subsocieties,
which receive identical levels of preferences for identical individuals,
due to invariance under k-replication.   q.e.d.

A second principle applied to a decomposable society might be called
"conservation of group welfare," or more succinctly, $\mathscr{I}$*-conservation*,
provided that for any decomposition of the economy between $\mathscr{I}$ and $\mathscr{J}$,
a social choice y is not Pareto inferior for $\mathscr{I}$ to a choice in $y_\mathscr{I} \in \mathscr{Y}_\mathscr{I}$.
 In effect, *coalition* $\mathscr{I}$ can assure itself of an alternative at least as good
as any alternative attainable by production, and trade only among
themselves. Hence, it would have its interests violated were it to receive
less. It is said that $\mathscr{I}$ *blocks* y whenever there is a y in $\mathscr{Y}_\mathscr{I}$ such that

$$\bar{y} \,\mathscr{R}_j\, y \qquad \text{for all} \quad j \in \mathscr{I},$$

$$\bar{y} \,\mathscr{P}_{j_0}\, y \qquad \text{for some} \quad j_0 \in \mathscr{I}.$$

Therefore, y is $\mathscr{I}$-conservative if and only if $\mathscr{I}$ does not block y. If y is
$\mathscr{I}$-conservative for all groups,

$$\mathscr{I} \subset \{1, 2,...\},$$

then y is *Edgeworth optimal* (Edgeworth [1881, pp. 34–45]). In game
theory, the set of Edgeworth optimal y's is called the *core*. The proof

that the core is nonempty appears to be difficult and it requires conditions that are obscure in nonmarket games (see Scarf [1967]). This chapter is restricted to economics, and the theory is developed in Section 11.

A particular instance of a decomposable economic system is that described in Section 1, where every individual i offers a trade x^{ij} under the presumption that all other x^{kj}, $k \neq i$, $j \neq i$, are fixed. A trade

$$(x^{ij}, \quad i, j = 1, 2, ...)$$

is in *trade equilibrium for i* provided that there is not an additional trade

$$\delta = (\delta^{ij}, \quad i, j = 1, 2, ...)$$

where δ^{ij} is the trade between i and j,

$$\delta^{ij} = -\delta^{ji},$$

such that

$$x + \delta \, \mathcal{P}_i \, x \quad \text{and} \quad x + \delta \, \mathcal{R}_j \, x \quad \text{for all} \quad j \neq i.$$

In words, if for each i there is no complex of added trades involving i and j, $j = 1, 2, ...$, that all the other j's will accept, then there is trade equilibrium. It is related to the greed process of Hurwicz [1960] (Problem D of Chapter 10 of the companion volume).

9 Remark   There is Pareto optimality if and only if there is trade equilibrium for all i.

Proof   Let

$$x^j = \sum_j x^i .$$

Trade equilibrium is equivalent to: there does not exist a trade $\bar{x}$ such that for any i

$$\bar{x}^i \, \mathcal{P}_i \, x^i, \quad \bar{x}^j \mathcal{R}_j \, x^j \quad \text{for all} \quad j,$$

$$\sum_{j=1}^{n} x^j = 0,$$

which is equivalent to the definition of Pareto optimality.   q.e.d.

Obviously, the condition of trade equilibrium is a stringent one insofar as each individual knows the preferences of others and yet does not account for his power to alter the trades x^{jk}, $j \neq i$, $k \neq i$. In certain cases, these conditions can be weakened. To do so we need a condition assuring contradiction of interests.

The required property is that for all j, preferences are quasi transferable from j at x in $\mathcal{Y}$. From our foregoing definition, this means that

$$x \mathcal{R}_i y \quad \text{for all} \quad i$$

and

$$x \mathcal{P}_j y \quad \text{for} \quad j$$

implies that there exists an $\bar{x}$ in $\mathcal{Y}$ such that

$$\bar{x} \mathcal{P}_i y \quad \text{for all} \quad i.$$

In effect, the extra preferences of j for x over y can be reallocated so that *all* other individuals benefit. Clearly, this is a property of the whole system, although it also relates to individual preferences. It amounts to saying that all individuals have some degree of opposing interests to j at the social position y. Obviously, this may not be true of all y in all social situations.

10 Remark If preferences are quasi transferable, then x is Pareto optimal if and only if there is at least one i in trade equilibrium at x.

Proof Clearly, if x is Pareto optimal, then all i are in trade equilibrium. On the other hand, if x is not Pareto optimal, then there is an $\bar{x} \in \mathcal{Y}$ such that

$$\bar{x} \mathcal{P}_i x,$$

$$\bar{x} \mathcal{R}_j x \quad \text{for all} \quad j.$$

Therefore, there is an $\bar{x} \in \mathcal{Y}$ for which

$$\bar{x} \mathcal{P}_j x \quad \text{for all} \quad j,$$

so that no j is in trade equilibrium. Taking the logical converse, if some j is in trade equilibrium, then x is Pareto optimal.   q.e.d.

Remark 10 weakens somewhat the stringency of trade equilibrium. Only one trader is required to combine complete knowledge of preferences with self-constraint with respect to economic power. It appears to verify a conjecture of Buchanan [1966] and Coase [1960] that a third party will always find it in its interest to effect Pareto optimality among the others. Nevertheless, it would be helpful to further reduce the information requirements, and the succeeding sections will do this. Quasi transferability plays a role hereafter, so first we develop the cases in which quasi transferability holds.

5. Quasi-Transferable Preferences in an Exchange Economy

The existence and optimality of competitive equilibrium and related results require the notion of quasi transferability. Before going into competitive theory in subsequent sections, we set forth the conditions that assure quasi transferability and the consequences of its absence.

In an exchange economy, as stated in the companion volume, the possibility set of trades is $\mathscr{Y} = \mathscr{X} \cap \mathscr{H}$. However, quasi transferability on such a set will be insufficient for our purposes. Instead, the definition will be applied to potential possibility sets due to trades imposed from outside the system. If y is such a trade, the possibility set is $\mathscr{Y} = (\mathscr{H} - y) \cap \mathscr{X}$. Preferences are *quasi transferable* if for any x, $x \mathscr{R}_i y$ for all i and $x \mathscr{P}_j y$ implies that there is an $\bar{x}$ in $(\mathscr{H} - \sum x^i) \cap \mathscr{X}$ such that $\bar{x} \mathscr{P}_i y$ for all i. In words, commodities can be redistributed from x so as to transfer benefit to all $i \neq j$ but without reducing too much the preference level of i.

The classic example of quasi transferability is that where each individual owns some of a good wanted by all. However, if goods are distinguished according to temporal or geographical location, such a good may not exist. Transferring benefit from one trader to another might occur only after transportation, and it would then be necessary to examine the availability of transport facilities.

Arrow [1951a] has provided a counterexample to quasi transferability, which can be stated as follows. Suppose a pauper lives on the wild onions growing in a farmer's drainage ditch. The farmer has no use for the wild onions, so that there is no way of transferring "goods" from the pauper to the farmer. This example poses difficulties for resource allocation. To anticipate succeeding sections, consider a price for wild onions that allows them to be exchanged for the farmer's produce. If the price is positive, the pauper cannot pay it. If the price is zero, he is likely to demand more than its current supply. Indeed, if more than one pauper is living off the wild onions, some agreement will have to be reached to avoid conflict over the onions.

There are two ways of avoiding the wild onion problem. The first is to assume away the pauper, and this represents the most common practice. However, since many consumers might end up as paupers, depending on the price system, the second alternative might be more attractive: assume away wild onions. For Theorem 11 below, there are no paupers. For Theorem 12, there are no wild onions.

An odd variant of the onion farmer is the following. Consider a consumer dedicated to the von Weizsäcker overtaking criterion and one with a Koopmans-type utility, $\sum u \alpha^t$. If the Koopmans type owns only goods before time t, and no factors of production, there is no way for him to transfer "goods" to the von Weizsäcker type. On the other hand, if the von Weizsäcker type as a secondary objective also prefers more utility at a given time to less, then there is quasi transferability.

Preferences are *convex* if $x \mathcal{P} y$ implies $tx + (1 - t)y \mathcal{P} y$ for all $0 < t < 1$. (Preferences are *strictly convex* if $x \mathcal{I} y$ implies $tx + (1 - t)y \mathcal{P} y$ for all $0 < t < 1$.) Preferences are *unsaturated* if for every $x \in \mathcal{X}$ there exists $y \in \mathcal{X}$ such that $y \mathcal{P} x$.

It is at first assumed that the individuals are independent in production and consumption. Theorem 11 shows that convexity of preference gives quasi transferability of preferences on internal points of the trade set.

11 Theorem *Let preferences $\mathcal{R}_i$ be independent (depend only on $x^i \in \mathcal{X}$, $i = 1, 2,...$). If preferences for $i \neq j$ are convex and unsaturated, and $\mathcal{P}_j(x)$ is open on line segments, then preferences are quasi transferable from j at points internal to the community trade set $\mathcal{X}$.*

Proof Consider $x \in \text{Int } \mathcal{X}$, $x \mathcal{P}_j z$, $x \mathcal{R}_i z$, $i \neq j$. Let $y^i \mathcal{P}_i x^i$ for all $i \neq j$.[2] Let

$$\bar{x}^i = t(y^i - x^i) + x^i, \qquad i \neq j,$$

Then $\bar{x}^i \mathcal{P}_i x^i$ for all i by virtue of preference convexity

$$\bar{x}^j = x^j - t \sum_{i \neq j} (y^i - x^i).$$

For t sufficiently small, $\bar{x} \in \mathcal{X}$. Also, openness of $\mathcal{P}_j(x)$ on line segments gives that $\bar{x} \mathcal{P}_j z$ for t sufficiently small.   q.e.d.

In many cases there may be a similarity of preferences in that an increase in certain commodities always leads to a higher level of preferences. Preferences have a *similarity* if

$$\mathcal{S} = \bigcap_i \bigcap_{x^i} (\mathcal{P}_i(x^i) - x^i) \neq \phi.$$

In words, there is a direction of change to a better position common to all trades and traders. An element $y \in \mathcal{S}$ is called a *direction of greater preference*. Preferences have an *essential similarity* if preferences have a similarity and if for z^i giving the minimum level of preference in $\mathcal{X}_i$, $x^i \mathcal{P}_i z^i$ if and only if

$$(x^i - \mathcal{S}) \bigcap \mathcal{X}_i \neq \phi;$$

[2] $y^i \mathcal{P}_i x^i$ whenever $y \mathcal{P}_i x$ whatever y^j, x^j, $j \neq i$. Similarly, $y^i \mathcal{R}_i x^i$ whenever $x_i \mathcal{R}_i y$ whatever y^j, $j \neq i$, $y^i \mathcal{I}_i x^i$ whenever both $y^i \mathcal{R}_i x^i$ and $x^i \mathcal{R}_i y^i$. It is hoped that this use of the same notion for two slightly different ideas is not inconvenient.

that is, any nonminimal level of preferences can be reduced in a direction negative to the similarity. For example, several traders may consume goods distinguished according to location. Different traders will not consume the same goods and transfer of welfare will occur only after the use of transport facilities. Hence, quasi transferability in general and similarity in particular require the existence of such facilities among those traders who are under consideration. In general, if each country has transport facilities and if, not accounting for location, there is an essential similarity, then there will be quasi transferability, accounting for location. When each trader has such facilities, there may be an essential similarity in that one preference level is superior to another if and only if there is some of one of the desired goods in some location.

A *Renoir good* is one preferred in the larger quantities by all traders. It is easy to verify that the Renoir good implies a similarity.

12 Theorem   *Suppose there is a Renoir good. Then there is a similarity. If there is a class of commodities $\mathcal{I}$ for which*

(i) $x^i \mathcal{P}_i y^i$

whenever

$$x^i_j \geqslant y^i_j, \quad j \in \mathcal{I},$$

$$x^i_{j_0} > y^i_{j_0}$$

for some

$$j_0 \in \mathcal{I}, \quad x_k = y_k, \quad k \notin \mathcal{I},$$

and

(ii)   *x is nonminimal on $\mathcal{X}_i$ if and only if there is some coordinate $j \in \mathcal{I}$ in which x can be reduced, then there is an essential similarity.*

Condition (ii) is to say that there must be an irreducible (possibly positive) amount of at least one good in order to have a nonminimal level of preference.

We can now give conditions that ensure quasi transferability even at points not internal to the trade set.

13 Theorem   *If preferences are convex, $\mathcal{P}_i(x)$ is open on line segments, and preferences have essential similarity, then preferences are quasi transferable.*

Proof   By hypothesis, if

$$x^i \mathcal{R}_i \bar{x}^i,$$

$$x^j \mathcal{P}_j \bar{x}_j,$$

x^j is nonminimal, and

$$x^j - y \in \mathscr{X} \quad \text{for} \quad y \in \mathscr{S}.$$

By convexity

$$sy \in \bigcap_i \bigcap_{x_i} (\mathscr{P}_i(x^i) - x^i) = \mathscr{S} \quad \text{for all} \quad 1 < s < 0.$$

Therefore

$$\bar{x}^i = x^i + \frac{s}{2^i} \, y \, \mathscr{P}_i \, \bar{x},$$

$$\bar{x}^j = x^i + s \left(1 - \frac{1}{2^j} + \frac{1}{2^n} \right) y \, \mathscr{P}_j \, \bar{x}^j$$

(where n is the number of traders, possibly ∞) for s sufficiently small. Clearly,

$$\sum_{i \neq j} \bar{x}^i + \bar{x}^j = \sum_j x^j, \qquad \bar{x}^i \in \mathscr{X}_i \quad \text{for all} \quad i.$$

Therefore,

$$\bar{\bar{x}} \in \mathscr{X} \quad \text{and} \quad \sum \bar{x}^j = \sum x^j. \qquad \text{q.e.d.}$$

Consider an economy with two commodities, food and labor. The trade set for all consumers, assumed identical, is illustrated in Figure 1. Whether or not labor is desirable, if it is not traded, we can reduce the food of one and give it to another. Zero preference is attained if and only if there is no food. Hence, there is quasi transferability, similarity, and essential similarity.

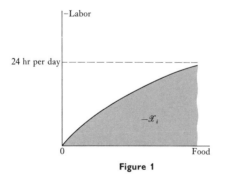

Figure 1

The fundamental lemma is an elaboration of the technique of Minkowski's theorem (Section 6 of Chapter 1) and it is a key tool of welfare economics. It states that the mathematical property of bounding a convex upper contour set by a hyperplane is the equivalent of maximizing preferences using the hyperplane as the budget plane.

Recall that positive components of trades represent outflows of goods, so that the smaller the value of a trade, the harder it is to have it accepted by others.

Preferences are *strongly quasi transferable* if there is a listing of all consumers $j(i)$, $i = 1, 2,...$, such that between any contiguous two $j(i)$, $j(i + 1)$, preferences are quasi transferable by trade only between the two.

14 Lemma   *Let $p\bar{x}^i \leqslant px^i$ for all $\bar{x}^i$ such that $\bar{x}^i \mathscr{P}_i x^i$, $i = 1, 2,...$, where p is a linear functional and either there is a finite number of i or p is continuous.*

Suppose

(1) *preferences are strongly quasi transferable,*
(2) *$\mathscr{P}_i(x)$ is open on line segments, and*
(3) *the social trade is an internal point of the sum of the individual trade sets, $\sum x^i \in \text{Int} \sum \mathscr{X}_i$.*

Then $p\bar{x}^i < px^i$ for all $\bar{x}^i$ preferred to x^i.

A basic problem with welfare analysis arises after a bounding hyperplane has been found, as in Figure 2, such that there is a continuous linear functional p for which $p(\bar{x}) \leqslant p(x)$ whenever $\bar{x} \mathscr{R}_i x$. Therefore trader i minimizes the cost of the budget, given his level of preferences. (Equivalently, he maximizes minus the cost of the budget.) Competitive choice requires that a trader also optimize his level of preferences subject to his budget constraint. Equivalently, anything better for the trader must require a larger value of outlay than of the commodities received. However, in Figure 2, it does not follow from cost minimization that the trader optimizes preferences. Consider that i is a consumer and p

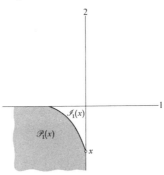

Figure 2

describes a budget constraint that society wishes to use to induce i to agree to x. This suggests the possibility that consumer i, given a price system, would find the position under consideration x in keeping with his budget constraint, where i's indifference curve is tangent to the 2-axis. But he would wish to move to the higher preference level also in keeping with the budget constraint. To put this in terms of Figure 2, *any* budget constraint compatible with x will include positions superior to x. Society cannot thereby induce i to adopt x. Put another way, minimizing budget cost subject to a constant preference constraint is not the same as maximizing preferences subject to a budget constraint. At best society must add a rationing device to persuade i to locate x. It then turns out that Lemma 14 is a key to determining when society does not need to place i at a point where it is necessary to have a rationing device that itself would be perpetrated on the basis of some special knowledge of i's preferences.

Hypothesis (3) is simply a statement that for every trade sufficiently small, there is some trader or group of traders who can make that trade. An example in which hypothesis (3) holds is where initial wealth of the community is positive for every good. Then we can increase or decrease in any direction the holdings of commodities by the community, provided the change is small. Thus, any "nearly" zero "trade" is consumable by the community.

Proof of Lemma 14 The community trade can be changed to $\bar{x}^i$, $i = 1, 2, \ldots$, such that

$$p\left(\sum_i \bar{x}^i\right) = p(\bar{x}) > p(x)$$

(by (3)). From finiteness of the x^i or else continuity of p,

$$p\left(\sum_i x^i\right) = \sum px^i$$

and

$$p\left(\sum_i \bar{x}^i\right) = \sum p\bar{x}^i.$$

Consequently, for some i_0

$$p(\bar{x}^{i_0}) < p(x^{i_0}).$$

This gives a trade with a cost greater than x^{i_0}. If

$$\bar{x}^{i_0} \mathscr{P}_{i_0} x^{i_0},$$

then

$$t\bar{\bar{x}}^{i_0} + (1 - t)\,\bar{x}^{i_0}\,\mathscr{P}_{i_0}\,x^{i_0}$$

for t nearly one, by virtue of openness of $\mathscr{P}_i(x)$ on line segments. Therefore,

$$p(x^{i_0}) \geqslant p(t\bar{\bar{x}}^{i_0} + (1 - t)\,\bar{x}^{i_0})$$

$$= tp(\bar{\bar{x}}^{i_0}) + (1 - t)\,p(\bar{x}^{i_0}).$$

Therefore,

$$p(x^{i_0}) > p(\bar{x}^{i_0}).$$

To extend to a contiguous i, suppose $\bar{x}^i\,\mathscr{P}_i\,x^i$. Then by quasi transferability, there is a change δ in $\bar{x}^i$ that can be transferred to i_0 to give i_0 a level of preference greater than x^{i_0} but that does not reduce i's preference level to that of x^i. Therefore,

$$p(x^{i_0} + \delta) < p(x^{i_0}) \qquad \text{or} \qquad p(\delta) < 0.$$

But also

$$\bar{x}^i - \delta t\,\mathscr{P}_i\,x^i$$

for small t (openness of $\mathscr{P}_i(\bar{x}^i)$), so that

$$p(\bar{x}^i - t\delta) \leqslant p(x^i),$$

or

$$p(\bar{x}^i) \leqslant p(x^i) + tp(\delta) < p(x^i) \qquad \text{for all} \quad \bar{x}^i \in \mathscr{P}_i(x^i).$$

Proceeding through $j(i)$, $j(i + 1)$, $j(i - 1)$, we have the conclusion of the theorem.   q.e.d.

Exercise 3 Show that factor-connected interindustry production as defined in the companion volume displays quasi transferability of net outputs.

6. Pairwise Optimality

In this section we show when the exploitation of mutual benefits within pairs of traders is equivalent to Pareto optimality. The amount of information is thereby reduced relative to trade equilibrium. No longer is any trader required to have knowledge of all trade preferences together. He simply needs to understand the possible gains between pairs of traders. We define a vestigial form of competitive equilibrium, competitive behavior, and show it to be equivalent to pairwise optimality. In Section 7 competitive behavior is seen to imply the decentralization of many production decisions from consumption decisions. Finally, optimality is shown even when there are geographical or temporal limits on trade.

A trade $x = (x^1,..., x^n)$ is said to be i–j *pairwise optimal* if

(i) $\sum_i x^i = 0, \qquad x^i \in \mathscr{X}_i$,
(ii) $y^i + y^j = 0, \qquad x^i + y^i \, \mathscr{R}_i \, x^i, \qquad x^j + y^j \, \mathscr{R}_j \, x^j$

implies

$$x^i + y^i \, \mathscr{I}_i \, x^i, \qquad x^j + y^j \, \mathscr{I}_j \, x^j.$$

A trade x is *pairwise optimal* if it is i–j pairwise optimal for all i, j. Pairwise optimal trades are those which are Pareto optimal for two traders, trades with others held fixed. Not only does pairwise optimality require relatively little information (normally only the preferences of two individuals), but it is easy to think of processes that lead to pairwise optimal solutions on the basis of trial and error without any a priori knowledge of preference (see Chapter 10 of the companion volume).

We will obtain conditions under which pairwise optimization implies Pareto optimality. A counterexample involving three independent traders appears in Figure 3, where there is pairwise optimality (at the zero trade) but not Pareto optimality. In Figure 3a, it is shown that 1 and 2 are pairwise optimizing, which follows if and only if

$$-\mathscr{P}_1(0) \cap \mathscr{R}_2(0) = \phi \qquad \text{and} \qquad -\mathscr{R}_1(0) \cap \mathscr{P}_2(0) = \phi.$$

Similarly, examination of Figure 3b, where $-\mathscr{R}_2(0)$ and $-\mathscr{R}_1(0)$ are graphed with $\mathscr{R}_3(0)$, reveals that 3 and 2 are pairwise optimal. However, 3 can simultaneously offer to trade x_1 with trader 1 and x_2 with trader 2, thereby improving the position of 1 and 2 and obtaining $x_1 + x_2$, which improves the position of 3. That pairwise optimality is insufficient appears to be due to the nonconvexity of preferences.

Not only is convexity required, but some smoothness of indifference curves is necessary. Consider three traders whose preferences to no trade are given by

(i) x^i for each trader i,
(ii) any nonpositive, nonzero trade,
(iii) any sum of x^i and a nonpositive trade, or
(iv) any convex combination of the foregoing   (Figure 4).

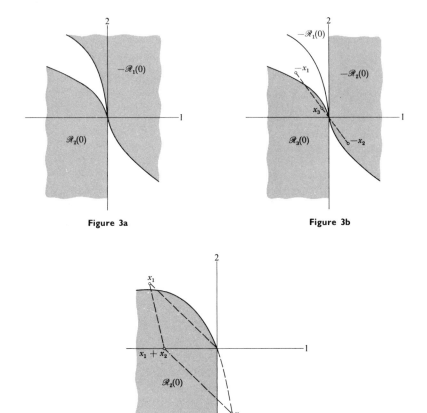

Figure 3a   Figure 3b

Figure 3c

In effect, the trader i likes proportions of x^i, and he likes to obtain additional positive quantities of the goods. It is assumed that

$$\sum_i x^i = 0,$$

so that the community can obtain a position better for each trader than that of no trade at all. On the other hand, for i, a position y^i is superior or equivalent to zero if and only if

$$y^i = t^i x^i - w^i, \qquad t^i \geqslant 0, \quad x^i \geqslant 0.$$

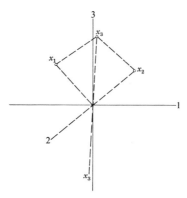

Figure 4

Therefore, if i and j can obtain trades superior to zero for one and not inferior for the other,

$$y^i + y^j = 0,$$

then

$$t^i x^i + t^j x^j - w^i - w^j = 0 \quad \text{or} \quad t^i x^i + t^j x^j = w^i + w^j = w \geqslant 0.$$

In order to make one trader better off, at least one t^i must be greater than zero, since otherwise

$$-w^i - w^j = 0, \quad w^i + w^j = 0, \quad w^i \geqslant 0, \quad w^j \geqslant 0$$

implies that

$$w^i = 0, \quad w^j = 0.$$

Therefore,

$$x^i + \frac{t^j}{t^i} x^j \geqslant 0.$$

If there are three goods, $\sum x^i = 0$, we need only choose x^i, $i = 1, 2, 3$, in a plane containing zero that otherwise has no points in common with the nonnegative orthant and for which

$$x^i + t x_j \not\geqslant 0, \quad t > 0$$

for all i, j. The trade x^i, $i = 1, 2, 3$, improves the position of all traders simultaneously. Even so, no pair of traders could do better than zero on their own. So long as there are at least three goods and at least three consumers, the example can be constructed. Only in the case of two goods would it necessarily follow that three coplanar vectors could not be arranged without

$$x^i + tx^j \not\geqslant 0 \qquad \text{for some} \quad t, i, j.$$

Let $x^{\sim i}$ be the not i coordinates of x. Preferences are *not malevolent* if

$$(\bar{x}^i, x^{\sim i}) \, \mathscr{R}_i \, x \qquad \text{and} \qquad (\bar{x}^{i_0}, x^{\sim i_0}) \, \mathscr{P}_{i_0} \, x$$

for all i implies

$$\bar{x} \, \mathscr{R}_i \, x \qquad \text{and} \qquad (\bar{x}^{i_0}, x^{\sim i_0}) \, \mathscr{P}_{i_0} \, x.$$

In words, there is not malevolence if making each individual better off separately makes the group better off together. If preferences are not not malevolent, they are *malevolent*.

Preferences are *not benevolent* if

$$\bar{x} \, \mathscr{R}_i \, x \qquad \text{for all} \quad i$$

and

$$\bar{x} \, \mathscr{P}_{i_0} \, x$$

implies that

$$(\bar{x}^i, x^{\sim i}) \, \mathscr{R}_i \, x \qquad \text{for all} \quad i$$

$$(\bar{x}^{i_0}, x^{\sim i_0}) \, \mathscr{P}_{i_0} \, x^{i_0}.$$

In words, there is not benevolence if bettering all individuals together requires at least bettering all individuals separately. Otherwise, some would be separately worse off, and since the others are separately better off, the former could be worse off due to the improvement in the position of others. If preferences are not not benevolent, they are *benevolent*. In words, there is benevolence if, short of acquiring a better situation for himself, individual i can be made better off only if some other individual (not the group) is made better off. Preferences are *independent* if preferences are neither malevolent nor benevolent. For convenience, write

$$x^i \, \mathscr{R}_i \, x^i \qquad \text{whenever} \quad (\bar{x}^i, x^{\sim i}) \, \mathscr{R}_i \, (x^i, x^{\sim i})$$

and the fixed x is clear from context.

15 Remark If preferences are not malevolent, Pareto optimal trades are pairwise optimal.

Proof Any improvement between two individuals does not deteriorate the position of others, so that such improvements cannot be possible from a Pareto optimal trade. q.e.d.

Preferences are *weakly convex* if $\mathscr{R}_i(x)$ is a convex set. They are *locally unsaturated* if $\mathscr{R}_i(x) \subset \overline{\mathscr{P}_i(x)}$. Evidently, $x \in B$ and $\mathscr{R}_i(x)$ and thus if Int $\mathscr{R}_i \neq \phi$, there is a price system p, such that $px \geqslant p\,\mathscr{R}_i(x)$. Preferences are *directional dense* at x if p is unique up to multiplication by a positive scalar. We then say that p is the *intrinsic* price system. Theorem 16 shows the equivalence of pairwise optimality and Pareto optimality.

16 Theorem *Let $\mathscr{P}_i(x)$ be open on line segments and let preferences be not benevolent, weakly convex, and locally unsaturated at the trade x^i for all i. Let*

$$\sum_i x^i \in \text{Int} \sum_{j=1}^{\infty} \mathscr{X}_j \,.$$

Let preferences for i be directional dense at x^i and for some j preferences are quasi transferable between i and all other j. Let there be a finite number of traders or else let $\sum_i \mathscr{P}_i(x)$ have interior points. Then x is Pareto optimal if it is i–j pairwise optimal for all j. In particular, if preferences are independent, x is pairwise optimal if and only if x is Pareto optimal.

The theorem gives a simple criterion for testing Pareto optimality. Simply find an j with directional dense preferences and make sure that he is pairwise optimizing with the others. In traditional terms, if all other of traders are on the contact curve with respect to j, then there is Pareto optimality. In particular, the case of bilateral monopoly, where one or more pairs of individuals face each other and pairwise optimize, is one of Pareto optimality. Objections to bilateral monopoly must be based on distributional considerations, not on the inefficiency of trade. The views of Pigou [1920, pp. 200–201] are not substantiated.

Proof The idea of the proof can be illustrated quite simply as in Figure 5, where the zero trade is pairwise optimal. The line $\mathscr{L}$ separates the two indifference curves $\mathscr{I}_1$ and $\mathscr{I}_2$, and indeed separates the better than zero sets for 1 and 2. If a third party exists whose indifference set is separated by $\mathscr{L}$, then necessarily any three trades x^i, $i = 1, 2, 3,...$, better than zero must each be entirely to one side of $\mathscr{L}$, as must be their sum. After the i–j pairwise optimal trade x, apply Minkowski's theorem, given that

$$\mathscr{P}_i(x^i) \cap (-\mathscr{R}_j(x^j)) = \phi \quad \text{and} \quad \mathscr{R}_i(x^i) \cap (-\mathscr{P}_j(x^j)) = \phi \quad \text{(no benevolence)}.$$

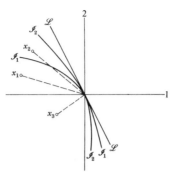

Figure 5

Since preferences are directional dense, there is a point y of $\mathscr{P}_i(x)$ that is an internal point of the commodity space. For every other point y, there is an s such that $t\bar{y} + (1 - t)\,y \in \mathscr{P}_i(x)$ for $0 < t < s$ (weak convexity and openness of $\mathscr{P}_i(x)$ on straight lines). Hence, y is an internal point of $\mathscr{P}_i(x)$. Hence, $\mathscr{P}_i(x)$ is a convex set with internal points, so that there is a linear functional for which

$$p(y^i) \leqslant -p(y^j) \qquad \text{for all} \quad y^i \in \mathscr{P}_i(x^i), \qquad y^j \in \mathscr{P}_j(x^j).$$

Since $\mathscr{R}_i$ is directional dense, p is determined up to a positive multiplicative constant, so that for all j (with which i pairwise optimizes),

$$p(\bar{x}^j) \leqslant p(x^j) \qquad \text{whenever} \quad \bar{x}^j\,\mathscr{R}_j\,x^j.$$

If there are an infinity of traders, $\sum \mathscr{P}_i(x)$ has interior points and p is continuous. Applying Lemma 14 to the whole economy, we get

$$p(\bar{x}^j) < p(x^j) \qquad \text{whenever} \quad \bar{x}^j\,\mathscr{P}_j\,x^j.$$

Since $\sum p(\bar{x}^j) = p(\sum \bar{x}^j) = 0$ whenever $\sum \bar{x}^j = 0$, we have $p(\bar{x}^j) = p(x^j)$ whenever $\bar{x}^j\,\mathscr{R}_j\,x^j$ and $\sum \bar{x}^j = 0$. Therefore, given x, $\sum_j \bar{x}^j = \sum_j x^j = 0$, and $\bar{x}^j\,\mathscr{R}_j\,x^j$, we cannot have $\bar{x}^j\,\mathscr{P}_j\,x^j$, whereupon x is Pareto optimal.
                                                                                                    q.e.d.

The proof of Theorem 16 also shows that competitive behavior is equivalent to pairwise optimality.

17 Theorem *Let preferences be weakly convex, quasi transferable, not benevolent, and locally unsaturated. Let*

$$\sum_i x^i \in \text{Int} \sum \mathscr{X}_i$$

and let i have preferences directional dense at x. Let there be a finite number of traders or else let $\sum_i \mathscr{P}_i(x)$ have interior points. Then x is i–j pairwise optimal for all j if and only if there is a linear functional p, unique up to a positive multiplicative constant, such that

$$p(\bar{x}^j) < p(x^j)$$

for all

$$\bar{x}^j \, \mathscr{P}_j \, x^j \qquad \text{for all} \quad j.$$

Proof It remains to verify sufficiency, which follows immediately from Theorem 28 below. q.e.d.

Trader j is said to follow a *noncompetitive policy* or *behavior* at x with respect to the price system p if there exists an

$$\bar{x}^j \, \mathscr{P}_j \, x^j \qquad \text{for which} \quad p(\bar{x}^j) \geqslant p(x^j).$$

Otherwise, j follows a competitive policy. (A competitive policy does not necessarily lead to a competitive equilibrium, since it is not required that $p(x^j) = 0$).

A monopolist follows a noncompetitive policy, since he would sell more at the going price were he not fearful of driving the price down. Similarly, a taxed producer would produce and sell more of a good were he not fearful that he would have to pay more of his income to the state.

Theorem 17 implies that the price system associated with individual i is the key one. This price system is the unique *separating price system* for i at x^i, for which

$$p(\bar{x}^i) < p(x^i) \qquad \text{whenever} \quad \bar{x}^i \, \mathscr{P}_i \, x^i.$$

It follows that noncompetitive behavior implies nonoptimality.

18 Corollary *Let preferences be independent, weakly convex, locally unsaturated, and quasi transferable. Let $\sum x_i \in \text{Int} \sum \mathscr{X}_i$. Let preferences for i be directional dense at x^i. If j follows a noncompetitive policy at x with respect to the separating price system for i at x^i, then x is not Pareto optimal. Conversely, if each j follows a competitive policy with respect to the continuous price system for i at x^i, then x is Pareto optimal.*

For example, let there be two traders i and j with directional dense preferences at x^i and x^j, respectively. If one attempts to deal with the other on a monopolistic basis, they will not pairwise optimize, and therefore the community trade will not be Pareto optimal.

As a second example, suppose that traders follow a competitive policy vis-à-vis the price system. If a tax is imposed (on all individuals) that is charged on goods held whose production cannot be changed, then the market equilibrium is Pareto optimal. Such a tax would be one on a fixed asset, for example, on the value of unimproved land, as suggested by Henry George. A land tax has no inefficiency associated with it. On the other hand, a tax on commodities traded is such that resale after purchase at best entails no further taxes and does not recoup the tax paid. Therefore, sellers and buyers follow competitive policies with respect to different price systems. According to the corollary, this leads to non-Pareto optimal trade, whereupon the tax places a burden on the economy above and beyond the amount collected (Joseph [1939], Little [1951]).

In general, we can check the Pareto optimality of government or business practices by simply checking each individual in comparison with the one with directional dense preferences. If pairwise optimization always occurs, or (what amounts to the same thing) policies are competitive with respect to i's separating prices system, then the community trade is necessarily not Pareto optimal.

Under certain conditions there may be bans on trades between i and j, due perhaps to a taboo or to the fact that i and j are located in different times or places. To analyze this case, let trades be allowed between (i, j) in the set of possible consumer pairs $\mathcal{T}$. $\mathcal{T}$ is *irreducible* if all trades are allowed, either directly or indirectly; that is, for every i–j, there is a "chain" of elements in $\mathcal{T}$ beginning in i and ending in j, (i, k), $(k, 1)$,..., $(m, j) \in \mathcal{T}$. A subset of traders $\mathcal{I}$ is called *universal* if for any k,

$$(k, j) \in \mathcal{T} \qquad \text{for some} \quad j \text{ in } \mathcal{I},$$

and if all trades (i, j), i in $\mathcal{I}$, $j \in I$, are allowed, either directly or indirectly. For example, if there are no bans on trade, $\mathcal{T}$ is the set of all trader pairs and any consumer j is universal. Theorem 19 shows how pairwise trading between chains of traders leads to Pareto optimality.

19 Theorem *Let $\mathcal{P}_i(x)$ be open on line segments. Let preferences be weakly convex, locally unsaturated, and not benevolent at the trade x^i for all i. Let $\sum \mathcal{P}_i(x)$ have interior points or else $\mathcal{T}$ be finite and let*

$$\sum_i x^i \in \text{Int} \sum \mathcal{X}_i.$$

Let preferences be directional dense at x^i for all i in $\mathscr{I}$, and quasi transferable between i and j for all pairs (i, j) in $\mathscr{T}$. Let $\mathscr{T}$ be irreducible, $\mathscr{I}$ universal. Then x is Pareto optimal if, for all i in $\mathscr{I}$, it is i–j pairwise optimal for all $(i, j) \in \mathscr{T}$. (There is equivalence between optimality and competitive behavior if preferences are independent). Alternatively, if preferences are independent, x is Pareto optimal if and only if there is a (unique) p such that $p\bar{x}^i < px^i$ for all $\bar{x}^i \mathscr{P}_i x_i$ for all i.

Proof Simply use the proof of Theorems 16 and 17, observing that the same p must be used for all i in $\mathscr{I}$. To see this, consider (i, j), $i \in \mathscr{I}, j \in \mathscr{I}$. Then there is a chain in $\mathscr{I}$ that leads from i to j. All along the chain each pair of traders must have the same (unique) separating hyperplane. q.e.d.

An application of Theorem 19 is the case of an economy over time where consumers in the same time period trade and intergenerational transfers take place between certain later generations and earlier ones. If there is one family, all of whose members, including descendants, are directional dense, then there is Pareto optimality if and only if there is pairwise optimality.

Samuelson [1958] and Cass and Yaari [1966] give examples of trades that are not Pareto optimal although they are pairwise optimal. Their examples depend on the assumption that to generation t, goods at time $t + 2$ and thereafter are of no use. Therefore, Pareto optimality requires that members of generation t hold zero quantities of such goods. On the other hand, should a person at time t hold claims on goods in time $t + 3$, he would have no way to negotiate with those who would find them useful, since time $t + 3$ traders would have nothing to give in return that would be of use to the generation at time t; only intermediation by an intervening generation could transfer the benefits. Preferences are not directional dense, since individuals of generation t are unaffected by different (nonnegative) prices of later goods. (Alternatively, from

$$x_{t+2} = 0,$$

consider the vectors

$$x = (\bar{x}_t, \bar{x}_{t+1}, -\bar{x}_{t+2}), \qquad x_{t+1} < 0, \quad i = 0, 1, 2.$$

Addition of ax is impossible for $a > 0$, whereas for $a < 0$, addition of ax leads to a lower level of preference.) As pointed out by the example in Figure 4 the failure of Pareto optimality is due to the failure of the property of directional density *not* to the ban on trades between individuals of different generations. They would have nothing to trade with each other, even if they could. In such cases, pairwise optimality is insufficient and at best the full competitive system is a method of obtaining a Pareto optimal trade.

Exercise 4   Interpret the results of this section for producer efficiency under increasing returns to scale, as in Section 6 of Chapter 3 of the companion volume.

Exercise 5   When would the linear functional in Theorem 17 be continuous?

Exercise 6   What restrictions could be placed on the commodity space so as to make the linear functional in Theorem 17 continuous in pointwise convergence?

7. The Separation of Production and Consumption

Before going on to competitive equilibrium, we consider some consequences of competitive behavior by consumers when production is operated separately. In the case of convex production sets, it is natural for producers to maximize profits. If the production set is not convex and the preferences on trades are consequently not convex, then the consumer prices still determine points of "tangency," among which are good points of production. Toward the end of the section, we take the opportunity to discuss the implications of nonconvex production sets and preferences for the producer sector when there are a large number of consumers.

One of the most remarkable aspects of competitive behavior is the separation of decisions relating to production and consumption. As it happens, an individual can consume as he pleases out of his income from labor and profits and then produce so as to maximize profits. No further coordination is needed. This is illustrated in Figure 6, where the consumer through production and trade can obtain $\mathscr{Y}^i$ and y^i is the optimal production. The line $\mathscr{L}$ is tangent to the indifference curve and the production set, and its normal p represents the intrinsic price system. Obtaining greater income amounts to locating on lines parallel to and to the right of $\mathscr{L}$. This is impossible. Attaining greater utility amounts to locating to the right of and above $\mathscr{I}_i(y^i)$, which requires greater income.

More generally, we must allow the possibility of exchange. Other factors, such as the economies of cooperation between producers and the utility of capital stock itself, assume importance. Because these factors

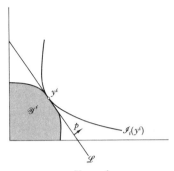

Figure 6

must be viewed simultaneously, it appears impossible to derive a price system for both. One cannot profit maximize and utility maximize with respect to the same price system, except in a particular way.

Consider all "inflows," $-\bar{x}^i$, that leave i no worse off than $-x^i$. Evidently,

$$-p(\bar{x}^i) \geqslant -p(x^i).$$

In this sense, $-p(x^i)$ can be regarded as income (or wealth) from production and exchange. It is maximized subject to the constraint of not decreasing the overall level of preference. For example, income might be maximized subject to a constraint on the amount of labor performed.

20 Remark If x is a competitive policy and if there are production goods $\mathscr{I}$ for which changes in x_i do not change preference, $i \in \mathscr{I}$, then the traders maximize profits, $-p(x_\mathscr{I})$, which is the difference between the value of (long-run) output and the cost of (long-run) inputs.

The information in Remark 20 suggests procedures for operation in the case of nonconvex (decreasing cost) industries. If there is not malevolence, then pairwise optimization is necessary for an optimum.

21 Theorem *If x is Pareto optimal, there is a directional dense convex set $\mathscr{Q}_j$ contained in $\mathscr{P}_j(x^j)$, and there is not malevolence, then there is a unique p such that for all $i \neq j$*

$$\lim \frac{p(x^{i,n} - x^i)}{|x^{i,n} - x^i|} \leqslant 0 \quad \textit{for any} \quad x^{i,n} \in \mathscr{R}_i(x^i)$$

such that

$$x^{i,n} \to x^i.$$

Proof If not, for $x^{i,n}$ close to x^i, $(x^{i,n} - x^i)/|\,x^{i,n} - x^i\,|$ is bounded away from $\{y \mid py = 0\}$, whereupon eventually $-x^{i,n} \in \mathcal{Q}_j \subset \mathcal{P}_j(x^j)$ and the trade $(x^{i,n} - x^i)$ from i to j make j better off without hurting i.

q.e.d.

Under the conclusion of Theorem 21, it is said that there is *quasi-competitive behavior for $i \neq j$*.

Industries producing goods from factors can be regarded as independent of the consumer i but their proceeds could certainly go to i. Since outflows minus inflows is profits, optimality requires that any production with nonzero profit have negative profit—at least in the limit. Hence, there must be profit maximization, or at most, marginal profits must be equal to zero. In either case, zero is equal to the derivative of profits with respect to output (using the cost-minimizing factor inputs), whence the rule, price equals marginal cost.

Under Pareto optimality, marginal costs equal average revenues.

22 Corollary *If x is Pareto optimal and there is a convex set contained in $\mathcal{P}_j(x^j)$ and directional dense in $x_{\sim \mathcal{J}}$, $\mathcal{R}_i$ constant on $x_{\mathcal{J}}$ for all i, then for $i \neq j$,*

$$\lim \frac{-p(x^{i,n} - x^i)}{|\,x^{i,n} - x^i\,|} \geq 0 \qquad \text{for } x^i \text{ fixed,}$$

$$x^{i,n} \to x^i, \quad x^{i,n}_{\sim \mathcal{J}} = x^i_{\sim \mathcal{J}}.$$

For example, if production is convex, then $-p(x^i)$ is profit maximizing. Even without convexity, optimality may require profit maximizing with respect to certain components y_j. Electric power generation may have increasing returns with respect to the size of the plant and the energy input but not both. Profits should be maximized with respect to energy input, and then minimized with respect to the overall inputs. In effect, current costs are minimized and investment is made so as to minimize long-run profits. Also, the demands of consumers with convex preferences should be met. Hence, the optimizing policy sets price equal to marginal cost and demand equal to supply. Even this may not be enough to determine uniquely the price and quantity of output.

It should be cautioned that if profits are negative, taxes will be needed to finance subsidies. Some of these may be noncompetitive and violate the conditions for efficiency.

We might think that quasi-competitive behavior would become competitive for an economy with large numbers of individuals. This would be in analogy to some results of Aumann [1966] for economies with a continuum of individuals. In particular, the out sets $\mathscr{Y}$ could be averaged as

$$\frac{1}{k}(\underbrace{\mathscr{Y} + \cdots + \mathscr{Y}}_{k\text{times}})$$

which would tend to the *convex hull* of $\mathscr{Y}$, namely, the smallest convex set containing $\mathscr{Y}$. If preferences were otherwise convex, then the induced preferences would be convex on this limiting production set. This idea is exploited in Problem E of Chapter 4.

Suppose that possible outputs are as in Figure 7. The most desired stock of the convex hull of $\mathscr{Y}$ is assumed to be

$$ty + (1 - t)\bar{y},$$

t an irrational number. No finite multiple of such individuals can pool their resources in such a manner as to obtain exactly this position for all. We might find that the margin of superiority obtained by moving from x along one's budget line may be diminished, but it does not altogether disappear. Only in the limit can the best position be obtained. Evidently, quasi-competitive behavior is all that can be expected until the limiting procedure is actually completed.

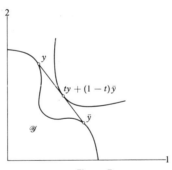

Figure 7

One individual can be placed at $\frac{1}{2}y + \frac{1}{2}\bar{y}$, but a separating line $\mathscr{L}$ does not give competitive behavior since $\bar{y}$ represents a more profitable output and each will tend to produce $\bar{y}$ and demand nonfeasible consumptions (Figure 8). Even rotating $\mathscr{L}$ to be a tangent at $\bar{y}$ will simply lead both parties to produce either $\bar{y}$ or y or $\frac{1}{2}y + \frac{1}{2}\bar{y}$ but to consume $ty + (1 - t)\bar{y}$, which is impossible. Competitive behavior could eventually result only in the case of an atomic world where only rational proportions were demanded.

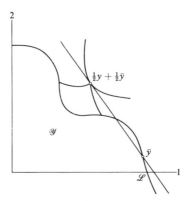

Figure 8

Exercise 7 For the public monopoly with decreasing marginal costs, what conditions must be imposed upon the demand curve in order to specify a unique efficient policy?

8. Competitive Equilibrium as an Economic System

Of the several conditions in the hypothesis of Theorem 19, the most serious restrictions are

(1) convexity of (induced) preferences, which excludes increasing returns to scale of production,

(2) independence of preferences, which excludes "externalities," and

(3) directional density, which limits differences in time of consumption by different consumers.

Movement from trade equilibrium to pairwise optimality preserves consumer efficiency only under these restrictive conditions. It is appropriate to consider economic systems ensuring Pareto optimality in the presence of one or more exceptions to the conditions (1)–(3). Assumptions (2) and (3) will be released in the next section and the competitive price equilibrium, will ensure optimality. In this section we consider the relationship between competitive behavior and the competitive system.

Recall that with directional density of preferences, x is Pareto optimal if and only if there is competitive behavior with respect to a linear functional p; that is, if and only if

$$p(\bar{x}^i) < p(x^i) \qquad \text{for all} \quad \bar{x}^i \in \mathscr{P}(x^i).$$

If also

$$p(x^i) = p(0) = 0 \qquad \text{for all} \quad i,$$

it is said that there is *competitive equilibrium* (C.E.). More generally, (p, x) is a competitive equilibrium pair of prices and trades if and only if

(i) $\sum x^i = 0$,
(ii) $\bar{x}^i \in \mathscr{P}(x^i)$ implies $p(\bar{x}^i) \neq p(x^i)$,
(iii) $p(x^i) = 0$.

We will show that competitive equilibrium arises under decentralized and nondiscriminatory behavior. In this section we will also indicate the connection between quasi-competitive behavior and competitive equilibrium. Later we will show that competitive equilibrium ensures Pareto optimality (Section 9), group conservation (Section 10), and efficient and nonexploitative foreign trade (Sections 11 and 12).

The requirement $p(x^i) = 0$ is that the value of outflow equal the value of inflow. This is a form of *Walras' Law*.

Since p is used solely for purposes of deriving exchange *ratios*, it would seem that sp would do as well, s any nonzero number. This is indeed the case, for we can multiply p by s and still have $sp(x^i) = 0$ if and only if $p(x^i) = 0$. Hence, we could pick some commodity as a *numéraire*, that is, standard of value, setting its price equal to one. Then the price vector would be uniquely specified. This will not be necessary, but rather, for mathematical reasons, all possible p (except, as it turns out, $p = 0$) will be considered and the property that the economy reacts in the same way to p and sp will be exploited (Chapter 4).

The definition of C.E. excluded from (ii) the phrase $p(\bar{x}^i) < p(x^i)$ whenever $x^i \neq 0$. Therefore, a competitive equilibrium trade is not necessarily a trade with competitive behavior. The motivation for this approach is to allow for waste products, which have prices of sign opposite to goods. It is not always clear which goods should have negative signs, since different individuals may have different views as to what a waste product is.

Usually, the definition of competitive equilibrium states that

$$p(\bar{x}^i) < p(x^i) \qquad \text{for} \quad \bar{x}^i \in \mathscr{P}_i(\bar{x}^i)$$

(Arrow and Debreu [1954]). However, this condition implies the one used above whenever preferences are locally unsaturated. In the other direction, suppose preferences are similar and suppose that $\mathscr{P}_i(x^i)$ is connected. Then possibly by multiplying p by minus one, we obtain

$$p(\bar{x}^i) < 0 \qquad \text{for} \quad \bar{x}^i \in \mathscr{P}_i(x^i).$$

23 Remark If $\mathscr{P}_i(x^i)$ is connected and for some listing of all consumers $(j), j = 1, 2,...$, between pairs $(ij), i(j + 1)$ preferences are similar, then $p(\bar{x}^i) < 0$, whenever $p(\bar{x}^i) \neq 0$ and $\bar{x}^i \in \mathscr{P}_i(x^i)$, so that competitive equilibrium implies competitive behavior.

Proof Let $\mathscr{S}_j$ be the similarity between j and $j + 1$. Simply let the price be negative for a direction of greater preference, $p(y) < 0$ for $y \in \mathscr{S}_j$. (It must be nonzero since otherwise an infinite quantity would be demanded.) Therefore x^i plus a positive addition of a direction of greater preference is on the negative side of the hyperplane,

$$\{x \mid p(x) = 0\}.$$

If any other superior bundle is on the other side, then there must be $\bar{x}^i \in \mathscr{P}_i(x^i)$ on the hyperplane (by connectivity) for which $p(\bar{x}^i) = 0$, contrary to the definition presented above. q.e.d.

A trade x is said to be *nondiscriminatory* if for any i,

$$x^i \mathscr{R}_i \sum_{j \neq i} -t_j x^j \qquad \text{for all} \quad 1 \geqslant t_j \geqslant 0.$$

This definition can be rationalized as follows. If x^{kj} is the trade from k to j, any other i presumes that he can always "share" k with j and obtain

$$s x^{kj} \qquad \text{for} \quad 1 \geqslant s \geqslant 0.$$

Therefore,

$$\sum_{k \neq i} s x^{kj} = -\sum_{k \neq i} s x^{jk}$$

is possible. Also, he presumes that if x^{ij} is acceptable to j, then so is $s x^{ij}$, since if j's preferences are convex, $s x^{ij}$ will be at least as good as no trade. Evidently,

$$-\sum_{i \neq j} s x^{jk} - s x^{ij} = s \sum_{k=1}^{n} -x^{jk} = -s x^j$$

is possible.

24 Theorem *A convex set $\mathscr{Q}_i$ directional dense at x^i and contained in $\mathscr{P}_i(x^i)$ implies that for the (intrinsic) price system p, and for a nondiscriminatory pairwise optimal trade x,*

$$p(x^j) \geqslant 0$$

for all j trading with i. Also, $p x^i \leqslant 0$.

In effect, at most i exploits the other traders relative to the competitive income.

Proof   Choose p so that

$$p(\bar{x}^i) \leqslant p(x^i) \qquad \text{whenever} \quad \bar{x}^i \in \mathcal{Q}_i \,.$$

If $p(y) < 0$ or $p(y + x^i) < p(x^i)$, directional density and convexity of $\mathcal{Q}_i$ imply that for some $1 > |s| > 0$, $sy + x^i \in \mathcal{Q}_i$.

Also, $sp(y) = p(sy) \leqslant 0$ or $s > 0$. Observe that $0 \leqslant st_j \leqslant 1$ if $0 < s < 1$ and $0 < t_j < 1$. Therefore,

$$x^i \, \mathcal{R}_i \sum_{j \neq i} -st_j x^j$$

so that $p(\sum_{j \neq i} -t_j x^j) < px^i$ cannot be. Therefore,

$$px^i \leqslant p\left(\sum_{j \neq i} -t_j x^j\right),$$

and letting $t_j = 0$ for all j, $px^i \leqslant 0$. Let $t_k = 1$ for $k \neq j$. Then we have

$$0 \geqslant px^i + p \sum_{k \neq j} x^k = p(-x^j).$$

Therefore, $0 \leqslant p(x^j)$.   q.e.d.

If there is quasi-competitive behavior and if $px_j = 0$ for all j, there is a *quasi-competitive equilibrium*.

25 Corollary   *If two traders have a convex set $\mathcal{Q}_i$ in $\mathcal{P}_i(x^i)$ that is directional dense at x^i, then for the intrinsic price system p, a nondiscriminatory pairwise optimal trade x is a quasi-competitive equilibrium.*

26 Corollary   *If two traders have preferences directional dense, all have preferences regular, weakly convex, quasi transferable, and $\mathcal{P}^i(x)$ open on line sements, and*

$$0 \in \text{Int} \sum \mathcal{X}_i \,,$$

then a nondiscriminatory, pairwise optimal trade x is a competitive equilibrium.

Proof   In the proof of Theorem 24, let $\mathcal{Q}_i = \mathcal{P}_i(x^i)$, and apply the fundamental lemma.   q.e.d.

9. Classical Welfare Economics

Welfare economics is the main substance of classical economics (as opposed to the more nearly positive neoclassical economics of Marshall, Menger, Jevons, Wicksell, Walras *et al.*). The fundamental proposition of welfare economics is the identity of a social optimum with decentralized decision making, a proposition that remains true only within certain economic environments. Specifically, there is a certain equivalence between competitive equilibrium and Pareto optimality. In this section, we show that equivalence and then discuss possible reasons for its failure.

For the case of two individuals and two goods, the basic ideas of this section are represented in the Edgeworth–Bowley box in Figure 9.

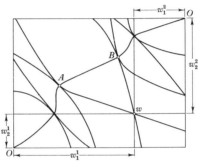

Figure 9

A single point such as w indicates the holdings of consumers 1 and 2. For example, w^i is the quantity of the jth good held by the ith individual. Therefore, every point in the box represents an allocation of goods to the consumers, and they can be ranked by these consumers. As usual, movements upward and to the right give higher levels of indifference for consumer 1. The indifference curves of consumer 2 are inverted and therefore concave to the origin. Movements downward and to the left represent movements to higher preference for consumer 2.

The Pareto optimal points are those where indifference curves of consumers 1 and 2 are tangent. The set of these form the "contract curve" $O_1 O_2$. From such a position, there can be no improvement for one that does not hurt the other. On the other hand, if the reference is to 2, those points which are Pareto superior to w are the ones in the interior of the lens bounded by the indifference curves passing through w. Of these Pareto superior points, those which are on the contract curve between A and B are also Pareto optimal. According to Edgeworth [1881], these were the points from which two trading individuals would chose. Therefore, the points on AB are called Edgeworth optimal, of which there will be more in the next section.

Here the welfare content of Pareto and Edgeworth optimal trades is emphasized because in a realistic situation, two traders may be restrained from efficient trades for fear of the repercussions from other traders. For example, a monopolist might be quite willing to discriminate in favor of a particular individual and thereby move to the contract curve, provided he were assured that his other customers would not demand the same terms and that the one buying on better terms did not sell to the others. In many practical situations, such assurance is not forthcoming. Therefore, the traders may not be on the contract curve even when there are many traders, if some have great influence over the price of one product.

A particular case that may represent some market conditions is that of competition, where the traders take prices as indicating the rates at which they can exchange goods. They then choose their trades so as to reach the highest level of preference. This is illustrated in Figure 10. Consumer 1 chooses along the budget line

$$\{x \mid p_1 x_1 + p_2 x_2 = p_1 w_1 + p_2 w_2\},$$

where (w_1, w_2) represents his initial wealth position. In the Edgeworth diagram, consumer 2 chooses along the same budget line. Let c_1 and c_2 be the total available goods. Then consumer 2 chooses from

$$\{y \mid p_1 y + p_2 y = p_1(c_1 - w_1) + p_2(c_2 - w_2)\},$$

which is represented in the diagram as

$$\{c - y \mid p_1 y + p_2 y = p_1(c_1(c_1 - w_1) + p_2(c_2 - w_2)\}$$
$$= \{c - y \mid p_1 w_1 + p_2 w_2 = p_1(c_1 - y_1) + p_2(c_2 - y_2)\}$$
$$= \{x \mid p_1 w_1 + p_2 w_2 = p_1 x_1 + p_2 x_2\}).$$

The price system leads to a competitive equilibrium provided the proposed trades are physically possible, that is, provided the two consumers choose the same point in the diagrammatic representation. This is not so for the budget line $\mathscr{L}_1$ (where 1 chooses z and 2 chooses y) but is so for $\mathscr{L}_2$ (where both choose x) in Figure 10. In particular, note that at a competitive equilibrium x there is tangency of 1 and 2's indifference curves, since they are mutually tangent to $\mathscr{L}_2$ at the same point. Therefore, the competitive choice is on the contract curve; the competitive equilibrium is Pareto optimal.

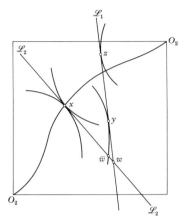

Figure 10

27 Theorem *If*

(i) *for some listing* $i(j)$, $j = 1, 2,...,$ *of all consumers, between pairs* $i(j)$, $i(j+1)$, *preferences are similar,*

(ii) $\mathscr{P}_i(x)$ *is connected for all* x,[3]

(iii) *and there is no benevolence,*

then for a competitive equilibrium (x, p), p *a continuous linear functional (or* p *only a linear functional if there are but a finite number of* i), x *is Pareto optimal.*

Theorem 27 is due to Arrow [1951a] and Debreu [1954] (see also Rader [1964]).

As an application, malevolence is no impediment to the efficiency of competitive equilibrium. The special cases of connected $\mathscr{P}(x)$ are

(i) $\mathscr{R}$ convex (Arrow and Debreu),

(ii) $\mathscr{R}$ monotonic (Koopmans and Bausch).[4]

Proof   Suppose

$$y \, \mathscr{P}_{i_0} \, x,$$

$$y \, \mathscr{R}_i \, x \qquad \text{for all} \quad i.$$

Then for x fixed,

$$y^i \, \mathscr{P}_{i_0} \, x^i,$$

$$y^i \, \mathscr{R}_i \, x^i \qquad \text{for all} \quad i \qquad \text{(no benevolence)}.$$

---

[3] If we adopt the Arrow–Debreu definition of competitive equilibrium, the hypothesis that $\mathscr{P}_i(x)$ is connected is not necessary.

[4] In Koopmans and Bausch [1959], the Arrow–Debreu definition of C.E. is used, so that in that framework, their theorem is general. The case of monotonic $\mathscr{R}$ easily gives the Arrow–Debreu C.E. from the one defined above.

Therefore,

$$p(y^{i_0}) < p(x^{i_0}) \qquad \text{(Remark 23 and Lemma 14)}$$

and

$$p(y^i) \leq p(x^i).$$

Summing, we get

$$p\left(\sum_i y^i\right) < p\left(\sum x^i\right) = 0 \qquad \text{(continuity of } p \text{ or finiteness of the } x^i\text{)}.$$

Therefore, it cannot be that

$$\sum_i y^i = 0,$$

that is, y is not in $\mathscr{X} \cap \mathscr{H}$. q.e.d.

Note that continuity of $\mathscr{P}$ is required only if the infinite sums are taken.

To approach this from the opposite direction, take a Pareto optimal point such as x in Figure 10. Then there is a line passing through x that is mutually tangent to the indifference curves. The set theoretic characterization of this line is

$$\mathscr{L}_2 = \{x \mid p_1 x_1 + p_2 x_2 = 0\}.$$

Let any w be on the line. Then

$$\mathscr{L}_2 = \{x \mid p_1 x_1 + p_2 x_2 = p_1 w_1 + p_2 w_2\}.$$

Therefore, from any w on the line, x is a competitive equilibrium with $\mathscr{L}_2$ as the budget line. Starting from some position such as x, we can obtain x simply by reallocating wealth in the horizontal good from 2 to 1 and then offering the consumers choice according to the price system associated with $\mathscr{L}_2$. Therefore, a Pareto optimum can be obtained by a competitive equilibrium, provided the initial distribution of income is appropriate.

A trade x is *sustainable* by a competitive equilibrium price system p if

(i) $p(\bar{x}^i) < p(x^i) = 0$ whenever $\bar{x}^i \mathscr{R}_i x^i$, $\bar{x}^i \neq x^i$,
(ii) $\sum x^i = 0$.

(The trade is *attainable* exactly when the competitive choice leads to that one trade alone. If there are several other trades, it is merely sustainable.)

28 Theorem   *If*

(i) $\mathscr{R}_i$ *is weakly convex, and* $\mathscr{P}_i(x)$ *is open on line segments,*
(ii)   *preferences are strongly quasi transferable and* $\sum_i \mathscr{P}_i(x)$ *has internal (interior) points,*
(iii) $\sum_{i=1}^{n} x_i \in \mathrm{Int} \sum \mathscr{X}_i$,
(iv)   *there is no malevolence,*

then a Pareto optimum x is sustainable by a competitive (continuous) price system p provided each individual is first transferred to x. Also, $\sum \mathscr{P}_i(x)$ *is directional dense if and only if at x, p is unique up to a multiplicative constant.*

The theorem is an extension of a theorem proposed by Arrow [1951] and Debreu [1954].

In the case of consumer benevolence, even where competitive equilibrium was not optimal, we could imagine that voluntary organizations redistributed income in order to attain optimality. Since for a given allocation there is one Pareto optimal and Pareto superior to that allocation, such voluntary schemes can supplement competitive equilibrium. Considering this theorem and the previous one, the effectiveness of competitive equilibrium in attaining economic efficiency is not necessarily invalidated by the existence of consumer interdependence, provided it is of the correct kind. This contradicts the view of Davis and Whinston [1965] that the greater the independence, the less appropriate the competitive mechanism.[5]

Combining Theorems 27 and 28 gives us the following result.

29 Theorem   *If*

(i) $\mathscr{R}_i$ *is convex, regular, and* $\mathscr{P}_i(x)$ *is open along line segments,*
(ii)   *preferences are strongly quasi transferable and independent and* $\sum \mathscr{P}_i(x)$ *has interior points,*
(iii) $\mathscr{X} \cap \mathscr{H}$ *is compact,*
(iv) $0 \in \mathrm{Int} \sum \mathscr{X}_i$,

then the set of Pareto optima is nonempty and is equivalent to the set of competitive equilibria with continuous p from the initial positions in $\mathrm{Int} \sum \mathscr{X}_i$.

---

[5] Their methodology, and that of Lipsey and Lancaster [1956] which it was based, depend on the theory of Lagrange multipliers, which does not appear to be a good tool for economic theory. (See Problems B–D.)

Only internal points are required if there are but a finite number of traders (although p will not be continuous). An example of $\sum \mathscr{P}_i(x)$ with internal points is the case of one i directional dense. Another example is where $\mathscr{P}_i(x)$ contains a point internal in the commodity space (apply convexity and $\mathscr{P}_i(x)$ open along line segments).

Proof As in Theorem 28, we have a competitive equilibrium. Since $\sum \mathscr{P}_i(x)$ has interior points, the separating linear functional can be chosen continuous. It remains to verify that the set of Pareto optima is nonempty. Simply apply Theorem 4 to

$$\sum x^i \in \operatorname{Int} \sum \mathscr{X}_i . \qquad \text{q.e.d.}$$

Proof of Theorem 28 If x is Pareto optimal, then there does not exist $\bar{x}$ such that

$$0 = \sum \bar{x}^i \in \sum \mathscr{P}_i(x^i) \qquad \text{(no malevolence)}.$$

Also, $\mathscr{P}_i(x)$ has internal points, since for any $y \in \mathscr{P}_i(x)$ and for any $\bar{x}$, $ty \in (1 - t)\, \bar{x} \in \mathscr{P}_i(x)$ for $t > 0$, t small (continuity on line segments). Therefore, applying Minkowski's theorem gives

$$p\left(\sum x^i\right) \geqslant p\left(\sum \bar{x}^i\right)$$

whenever

$$\bar{x}^i \in \mathscr{P}_i(x^i) \qquad \text{for all} \quad i.$$

Applying Lemma 14,

$$p(x^i) > p(\bar{x}^i) \qquad \text{for all} \quad \bar{x}^i \mathscr{P}_j x^i.$$

Allocating x^i to each i gives a competitive equilibrium. q.e.d.

The foregoing shows an equivalence between competitive equilibria and Pareto optima. This is the main content of classical welfare economics, that the invisible hand of a competitive price system leads to optimality, and indeed any optimum desired can be so obtained. Consequently, a planner might wish to move the economy in Figure 10 from x to z, say, because consumer 2 was of the bourgeoisie or a non-Aryan or a nonwhite or what have you. Nevertheless, he would not be obliged to drop the competitive system, which involves a large degree of decentralization. As such, Theorem 28 constitutes a refutation of the Marxist call for centralization to implement redistribution and might be characterized as the liberal reformer's theorem. Of course, this theorem should be qualified with the statement that the method of

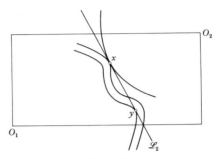

Figure 11

transfer may itself involve inefficiencies, say, in the case of the use of income taxes or excise taxes, which involve a burden above and beyond the cost of their collection.

It should be apparent that the argument for obtaining a Pareto optimum from a competitive equilibrium depends essentially on the convexity of preferences. This is illustrated in Figure 11, where x is Pareto optimal. When allowed to choose along $\mathscr{L}_2$, consumer 2 chooses x and consumer 1 chooses y. Hence, the competitive equilibrium does not obtain x. From any initial position on $\mathscr{L}_2$ there is at best some other line that gives competitive equilibrium but not at x.

Other qualifications include: the consumers must be independent to some extent (that is, there must be limits on externalities) and there must be well-defined commodity classifications with the physical possibility of *appropriating* their services. The independence required is as follows. If there is malevolence, that is, if consumer preferences are negatively related, we cannot be assured that a Pareto optimum can obtained by a competitive equilibrium. If there is benevolence, that is, if consumer preferences are positively related, we cannot be assured that a competitive equilibrium is Pareto optimal. The latter qualification is easy to understand since a reallocation may lead the "loved" consumers to a better position without hurting the "lovers."

These exceptions are well illustrated in Meade's (Bator [1958]) examples of the beekeeper and the apple orchard, which display joint outputs and in and of themselves pose no problems. For example, the competitive equilibrium would normally require the processes to be operated jointly, possibly as a partnership hiring the labor of the two individuals, or equally well, as separate enterprises, say, with half and half of each of the orchard and the bees in each firm, allocating the labor equally. However, if it is impossible to keep the bees and the apple trees apart, that is, there is an inappropriability, then there is no incentive for the two producers to get together. Each could not expect an optimum from competitive equilibrium, whenever the initial position separates the ownership of the two estates. Therefore, a competitive equilibrium with the right initial distribution of wealth could be expected to lead to an optimum, but not necessarily one from any distribution of wealth.

The removal of inappropriabilities, for example, industrial wastes or air pollution, is often the object of economic policy. Even if there is no inappropriability, due to equal holdings of bees and apple orchards, difficulties still arise whenever the beekeeper is better at beekeeping than the apple grower. It is as if the two have interrelated preferences. An increase in output by the beekeeper, whether or not it makes him better off, will make the apple grower better off—and vice versa. A division of the estates might be a solution, but this would be suboptimal, since the beekeeper is better at running his operation. Hence, some kind of merger is required—which is not within the competitive framework. The externality invalidates the optimality of competitive equilibrium. Of course, if there were divisible and marketable labor goods, beekeeping and apple growing, then the apple grower would think about going into the bee business and the beekeeper would think about going into apple growing, one with the same expectation of return as the other. In this case, the arrangement of ownership would not constrain them from using the joint production process separately and efficiently, and the classical equivalence would not be invalidated.

The foregoing interpretations of Bator's example illustrate the view that of the four concepts often discussed by welfare economists, increasing returns, inappropriabilities, joint processes, and externalities, one is a combination of the others. The apple–bee externalities normally arise because of a combination of a joint process and an inappropriability, or of an indivisibility (that is, increasing returns), a joint process, and an inappropriability.

Another example is afforded by national defense, normally regarded as a classic *public good*, whereby benefits accrue to a group from a simple activity. Evidently, the per capita cost of defense of the United States is much less than that of Luxembourg, due to the oddity of strategic position. (The area increases by the square of the boundary of defense.) Also, benefits accrue to individuals and they can be charged the marginal cost, but because of the increasing returns aspect, such charges cannot be expected to cover total costs. Indeed, for those in the center of the defense area, the marginal cost of defense may well be zero, which is the extreme case of a public good. It is not true that the benefits accrue without choice by the defenders. Any given individual could be left undefended and subject to invasion by a foreign power. The foreign power might even be transported to that individual at cost of the would-be defender in order to penalize the individual for not paying his "share." Therefore, those in the center may be forced to pay a nonzero price, even though the marginal cost is zero. This may prompt an inappropriate choice of the amount of defense.

It must be admitted that in some instances, externalities could be analyzed in and of themselves, as in the interindustry analysis of Marshall [1890], Pigou [1920], and Chipman [1966]. Presumably the properties of these externalities should be derived from other more basic phenomena.

It is not enough to know that the competitive equilibria and Pareto optima are more or less equivalent. We must also know that the competitive equilibrium is a complete social system. Theorem 29 gives that there is some distribution of wealth at which equilibrium exists, namely, a Pareto optimal one. However, nothing has been said about the set of initial positions from which a competitive equilibrium (with voluntarism in the presence of benevolence) does exist. If this set is small, then there must be some agency or mechanism to ensure that the initial distribution is placed in this set. The theory developed is sufficiently important to devote a chapter to its exposition (Chapter 4).

Exercise 8 In finite-dimensional space, how can the results of Theorems 27–29 be improved?

PROBLEMS

E. Public Goods I

Suppose the state has power over a production set $\mathcal{Y}$. Show that the choice of a Pareto optimal production with given equilibrium prices leads to a Pareto optimal production. (Hint: Simply restate the proof of Theorem 27 except that $\sum x^i = y$.)

This problem was due in part to Barone [1908], Lange [1938], and Lerner [1946], and was solved by Foley [1967]. Several of the other results of welfare economics are extended.

F. Public Goods II

It is alleged that a public project should be developed at some level if it can yield a positive profit. Assume two traders, one playing the role of the state, and two goods.

(i)   Find a case of a Pareto optimal trade where an increase in one good provided by the state trade can lead to a better position for the state trader.

(ii)   How does transferability of utility, where u_i is linear in one good for all i, change the answer in (i)?

G. Excise Taxes I

Suppose there is one consumer; let him be taxed at the rate t_i on the ith good. Then return the goods taxed to him in the form of a subsidy. Presuming competitive choice, show that for any level of preference there is at most one θ for which the final outcome from tax θt gives the level of preference. (Hint: Define preferences on taxes and prove continuity on line segments. Assume uniqueness of equilibrium with regard to a given tax structure.)

This problem was solved by Foster and Sonnenschein [1970].

H. Equilibrium with a Countable Number of Traders

Let there be goods $1, 2,\dots$. Let consumer i hold one unit of good i only. Suppose that x units of good i can be transferred into λx units of good $i + 1$, $0 < \lambda < 1$. Let $u_i(c) = c_i^\sigma c_{1+i}^{1-\sigma}$ for $c = (c_1, c_2,\dots)$.
Show that in equilibrium

(i) $p_i = \lambda p_{i+1}$,
(ii)   no transfers take place among individuals,
(iii)   the trade is nonoptimal,
(iv)   the price system is discontinuous.

This is a modification due to David Gale of the problem of Samuelson [1958] and Cass and Yaari [1966].

UNSOLVED PROBLEM

I. Interdependent Preference II

If there is benevolence that occurs because another individual is better off, under what conditions on preferences is Pareto optimality ensured by pairwise optimality or by or by competitive equilibrium with voluntary transfers of wealth from one trader to another?

A partial answer appears in Bergstrom [1971].

10. Neoclassical Welfare Economics

Here we show that competitive equilibrium is equitable, Edgeworth optimal, and invariant. Under nonconvexity of the production set, where competitive equilibrium does not exist, there is doubt about the existence of Edgeworth optimal consumptions when more than one good is subject to increasing returns to scale. Under convexity assumptions, it will be shown that the competitive equilibrium is the only outcome that is both Edgeworth optimal and invariant. As will be seen in Chapter 4, competitive equilibrium exists and therefore Edgeworth optimal consumptions exist under the appropriate continuity and convexity assumptions.

In classical welfare economics, the distribution of income remained arbitrary. Even when there is consumer efficiency, however, an incorrect distribution of income necessarily involves theft. Hence, many of the neoclassical economists attempted to resolve the indeterminacy of income distribution. For example, J.B. Clark [1890] formulated a theory to explain the "correct" distribution of benefits on the basis of productivity considerations. This theory is an important part of the economics of the firm and the industry. Nevertheless, although Clark's theory restricted the possibilities for distribution of benefits, it was really no more restrictive than the classical approach. Clark's theory merely said that benefits must be distributed according to rules such that the benefits are competitive. This is simply a requirement of consumer efficiency and leaves the distribution of initial wealth undetermined. A more successful approach was suggested by Edgeworth [1881]. Formal proofs for his conjectures and rough arguments were absent for almost a century until recent work by Scarf [1962] (also Shubik [1959]). Improvements were made by Debreu and Scarf [1963]. Extension to cases of a continuum of traders was attained by Aumann [1965, 1966] and Vind [1964].

Suppose there are basically two kinds of consumers, as illustrated in Figure 9, although there may be large numbers of these consumers. The problem is to ascertain just where on the contract curve the consumers will locate after trading. Notwithstanding reservations about being on the contract curve at all, there are some appealing notions about how trading might take place.

It is required that the trade that might be obtained lead to consumptions for which no particular consumer nor any group of consumers could do better on the basis of their own resources without trading with the others. Such trades form what is called the *core*. From the point of view of welfare economics, they are *Edgeworth optimal*.

Edgeworth optimal trades lead to the same level of preference for consumers of the same type (Debreu and Scarf [1963]). This can be shown simply by breaking off the consumers who are treated worse and letting them trade among themselves without trading with the others. For example, suppose there are an even number of each type of consumer. Take the half of each type of consumer who are relatively worse off. For each such worse-off consumer, associate one of the better-off consumers. Then the coalition of worse-off consumers can obtain, for each consumer in the coalition, a trade halfway between that which he formerly had and that which the associated better-off consumer had. This trade turns out to be physically possible, and by convexity of preferences it is no worse for any of the consumers in the coalition and is better for some. Hence, in the core, consumers of the same type are equally well off. Under strict convexity they are actually awarded the same consumption.

Whenever consumers with the same preferences and initial wealth are given the same level of preference, the consumptions are *absolutely equitable*. It is not true that all Pareto optimal points are absolutely equitable, as for example in Figure 10, if there are four consumers, two of each type. One pair of type 1 and type 2 might locate at x and the other pair at y. Hence, the notion of Edgeworth optimality seems to be an advance over the more general notion of Pareto optimality, at least in this respect.

Recall that an economy is a replica provided each consumer is reproduced exactly k times. For example, it is argued above that Edgeworth optimal allocations are absolutely equitable for a k-replica of consumers of types 1 and 2 provided k is greater than or equal to 2. (Actually, there is no need for the restriction to two types of consumers.)

30 Theorem (Debreu and Scarf) *Let preferences be independent and either convex or weakly convex and quasi transferable. Then Edgeworth optimality for a k-replica, $k > 1$, implies absolute equity.*

Proof   Renumber individuals so that the first set of individuals $\mathscr{I}_1$ are those who are worse off for types $i = 1, 2,..., n$, and whose composition make a 1-replica. Similarly, one more each of types $1, 2,..., n$ are denoted $\mathscr{I}_2$, and so on. If there is quasi transferability at x, "allocate" from a consumer who is made better off than the comparable member of the 1-replica $\mathscr{I}_1$ and make everyone *else* better off at $\bar{x}$, and everyone better than at x^i, $i \in \mathscr{I}_1$. Taking convex combinations gives

(i) $(\sum_{j \text{ of type } i} (1/k) \bar{x}^j) \mathscr{P}_i x^i$

since $\bar{x}^i \mathscr{P}_i x^i$ and there is weak convexity. If there is not quasi transferability, then we have instead

(ii) $\left(\Sigma_{j \text{ of type } i} (1/k) x^j\right) \mathscr{R}_i x^i$ for all i, by weak convexity,

and

$$\left(\sum_{j \text{ of type } i_0} \frac{1}{k} x^j\right) \mathscr{P}_{i_0} x^{i_0} \qquad \text{for some}\quad i_0\,,$$

since $x^j \mathscr{R}_i x^i$ for all j of i's type and $x^j \mathscr{P}_{i_0} x^{i_0}$ for some i_0 and all j of the same type as i_0 and there is convexity.

Consider the trade

$$y^i = \left(\sum_{j \text{ of type } i} \frac{1}{k} x^j\right), \qquad \sum_{i \in \mathscr{I}_1} y^i = \frac{1}{k} \sum_j x^i = 0.$$

It is possible for the 1-replica and blocks x. This is a contradiction, whereupon it must be true that people of the same type are treated equivalently.   q.e.d.

31 Remark If there is strict convexity, it can be shown that the quantities are actually identical for traders of the same type. In any case, we can average trades and thereby attain a given level of preference for each type with identical trades.

We show that the competitive allocation is Edgeworth optimal for all k-replicas (Theorem 32). Consider the Pareto optimum x, which is also a competitive equilibrium in Figure 10. (The initial position is given by w.) Keep in mind that in the end, consumers of each type are awarded the same consumptions. In order to move to a better position for consumer 2, we must move downward and to the left of the indifference curve for 2 passing through x. In order to give this new consumption, say y, to consumers of type 2, consumers of type 1 must all be placed somewhere on the line containing y and w, namely, $\mathscr{L}_2$.

A positive multiple of the award y to consumer 2, namely, by the number of consumers being awarded y, and a positive multiple of the award x to consumer 1, namely, by the number of consumer 1's in the bargain, must be the negative of one another. Since the multiples are positive, it follows that the award to consumers of type 1 must be upward and to the left of w on the line $\mathscr{L}_2$. It is clear that such consumptions are inferior to x for consumer type 1, and therefore no coalition of consumers of type 1 and 2 would obtain y for type 2 without hurting type 1.

32 Theorem (Shapley) *If $\mathscr{R}_i(x)$ is connected, there is not benevolence, and preferences are similar for contiguous pairs, then a competitive equilibrium trade with a continuous price system is Edgeworth optimal.*

If there are but a finite number of consumers, the continuity assumption on prices is not needed.

Proof Let (x, p) be the competitive equilibrium and apply Remark 23 and Lemma 14. If

$$\bar{x}^i \mathscr{R}_i x^i, \qquad p(\bar{x}^i) \leqslant p(x^i),$$

and if

$$\bar{x}^{i_0} \mathscr{P}_{i_0} x^{i_0}, \qquad p(\bar{x}^{i_0}) < p(x^{i_0}).$$

Therefore,

$$\sum_{i \in \mathscr{S} \sim i_0} p(\bar{x}^i) + p(\bar{x}^{i_0}) > \sum_i p(x^i) = p\left(\sum x^i\right) = 0 \qquad \text{(continuity of } p\text{)}.$$

Therefore,

$$p\left(\sum_{i \in \mathscr{S}} \bar{x}^i\right) < 0 \qquad \text{or} \qquad \sum_{i \in \mathscr{S}} \bar{x}^i \neq 0.$$

Therefore, x is Edgeworth optimal. q.e.d.

Even the simple result of Shapley is of importance. For example, if one or more countries move from international free trade to autarky, each country loses relative to the initial distribution of benefits. On the other hand, a redistribution of wealth internally can obtain any Pareto optimum under autarky, after which there would be no further trade. Thereafter, a country can trade externally and be assured of improving the position of all its consumers.

33 Corollary *If $\mathscr{R}_i$ is connected, preferences are similar for contiguous pairs $i, i + 1$, and there is not benevolence, then competitive equilibrium between groups can always attain as much as a Pareto optimum for a separated group, with a possible redistribution of wealth within the group, while a separated group can never do better for all its members than does the competitive choice.*

Proof Apply Theorems 28 and 32. q.e.d.

Alternatively, breaking off any given group, together with all its wealth, can never make the remaining group better off. Obviously, Corollary 33 gives a basis for minority rights in the economic sphere.

A theorem of Scarf [1967] gives a very general characterization of "games" with nonempty cores. A *game* is specified if for each coalition $\mathscr{S}$, $\mathscr{V}_{\mathscr{S}}$ is the set of utilities $u^{\mathscr{S}}$ attainable for its members. A collection of coalitions t is a balanced collection if there exist $\delta_{\mathscr{S}} \geqslant 0$ such that

$$\sum_{\substack{\mathscr{S} \in t \\ \mathscr{S} \supset \{i\}}} \delta^{\mathscr{S}} = 1.$$

A game is *balanced* if for each balanced collection t and for any u satisfying $u_{\mathscr{S}} \in \mathscr{V}_{\mathscr{S}}$ for all $\mathscr{S} \in t$, then $u \in \mathscr{V}_{\cup_{i=1}^{n}\{i\}}$. The *weak core* is an imputation, $u \in \mathscr{V}_{\cup_{i=1}^{n}\{i\}}$, such that there is no $\mathscr{S}$ and $u^{\mathscr{S}} \in \mathscr{V}_{\mathscr{S}}$ with $u^{\mathscr{S}} \gg u_{\mathscr{S}}$. There is a sense in which the following result is the best possible (see Problem I).

34 Theorem (Scarf). *If*

    (i)   *there is a finite number of individuals,*
    (ii) *the set of utilities attainable by any coalition is closed and bounded from above,*
    (iii) *the game is balanced,*

then the weak core is nonempty.

The proof is an elaborate but elegant algorithm and the reader is referred to the original article by Scarf [1967].

35 Theorem *If there are quasi-transferable preferences for all subsets of consumers $\mathscr{S}$, the weak core equals the strong core.*

Proof If for x and y feasible, $x \mathscr{R}_i y$ for all $i \in \mathscr{S}$, $x \mathscr{P}_j y$ for some j, then there is a z feasible for $\mathscr{S}$ such that $z \mathscr{P}_i y$ for all i. Hence, anything that cannot be blocked by something better for all in $\mathscr{S}$ also cannot be blocked by something better for one and no worse for all in $\mathscr{S}$. q.e.d.

As an example of a balanced game other than one where there is competitive equilibrium, consider an economy with a single commodity and with factors of production x^i, $i = 1,...,n$. Let the maximum output be given by f. For a given coalition, attainable output is limited by $f(\sum_{i \in \mathscr{S}} x^i)$. The distribution of output among individuals is a *game with transferable utility*, since utility may be taken to be the quantity of the single commodity required, whereupon we can transfer utility from one individual to another.

36 Theorem (Shapley) *If $x \geqslant y$ and $\delta \geqslant 0$ imply*

$$f(x + \delta) - f(x) \geqslant f(y + \delta) - f(y)$$

and $f(0) = 0$, then the game with transferable utility has a nonempty core.

Proof Order individuals i_1, i_2 ,... . Give i_1 ,$f(x^{i_1})$ and i_2 ,$f(x^{i_1} + x^{i_2}) - f(x^{i_1})$. In general, give i_n ,$f(\sum_{i=1}^{n} x^{i_1}) - f(\sum_{1+j}^{n-1} x^{i_j})$. Such an allocation is feasible and it cannot be blocked. q.e.d.

The function f is *convex* if $-f$ is concave.

37 Corollary *If f is convex, $f(0) = 0$, and there is only one factor of production, then the game with transferable utility has a nonempty core.*

Proof For $x \geqslant y$,

$$f(x + \delta) - f(x) \equiv \int_{x}^{x+\delta} f' \, dz$$

$$\geqslant \int_{y}^{y+\delta} f' \, dy = f(y + \delta) - f(y)$$

since f' is decreasing in x, almost everywhere. q.e.d.

Scarf [1967] has shown that convexity is necessary if the core is to exist whatever the distribution of wealth.

Note that superadditivity of production may suffice for the core to exist under increasing returns to scale, if there is a single factor. In Figure 12a, there is superadditivity but not convexity, which is illustrated in Figure 12b. Nevertheless, the core exists. Since the average product increases, the community can award to each individual the average product multiplied by the amount of the factor he contributed. No subgroups

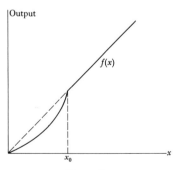

Figure 12a

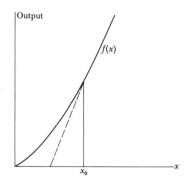

Figure 12b

can attain a higher average product and thereby block the allocation.

Convexity appears to be the traditional concept of a public utility where marginal costs are decreasing and then constant. In contrast, in Figure 12a there will be a discontinuity in marginal costs, and at the discontinuity marginal costs increase.

Theorem 36 and Corollary 37 state that a public utility can assure enough to its subscribers to improve the position of any member or group relative to what it could get alone, provided it devotes the same resources to the public utility.

The caveat of the preceding paragraph is not a trivial one, and it can be seen that there is no core in cases where several public utilities are competing for resources. To see why superadditivity or convexity do not ensure the existence of Edgeworth optimal allocations when there are more than one good, consider a three-person, three-good economy. Let consumer 1 like goods 2 and 3, and be indifferent regarding the proportions consumed of each. Similarly, let consumer 2 like 3 and 1, and consumer 3 like 1 and 2. Let commodities be produced from a single factor by identical production functions f, with increasing returns to scale, and let each consumer have an initial endowment of the factor x. Then coalition $\{i, j\}$ will produce only commodity k, $i \neq j$, $k \neq i$, $k \neq j$. For the case of equal division of production, the coalition $\{1, 2, 3\}$ must assure each party at least $\frac{1}{2}f(2x)$ of the desired good. Obviously, producing all three goods is inefficient. Should we produce as much as $f(2x)$ of good i, then we must produce $\frac{1}{2}f(2x)$ of j, since otherwise the consumer not liking j can entice one of the others to join him. Of course, it is impossible to produce $f(2x)$ of i and $\frac{1}{2}f(2x)$ of j. Reducing the scale of output in good i will reduce the ratio of output to input in good i without bringing the input–output ratio in good j to an acceptable level. Of course, we cannot increase the scale of output of j without violating one person's benefit required to keep him from bidding away another from the arrangement. Formally, for increasing returns to scale, we cannot simultaneously solve

$$f(tx) + f((1 - t)x) \geq \tfrac{3}{2}f(2x),$$

$$f(tx) \geq \tfrac{1}{2}f(2x),$$

$$f((1 - t)x) \geq \tfrac{1}{2}f(2x).$$

To remedy this we might imagine a production of one of the goods at the level of $(2x)$, the one to be so produced to be determined by a random device. However, this would be unacceptable if there were (sufficient) risk aversion on the part of the consumers.

A possible way out is for each person to regard coalitions as being assigned probabilities of formation. In this way, they apply the rule that should i make an offer to j to leave the coalition $\{1, 2, 3\}$, it is quite likely that k will do so also. Then the payoffs for coalitions $(1, 2)$, $(2, 3)$, and $(3, 1)$ would be greatly reduced in threat against $(1, 2, 3)$. Without application of the categorical imperative, the resolution of conflict would be impossible. This point of view will be discussed more fully in the next chapter, where a method of conflict resolution will be indicated. Hopefully, that method will have both positive and normative content.

The last result of this section is that *competitive equilibrium is the only allocation of consumer benefits that is in the core for all k-replicas*. Consider a point x that is on the contract curve, as in Figure 13. It is assumed

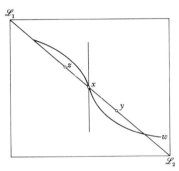

Figure 13

that x is not a competitive equilibrium. This is shown by the small line segment through x that indicates the tangency to indifference cores. That tangent line is not the line between x and w. It will be shown that there exists a sufficiently large k, such that a coalition in the k-replica blocks any movement of consumers from w to x. The proposal is to award y to consumers of type 1 and z to consumers of type 2 where z minus w is a rational multiple of y minus w. From their position relations to the tangent line, type 1 prefers y to x, and type 2 prefers z to x. Since rational numbers are ratios of integers,

$$(z - w) = \frac{m}{n}(y - w)$$

where n and m are integers, or

$$n(z - w) = m(y - w).$$

Therefore, moving m consumers of type 1 from w to y can be accomplished by moving n consumers of type 2 from w to z. Choose k to be the larger of n or m; then the proposed coalition is possible for the k-replica of the economy. Clearly, the coalition of m consumers of type

1 and n consumers of type 2 blocks the allocation and x is not in the core for this k-replica of the economy. This completes the argument, which is the basic result proposed by Edgeworth and demonstrated by Scarf. Of course, the argument becomes more difficult in the case of more than two consumer types.

Not only should a social optimum be such that no minority group is damaged beyond what it can do on its own, but also the social choice should be *invariant* to replication of the economy. That is to say, replicating the economy exactly by a factor of k should not lead to any change in preference level per type of consumer, unless production possibilities per consumer are changed, which is excluded by the assumption of no increasing returns to scale or externalities between the consumers. Essentially, invariance under k-replication requires that no consumer benefit merely because his wealth and his productive "talents" are orginized under one house. This would seem to exclude as ill-gotten gains entirely due to a monopoly position. The position would disappear as the economy were replicated by factors of k, and a solution for a social optimum that allowed monopoly gains would not be invariant to k-replication.

38 Theorem   (Debreu and Scarf)   *If*

(i)   *there are a finite number of traders,*
(ii)   *preferences are strongly quasi transferable, weakly convex, and independent, and $\mathscr{P}_i(x)$ is open on line segments,*
(iii) $0 \in \operatorname{Int} \sum \mathscr{X}_i$,

then only the competitive equilibrium is both Edgeworth optimal and invariant.

Theorem 38 denies the necessity for reform once a proper income distribution has been effected. It is the Theorem of the Great Conservative. There is another proof due to Vind [1965].

Proof   Define the convex set from the $\mathscr{P}_i(x^i)$, $i = 1,..., n,$

$$\varDelta = \left\{ \sum t_i \bar{x}^i \,\middle|\, \bar{x}^i \in \mathscr{P}_i(x^i) \quad \text{for all} \quad t_i \geqslant 0, t_i = 1 \right\}.$$

In particular,

$$\mathscr{P}_i(x^i) \subset \varDelta \qquad \text{for all} \quad i.$$

To show that $0 \notin \Delta$, consider any $\sum t_i \bar{x}^i \in \Delta$. Take k sufficiently large such that for each i there is an $m_i \leqslant k$ for which

$$\bar{x}^i = \frac{k}{m_i} t_i \bar{x}^i \, \mathscr{P}_i \, x^i$$

(openness of $\mathscr{P}_i(x)$ on line segments applied to $[\bar{x}^i, 0]$ for $1 > (k/m_i) t_i$ nearly 1).

Consider the coalition made up of m_i of individuals of type i. Then

$$\sum m_i \bar{x}^i = \sum k t_i \bar{x}^i = k \left(\sum t_i \bar{x}^i \right) = 0,$$

and x is blocked by the coalition. This is a contradiction, so that it must have been that $0 \notin \Delta$. Also, $\mathscr{P}_i(x)$ has internal points. For any $y \in \mathscr{P}_i(x)$ and any $\bar{x}$, $ty + (1 - t)\bar{x} \in \mathscr{P}_i(x)$ for $t > 0$, t small (continuity on line segments). Next, apply Minkowski's theorem to obtain a separating linear functional p for which

$$0 = p(0) \geqslant p(\Delta) \quad \text{or} \quad 0 \geqslant p(\mathscr{P}_i(x)) \quad \text{or} \quad p(\bar{x}^i) \leqslant 0$$

whenever $\bar{x}^i \, \mathscr{P}_i \, x^i$. Applying Lemma 14 for all i, we have

$$p(\bar{x}^i) < 0$$

whenever $\bar{x}^i \, \mathscr{P}_i \, x^i$. This gives the competitive equilibrium.   q.e.d.

In general, it cannot be said that a competitive equilibrium is uniquely determined. That is to say, for a given wealth distribution there may be several price systems that attain an equilibrium and that lead to different levels of preference, at least for some consumers.

An example is given in Figure 14, from which we can see that the wealth distribution w may lead to x or y as competitive equilibria,

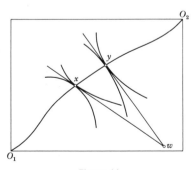

Figure 14

depending on which price system is used. Uniqueness of equilibrium results only in the unlikely event that for all prices, goods are gross substitutes for each other, that is, when an increase in the price of one good leads to an increase in the excess demand for all other goods (Chapter 5). Hence, social choice, although greatly restricted, has not been completely determined.

The convexity assumptions have excluded the very returns to scale that seem the source of much public action. The economies of scale provided a surplus of value over what subgroups could get, attributable completely to the existence of the large society and presumably at its disposal. This introduces difficulties into the notion of a social optimum. Even so, the theorems may be of some value in guiding policy for that (substantial) amount of economic activity not normally viewed as being a natural monopoly. In this case we are tempted to derive the percentage of government control in natural monopolies as opposed to industries with more or less convex production sets, for example, transportation, postal service, communications, and perhaps metal fabrication and automobiles, versus agriculture, oil, trucking, shipbuilding, textiles, watchmaking.

It is possible that everything began with Adam and that we would not wish to question the intergenerational transfers of wealth. Then, provided that all human economic affairs had been formerly dictated by competitive choice, the competitive method of economic organization should be sustained. However, the world since Adam has not been competitive. Conquest has been an especially important determinant of the distribution of wealth. We might think that the Scarf theorem justifies searching out the descendants of Esau and returning to them the inheritance now enjoyed by Jacob's descendants. Apart from the practical difficulty of redressing ancient woes, it must be emphasized that Scarf's theorem determines not a social welfare function, but only a social optimum. Therefore, if the course of human history has been other than optimal, there does not appear any way of comparing the suboptimal situations among which we must then necessarily choose.

Nevertheless, two positive points may be made. First, if the ideal distribution of wealth is one determined for a given generation, then the Scarf theorem applies to show that it will be ideal for future generations, even though changes are wrought by inheritance, provided we accept the manner in which fathers pass their inheritance to their sons. This follows by virtue of the fact that future as well as present commodities are accounted for in the definition of Edgeworth optimality. In effect, the competitive order is a going concern, from the point of view of welfare economics. From a political viewpoint, it may be otherwise.

Occasionally, the rich must bribe the poor to avoid revolution, as in Byzantium of old (Gregoire [1966]), but in economies where opportunity and wealth have not been overwhelmingly based on land the distribution of which is necessarily arbitrary, this kind of revolution has not proved important; examples are the United States, the Netherlands, and perhaps Belgium. Apparently, the distribution of talents and enterprise is sufficiently great that revolt by the poor is not the main problem in a relatively free economy.

A second possibility is that in a highly industrialized economy, the distribution of wealth may be determined by labor, enterprise, and past savings from labor and enterprise rather than by the former ownership of land, which presumably resulted from conquest. In this case, the competitive economy at the given distribution of wealth would be (nearly) optimal. However, the rule does not apply when there are groups who have been excluded from the competitive economy in the near past, as in the case of the American Negro.

Exercise 9   How can Theorem 32 be improved by assuming a finite number of commodities?

Exercise 10   Show that the game in Theorem 36 is balanced.

PROBLEMS

J. The Core Exists I

There is transferable utility provided only that for constants $f^{\mathscr{S}}$, the only constraints are

$$\sum_{i \in \mathscr{S}} u_i \leqslant f^{\mathscr{S}} .$$

Show that the core exists if and only if the game is balanced. (Hint: Minimize $\sum_{i=1}^{n} u_i$ subject to $\sum_{i \in \mathscr{S}} u_i \geqslant f^{\mathscr{S}}$ for all $\mathscr{S}$.)

The solution to this problem is due to Shapley and to Bondareva (Scarf [1967]).

K. The Core Exists II

Show that with weakly convex preferences, the exchange economy with independent consumers forms a balanced game. Use this fact to construct a proof of the existence of competitive equilibrium.

L. Games with Transferable Utility

Show that a game with transferable utility has a convex core.

UNSOLVED PROBLEM

M. The Core Exists III

In a single good, many factor economy, what conditions additional to superadditivity of f and $f(0) = 0$ are sufficient for the existence of the core?

11. Compensation in Small Countries

The general imposition of subsidies and taxes, when based on productive services, leads to inefficiency (Section 6). An exception is a tax on the (unimproved) value of land or other fixed resources. Therefore, the question of attaining social optimality by the payment of subsidies is not entirely answered by Theorem 28. The rest of this chapter is concerned with the nature of subsidies needed to improve the position of all consumers.

A special case in which Theorem 28 applies with practical force is a *small country* in international trade, defined as a country that can buy and sell at the international price p without fear of changing that price. Here we show that in contrast to tariffs, which are inefficient, taxes on factors or goods involve no short-run welfare loss. Also, it will be shown that in one sense, the higher the tariffs, the greater the welfare loss. Questions of proper income distribution in international trade are deferred to Section 12, where large countries are treated.

It is assumed that production may be the result of the use of factors that are not traded internationally, which will have the price system w. Home factors are assumed to be fixed in quantity and therefore not subject to short-run fluctuation. Imagine that they represent fixed quantities of labor or capital.

Let

z = trades for production alone, independent of preferences,

x = trades for consumer value,

y = supplies of factors of production.

Of course, $x + z$ is the country's world trade position, and z is produced from y. In addition, there are the price systems

p for trades z and x, and

w for stock y, where by definition $w(y) = p(z)$;

that is, total profits are allocated to factors.

Presuming full employment of factors, three instruments of state policy come to mind: taxes on factor income, taxes on goods, and taxes on imports. Of course each of these policies has a negative side, namely, a subsidy. The theory is the same, whether the tax is negative or positive.

Following Kreuger and Sonnenschein [1967], we posit that a policy leads to *no potential loss* if the government obtains revenues that can be used in the foreign market to purchase goods that in turn can be granted in subsidy, so as to restore all individuals to a position at least as good as the one before the policy. Otherwise, there is a potential loss. This is the Hicks–Kaldor criterion. Only if the no-policy situation also leads to no potential loss with respect to the policy can it be said that the notion of potential loss has welfare content. Otherwise, the policy would lead to a loss with respect to the initial position of consumers, but the new situation would be better than anything without the policy, that is comparable with regard to the distribution of benefits among consumers.

39 Theorem   *Taxes on factor wages involve no potential loss.*

This proposition is a version of the theorem of Hotelling [1938].

Proof   Taxes on factor income must not affect the wages firms pay, for only at those wages can the factor market be equilibrated, given the factor supplies. Therefore, the only effect of the taxes on factor income is to reduce the income of factors and their demands for goods. Presuming that all industries are subject to international competition, either because they export to the international market or because they import some quantity of foreign goods, there is no change in prices of goods. All the loss in factor income accrues to the state and the state may use the proceeds to restore individuals to the position at which they would have been, simply by buying and distributing among individuals goods equal to the goods bought without tax minus goods bought after the tax.   q.e.d.

Theorem 39 applies equally well to negative as to positive taxes. Therefore, reversing taxes on factors leads to no potential loss. Taxes or subsidies on factor wages are efficient methods of *distribution of welfare.*

40 Remark   A tax–tariff policy leads to a potential loss if and only if government revenues are insufficient to purchase at the international price system, the goods purchased by consumers before the policy.

Proof   The government can always buy effectively at the international price system, since anything in excess of it is collected by the government as a tax and therefore the extra charge is illusory. Whatever the government purchases can be parceled out to consumers via subsidies on factor wages.   q.e.d.

In particular, Remark 40 applies to show that reversal of a tax–subsidy scheme leading to a potential loss leads to a gain. Therefore, the notion of potential loss is not dependent on the socially preferred distribution of benefits.

41 Theorem   *Taxes on goods do not change output decisions and no potential loss occurs.*

The rationale for the theorem is that the equilibrium of the factor market and the preservation of factor wages normally require that producers obtain a particular profit that must be invariant to price changes.

Taxes on goods force consumers to pay higher prices but do not affect the effective price of goods to produce since this is determined by the international market, subject to whatever tariff restrictions are in effect. Normally, increases in the price of goods from p to $\bar{p}$ will influence consumers to decrease their purchases of the taxed goods, so that the state will obtain revenues less than the amount that the consumers originally paid. That is to say,

$$(\bar{p} - p)(\bar{x} - x) < 0$$

where x is the consumer's purchases under p and $\bar{x}$ is the consumers' purchases under $\bar{p}$. Nevertheless, the state will be able to make purchases sufficient to restore consumers to their old position.

Proof   The value of the consumers' old purchases, possibly after some income transfers, will be

$$p(x) = w(y)$$

but for the new purchases with the new price system $\bar{p}$ it will also be

$$\bar{p}(\bar{x}) = w(y).$$

In order to return the consumers to their old position x, the state must purchase internationally the amount $x - \bar{x}$ at a cost of $p(x - \bar{x})$.

The state's new revenues are $(\bar{p} - p)\bar{x}$. The state can buy goods on the international market at price p. Since

$$p(x - \bar{x}) - (\bar{p} - p)(\bar{x}) = p(x) - \bar{p}(\bar{x}) = 0,$$

it is possible to restore the economy to $\bar{x}$. Therefore, there is neither a potential loss nor a potential gain.   q.e.d.

A theorem of Samuelson [1938] (see also [1962]) is:

42 Theorem   *If and only if the tariff leads to a less profitable production, there is a potential loss from a tax–subsidy scheme, and it is an inferior method of increasing factor income.*

Proof   The imposition of a tariff has two effects. First, there are changes in factor wages in order to preserve zero profitability of industries. Second, the state obtains revenues from imported goods. Let

$$\bar{p}_i > p_i$$

only for import industries, since there is no point in placing a tariff on an exported good. Also, wages change to $\bar{w}$. If $\bar{x}$ is the new demand for goods and $\bar{z}$ is the new home supply, then the state receives the tariff times imports which is equal to

$$0 \leqslant (\bar{p} - p)(\bar{x} - \bar{z}) = \bar{p}(\bar{x} - \bar{z}) - p(\bar{x} - \bar{z}) = -p(\bar{x} - \bar{z}).$$

Factor income changes from w to $\bar{w}$, where

$$\bar{p}\bar{x} = \bar{p}\bar{z} = \bar{w}y.$$

An alternative state policy is to tax by the amount $(\bar{p} - p)$, yielding revenues $(\bar{p} - p)\bar{x}$, and to subsidize so as to obtain the same factor income as under the tariff, which sums to $\bar{w}y$. The subsidy would be equal to

$$\bar{w}y - wy = \bar{p}\bar{x} - px.$$

The remaining revenues would be equal to

$$(\bar{p} - p)\bar{x} - \bar{p}\bar{x} + px = px - p\bar{x} = p(x - \bar{x}) = p(z - \bar{x}).$$

Factor income would be as high as under the tariff and the revenues would be higher by the amount

$$p(z - x) + p(\bar{x} - \bar{z}) = p(z - \bar{z}) \geqslant 0. \qquad \text{q.e.d.}$$

A tariff proposed is one of *divergence* if the new tariff, $p - \bar{p}$, is proportional to the old, δ^2.

43 Theorem   *If profits are reduced by a divergence tariff, then in fact they yield less consumer welfare than a tax–subsidy scheme supplementing the old tax–tariff system.*

This is a version of the so-called price divergence theorem (Kreuger and Sonnenschein [1967]). The farther the prices diverge from free trade, the greater the potential loss.

Proof In the general case, where taxes and tariffs already exist, the increase in state revenues due to a tariff is given by

$$(\bar{p} - p)(\bar{x} - \bar{z}) + \delta^1(\bar{x} - x) + \delta^2(\bar{x} - x) - (\bar{z} - z) + \delta^3(\bar{g} - g)$$

where δ^1 is the prevailing tax on goods, δ^2 is the former level of tariffs, and δ^3 is the level of taxes on factor income. It is conceivable that the increase in revenues is sufficiently large and positive to give the tariff and a potential gain. However, a tax–subsidy combination can always accomplish the same thing or do better, even with the given tariff. This can be accomplished by taxing goods by $(\bar{p} - p)$ and subsidizing the factors of production, which increases state revenues by

$$(\bar{p} - p)\bar{x} - \bar{p}\bar{x} + px + \delta^1(\bar{x} - x) + \delta^2(x - \bar{x}).$$

These revenues are greater than those due to the tariff provided that $\delta^2(\bar{x} - x)$ is not less than

$$\delta^2((\bar{x} - x) - (\bar{z} - z)),$$

or, provided

$$\delta^2(\bar{z} - z) \geqslant 0.$$

If

$$t\delta^2 = (\bar{p} - p),$$

then

$$\delta^2(\bar{z} - z) \geqslant 0. \qquad \text{q.e.d.}$$

In Theorems and Remark 40–43, there is an arbitrariness of the consumer regimes. The results would have been modified if the state were restricted to tax–subsidy–tariff schemes and competitive choice were required. To be specific, we could no longer appeal to Remark 40. The state could place consumers at their old positions but if the home price of i were higher than the international price relative to other goods, consumers would try to substitute other goods. They would replace foreign sellers, reduce government revenues from tariffs, and hence undermine the basis of the original subsidy. In place of Remark 40, in the case of $\sum_i \mathscr{P}_i(x^i)$ directional dense at $\sum_i x^i$, a tax–subsidy scheme would lead to no potential loss if and only if

(i) government revenues were sufficient to purchase at the international price system the goods purchased by consumers before the policy, and

(ii) the home consumer price system was a positive multiple of the international price system. Hence, taxes on fixed factor endowments and sales taxes of the same proportion on all industries would have no potential loss.

The proofs of the theorems of this section involved sales taxes that left consumer price ratios unchanged. Therefore, even if a competitive consumer regime is imposed, the theorems remain valid. Taxes that changed the price ratios for consumer goods would involve a potential loss. Examples would be differential sales taxes, taxes on a particular industry (for example, corporation income taxes), or tariffs (which raise prices of imported goods only).

A loss of income that nevertheless restored consumer prices to the international level might lead to improved consumption. An example would be an increase in tariff from a nonproportional sales tax. There would be a loss in industry income, including tax revenues (Theorem 42), but it could be that the international price system would be restored and consumer welfare improved. All that Theorem 43 says is that there is a sales tax with the old tax–subsidy–tariff system that would be still better (even without directional dense $\sum_i \mathscr{P}_i$).

12. Compensation in Large Countries

A problem often cited with the application of modern welfare economics to international trade is that even though transfers can be made to improve everyone, with the introduction of free trade, these transfers *may* be international (Samuelson [1938], Kemp [1962], Samuelson [1962], Scitovsky [1942]). Some suggestions along these lines for the two-good case were offered by Samuelson [1962]. It will be seen that the redistribution can take place internally to the country. Incidentally, the analysis applies to intersociety economies other than those in international trade.

The problem with internal transfers is that they disturb international prices. Hence, it is necessary to derive a way of computing subsidies first and deriving the resulting prices later. Let a distribution of trades (and resulting goods and services) among members of each of several groups be given for each of the groups, acting alone (in autarky). Now redistribute obligations and claims in trade so that without trade exactly these goods and services are obtained. Whenever traders are rational and not benevolent, if the original trades were Pareto optimal (under autarky), there will be no incentive for further trade within the group. In any case, as trade takes place within and between groups, no consumers will agree to a trade that will worsen his position.

44 Remark A level at least equal to that of autarky will be attained by the foregoing procedure, whatever the original position under autarky.

The transfers relevant to the remark amount to administered economies for each society in autarky. To be at all amenable to policy purposes, they should be stated in value terms, as money subsidies. Under the appropriate assumptions of convexity and closedness of the "better than" sets of trades for consumers, a competitive equilibrium will exist (Chapter 4). Now compute the value of the transfers of obligations and transfer the money values instead of the actual quantities of (present and future) commodities. Consumers will then choose the same trades with the value of transfer as with the quantity transfer, provided there are no monopolies or other imperfect competitors. Evidently, there will result the same competitive equilibrium in *world free trade*, as before.

45 Theorem *Under the hypothesis of Theorem 29, if there are no monopolists or imperfect competitors, then world free trade obtains a level of trade at least as good as autarky provided appropriate redistributions of wealth (in value terms) take place internally to each country.*

46 Corollary *Under world free trade, international transfers are necessary only for a transfer of welfare from one country to another.*

Economists in policy recommendations are sometimes cavalier about wealth redistribution. This is certainly the case in international trade. There are at least two rationalizations. First, free world trade is Edgeworth optimal (Theorem 32). Second, only world free trade is both Edgeworth optimal and invariant.

In conclusion, although inner country redistribution can be a tool of obtaining at least the distribution of benefits under autarky, economic theory strongly advises against internal redistribution to special groups except on the grounds that the initial wealth of certain groups is unjust. For example, if labor were to do worse under international free trade than without it, economic theory would recommend redistribution to labor only if it were justified *before* the imposition of free trade, perhaps on the grounds that laborers were descendants of those whose hereditary property rights had been violated by conquest or slavery. To turn the issue a little differently, farmers in an industrial society may be made worse off after free trade with an agricultural society. They should not be compensated for a loss of a quasi-monopolistic position.

PROBLEMS

N. Divergent Tariffs

Do divergent tariffs necessarily lead to decreases in welfare for large countries in international trade?

O. Optimal Tariffs I

When for a large country is a tariff superior by the Pareto relation to free trade? (See Mundell [1968, pp. 62–64] and Kreuger and Sonnenschein [1967].)

Appendix

A SUMMARY OF WELFARE ECONOMICS

	Preferences are									
Theorems[a]	Weakly convex	Similar	Quasi transferable	Directional dense	$\mathscr{R}_i(x)$ connected	Interior $\mathscr{P}_i(x) \neq \phi$	$\mathscr{P}_i(x)$ open on straight lines	No benevolence	No malevolence	$\Sigma x_i \epsilon$ Int $\Sigma \mathscr{X}_i$
1. Pair ↔ P.O.	×		×	×		×		×	×	×
2. C.E. → P.O.		×			×	×		×		
→ Eq.[b]										
→ Inv.[b]										
→ E.O.		×			×	×		×		
3. E.O. → P.O.[b]										
→ Eq.										
for k-multiples										
$k > 1$	×	×						×	×	
→ C.E.										
(for large numbers)	×	×				×		×	×	×
4. Inv. → Eq.[b]										
5. Inv. + E.O. ↔ C.E.	×	×				×		×	×	×
6. P.O. → C.E.										
(with a possible										
wealth redistribution)	×	×					×		×	×

[a] Inv., invariant; Eq., absolutely equitable; E.O., Edgeworth optimal; P.O., Pareto optimal; Pair, pairwise optimal.

[b] By definition.

II

Statics

3

Bargaining

Almost every specie of social and political contract is affected with an indeterminantness—an evil which is likely to be much more felt when, with the growth of intelligence and liberty, the principle of contract shall have replaced both the appeal to force and the acquiescence in custom. The whole creation groans and yearns, desirating a principle of arbitration, an end of strifes.

Edgeworth
in Mathematical Psychics, 1881

1. The Generalized Core

Much of economic behavior is the result of bargaining: trades at market; price and output collusion among oligopolists; even political agreements about economic affairs. Because we can hardly escape from bargaining, we naturally put great hopes in the theory of bargaining as a foundation for a positive theory of economics. For this purpose von Neumann and Morgenstern [1944] set forth a theory of games, which has since been greatly modified and developed. Unfortunately, this theory of games presents a bewildering variety of solutions, many of which do not exist in certain interesting cases and none of which is really unique (Aumann [1967]). Therefore, it seems best to start again and develop bargaining theories that are more closely related to economic situations. This chapter is a brief attempt in that direction. Mainly, we will show how a solution can be defined (Sections 1–3). Application is made to some three-person games (Section 4). For large games, in Section 5 competitive equilibrium is shown for a certain class of solutions that may or may not include the solution recommended in the earlier part of the chapter.

In this chapter we are concerned with coalition formation as a prospective event. Ordinarily it and its choice of "payoff" occur with a certain probability. These probabilities depend on which coalitions fail to form and in turn determine the expected return to individuals in case one or more coalitions fail.

Given that coalitions t in s fail to come to agreement, each coalition $\mathscr{S} \in s \sim t$ presents "believable" utilities $u^{\mathscr{S}}$ that the coalition can attain on its own ($u^{\mathscr{S}} \in \mathscr{V}^{\mathscr{S}}$). For example, often $u_i^{\mathscr{S}} = 0$ for $i \notin \mathscr{S}$. (If desired, normalize utility so that zero reflects a no-trade situation.) In $\mathscr{V}^{\mathscr{S}}$, given that coalitions in $s \sim t$ occur, there is a (credible) response $u^{\mathscr{S}, s \sim t}$. In contrast, if the coalition could choose $u^{\mathscr{S}, s \sim t}$ freely, then it would be chosen to maximize the coalition's final payoff. Such an optimal response would not be credible, since it would be offered on the expectation that there would be no contingency, only $s \sim t$ occurs.

All further bargaining assumes credible response to failure of agreement. This is the idea of rational expectations as applied in economic analysis (Muth [1961]). In contrast, the core involves many possible responses, any of which is sufficient to reject a solution, whereas at most one can be the credible response.

A response may be a probability *mixture* of utilities from alternative plays or trades.

1 Remark   For traders with weakly convex preferences, convex trade sets, and von Neumann–Morgenstern utility, for every mixed response, there is one that is at least as good and that is the utility of a single certain trade.

Proof   By Theorem 16 of Chapter 6 of the companion volume, von Neumann–Morgenstern utility is concave when restricted to the space of trades with certainty.

For trades $x(k)$, let $\sum \rho_k \circ x(k)$ be a *mixed trade*:

$$u\left(\sum \rho_k \circ x(k)\right) = \sum \rho_k u(x(k)) \leqslant u\left(\sum \rho_k x(k)\right)$$

where $\sum \rho_k x(k)$ is a "sure" trade, which is clearly possible for the coalition whenever each $x(k)$ separately is possible.   q.e.d.

2 Remark   The core with mixed trades awards the same utilities as the core without mixed trades.

Proof   Apply Remark 1.   q.e.d.

Given that only coalitions in $\mathcal{a}$ occur, there are probabilities of each coalition, $\mathcal{S} \in \mathcal{a}$, denoted $p_{\mathcal{S},\mathcal{a}}$. The expected payoff given that only $\mathcal{a}$ occurs is

$$Eu^{\mathcal{a}} = \sum_{\mathcal{S} \in \mathcal{a}} u^{\mathcal{S},\mathcal{a}} p_{\mathcal{S},\mathcal{a}} \qquad \text{where} \quad u_i^{\mathcal{S},\mathcal{a}} = 0 \qquad \text{for} \quad i \notin \mathcal{S}.$$

We must specify that a coalition $\mathcal{S}$ attains at least $(Eu^{\mathcal{a}\sim\mathcal{S}})_{\mathcal{S}}$ for its members. If this is impossible, the coalition has zero probability in $\mathcal{a}$. In order for one coalition to have non zero probability, we only need specify that if there is an i contained in coalitions with summed probabilities $p(i)$, then the singleton $\{i\}$ occurs with probability $1 - p(i)$. A *probabilistic collection* is a set of numbers $(p_{\mathcal{S}}, \mathcal{S} \in \mathcal{a})$ such that $\sum_{\mathcal{S} \in i} p_{\mathcal{a}} = 1$ and $p_{\mathcal{S}} \geqslant 0$.

Let $\mathcal{N} = \bigcup_{i=1}^{n} \{i\}$ and $\mathcal{n} = \{\mathcal{S} \mid \mathcal{S} \subset \mathcal{N}\}$.

If $u \geqslant Eu^{\mathcal{n}\sim\mathcal{N}}$ and if u is Pareto optimal, there exists a *generalized core* of which u is a member.

3 Theorem   *For every collection of credible responses* $u^{\mathcal{S},\mathcal{n}\sim\mathcal{N}} \in \mathcal{V}^{\mathcal{S}}$, *there is a generalized core if*

(i) $\mathcal{V}^{\mathcal{N}}$ *contains* $\sum_{\mathcal{S}} p_{\mathcal{S}} u^{\mathcal{S}}$ *for any* $u^{\mathcal{S}} \in \mathcal{V}^{\mathcal{S}}$ *and for any probabilistic combination* $(p_{\mathcal{S}}, \mathcal{S} \in \mathcal{n} \sim \mathcal{N})$,

(ii) $\mathcal{V}^{\mathcal{N}}$ *is closed and bounded from above,*

(iii)   *probabilities of coalition formation are agreed upon by all players.*

Proof $Eu^{\mathcal{a}\sim\mathcal{N}} \in \mathcal{V}^{\mathcal{S}}$ by (i) and (iii). Apply Theorem 4 of Chapter 2.
                                                                            q.e.d.

It is crucial to have agreement on probabilities of outcomes, for otherwise even transferable utility games would have no generalized cores.

One peculiarity that reflects on the core as a game solution is that a member of the core is not necessarily a member of the generalized core. Consider a three-person game where each individual alone attains utility 0, where 1 and 2 attain $(1, 1, 0)$, where 2 and 3 attain $(0, 1, 1)$, and where 3 and 1 attain $(1, 0, 3)$. The community can attain anything the smaller coalitions can, as well as the utility $(1\frac{1}{4}, 1\frac{1}{4}, 1\frac{1}{4})$, which is the core. If each coalition is regarded as equally likely, the expected utility of failure of agreement among the committee of all is

$$u = \tfrac{1}{3}(1, 1, 0) + \tfrac{1}{3}(0, 1, 1) + \tfrac{1}{3}(1, 0, 3) = (\tfrac{2}{3}, \tfrac{2}{3}, 1\tfrac{1}{3}).$$

Hence, the generalized core consists of that vector alone and is different from the core (which is also unique). Note that the game can be made to have convex $\mathscr{V}^{\mathscr{S}}$ with the same conclusions holding. The core is unrealistic because Mr. 3 is willing to take great risks to attain the coalition $(1, 3)$.

Exercise 1 Let the probability of a coalition be a continuous function of the responses. Define a generalized core and show that it exists. (Hint: Use Brouwer's theorem, Lemma 7 of Chapter 3 of the companion volume.)

2. Coalition Probabilities

The generalized core would seem to be highly sensitive to the probabilities assigned to various coalitions, whereupon for any solution there should be a set of probabilities that would disqualify it. This is certainly the case for games with transferable utility, a special case of most classes of games. Hence, it is important to find a unique specification.

Given $(u^{\mathscr{S},\jmath}, \mathscr{S} \in \jmath)$, let $\mathscr{S}$ *block* $\mathscr{T}$ if $u^{\mathscr{S},\jmath}_{\mathscr{S} \cap \mathscr{T}} > u^{\mathscr{T},\jmath}_{\mathscr{S} \cap \mathscr{T}}$. If no $\mathscr{T} \in \jmath$ blocks $\mathscr{S}$, then $\mathscr{S}$ *blocks* $\mathscr{S}$. Let $\ell_{\jmath}(\mathscr{S})$ be the set of coalitions in $\jmath$ that block $\mathscr{S}$. Let $n(\ell)$ be the number of coalitions in ℓ. Define

$$p_{\mathscr{S}} = \sum_{\mathscr{T} \in \ell_{\jmath}^{-1}(\mathscr{S})} p_{\mathscr{T}} \, \frac{1}{n(\ell_{\jmath}(\mathscr{T}))}$$

so that the *transition probability* of passing from $\mathscr{T}$ to $\mathscr{S}$ is $a_{\mathscr{S}\mathscr{T}} = 1/n(\ell_{\jmath}(\mathscr{T}))$ if $\mathscr{S}$ blocks $\mathscr{T}$ and zero otherwise. Listing the transition probabilities results in a Markov matrix $A_{\jmath}(\geqslant 0)$ such that

$$p = pA^{\jmath}, \quad A^{\jmath}v' = v'$$

for p the vector $(p_{\mathscr{S}}, \mathscr{S} \in \jmath)$ and $v = (1, 1, ..., 1)$. It is known that $(v/n(\jmath))(A^{\jmath})^{n} \to p$ where $p = pA^{\jmath}$ (Problem A).

Lim $v/n(\jmath) A^{n}$ is defined as the *neutral blocking probability* vector. In effect, $p_{\mathscr{S}}$ are the final probabilities, assuming an initial state of equal probabilities between each coalition. Under some conditions, such as $A^{\jmath}$ indecomposable, p is independent of the initial vector, so that

$x(A^a)^n \to p$ for any probability vector x, but in general this is not the case. Theorem 4 shows the existence of probabilities of coalitions.

4 Theorem *If*

(i)   *coalition probabilities are the neutral blocking probabilities,*

(ii) *for every* $(Eu^{a,\mathcal{S}}, \mathcal{S} \in \mathfrak{d})$ *there is a unique generalized core specified by the law* $f^{\mathcal{S}}(Eu^{\mathcal{T} \sim a})$,

(iii) *if no coalitions form, there is a unique (expected) outcome of utilities,*

then for all $\mathfrak{d}$ there are unique probabilities $p_{\mathcal{S},a}$ and credible responses $u^{\mathcal{S},\mathcal{T}} = f^{\mathcal{S}}(Eu^{a \sim \mathcal{S}})$.

Let n be the set of all coalitions in $\mathcal{N} = \bigcup_{i=1}^{n} \{i\}$. The conclusion is to be interpreted as giving a solution for the game, namely,

$$u^{\mathcal{N},n} = f^{\mathcal{N}}(Eu^{n \sim \mathcal{N}}).$$

Once $f^{\mathcal{S}}$ is specified, the solution is uniquely determined. Hypothesis (iii) can be satisfied by taking expected utilities over the Nash non-cooperative solutions (Chapter 3 of the companion volume).

Proof Utilities $u^{\mathcal{S},a}$ can be specified for all i by $f^{\mathcal{S}}(Eu^{\mathcal{S},a}) = f^{\mathcal{S}}(0)$ and $p_{\mathcal{S},a} = 1$. (If $\mathcal{S} = \{i\}, f^{\{i\}}(0) = \max\{u^i \mid u^i \in \mathcal{V}^i\}$.) Also, if $u^{\mathcal{T},a \sim \mathcal{S}}$ is determined for all $\mathcal{S}, \mathcal{T}$ in $\mathfrak{d} \sim \mathcal{S}$, then so is $p_{\mathcal{T},a}$, and therefore $u^{\mathcal{T},a}$ for all $\mathcal{T}$ in $\mathfrak{d}$. Evidently, $n(\mathfrak{d} \sim \mathcal{S}) = n(\mathfrak{d}) - 1$. Therefore, for n, given that for all the $\mathfrak{d}$ with n coalitions, responses and probabilities have been determined, then those for sets with $n + 1$ coalitions are determined. Clearly, for $n = 0$, utilities and probabilities are determined as in (iii). Hence, they are determined for all $\mathfrak{d}$.   q.e.d.

It might be objected that only $u^{\mathcal{S},a}_{\mathcal{S} \cap \mathcal{T}} \gg u^{\mathcal{T},a}_{\mathcal{S} \cap \mathcal{T}}$ is sufficient to move from $\mathcal{S}$ to $\mathcal{T}$. In that case, it is said that $\mathcal{T}$ *strictly blocks* $\mathcal{S}$.

Letting $\ell_{\mathfrak{d}}^*(\mathcal{S})$ be the set of coalitions in $\mathfrak{d}$ that strictly block $\mathcal{S}$, we could define

$$q_{\mathcal{S}} = \sum_{\mathcal{T} \in \ell_{\mathfrak{d}}^{*-1}(\mathcal{S})} q_{\mathcal{T}} \frac{1}{n(\ell_{\mathfrak{d}}^*(\mathcal{T}))}.$$

The *neutral strictly blocking* probabilities would be defined in the obvious way and Theorem 4 would be restated. The same is true where we consider a transition to have positive probability when

$$u^{\mathcal{S},a}_{\mathcal{S} \cap \mathcal{T}} = u^{\mathcal{S},t}_{\mathcal{S} \cap \mathcal{T}}.$$

There is no obvious reason for preferring one or another of these schemes. Hence, it is to be hoped that the outcome is the same whichever is adopted. That this is not true can be seen for only one pair $\mathscr{S}$, $\mathscr{T}$, for which $u^{\mathscr{S},\delta}_{\mathscr{S}\cap\mathscr{T}} > u^{\mathscr{S},\delta}_{\mathscr{S}\cap\mathscr{T}}$ but not $u^{\mathscr{S},\delta}_{\mathscr{S}\cap\mathscr{T}} \gg u^{\mathscr{S},\delta}_{\mathscr{S}\cap\mathscr{T}}$. A^δ is altered to $A^\delta + \Delta A^\delta$ where ΔA^δ has zero except for the row for $\mathscr{T}$, where all nonzero entries except for $\mathscr{S}$ are increased and that for $\mathscr{S}$ is decreased. Then

$$p(A^\delta + \Delta A^\delta) = p + p\,\Delta A^\delta \neq p \qquad \text{since} \quad p\,\Delta A^\delta \neq 0.$$

PROBLEM

A. Markov Matrices

Let $Av = v$, $v = (1, 1,..., 1)$. Show that $(v/n)\,A^n$ converges. Let A be indecomposable. Show that for any $p \geqslant 0$, $pv = 1$, $pA^n \to q$.

3. The Nash Law of Division

If utility is *transferable*, where for some *value* $v_\mathscr{S}$,

$$\mathscr{V}^\mathscr{S} = \left\{ u^\mathscr{S} \,\middle|\, \sum_i u_i^\mathscr{S} = v_\mathscr{S} \right\}.$$

The difference

$$v_\mathscr{S} - \sum_{i\in\mathscr{S}\in\delta} Eu^{\mathscr{S},\delta\sim\mathscr{S}}$$

is called the social dividend (Harsanyi [1963]). Rules must be specified for its distribution.

In general, whenever $u^{\mathscr{S},\delta} > (Eu^\delta)_\mathscr{S}$, the law $f^\mathscr{S}$ must be determined. This is an *n*-person bargaining game, with fixed nonagreement payoffs. By utilizing the axioms of Nash (Chapter 10 of the companion volume), we can obtain a unique *solution*.

5 Theorem *Let x_i be the unique threat for nonagreement i, $\bar{u}_i$ the expected utility of x_i, and*

$$\pi_i = u_i - \bar{u}_i.$$

Let $V^\mathscr{S}$ be convex and $\mathscr{S}'$ the maximum set of players for which $\pi_i > 0$ is possible for all $i \in \mathscr{S}'$. If the agreement is Pareto optimal, symmetric, invariant to increasing linear transformations, and independent of irrelevant alternatives, then it maximizes

$$\prod_{i\in\mathscr{S}'} \pi_i.$$

The law of division in Theorem 5 will be referred to as the *Nash division law*.

Proof   If $\pi_i > 0$ for all $i \in \mathscr{T}$ and $\hat{\pi}_i > 0$ for all $i \in \mathscr{T}'$, then

$$\tfrac{1}{2}\pi_i + \tfrac{1}{2}\hat{\pi}_i = \tfrac{1}{2}(u_i - \bar{u}_i) + \tfrac{1}{2}(\hat{u}_i - \bar{u}_i)$$
$$= \tfrac{1}{2}u_i + \tfrac{1}{2}\hat{u}_i - \bar{u}_i > 0 \qquad \text{for all} \quad i \in \mathscr{T} \cup \mathscr{T}'.$$

Hence, a maximum $\mathscr{S}'$ exists. Simply repeat the proof of Theorem 3 of Chapter 10 of companion volume in $\mathscr{E}^n$-space rather than $\mathscr{E}^2$, n the number of traders in $\mathscr{S}'$.   q.e.d.

6 Remark   For games with transferable utility, the Nash division law specifies equal division of the social dividend.

A *generalized Zeuthen process*, whereby the player with the smallest bearable probability of capitulation will make the first concession, and so on, will lead to product maximization in the n-person as well as in the two-person game. This follows because given the utility of others, each pair will maximize the product.

7 Theorem   *The generalized Zeuthen process leads to maximization of*

$$\prod_{i \in \mathscr{S}'} \pi_i \, ,$$

$\mathscr{S}'$ *the maximum subset of* $\mathscr{S}$ *over which* $\pi_i > 0$ *for all* $i \in \mathscr{S}'$ *is possible.*

The noncooperative equilibrium nonbargaining strategies can be shown to be equilibrium threat strategies for the foregoing bargaining game. Equivalently, it is never in one's interest to reduce the utility of his threat, which is a generalization of Remark 5 of Chapter 10 of the companion volume.

8 Remark   Increases in the response of i alone increase his final payoff.

Proof   Consider a change in $\bar{u}_i$ to $\bar{v}_i$. Let

$$u = \max_{u^{\mathscr{S}} \in \mathscr{V}\mathscr{S}} \prod_{j \in \mathscr{S}} (u_j - \bar{u}_j), \qquad v = \max_{v^{\mathscr{S}} \in \mathscr{V}\mathscr{S}} \left[(v_i - \bar{v}_i) \prod_{j \neq i} (v_j - \bar{u}_j) \right].$$

Evidently, utilities after the change in i's strategy can be attained before, and utilities before can be attained afterward. Therefore

$$u \geqslant v \left(\frac{v_i - \bar{u}_i}{v_i - \bar{v}_i} \right) \qquad \text{and} \qquad v \geqslant u \left(\frac{u_i - \bar{v}_i}{u_i - \bar{u}_i} \right),$$

with equality only if there is no change in u_j , $j \in \mathscr{S}'$. In the case of a change in u_i ,

$$v \left(\frac{u_i - u_i}{u_i - \bar{v}_i} \right) > v \left(\frac{v_i - \bar{v}_i}{v_i - \bar{v}_i} \right)$$

or

$$(u_i - \bar{u}_i)(v_i - \bar{v}_i) > (v_i - \bar{u}_i)(u_i - \bar{v}_i)$$

or

$$-\bar{u}_i v_i - u_i \bar{v}_i > -v_i \bar{v}_i - \bar{u}_i u_i$$

or

$$\bar{u}_i(u_i - v_i) - \bar{v}_i(u_i - v_i) > 0$$

or

$$(\bar{u}_i - \bar{v}_i)(u_i - v_i) > 0.$$

Evidently, either no change in utility results or

$$\bar{u}_i - \bar{v}_i < 0 \qquad \text{if and only if} \quad u_i - v_i < 0. \qquad \text{q.e.d.}$$

UNSOLVED PROBLEM

B. The Solution under Replications

Show that the solution tends to the competitive equilibrium under replication.

4. Solutions for Some Three-Person Games

Hereafter, the generalized core chosen by the Nash law of division will be called the solution. It can be computed for important special cases of three traders with transferable utility. The solution reveals much variety and even paradoxes.

In the normalized three-person game, with values $v_{\mathscr{S}}$, $\mathscr{S} \subset 1 \cup 2 \cup 3$,

$$\mathscr{V}^i = \{0\}, \qquad i = 1, 2, 3,$$

$$\mathscr{V}^{ij} = \{(u^i, u^j) \mid u^i + u^j = v_{ij}\},$$

$$\mathscr{V}^{123} = \left\{ (u^1, u^2, u^3) \,\middle|\, \sum u^i = v_{123} \right\}.$$

Clearly, all $\mathscr{V}^{\mathscr{S}}$ are convex and closed. The social dividend is divided equally. Therefore, the coalitions are ranked according to their average values where the larger in rank blocks the smaller. Hence, the possible probability combinations are large.

Without loss of generality, let

$$v_{12} \geqslant v_{23} \geqslant v_{31} \geqslant 0.$$

Together with any other coalition, the singletons are of zero probability or else of equal utility (if $u_{ij} = 0$). Hence, they do not figure in the solution. Given that $(1, 2, 3)$ fails, we need only compute the award of (i, j).

In the following two games, Mr. 2 is most powerful but his power is somewhat limited.

$v_{12} > v_{23} > v_{31}$ and $v_{31} \geqslant \frac{1}{2}v_{12}$:

	1	2	3
$(1, 2)$	$\frac{1}{2}v_{12} - \frac{1}{4}v_{23}$	$\frac{1}{2}v_{12} + \frac{1}{4}v_{23}$	0
$(2, 3)$	0	$\frac{1}{2}v_{23} + \frac{1}{4}v_{12}$	$\frac{1}{2}v_{23} - \frac{1}{4}v_{12}$
$(3, 1)$	$\frac{1}{2}v_{31} + \frac{1}{4}v_{12}$	0	$\frac{1}{2}v_{31} - \frac{1}{4}v_{12}$

We explain the table for this case only, the other follow in like manner. If $(1, 2)$ fails, $(2, 3)$ occurs with probability one. Therefore, player 2 must be mollified. The social dividend is $v_{12} - \frac{1}{2}v_{23}$, which is split evenly between 1 and 2. Clearly, Mr. 2 receives

$$\tfrac{1}{2}(v_{12} - \tfrac{1}{2}v_{23}) + \tfrac{1}{2}v_{23} = \tfrac{1}{2}v_{12} + \tfrac{1}{4}v_{23}.$$

Mr. 1 gets the rest of v_{12}. If $(2, 3)$ or $(3, 1)$ fails, then Mr. 2 or 1, respectively, must be given extra, since $(1, 2)$ will occur with probability one. The computations follow easily.

$v_{12} > v_{23} > v_{31}$, $v_{31} < \frac{1}{2}v_{12}$,   but $v_{23} \geqslant \frac{1}{2}v_{12}$:

	1	2	3
$(1, 2)$	$\frac{1}{2}v_{12} - \frac{1}{4}v_{23}$	$\frac{1}{2}v_{12} + \frac{1}{4}v_{23}$	0
$(2, 3)$	0	$\frac{1}{2}v_{23} + \frac{1}{4}v_{12}$	$\frac{1}{2}v_{23} - \frac{1}{4}v_{12}$
$(3, 1)$	0	0	0

In the next game, Mr. 2 has overwhelming power.

$v_{12} > v_{23} > v_{31}$ and $v_{23} < \frac{1}{2}v_{12}$:

	1	2	3
(1, 2)	$\frac{1}{2}v_{12} - \frac{1}{4}v_{23}$	$\frac{1}{2}v_{12} + \frac{1}{4}v_{23}$	0
(2, 3)	0	0	0
(3, 1)	0	0	0

In the next three games, traders 1 and 2 are especially well matched and have little to gain from Mr. 3. For example, let shoes be usable only in pairs. Mr. 1 might own only left shoes Mr. 2 only right shoes, but Mr. 3 might own equal numbers of some left shoes and right shoes.

$v_{12} > v_{23} = v_{31}$ and $v_{33} > \frac{1}{2}v_{32}$:

	1	2	3
(1, 2)	$\frac{1}{2}v_{12}$	$\frac{1}{2}v_{12}$	0
(2, 3)	0	$\frac{1}{2}v_{23} + \frac{1}{4}v_{12}$	$\frac{1}{2}v_{23} - \frac{1}{4}v_{12}$
(3, 1)	$\frac{1}{2}v_{31} + \frac{1}{4}v_{12}$	0	$\frac{1}{2}v_{31} - \frac{1}{4}v_{12}$

$v_{12} > v_{23} = v_{31}$ and $v_{31} < \frac{1}{2}v_{12}$ but $v_{23} \geqslant \frac{1}{2}v_{12}$:

	1	2	3
(1, 2)	$\frac{1}{2}v_{12}$	$\frac{1}{2}v_{12}$	0
(2, 3)	0	$\frac{1}{2}v_{23} + \frac{1}{4}v_{12}$	$\frac{1}{2}v_{23} - \frac{1}{4}v_{12}$
(3, 1)	0	0	0

$v_{12} > v_{23} = v_{31}$, $v_{31} < \frac{1}{2}v_{12}$,   and $v_{23} < \frac{1}{2}v_{12}$:

	1	2	3
(1, 2)	$\frac{1}{2}v_{12}$	$\frac{1}{2}v_{12}$	0
(2, 3)	0	0	0
(3, 1)	0	0	0

The following game is essentially the *shoe game* where trader 2 owns only right shoes and traders 1 and 3 own only left shoes. Shoes are usable only in equal proportions of left and right shoes.

$v_{12} = v_{23} > v_{31}$:

	1	2	3
(1, 2)	$\frac{1}{2}v_{12} - \frac{1}{4}v_{23}$	$\frac{1}{2}v_{12} + \frac{1}{4}v_{23}$	0
(2, 3)	0	$\frac{1}{2}v_{23} + \frac{1}{4}v_{12}$	$\frac{1}{2}v_{23} - \frac{1}{4}v_{12}$
(3, 1)	$\frac{1}{2}v_{31}$	0	$\frac{1}{2}v_{31}$

The symmetric game is the last one given. As we will see, it has a trivial solution.

$v_{12} = v_{23} = v_{31}$:

	1	2	3
(1, 2)	$\frac{1}{2}v_{12}$	$\frac{1}{2}v_{12}$	0
(2, 3)	0	$\frac{1}{2}v_{23}$	$\frac{1}{2}v_{23}$
(3, 1)	$\frac{1}{2}v_{23}$	0	$\frac{1}{2}v_{31}$

The probabilities of (i, j) given that $(1, 2, 3)$ fails are as follows.

$v_{12} > v_{23} > v_{31}$ and $\frac{1}{4}v_{12} > \frac{1}{4}v_{23} + \frac{1}{2}v_{31}$:

  (1, 2) blocks (2,3),
  (2, 3) blocks (3, 1)   (if $v_{23} \geqslant \frac{1}{2}v_{12}$),
  (1, 2) blocks (3, 1),
  so that $p(1, 2) = 1$.

$v_{12} > v_{23} > v_{31}$ and $\frac{1}{4}v_{12} = \frac{1}{4}v_{23} + \frac{1}{2}v_{31}$:

  (1, 2) blocks (2, 3),
  (2, 3) blocks (3, 1),
  and $p(1, 2) = 1$.

$v_{12} > v_{23} > v_{31} > v_{31} \geqslant \frac{1}{2}v_{12}$ and $\frac{1}{4}v_{12} < \frac{1}{4}v_{23} + \frac{1}{2}v_{31}$:

  (1, 2) blocks (2, 3),
  (2, 3) blocks (3, 1),
  (3, 1) blocks (1, 2),
  so that $p(i, j) = \frac{1}{3}$.

$v_{12} > v_{23} = v_{31}$ and $\frac{1}{4}v_{12} > \frac{1}{2}v_{31}$:

    (1, 2) blocks (2, 3) and (3, 1),
    so that $p(1, 2) = 1$.

$v_{12} > v_{23} = v_{31}$ and $\frac{1}{2}v_{12} = v_{31}$:

    $p(i, j) = \frac{1}{3}$.

$v_{12} > v_{23} = v_{31}$ and $\frac{1}{4}v_{12} < \frac{1}{2}v_{31}$:

    (2, 3) and (3, 1) block (1, 2),
    and $p(2, 3) = p(1, 2) = \frac{1}{2}$.

$v_{12} = v_{23} > v_{31}$ and $\frac{1}{4}v_{21} = \frac{1}{2}v_{31}$:

    $p(i, j) = \frac{1}{3}$.

$v_{12} = v_{23} > v_{31}$ and $\frac{1}{4}v_{21} < \frac{1}{2}v_{31}$:

    $p(3, 1) = 1$.

$v_{12} = v_{23} = v_{31}$:

    $p(i, j) = 1/3$.

Final utilities are computed as

$v_{12} > v_{23} > v_{31}$ and $\frac{1}{4}v_{12} > \frac{1}{4}v_{23} + \frac{1}{2}v_{31}$:

$$u_1 = \tfrac{1}{3}v_{123} + \tfrac{1}{6}v_{12} - \tfrac{1}{4}v_{23} ,$$
$$u_2 = \tfrac{1}{3}v_{123} + \tfrac{1}{6}v_{12} + \tfrac{1}{4}v_{23} ,$$
$$u_3 = \tfrac{1}{2}v_{123} - \tfrac{1}{3}v_{12} .$$

$v_{12} > v_{23} > v_{31}$, $v_{31} \geqslant \frac{1}{2}v_{12}$,   and $\frac{1}{4}v_{12} < \frac{1}{4}v_{23} + \frac{1}{2}v_{31}$:

$$u_1 = \tfrac{1}{3}v_{123} + \tfrac{5}{36}v_{12} - \tfrac{7}{36}v_{23} + \tfrac{1}{6}v_{31} ,$$
$$u_2 = \tfrac{1}{3}v_{123} + \tfrac{5}{36}v_{12} + \tfrac{5}{36}v_{23} - \tfrac{1}{6}v_{31} ,$$
$$u_3 = \tfrac{1}{3}v_{123} - \tfrac{5}{18}v_{12} + \tfrac{2}{36}v_{23} - \tfrac{1}{18}v_{31} .$$

The other cases can be computed easily.

Example 1 There are two traders, one owing K of capital and the other L of labor, with production according to $f(K, L)$, $f(K, 0) = 0$, $f(0, L) = 0$. They then split equally, each taking $\frac{1}{2}f(K, L)$. Another capitalist enters as a third party. Then, letting the capitalists be 1 and 3, $v_{1,2} = v_{2,3} > v_{3,1} = 0$. Hence, the payoffs are

	1	2	3
(1, 2)	$\frac{1}{2}f(K,L)$	$\frac{1}{2}f(K,L)$	0
(2, 3)	0	$\frac{1}{2}f(K,L)$	$\frac{1}{2}f(K,L)$
(3, 1)	0	0	0

and (1, 2) and (2, 3) are equally probable. Hence, final payoffs are

$$u_1 = \tfrac{1}{3}f(2K,L) - \tfrac{1}{12}f(K,L),$$

$$u_2 = \tfrac{1}{3}f(2K,L) + \tfrac{1}{6}f(K,L),$$

$$u_3 = \tfrac{1}{3}f(2K,L) - \tfrac{1}{12}f(K,L).$$

The new capitalist would have not his marginal product

$$[f(2K,L) - f(K,L)],$$

but a share of it ($\frac{1}{3}$) and of the product of the others.

Example 2 If instead the new capitalist had only $\bar{K}$ small, so that $f(\bar{K}, L) < \frac{1}{2}f(K, L)$, then we would have

	1	2	3
(1, 2)	$\frac{1}{2}f(K,L)$	$\frac{1}{2}f(K,L)$	0
(2, 3)	0	0	0
(3, 1)	0	0	0

and $p_{(12)} = 1$, so that

$$u_1 = \tfrac{1}{3}f(K + \bar{K},L) + \tfrac{1}{6}f(K,L)$$

$$u_2 = \tfrac{1}{3}f(\bar{K} + K,L) + \tfrac{1}{6}f(K,L)$$

$$u_3 = \tfrac{1}{3}f(K + \bar{K},L) - \tfrac{1}{3}f(K,L) = \tfrac{1}{3}\Delta f.$$

The new capitalist would get only one third of his marginal product.

In the three-person game, bargaining outcomes are higly dependent on relative coalitional strengths.

Example 3 A theory of duopoly or triopoly can be developed along these lines. In contrast to the Nash cooperative solution, optimal threats are not used.

For equal parties, profits would be maximized and distributed equally. However, if the parties have different cost curves and are unequal, the solution is more complicated.

In the absence of coalition formation, the Cournot solution obtains. Assume that utility is linear in money. If only two firms collude, they will restrict output, and the share of the third will increase. In effect, they will operate like a single firm, dividing equally the increase in profit. As a simple case, assume that each has a constant amount of the good to be sold $\bar{x}_i$. The Cournot solution gives incomes px_i where $p = f(\sum_i x_i)$ and x_i is sold by i. This requires that

$$-f'x_i = p = f\left(\sum_i x_i\right) \quad \text{if} \quad x_i < \bar{x}_i \quad \text{or} \quad \frac{1}{x_i} = -\frac{f'}{f}.$$

Evidently, $1/x_j = 1/x_i$ unless $x_i = \bar{x}_i$. Hence, unequal quantities imply that the smaller two sell all of their product and the largest establishes the monopoly.

The game is not one with transferable utility, but the analysis is easy. For simplicity's sake, let $\bar{x}_1 = 4$, $\bar{x}_2 = 3$, $\bar{x}_3 = 2$, and $f(x) = 9 - x$, so that if all goods are sold, $p = f(x) = 0$. Then for the Cournot solution,

$$x_1 = -\frac{f}{f'} = f = 9 - (\bar{x}_2 + \bar{x} + x_1)$$

or

$$2x_1 = 9 - (3 + 2) = 4$$

or

$$x_1 = 2, \quad \text{which is not possible.}$$

Evidently,

$$x_2 = x_1 \quad \text{and} \quad x = 9 - \bar{x}_3 + 2x$$

or

$$3x_1 = 9 - 2 = 7$$

or

$$x_1 = p = 2\tfrac{1}{3}.$$

The payoffs are

$$\bar{u}_1 = 5\tfrac{4}{9},$$

$$\bar{u}_2 = 5\tfrac{4}{9},$$

$$\bar{u}_3 = 4\tfrac{2}{3}.$$

Given that 2 and 3 collude,

$$x_2 + x_3 = f - 9 - \bar{x}_1 + x_1 + x_2$$

or

$$2(x_2 + x_3) = 5$$

or

$$x_2 + x_3 = 2\tfrac{1}{2}, \quad \text{which is not possible.}$$

Instead, 1 must also cut back $x_1 = x_2 + x_3$, so that $3(x_2 + x_3) = 9$ or $x_2 + x_3 = 3 = p$. Total profit is $p(x_2 + x_3) = 9$, which is insufficient to take the initiative from 1 and 2 since the Cournot payoffs were $5\,4/9 + 4\,2/3 = 10\,1/9$.

Given that 1 and 3 collude,

$$2(x_1 + x_3) = 9 - \bar{x}_2 = 5$$

or

$$x_1 + x_3 = 2\tfrac{1}{2}, \quad \text{which is not possible.}$$

therefore,

$$x_2 = (x_1 + x_3)$$

and

$$3(x_1 + x_3) = 9 \quad \text{or} \quad x_1 + x_3 = 3 \quad \text{and} \quad p(x_1 + x_3) = 9,$$

which is again insufficient to overturn the Cournot solution.

If 1 and 2 collude, $2(x_1 + x_2) = 9 - \bar{x}_3 = 7$ or

$$x_1 + x_2 = 3\tfrac{1}{2}.$$

Or $p(x_1 + x_2) = 12\tfrac{1}{4}$. Hence,

$$u_1 = 6\tfrac{1}{8},$$
$$u_2 = 6\tfrac{1}{8},$$
$$u_3 = 7.$$

The monopoly price is $4\tfrac{1}{2}$ and the total profit is $(4\tfrac{1}{2})^2 = 20\tfrac{1}{4}$. The social dividend is

$$20\tfrac{1}{4} - 19\tfrac{1}{4} = 1.$$

Hence, final payoffs are

$$u_1 = 6\tfrac{11}{24},$$
$$u_2 = 6\tfrac{11}{24},$$
$$u_3 = 7\tfrac{1}{3}.$$

There are two paradoxes. First, one's extra goods get him nothing. Goods that never enter the market are not very interesting to competitors. Second, by being the weakest, three thrusts the responsibility of price leadership on one and two, and thereby obtains more profits than the others. If 1 and 2 were to merge, then the Cournot solution would be the same as that when 1 and 2 colluded. The final outcome would be the same, $u_1 + u_2 = 12\frac{22}{24}$ $u_3 = 7\frac{1}{3}$. If instead 1 and 2 broke up into subsidiaries, they would attain a more equitable share of the monopoly profits. Evidently, such information should be defined into the game. It is not easy to see how it can be done.

Exercise 2 In which of the foregoing three-person games will transferable utility have a core?

Exercise 3 Compute the cores for several of the foregoing three-person games and compare with the generalized core.

PROBLEMS

C. Nonmarket Economies I

Let there be one owner of a factor and let the quantities of the other factors be divided evenly among m others. Assume one good in which utility is linear. What are

   (i)   the core?
  (ii) the generalized core?
 (iii) the competitive equilibrium?

Parts (i) and (iii) were solved by Shapley and Shubik [1967].

D. Nonmarket Economies II

Suppose utility is linear in wealth and a given wealth is to be distributed by a ruling of majority vote. What are

  (i) the core?
 (ii) the generalized core?

Part (i) was solved by Shapley and Shubik [1967].

5. Solutions in Large Markets

It is hoped that the solution tends to the core under replication. In lieu of this result, it is best to set out weak conditions that will give competitive equilibrium as the limiting state.

9 Theorem *Let*

(i) *preferences be regular, complete, weakly convex, strongly quasi transferable, and $\mathscr{P}_i(x)$ open on line segments,*

(ii) *type i traders be directional dense,*

(iii) $0 \in \operatorname{Int} \sum_{i=1}^{n} \mathscr{X}_i$,

(iv) *either there are but a finite number of consumer types or $\sum \mathscr{P}_i(x')$ has interior points.*

If an absolutely equitable, Pareto optimal trade under k-replication is unblocked by

(a) *any coalition with $k - 1$ of all types except i and k of type i, or*

(b) *any coalition with $k - 1$ of types other than j and k of type j, $j \neq i$,*

then all limiting points ($k \to \infty$) are competitive equilibria.

The proof is a tighter version of that of Theorem 23 of Chapter 2. The essential point is that because of directional density at x, if $x \mathscr{R}_i x + ty$ for $t > 0$, t small, then $px \leqslant p(x + ty)$ for p the intrinsic price system at x. Application would be to a system where only majority coalitions or only coalitions with at least $(k - 1)n$ members are allowed to block.

Proof Let $x(k) = (x^j(k), j = 1, 2,...)$ be the award in a k-replication; $x^j(k_q) \to x^j$ for all j. Clearly, $\sum x^j = 0$. Also, x cannot be blocked by coalitions as described in (a) and (b), since if so, x would be strictly blocked (quasi transferability) and $x(k_q)$ would be blocked for large q (openness of $\mathscr{P}_j^{-1}(y^j)$).

We first consider the equal-treatment trade with the same level of preference as the one hypothesized (weak convexity).

The coalition described in (b) can attain x^j for j, x^l for $l \neq i$, and for i,

$$\frac{1}{k-1}\left[-(k-1)\sum_{\substack{l \neq j \\ i \neq k}} x^l - kx^j\right] = \frac{1}{k-1}\left[-(k-1)\sum_{l \neq i} x^l - x^j\right]$$

$$= -\sum_{l \neq i} x^l - \frac{1}{k-1}x^j$$

$$= x^i - \frac{1}{k-1}x^j.$$

Therefore, $x^i \mathscr{R}_i x^i - (1/k - 1) x^j$. Hence, for small t, $x^i \mathscr{R}_i x^i - tx^j$ (openness and convexity of $\mathscr{P}_i(x - tx^j)$ on line segments). Therefore, $px^i \leqslant p(x^i - tx^j)$ (directional density) or $-tpx^j \geqslant 0$ or $px^j \leqslant 0$.

For the case of $j = i$, the foregoing argument can be modified to apply to awards of x^j for $j \neq i$, and

$$\frac{1}{k}\left[-(k-1)\sum_{j \neq i} x^j\right] = \frac{k-1}{k}x^i = x^i - \frac{1}{k}x^i.$$

This shows that $-px^i/k \geqslant 0$ or $px^i \leqslant 0$. Hence, $px^j = 0$ for all j, and by Pareto optimality there is a competitive equilibrium.

Returning to the original nonequal-treatment trade, it is easy to show that the value of all trades is zero.   q.e.d.

The usual view of economic theory is to exclude analysis of very large coalitions, the idea being that these are more in the realm of political science than economics. Often, Pareto optimality is not a consequence of individual bargaining, and social bargaining is also required. Some exceptions are studied in Section 6 of Chapter 2. Nevertheless, it is clear that monopoly power is often exercised in an inefficient manner The means for making decisions for large coalitions are not readily available. Therefore, the bargaining games as presented may not adequately represent the economic world. Restrictions must be placed on coalition sizes; in particular, there is no committee at large to meet to make trades efficient.

An instance of an economic system would be one where contracts are made between pairs of individuals. If trade were to proceed between any collection of individuals, then we might expect them to be pairwise optimal as well as Pareto optimal. This would lead to a trade that no group could better by holding its obligations fixed. Evidently, after trading to x, the zero transfers would be in the core. Of course, the competitive equilibrium (before the trade x) would be such a solution. Incidentally, there would be no requirement that each group actually meet. Some traders might act as bokers analogously to the trade in trade equilibrium of Section 4 of Chapter 2.

In the more restricted case of trades within pairs of individuals, it might be that each pair bargains to a Nash position, holding obligations with others fixed. On the other hand, it might be that each trader thinks that he will be allowed to provide the trades of any other trader. This would be a *weak* version of the *nondiscrimination* of Chapter 2.

10 Theorem *If under the hypothesis of Theorem 9 for limits of a pairwise optimal, then weakly nondiscriminatory k-replicas are quasi-competitive equilibria.*

Proof Let i have directional dense preferences. Since each i of the same type can have the trades of others, there is absolute equity, as in the proof of Theorem 9, and this be can accomplished by equal treatment. Clearly, $x^i - (1/k - 1) x^j$ is possible for i, for all j. Hence, as in the proof of Theorem 9 for limiting points x,

$$px^i \leqslant p \left(x^i - \frac{1}{k-1} x^j \right) \quad \text{or} \quad px^j \leqslant 0.$$

Also, $px^i \leqslant p(x^i - (1/kx^i))$ or $px^i \leqslant 0$. Hence $px^j = 0$ for all j.   q.e.d.

A generalization of pairwise optimality appears in the case where a trader i assumes that the other traders will pairwise optimize. In effect, trader i makes contracts with j, assuming that the remainder of the economy will pairwise optimize between them, possibly according to the rules of weak nondiscrimination. At least for k sufficiently large, this amounts to assuming competitive behavior on the part of the rest of the economy. The trader i then acts as a classical monopolist–monopsonist. He can make only those contracts that are

(i)   favorable to the other party, and
(ii)   not bettered somewhere else.

Evidently, the rest of the economy abides by the competitive price system and the would-be monopolist-monopsonist must transact at the going price system. His power lies in the fact that he can influence that system.

Difficulties with the approach above are:

(1)   There may be more than one monopolist-monopsonist, so that the assumption that the others are competitive is not supported by experience. If these operate in entirely separate markets, there is no problem. Otherwise, there may be an "oligopoly" problem.

(2)   There may be a multiplicity of competitive equilibria associated with a given action of the monopolist. This necessiates the negotiation among several monopolists or dynamic manipulation of markets if there is only one.

PROBLEM

E. Equal Treatment

Show that if preferences are weakly convex and if for some $n > 0$, any coalition with n members of each type is allowed, there is absolute equity for k-replicas, $k > n$.

This problem is due to Alan Kirman.

4

General Equilibrium

> In the general case, demand[s] are functions of $m - 1$ variables which are too numerous [for] space. Therefore, the [equilibrium] problem when generalized can only be formulated and solved algebraically [*sic*], not geometrically. It should be recalled that what we have in mind is—to formulate scientifically the nature of the problem which actually arises in the market where it is solved empirically. Not only is the algebraic solution as good as the geometrical solution, but—the analytical form of mathematical expression is [one of] general and scientific *par excellence*.
>
> Léon Walras
> in ELEMENTS OF PURE ECONOMICS, 1877
> as translated by W. Jaffé, 1953

1. Existence of Competitive Equilibrium I

The existence of equilibrium is of importance to both normative and positive economics. Within the context of welfare economics, it is not enough to know that the competitive equilibria and Pareto optima are more or less equivalent. We must also show that the competitive equilibrium is a complete social system. Theorem 11 of Chapter 2 gives that there is some distribution of wealth at which equilibrium exists, namely, a Pareto optimal one. However, nothing has been said about the set of initial positions from which a competitive equilibrium does exist. If the set were small, then there would have to be some agency or mechanism to ensure that the initial distribution is placed in the set.

From a positive viewpoint, theories of the economy are often equilibrium theories, and therefore it is absolutely necessary to know that the equilibrium exists. Furthermore, it is desirable to avoid indeterminacy in the theory, so that ideally equilibrium should be unique. Failing that, it should be at least locally unique. For economic theories that are about disequilibrium situations, it may nevertheless be interesting to know whether the equilibrium exists, since the system may well tend to equilibrium. Uniqueness or local uniqueness of equilibrium would then amount to an asymptotic determinacy of the theory.

In proving the existence of equilibrium, various convexity assumptions are used, just as in welfare economics. Therefore the generality of positive economics theory is not great as it stands, especially insofar as it assumes competition. In the case of monopolies or oligopolies, it will be seen that some kinds of nonconvexities of production are admissible, but only at the cost of excluding other possibilities, such as backward-bending demand curves.

In this section, the existence of the core (Theorem 38 of Chapter 2) is used to show the existence of competitive equilibrium. Somewhat better results can be obtained by analysis of competitive choice. In Sections 2 and 3 conditions are given for the continuity and convexity of excess demand. These properties are used to show competitive equilibrium in Section 4. In Sections 5–7, monopolies, oligopolies, and other noncompetitive individuals are integrated into the economy. Conditions for equilibrium are set forth. In Sections 8 and 9, the local uniqueness of equilibrium is shown for almost all wealths. Conditions for the uniqueness of equilibrium are put off until Chapter 5, since they apply only to very special cases. In the first four sections of this chapter, an infinite time horizon is given special consideration.

Before proceeding, it is well to realize that the existence theorems are not self-evident, as some have claimed. Indeed, the methods are applied in Section 5 to very general economies with monopoly, oligopoly, and consumer interrelationships to show that millions of people trading millions of commodities can come to a physically possible solution to trades. Agents simply take a certain collection of prices as given and act without any account of their influence on others. That the solution is also optimal under certain general conditions makes the theory of competitive equilibrium one of the most powerful in all of science.

Let

$\mathscr{A} = \{x \mid$ there exists a continuous, linear functional

p, such that there is an $\bar{x}$ for which

$$p(\bar{x}^i) = p(x^i), \quad p(\bar{x}^i) \neq p(\bar{\tilde{x}}^i) \quad \text{for} \quad \bar{\tilde{x}}^i \in \mathscr{P}_i(x^i)\}.$$

It will be shown that

$$\mathscr{X} = \times_i \mathscr{X}_i \subset \mathscr{A}.$$

At this stage of the analysis, the simplest proof is based on the core for a finite number of traders. The method is due to Scarf. Related work has been done by Mantel [1968], Hansen [1968], Peleg and Yaari [1970], and Bewley [1969].

The core exists (Theorems 34 and 35 of Chapter 2). The points Edgeworth optimal are compact and decreasing under replication, so that there is an invariant point in the core. Such a point is a competitive equilibrium (Theorem 38 of Chapter 2).

1 Theorem   *There is a competitive equilibrium, and* Int $\mathscr{X} \subset \mathscr{A}$, *if*

(i)   *there are but a finite number of traders,*
(ii)   *induced preferences are regular, weakly convex independent,* $\mathscr{P}(x)$ *is open on line segments, complete, and strongly quasi transferable,*
(iii) $0 \in$ Int $\sum \mathscr{X}_i$,
(iv)   *in any given time period the physically attainable capital stocks are bounded,*
(v)   *the commodity space is completely separable.*

Proof   There is a regular utility function ((ii) and (v)) with

$$\mathscr{V}_{\mathscr{S}} = \left\{ u^s(x^s) \,\middle|\, \sum_{i \in s} x^i = 0, \quad x_i \in \mathscr{X}_i \right\}$$

that can be shown to have the property

$$u^{s,n} \to u^s \quad \text{implies there exists} \quad \bar{u}^s \in \mathscr{V}_{\mathscr{S}}, \quad \bar{u}^s \geqslant u^s.$$

Hence, Scarf's theorem can be applied to $\mathscr{V}_{\mathscr{S}}$ augmented with any lesser utility vectors. These augmented sets are closed and bounded from above (iv). Also, the game is balanced (Problem K of Chapter 2). Therefore, the weak core exists. Also, the core exists.

The compactness of the core is shown as follows. Let $\mathcal{N} = \bigcup_{i=1}^{n} \{i\}$. Let $u^m \in \mathcal{V}_{\mathcal{N}}$, $u^m \to u$. Then u is in the core since $\bar{u} > u$ implies there exists $\bar{u} \gg u$ (quasi transferibility) and therefore $\bar{u} \gg u^m$ for large m. Hence u^m could not have been in the core.

Let $\mathcal{C}_p$ be the core for the p-replica. Then $\cap \, \mathcal{C}_p \neq \varnothing$, and applying the Debreu–Scarf theorem gives that $\cap \, \mathcal{C}_p$ are the competitive equilibria.

q.e.d.

In Theorem 1, we can directly incorporate separated production in the form of a common convex production set with constant returns to scale (Debreu and Scarf [1963]). Alternatively, we can refer to Chapter 5 of the companion volume for the properties on original production and preferences compatible with the hypothesis of Theorem 1.

In "constructing" equilibrium prices and quantities, their mere existence is not the only question of interest. Are the prices positive? Over time, are they an infinite vector $(p^1, p^2,...)$ or some other abstract linear functional? Are they stationary, $(p^1, p^2, p^3,...) = \alpha(p^2, p^3,...) = (p, p\alpha^1, p\alpha^2,...)$? The last question is largely unanswered (see Chapter 6, Section 3), even though an affirmative answer is the basis of part of intertemporal economic theory (Chapter 11 of the companion volume). The first question is easily answered whenever the conditions of Remark 26 of Chapter 2 are satisfied. For goods with positive marginal utility or marginal productivity, yes; otherwise, no.

The nature of prices over infinite time remains a problem. Minkowski's theorem is proved by a highly abstract construction involving an uncountable algebraic (Hamel) base and the Axiom of Choice. It is possible that a price system thereby discovered can be described only in an infinite, possibly uncountably infinite, number of sentences. Consequently, consumers may not regard the price system as an efficient method of transferring information. In general, can the budget set be described in a finite, or at least in a countable, number of sentences?

In abstract linear topological spaces, a linear functional is continuous if it bounds a convex set with nonempty interior. As usual, let $\mathcal{X}$ be the trade set. The following theorem gives a criterion for a nonempty interior of the upper contour set.

2 Theorem $\mathcal{R}(x)$ *has nonempty interior if* $\mathcal{R}$ *is unsaturated and continuous on line segments,* $\mathcal{P}(x)$ *is open in the interior of* $\mathcal{X}$, *and* $\mathcal{X}$ *is convex with small convex neighborhoods and nonempty interior.*

Proof We have, $\mathcal{P}(x) \cap$ (interior of $\mathcal{X}$) is open. To show that it is non-empty, observe that $\mathcal{X}$ is locally convex, so that the interior of $\mathcal{X}$ is identical with Int $\mathscr{X}$ (Kelly and Namioka [1963, p. 110]). Also, for $\mathscr{X}$ convex, $y \in \mathscr{X}$,

$$x \in \text{Int } \mathscr{X}, \qquad ty + (1 - t)x \in \text{Int } \mathscr{X} \qquad \text{for} \quad t > 0$$

(Kelly and Namioka [1963, p. 15]). Finally, by openness of $\mathscr{P}_i(x)$ on line segments, if $y \in \mathscr{P}(x)$,

$$\bar{x} \in \text{Int } \mathscr{X}, \qquad ty + (1 - t)\bar{x} \in \mathscr{P}(x) \cap \text{Int } \mathscr{X} \qquad \text{for small} \quad t > 0. \qquad \text{q.e.d.}$$

Theorem 2 can be applied to the topology of pointwise convergence to obtain a relatively strong condition sufficient for a price system to be an infinite vector of prices. A result suggested by Peleg is as follows.

3 Remark A linear functional p is continuous in pointwise convergence, on a subset $X_{t=1}^{\infty} \mathscr{X}_t$ of a linear topological space, $\mathscr{X}_t$ contained in a finite-dimensional Euclidean space, if and only if

(i) $f(x) = \sum p^t x^t$, $x = (x^1, x^2, ...)$,
(ii) $\sum_x \sup_{t \in \mathscr{X}_t} p^t x^t$ is finite except for a finite number $\mathscr{X}_t$.

Proof Such a p clearly defines a linear functional continuous in pointwise convergence. On the other hand, consider

$$f(x) = \sum_{t < T} f(x^t) + f(0,..., 0, x^{T+1},...).$$

By continuity,

$$f(0,..., 0, x^{T+1},...) \to 0, \qquad T \to \infty,$$

so that

$$f(x) = \sum_{t=1}^{\infty} f(x^t) = \sum p^t x^t \qquad \text{(linearity of } f \text{ in finite space)}.$$

Also, suppose that $\sum \sup x^t \in \mathscr{X}_t p^t x^t$ is infinite for every infinite set of subscripts t_i, $i = 1, 2,....$ Then let $f(x^t_i) = 2^{t_i}$, and

$$f(0,..., 0, x^{t_i}, 0,..., 0, x^{t_{i+1}}) = \sum_{j \geq i} f(x^{t_j}) = \sum_{j \geq i} 2^j$$

is infinite, which cannot be. q.e.d.

Weaker conditions will be given in section 4 for the existence of infinite vector prices. Also, an infinite number of traders will be permitted, as well as partial orderings.

2. Continuity of Excess Demand

The continuity of the excess demand function or correspondence is used in many mathematical arguments, including that for the existence of equilibrium. It is therefore surprising that continuity was not proved for demand until Arrow and Debreu]1954] studied competitive equilibrium.

The *excess demand correspondence* for p in $\mathcal{S}$ is defined as

$$\mathscr{E}^i(p) = \{x^i \mid p(\bar{x}^i) \not\!\!\!> p(x^i) = 0 \quad \text{for all} \quad \bar{x}^i \in \mathscr{P}_i(x^i), \quad x^i \in \mathscr{X}^i\}.$$

Letting $\mathscr{H}(p) = \{x^i \mid p(x^i) = 0\}$, we get

$$\mathscr{E}^i(p) \subset \mathscr{H}(p) \cap \mathscr{X}_i.$$

The community *excess demand correspondence* is $\mathscr{E}(p) = \sum_i \mathscr{E}^i(p)$. Clearly, if $0 \in \mathscr{E}(p)$, there is a competitive equilibrium.

These ideas facilitate the proof of a quite general existence theorem, which in turn illustrates the need for continuity. A version of the two-trader, two-good equilibrium theory is as follows.

Indifference curves are drawn in Figure 1 to illustrate (induced) preferences $\mathscr{R}_i$. Since x^i represents the net outflow, smaller x^i are preferred to larger ones. Hence, the direction of higher indifference classes points toward the nonpositive orthant.

In Figure 1, $\mathscr{E}(p)$ is constructed for the price vectors p. The direction of p is indicated by the arrow based at the origin, Op. The set of all points that have a zero inner product with p, namely, $\mathscr{H}(p)$, comprises exactly those points whose direction from the origin is perpendicular to that of p. Hence, $\mathscr{H}(p)$ is the line perpendicular to p that passes through the origin. The box indicates the set of x^i that are in

$$\mathscr{X}_i \cap -\mathscr{X}_j.$$

Therefore, $\mathscr{E}_i(p)$ is the set of points on $\mathscr{H}(p)$ that are in the box and that are on the indifference curve with the highest index that has a nonempty intersection with $\mathscr{H}(p)$; in fact, the two line segments are interposed upon each other at these points.

In Figure 1 there appears the locus of all points in $\mathscr{E}_i(p)$ for all possible $p \neq 0$, as indicated by the dashed curves and the shaded region between. The locus was constructed by taking all possible lines $\mathscr{H}(p)$ through the origin and finding the x^i that give the optimum vector under $\mathscr{R}_i$ in the box and on $\mathscr{H}(p)$. In the case of two commodities, this locus is a convenient representation of $\mathscr{E}_i$, since the value of $\mathscr{E}_i$ on any p can be

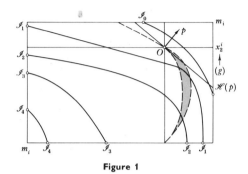

Figure 1

ascertained by taking the ray perpendicular to p and finding the points on the locus that intersect the ray. The sole exception is the origin, since it can be considered as being in $\mathscr{E}_i(p)$ for only some of the p, but is in the intersection of $\mathscr{H}(p)$ with the locus for all p. Hence, direct inspection of the indifference curves must be made to decide whether O is in $\mathscr{E}_i(p)$. Unfortunately, this procedure does not work for higher dimensions (that is, more goods than two) since the hyperplane may have more points than the origin in common. Nevertheless, the locus in Figure 1 is convenient for illustrating ideas about competitive equilibrium.

The foregoing reasoning points out the usefulness of upper semicontinuity of excess demand.

The following result on the continuity of excess demand is due to Arrow and Debreu [1954].

4 Lemma *Let preferences be regular, $\mathscr{P}_i^{-1}(x)$ be open in the pointwise topology, $\mathscr{P}_i(x)$ open on line segments. For some linear topological space, let $\mathscr{P}_i(x)$ be open in the interior of $\mathscr{C}_i$, $\mathscr{C}_i$ compact in pointwise convergence, convex, and $0 \in \text{Int}\,\mathscr{C}_i$. Then $\mathscr{E}$ is upper semicontinuous in pointwise convergence on the infinite vectors whose values px are bounded by 1.*

Proof Clearly, $\mathscr{R}$ takes a maximum on compact sets and $\mathscr{H}(p) \cap \mathscr{C}_i$ is compact; therefore, $\mathscr{E}^i(p)$ is defined.

Let $p^n \to p$ pointwise. Then $p^n x^n = 0$ implies $px = 0$, so that $x^n \to x$ for $x^n \in \mathscr{E}^i(p^n)$ implies that there is an $\bar{x} \in \mathscr{E}^i(p)$ such that $\bar{x}\,\mathscr{R}_i\,x$.

To show that $\bar{x}\,\mathscr{I}_i\,x$, suppose $\bar{x}\,\mathscr{P}_i\,x$. A contradiction results by deriving $\bar{x}^n \in \mathscr{E}^i(p^n)$, $\bar{x}^n\,\mathscr{P}_i\,y\,\mathscr{P}_i\,x$. $\mathscr{P}_i^{-1}(x)$ is open on line segments and in the interior of $\mathscr{C}_i$, which equals the internal points of $\mathscr{C}_i$ (Kelly and Namioka [1963, p. 110]). Also, $s\bar{x} \in \text{Int}\,\mathscr{C}_i$ for $0 < s < 1$, and $s\bar{x}\,\mathscr{P}_i\,y$ for s near 1.

There is an $\bar{x}^n \in \text{Int } \mathscr{C}_i \cap \mathscr{H}(p^n)$ tending to $s\bar{x}$. To see this, observe to some $p_k(t) \neq 0$. Since $p^n\bar{x}$ is finite, it is possible to define

$$y_k^n(t) = -\frac{sp^n\bar{x}}{p_k^n(t)}, \qquad y_i^n(s) = 0$$

whenever either $s \neq t$ or $i \neq k$. Then $y^n \to 0$, $s\bar{x} \to \bar{x}$, so that $s\bar{x} + y^n \to x$. Also, $p^n(s\bar{x} + y^n) = 0$, and $s\bar{x} + y^n$ is in the interior of $\mathscr{C}_i$ for n large. Evidently, if $s\bar{x} \mathscr{P}_i y \mathscr{P}_i x$, then $\bar{x}^n \mathscr{P}_i y$ for large n. Therefore, there are $\bar{x}^n \in \mathscr{E}_i(p^n)$, $\bar{x}^n \mathscr{P}_i y$ for large n, which gives $x \mathscr{R}_i y \mathscr{P}_i x$, which is the contradiction.   q.e.d.

An example of a linear topological space is $\bigcup_{k=1}^{\infty} k\mathscr{C}$, for $\mathscr{C}$ compact and convex with the $\geqslant$-*topology*: $x^n \to x$ if there are y, z, t^n, s^n such that

$$x + t^n y \geqslant x^n \geqslant x + s^n z, \qquad t^n, s^n \to 0.$$

Exercise 1   Let py be maximized in y. Show that the *supply correspondence* $\mathscr{S}(p) = \{y \mid py \geqslant p\bar{y} \text{ for all } \bar{y} \in \mathscr{Y}\}$ is upper semicontinuous and $p\mathscr{S}(p)$ is continuous. When is production described by such a set $\mathscr{Y}$?

PROBLEMS

A. Continuity of Excess Demand I

Suppose consumer preferences are strictly convex and complete on those coordinates on which they vary, and production from inputs on the other coordinates satisfies constant returns to scale, a Leontief technology, and strong convexity.

Show that excess demands are continuous on the set of prices upon which all industries operate. (What additional assumptions are needed ?)

B. Continuity of Excess Demand II

In Problem *A*, substitute for strict convexity and completeness, preferences are finite unions of finite intersections of strictly convex and complete preferences.

Show that excess demands are continuous on the set of prices upon which all industries operate.

C. Competitive Equilibrium and Nonconvex Preferences

(i)   The *convex hull* of $\mathscr{A}$, denoted by $\mathscr{A}^0$, is the smallest convex set containing $\mathscr{A}$. Show that

$$\mathscr{A}^0 = \left\{ x \mid x = \sum t_i x_i, \quad t_i \geqslant 0, \quad \sum t_i = 1, \quad x_i \in \mathscr{A} \right\}.$$

(ii)   Let $\mathscr{A}^0$ be a subset of $\mathscr{E}^n$. Show that

$$\mathscr{A}^0 = \left\{ x \,\middle|\, x = \sum_{i=1}^{n+1} t_i x_i, \quad t_i \geq 0, \quad \sum t_i = 1, \quad x_i \in \mathscr{A} \right\}.$$

(Hint: Let an $x_k, \ldots, x_p$ be a *convexly independent* collection if no x_q is a convex combination of the others. Observe that any $m + 1$ convexly independent vectors define a *simplex* $\mathscr{S}$, such that vectors on the boundary of the simplex can be expressed as convex combinations of m of the convexly independent vectors. Use this fact to prove that a convex combination of the $m + 1$ convexly independent vectors and an $(m + 2)$nd vector is necessarily a convex combination of the $m + 1$ original vectors or of m of the convexly independent vectors and the added one. Use this to show that there are at most $n + 1$ vectors in a convexly independent collection.)

(iii)   Let $\mathscr{A}$ be compact. Show $\operatorname{Bnd} \mathscr{A}^0 \subset (\operatorname{Bnd} \mathscr{A})^0$. (Hint: Use the fact that the convex hull of a compact set is compact (Kelly and Namioka [1963, p. 114]).)

(iv)   Let $\mathscr{C}$ be a compact, convex set. Show that if $x \mathscr{P} y$, then $\operatorname{Bnd}(\mathscr{R}(x) \cap \mathscr{C})^0 \cap \operatorname{Bnd}(\mathscr{R}(y) \cap \mathscr{C})^0 = \varnothing$ whenever $\mathscr{R}$ is continuous and $z \mathscr{R} y$, $y \mathscr{P} x$ imply $y \mathscr{P} x$.

(v)   Let $\mathscr{R}$ be continuous and locally unsaturated and let $\operatorname{Bnd}(\mathscr{R}(x) \cap \mathscr{C})^0$ define equivalence classes denoted $\mathscr{J}(y)$ for $y \in \operatorname{Bnd}(\mathscr{R}(x) \cap \mathscr{C})^0$. Show that $\mathscr{J}(y)$ is a continuous correspondence. (Hint: Use (ii) to show that the convex hull of a continuous correspondence is continuous.) Show that $\mathscr{J}(y)$ is defined for all y.

(vi)   Let $x \mathscr{S} y$ if $x \in (\mathscr{R}(z) \cap \mathscr{C})^0$ and $y \in \operatorname{Bnd}(\mathscr{R}(z) \cap \mathscr{C})^0$. Let $x \mathscr{Q} y$ if $x \mathscr{S} y$ or $x \mathscr{J} y$. Show that $\mathscr{Q}$ is transitive or complete whenever $\mathscr{R}$ is transitive or complete, respectively.

(vii)   Show that $\mathscr{Q}$ is locally unsaturated and continuous.

(viii)   Show that if x is a competitive choice with respect to p, $x = \sum t_i x_i$, $x_i \in \operatorname{Bnd} \mathscr{R}(x)$, then $p x_i = p x$.

(ix)   Show that for $\varepsilon > 0$ and for any $x \in \operatorname{Bnd}(\mathscr{R} \, y \cap \mathscr{C})^0$, there exists an n such that the distance of x from $\sum_{n\text{times}} \operatorname{Bnd}(\mathscr{R}(y) \cap \mathscr{C})$ is less than ε.

(x)   When is there a $\mathscr{C}$ sufficiently large that $(\mathscr{R}(y) \cap \mathscr{C})^0 = \mathscr{R}(y)^0 \cap \mathscr{C}$?

(xi)   In case of (vi) and competitive choice, with n large enough for (v), it is said that there is an *ε-competitive choice*. If there is an equilibrium among several types of traders' convex hull preferences, and if the choices from the convex hull preferences are ε-competitive choices, then there is *ε-equilibrium*. The interpretation is that for large numbers of traders,

traders can be given equilibrium values plus or minus small quantities of various goods. Show that there is an ε-equilibrium and that it can be attained with only small disturbances for each person. (Is transitivity required? Can production be incorporated by the principle of equivalence?)

(xii) What can be said about the relationship between Pareto optimality and ε-equilibrium?

The problem is due to Starr [1969], who provides several parts of the proof.

3. Convex-Valued Excess Demand

The argument in Figure 1 requires that $\mathcal{E}_i(p)$ be a convex set, that is, $\mathcal{E}_i$ be *convex valued*. Also, if $\mathcal{E}_i(p)$ is a single point, it is *single valued*. The case of complete preference orderings is easy; more care must be taken with partial orderings.

5 Lemma *If preferences are weakly (strictly) convex and complete, then $\mathcal{E}_i$ is convex valued (single valued).*

Proof If preferences are convex, then

$$tx + (1 - t)\bar{x} \, \mathcal{R}_i \, x \qquad \text{whenever} \quad x \in \mathcal{E}^i(p), \quad \bar{x} \in \mathcal{E}^i(p).$$

Therefore $\mathcal{E}^i(p)$ is convex.

Applying $\mathcal{E}(p) = \sum_i \mathcal{E}^i(p)$ gives the theorem.   q.e.d.

The results following are designed to admit partial orderings. The reader may go on to the next section, always reading "convex" for "acyclic." The purpose of the rest of this section is to incorporate partial orderings into the theory of equilibrium, just as was done for welfare economics in Chapter 2. In the case of partial orderings, which are themselves defined as unions and intersections of complete orderings, the choice sets $\mathcal{E}(p)$ can be shown to obtain a certain property that is here a sufficient substitute for convexity. First, observe that for a union of partial orderings

$$\bigcup_{\alpha \in \mathscr{A}} \mathscr{R}_\alpha$$

the choice set is the intersection of those for each $\mathscr{R}_\alpha$:

$$\mathcal{E}(p) = \bigcap_{\alpha \in \mathscr{A}} \mathcal{E}^\alpha(p).$$

As in Chapter 1, the standard procedure of showing $\mathscr{E}(p)$ nonempty is to apply the finite intersection property of compact sets to a decreasing sequence of $\mathscr{E}(p)$. Therefore, it is appropriate to treat first the case of intersections.

An *acyclic* set $\mathscr{A}$ is one for which certain groups associated with $\mathscr{A}$, so-called Vietoris homology groups, are zero (Hocking and Young [1961, pp. 346–347]). The groups cannot be explained here, and therefore this discussion may seem mysterious. A basic result is borrowed from the theory derived by Vietoris in which the term acyclic can be paraphrased as "sufficiently nice for present purposes."

6 Lemma   *If $f: \mathscr{A} \to \mathscr{B}$, $\mathscr{A}$ compact, f continuous, $f^{-1}(b)$ acyclic for all $b \in \mathscr{B}$, $\mathscr{B}$ acyclic, then $\mathscr{A}$ is acyclic.*

7 Remark   A convex set is acyclic.

Finally, it will be necessary to prove the following lemma.

8 Lemma   *If $\mathscr{R}$ is a finite intersection of complete weakly convex orderings, and if on the choice set $\mathscr{E}(p)$ these orderings are continuous and quasi transferable for those which take more than one value on $\mathscr{E}(p)$, then $\mathscr{E}$ is acyclic valued with $u^{-1}(e)$ convex.*

In Figure 2 the $\geqslant$-ordering is optimized on the set $\mathscr{A}$ by choosing points on the "arc" ab. Evidently, ab is not convex, but in fact it is homeomorphic to a convex set, which for purposes of proving the existence of equilibrium is quite enough.

The homeomorphism can be derived by evaluating the coordinates of points of ab and then showing them to be mapped into an interval. This is the kind of procedure involved in Lemma 8. For example, if $p_i = 0$, the efficiency partial order requires that the ith good be consumed

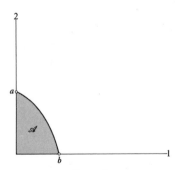

Figure 2

in the maximum quantity admissible. If $p_i \neq 0$, one can reduce one's consumption of i in order to consume other goods j, p_j of like sign with p_i. Hence, for $p \gg 0$, the hypothesis of the theorem is satisfied for the efficiency order. This result can be extended to the intertemporal efficiency partial orderings, since there we have a net of orderings that are *decreasing*, that is to say, $\mathscr{R}_\alpha \supset \mathscr{R}_\beta$ whenever $\alpha < \beta$.

9 Lemma   *The intersection of a decreasing net of acyclic sets is acyclic.*

10 Corollary   *The choice $\mathscr{E}(p)$ is acyclic whenever the partial ordering is the union of decreasing finite intersections of complete orderings that are continuous, weakly convex, and quasi transferable, each taking more than one value on $\mathscr{E}(p)$.*

Proof of Lemma 8 $\mathscr{E}(p)$ is compact (Theorem 7 of Chapter 2). Evaluate $u(\mathscr{E}(p))$ where u_i is the continuous representation of $\mathscr{R}_i$, $\mathscr{R} = \bigcap_{i=1}^{n} \mathscr{R}_i$.

Evidently, $u^{-1}(u_1, ..., u_m)$ is a convex set and therefore acyclic. Define

$$u^m = u, \qquad u^{i-1} = (u_i, ..., u_i, \bar{u}_{i+1}, ..., \bar{u}_m).$$

The u^i can be regarded as functions of the u^{i+1} mapping u^{i+1} and leaving the other u^j unaltered. Also, given $(u_1, ..., u_i)$, u_{i+1} takes a value on all of the interval

$$(\min_{u_1, ..., u_i \text{fixed}} u_{i+1})(\max_{u_1, ..., u_i \text{fixed}} u_{i+1}).$$

Therefore $(u^i)^{-1}(u_1, ..., u_i)$ is an interval in $(\prod_{j=i+1} u^j)(\mathscr{E}(p))$. (By continuity, the inverse image is closed in the interval, and by quasi transferability, it is open in the interval, since decreasing one component always allows us to increase another component.) Now

$$\left(\prod_{j=1}^{m} u^j\right)(\mathscr{E}(p))$$

is acyclic (as a single point) and by induction,

$$\prod_{j=i}^{m} u^j(\mathscr{E}(p))$$

is acyclic. In particular, $\mathscr{E}(p)$ is acyclic.   q.e.d.

4. Existence of Competitive Equilibrium II

Here conditions assuring equilibrium are given and a counterexample
is presented. For bounded choice, existence is easily shown from the
Lefschetz fixed-point theorem, which is then extended to the unbounded
case. Turning to Figure 9 of Chapter 2, we can see that as prices change,
the competitive choices trace out a locus for traders 1 and 2. If the two
loci intersect, then there is a competitive equilibrium trade. If they are
discontinuous, however, an intersection might not occur and there
might be no equilibrium. At the end of this section, a discontinuous
locus is derived from nonconvex preferences.

In the case where the contract curve in Figure 9 of Chapter 2 is a
curve, an argument for equilibrium can be stated as follows. Given w,
a line from w to O_1 is above the tangent line at O_2. Above, at O_2, the line
wO_2 is below the tangent line at O_2. Somewhere between they intersect.
More generally, for a consumption (for 1) of minimal preference level x,
with p the separating linear functional at x, $p(x) \leqslant p(w)$, whereas at
the highest level of preference (for 1) y, q the separating linear functional
at y, $q(y) \geqslant q(w)$. Since y is on the boundary of $\mathscr{X}_1 \cap (-\mathscr{X}_2)$, the
possibilities open (to 1), so that somewhere between there is an $\bar{x}$ on
the contract curve for which $p(\bar{x}) = p(\bar{w})$. This would follow provided p
were continuous on the contract curve, which it is if there is directional
density. We then apply the intermediate value theorem to

$$h(x) = p_x(x) - p_x(w),$$

for p_x the separating linear functional at x. Representing the contract
curve on the horizontal axis is

$$h(x) \leqslant 0, \qquad h(y) \geqslant 0 \qquad \text{(Figure 3)}.$$

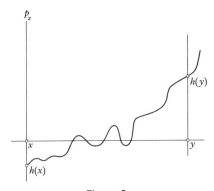

Figure 3

The intermediate value theorem for continuous functions applies. There is some point between x and y at which

$$h(x) = p_x(x) - p_x(w) = 0,$$

which gives the competitive equilibrium. This method must be generalized to allow for more than two traders, more than two goods, and other than directional dense preferences. To do so requires a more advanced fixed-point theorem.

There are several possible approaches to the problem, as in Wald [1936], von Neumann [1937], Arrow and Debreu [1954], McKenzie [1959], Gale [1955], Nikaido [1956], Debreu [1952], and Negishi [1960] (Moore [1968]). The existence theorem described by Rader [1964, 1968] appears to be one of the most general.

11 Theorem *Suppose*

(i) *preferences are independent, and regular (or $\mathcal{P}^{-1}(x)$ is open) in pointwise convergence,*

(ii) *$\mathcal{P}(x)$ is open on line segments and intersects the interior of the trade set (in a linear topological space),*

(iii) *preferences are either complete and weakly convex, or decreasing unions of finite intersections of preferences variable on $\mathcal{E}_i(p)$ and complete, weakly convex, and locally unsaturated,*

(iv) *the community trade possibility set $\mathcal{X} \cap \mathcal{H}$ is bounded and closed,*

(v) *for large t, $|p^n(t+1)|/|p^n(t)| \to \infty$ and $|p^n(t+1)| \to \infty$ implies that excess demands of some consumer i cannot remain finite.*

Then a competitive equilibrium with price system p, $p(x) = \sum_{j=0}^{\infty} p_j x_j$, exists from an initial point x in Int $\mathsf{X}_i \mathcal{X}_i$; *that is,*

$$\mathcal{A} \supset \underset{i}{\mathsf{X}} \operatorname{Int} \mathcal{X}_i.$$

Condition (v) would be satisfied if either

(a) one of the time $t+1$ prices is positive, a proportion of the commodity involved survives from period t to $t+1$, and the consumer tries to make arbitrarily large profits by buying in time t and selling in time $(t+1)$, or

(b) one of the time $t+1$ prices and one of the time t prices are positive and the consumer's marginal rate of substitution for the two goods tends to infinity only if the consumption of one commodity tends to infinity.

If there is a finite time horizon t_0, (v) is satisfied trivially for $t > t_0$, since there will be no prices against which we can test the contrary. The restriction of initial positions to the interior of $X_i \mathscr{X}_i$ is fairly serious for the case of a large number of commodities, all of which, even in a production economy, no consumer can expect to obtain on his own. In order to dispose of this difficulty, proof of Theorem 11 is delayed. The following theorem shows existence without restriction of the initial position to the interior of the trade set.

12 Theorem   *Suppose*

(i)   *preferences are regular (or $\mathscr{P}_i^{-1}(x)$ is open) in the pointwise topology, and for some listing of all consumers $i(j)$ ($j = 1, 2,...$), $i(j)$ and $i(j + 1)$ have similar preferences,*

(ii)   *$\mathscr{P}_i^{-1}(x)$ is open on line segments and open in the interior of the trade set (for some linear topological space),*

(iii)   *preferences are either complete and weakly convex, or decreasing unions of finite intersections of preferences complete, weakly convex, quasi transferable, and variable on $\mathscr{E}^i(p)$,*

(iv)   *locally unsaturated, and strongly quasi transferable,*

(v)   *$\mathscr{X} \cap \mathscr{H}$ is closed and bounded,*

(vi)   *for large t, $|p(t + 1)|/|p(t)| \to \infty$ and $|p(t + 1)| \to \infty$ implies that excess demands of some consumer i cannot remain finite.*

Then the competitive equilibrium with price system p, $p(x) = \sum_{j=0}^{\infty} p_j x_j$, exists for all x in $X_i \mathscr{X}_i$.

Theorem 12 removes a serious restriction to the proof of the existence of a competitive equilibrium along lines first developed by McKenzie [1959].

Proof   Let each individual's wealth be enhanced by a multiple of $w \gg 0$,

$$0 \in \text{Int } \mathscr{X}_i$$

for wealths $w^i + (1/2^i) w$, $i = 1, 2,....$ For each m, theorem 11 applies to give an equilibrium pair $(x(m), p^m)$. Let p^m be multiplied by $k^m > 0$, so that

$$|(k^m p^m(s), \quad s \leqslant t_0)| = 1,$$

t_0 sufficiently large for condition (vi). Then the $k^m p^m(t)$ are bounded for given t by induction on condition (vi). Hence, there is a subsequence $(x(m), k^m, p^m)$ pointwise convergent to $p(x)$. Since $|(p^m(s), s \leqslant t_0)| = 1$,

$$|(p(s), s \leqslant t_0)| = 1 \qquad \text{and} \qquad p \neq 0.$$

To show that p is a competitive price system giving the equilibrium $\bar{x}$, choose p so that $p(y) < 0$ for some $y \in \mathcal{S}$. Suppose $\bar{x}^i \mathcal{P}_i x^i$. $\mathcal{P}_i^{-1}(\bar{x}^i)$ is open and contains $x^i(n)$ for large n, so that

$$\bar{x}^i \mathcal{P}_i x^i(n)$$

for n sufficiently large. Then Remark 23 of Chapter 2 applies to show that

$$p(\bar{x}^i) \leqslant p(x^i(n)) = 0.$$

Therefore

$$p(\bar{x}^i) \leqslant p(x^i) = \lim p(x^i(n)) = 0$$

(since $\sum_i y_i^n = 0$, $y^n \to y_i$ implies $\sum_i y_i = 0$). Applying Lemma 14 of Chapter 2, we get $p(\bar{x}^i) < p(x^i) = 0$, so that x is the competitive choice. That it is an equilibrium is verified by the fact that

$$\sum_i x^i = \lim \sum_i x^i(n) = 0. \qquad \text{q.e.d.}$$

The rest of this section is concerned with the proof of Theorems 11 and the presentation of an example in which there is no equilibrium.

Let the time t components of trades in $\mathcal{X} \cap \mathcal{H}$ be bounded in absolute value by $k(t)$. The proof of Theorem 11 is facilitated by limiting attention to a bounded set

$$\mathcal{C} = \{x \mid |x(t)| \leqslant k(t) + \epsilon\}.$$

Define

$$\mathcal{C}_i = \mathcal{C} \cap \mathcal{X}_i, \quad \text{Int } \mathcal{C}_i = \text{Int } \mathcal{C} \cap \text{Int } \mathcal{X}_i \quad (\text{Int } \mathcal{C} = \{x \mid |x(t)| < k(t) + \epsilon\}).$$

Choose $k(t)$ so that for all i, all feasible trades appears in the interior of $\mathcal{C}_i$.

Lemma 13 shows how the existence of equilibrium in a bounded trade set implies existence in an unbounded trade set.

13 Lemma *Let preferences be locally unsaturated (in uniform convergence), weakly convex, $\mathcal{P}_i(x)$ open on line segments for some listing of all consumers $i(j)$, $j = 1, 2, ..., i(j)$, $i(j + 1)$, have similar preferences. If (x, p) is a competitive equilibrium for preferences defined on*

$$\mathcal{C}_i \supset \mathcal{X}_i \cap \sum_{j \neq i} \mathcal{X}_j (\subset \mathcal{X}_i),$$

then it is a competitive equilibrium defined on $\mathcal{X}_i$.

Proof If $\bar{x}^i \mathcal{R}_i x^i$, $\bar{x}^i \notin \mathcal{X}_i \cap -\sum_{j \neq i} \mathcal{X}_j$, and $p(\bar{x}^i) \leqslant p(x^i)$, then $t\bar{x}^i + (1 - t) x^i$ is in $\mathcal{C}_i$ for small $t > 0$. Also,

$$p(t\bar{x}^i + (1 - t)x^i) < p(x^i) = 0,$$

so that local unsaturation at $t\bar{x}^i + (1 - t) x^i$ applies to give $\bar{x}^i \mathcal{P}_i x^i$,

$$p(\bar{x}^i) < 0.$$

Apply Remark 26 of Chapter 2 to obtain a contradiction. Therefore $p(\bar{x}^i) \leqslant p(x^i)$ whenever $\bar{x}^i \mathcal{R}_i x^i$.

Apply Lemma 14 of Chapter 2 to obtain

$$p(\bar{x}^i) < p(x^i) \qquad \text{whenever} \quad \bar{x}^i \mathcal{P}_i x^i. \qquad \text{q.e.d.}$$

In Figure 1 each individual i chooses $\mathcal{E}^i(p)$, given p. To get $\mathcal{E}$, we need only sum the $\mathcal{E}_i$, as in Figure 4 for two individuals i and j. $\mathcal{E}^i$ and $\mathcal{E}^j$ are derived as in Figure 1; they are then summed along the lines through the origin. For example, for p illustrated in Figure 4, take $\mathcal{H}(p)$ and find the value of $\mathcal{E}^i$, namely A, and the value of $\mathcal{E}^j$, also A; adding the two gives $2A$, which is on the cross-hatched line giving the locus of $\mathcal{E}^i + \mathcal{E}^j = \mathcal{E}$ (for the two-person economy). It has been seen that this locus is a closed set (Lemma 5). Also, the convexity of induced preferences implies that the trades chosen by any one individual form a convex set (Lemma 6) (in Figure 4 only one point has been chosen for each p, which gives, of course, the convex set).

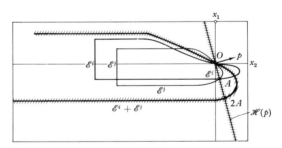

Figure 4

In the two-dimensional case, the community's net demand seems to be of the same general form as the net demand for any one individual. By rotating the hyperplane and trying to construct counterexamples, the reader may convince himself that for the closed path to have the properties outlined, namely, for it to have at most two points in common for each $\mathcal{H}(p)$ (that is, the origin (possibly) and one other) but to have at least one point for each $\mathscr{H}(p)$, the origin must be in the path. Such experiments give a similar result for closed convex sets on $\mathscr{H}(p)$. This can be reasoned as in Figure 5: $\mathscr{E}(p)$ is perpendicular to p. Beginning at p, and proceeding in a circular fashion to $-p$, $\mathscr{E}(p)$ must proceed to $\mathscr{E}(-p)$. However, if $\mathscr{E}(\bar{p}) \neq 0$ along the way, this is impossible, since $\mathscr{E}(-p)$ is "pointing" the wrong way. Hence for some $\bar{p}$

$$0 \in \mathscr{E}(\bar{p}),$$

that is to say, there is an equilibrium. The n-dimensional case is more complicated, but this intuitive two-dimensional point of view will be quite helpful in constructing a proof of the existence of equilibrium.

Let $\mathscr{S}^{n-1}$ be the $n-1$ sphere: $\mathscr{S}^{n-1} = \{x \mid x \in \mathscr{E}^n, \mid x \mid = 1\}$.

The following lemma is the needed generalization of the argument in Figure 5 to Euclidean n-space. Its proof follows from a fixed-point theorem on n spheres.

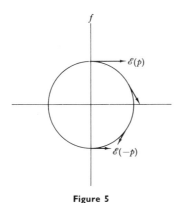

Figure 5

14 Lemma *If $\mathscr{E}$ is convex (or acyclic) valued and upper semicontinuous, taking $\mathscr{S}^{n-1}$ into $\mathscr{C} \subset \mathscr{E}^n$ compact, and if*

(1) $\mathscr{E}(p) = \mathscr{E}(-p)$,
(2) $p(\mathscr{E}(p)) = 0$,

then there exists a $p \in \mathscr{S}^{n-1}$ for which $0 \in \mathscr{E}(p)$.

Proof   If

$$\mathscr{E}(p) \neq 0 \quad \text{for} \quad p \in \mathscr{S}^{n-1},$$

then define

$$\mathscr{E}(p) = \mathscr{E}(p/\mid p \mid)$$

so that $\mathscr{E}$ maps $\mathscr{E}^n \sim 0$ into itself.

Clearly,

$$p(\mathcal{F}(p)) = p \frac{\mathcal{E}(p)}{\|\mathcal{E}(p)\|} = \frac{1}{\|\mathcal{E}(p)\|} p(\mathcal{E}(p)) = 0,$$

$$\mathcal{F}(p) = \mathcal{F}(-p).$$

Clearly, $\mathcal{F}$ maps $\mathcal{S}^{n-1}$ onto $\mathcal{S}^{n-1}$ and $\mathcal{F}$ is upper semicontinuous, compact, and convex (acyclic) valued on the sphere $\mathcal{S}^{n-1}$. The generalized Lefschetz fixed-point theorem as applied to general compact, metric spaces (Eilenberg and Montgomery [1946]) gives that $\mathcal{F}(p)$ has a fixed point on $\mathcal{S}^{n-1}$, that is,

$$p \in \mathcal{F}(p).$$

However,

$$p(\mathcal{F}(p)) = p(p) \neq 0,$$

which is a contradiction.   q.e.d.

Incidentally, the Lefschetz fixed-point theorem is related to the intermediate value theorem. Consider g on the circle without a fixed point. In Figure 6, where the circle is represented, begin at a point a and proceed

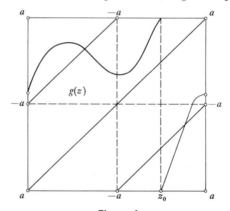

Figure 6

around the circle as though along an interval until we return to a. The function g in Figure 6 is continuous. The apparent discontinuity at z_0 is only apparent, since the value of g at both the top and the bottom of the box is a. Exactly on the 45° diagonal we have $g(z) = z$. By virtue of the fact that g does not cross the 45° diagonal, it does not have a fixed point. However, g in Figure 6 does cross the subdiagonal $(-z, -z)$ where $g(z) = -z$. In fact, this happens because

$$g(a) = g(-a).$$

In order to get from $g(a)$ to $g(-a)$, g must cross either the $(a, -a)$ diagonal or the (a, a) diagonal somewhere between a and $-a$. This can be demonstrated rigorously from the intermediate value theorem for continuous functions. Hence, there is a point for which

$$g(z) = z$$

or else there is a point for which

$$g(z) = -z.$$

In the latter case, by virtue of the fact that

$$g(-z) = g(z), \qquad g(-z) = -z.$$

Hence, in both cases, one of which must occur if

$$g(a) = g(-a),$$

there is a fixed point.

Proof of Theorem 11   Lemmata 4 and 14 give p^t, for which $x^{it} \in \mathscr{E}^i(p^t)$ and $\sum_i x_j^{i,t}(s) = 0$ for $s \leqslant t$. As in the proof of Theorem 12, there are pointwise limits of subsequences of (x^t, p^t). (Again property (v) of the hypothesis of Theorem 11 applies.) Now $p_j{}^t x_j{}^t \to p_j x_j$ and

$$\sum_j p_j^t x_j^t = 0 \qquad \text{imply} \qquad \sum_j p_j x_j = 0.$$

Hence, $p(x^i) = 0$ for each i. Also, if $\bar{x} \mathscr{P}_i x^i$, $\bar{x} \mathscr{P}_i x^{t,i}$ for large t and $p^n \bar{x} < 0$. Hence, $p \bar{x} \leqslant 0$. Applying Lemma 14 of Chapter 2 gives $p \bar{x} < 0$. Finally,

$$\sum x_j^t = 0 \qquad \text{implies} \qquad \sum x_j = 0.$$

(Apply Lemma 13 and the theorem is proved.)   q.e.d.

A situation where a competitive equilibrium does not exist is easily found. Suppose the aggregation of all net demands except those of individual k gives a path like that in Figure 4. This is reproduced (dashed lines) in Figure 7b. Unlike the indifference curves for i in Figure 1, the indifference curves for k are assumed to be concave in

Figure 7a. Rotate $\mathscr{H}(p)$ to find the $\mathscr{E}^k(p)$, which happen always to lie on the boundary of

$$\mathscr{X}_k \cap -\sum_{i \neq k} \mathscr{X}_i \, .$$

The locus of $\mathscr{E}^k(p)$ is shown by the cross-hatched line in Figure 7a. This locus displays a discontinuity. $\mathscr{E}_k$ (on a smaller scale) is reproduced in Figure 7b. Summing $\mathscr{E}^k$ and $\mathscr{E}^i$ gives $\mathscr{E}$. (Summation is made along each $\mathscr{H}(p)$, as in Figure 4.) The locus of $\mathscr{E}$ has a discontinuity, which derives from the discontinuity of the locus of $\mathscr{E}^k$. Note that $0 \notin \mathscr{E}(p)$ for all p. Hence, there cannot be an equilibrium.

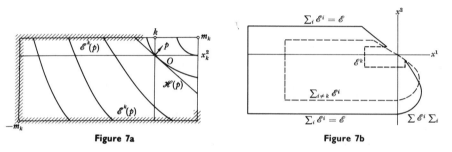

Figure 7a   Figure 7b

The convexity of indifference curves of k (or the nonconvexity of $\mathscr{R}_k(x^k)$, $x^k \in \mathscr{E}^k(p)$) gives rise to the gap in k's demand locus. This gap may arise from either economies of scale of nonconvex preferences. Recalling Figure 7 of Chapter 4 of the companion volume, there is some doubt on the existence of competitive equilibrium vis-à-vis the distribution of population over space. Discontinuity of the original preferences might have the same effect.

Exercise 2   In the finite-dimensional case, how might Theorems 11 and 12 be improved?

Exercise 3   If also $\mathscr{P}_i(x)$ is open in pointwise convergence, show that $\mathscr{E}(p)$ is upper semicontinuous on all infinite vectors. (Hint: Show that $x(m, n) \to_{m \to \infty} 0$ implies there exists an m_n such that $x(m_n, n) \to_{n \to \infty} 0$. Such a choice of m_n is called *diagonalizing* a double sequence.)

Exercise 4   In $\mathscr{E}^n$ prove Lemma 2 for the case when $\mathscr{E}$ is upper semicontinuous but there is not local unsaturation. (Hint: Show that the set of "equilibrium" prices is compact and decreasing with increases in $k(t)$ in the definition $\mathscr{C}_i$.)

PROBLEMS

D. Nondiscrimination

1. Let $\phi_i(x^i) = \bigcup_{k \geqslant 0} k \mathcal{R}_i(x^i) \cap \mathcal{C}, \phi = (\phi_i)$.
Show that

(i) ϕ is continuous,
(ii) ϕ is convex valued.

(Hint: Use continuity and local unsaturation of preferences.)

2. Let $(\gamma_{ij}, j = 1, 2, ..., n)$ be the trades between i and j that optimize $\mathcal{R}_i$ on

$$\{x_i\} - \sum_{j \neq i} \phi_j(x^j).$$

Show that γ_{ij} is convex and upper semicontinuous.

3. Let $\Gamma_i = \{x_i\} + \sum_{j \neq i}(\gamma_{ij} - \gamma_{ji})$.

(i) Show that for $x \in \mathcal{X}$,

$$\Gamma(x) \subset \mathcal{X}.$$

(Hint: Assume $\mathcal{X}_i + \mathcal{X}_i \subset \mathcal{X}_i$. Interpret the assumption's significance for the production set.)

(ii) Show that Γ has a fixed point on x.
(iii) Show that the fixed point defines a nondiscrimination trade.

E. The Existence of Competitive Equilibria

Continuing Problem D, show that

(i) $0 \notin \sum_j \bigcup_{t > 0} t \mathcal{P}_j(x^j)$,
(ii) there exists a linear functional p for which $p(\bar{x}^i) > p(x)^i$ whenever $\bar{x}_i \mathcal{P}_i x^i$,
(iii) there exists a competitive equilibrium.

This problem gives a proof of competitive equilibrium that does not require an analysis of excess demand. Full continuity of preferences is used. What assumptions are employed other than those listed in Theorem 12?

UNSOLVED PROBLEM

F. Large Numbers of Traders

Hildenbrand [1968] has shown that for sufficiently large numbers of similar consumers, for any member of the core, there is a price system such that excess demands are nearly zero. What conditions can ensure the existence of the core for large numbers?

5. Existence of General Equilibrium

With assumptions slightly stronger than in the last section, equilibrium can be shown by means of Kakutani's fixed-point theorem. The advantage of the proof is that it can be easily extended to show equilibrium where many, not necessarily competitive, forms of market organization coexist. This leads to the notion of general equilibrium in a socioeconomic system. In what follows, we first define social equilibrium and then combine the competitive and social equilibrium concepts.

The structure of a social equilibrium is quite simple. Let a social system be such that for given *actions* $a_i \in \mathcal{A}_i$, by the ith agent, there result choices by i; $\mu_i(a_i) \in \mathcal{A}_i$. Social equilibrium occurs whenever $a \in \mu(a)$. Existence of social equilibrium is simply a well-known fixed-point theorem. For a proof see Debreu [1952] and Eilenberg and Montgomery [1946].

15 Lemma *If μ_i be acyclic (convex) valued and upper semicontinuous and $\mathcal{A}_i$ is compact and convex, then there is a social equilibrium.*

On the basis of Lemma 15, one strategy is to list the various kinds of behavior and ascertain that μ_i is upper semicontinuous. However, a more general procedure is available.

The following sectors interact:

(1)   The competitive sector reacting to prices p and voluntaristic transfers t,

(2)   disjoint Cournot sectors, submembers reacting to demands and supplies of each member $\mathscr{E}_i$, in the relevant components, but otherwise taking prices as given,

(3)   contractual oligopolies, where $\mathscr{E}_i$'s are offered in certain components, according to rules of bargaining, and otherwise prices are given, and

(4)   special cases of (2) and (3), namely, monopolies.

Let e_{ij} be the "flow" of trade from i to j. Evidently, just two sets of variables p and $(e_{ij}, i, j = 1, ..., n)$, generate all the information of the model (since $\sum_j e_{ij} = e_i \in \mathscr{E}_i$ and the t_{ij}'s can be computed as $e_{ij} p$). Let ϕ_{ij} be the trade from i to j given $(e_{ij}) = E$ and p. Hence, there is the law

$$(E, p) \to (\phi, \mathscr{E}).$$

The equilibrium problem is a generalization of that of Lemmata 14 and 15, namely, to find $(\bar{E}, \bar{p})$ for which

$$\bar{E} \in \phi(\bar{E}, \bar{p}) \qquad \text{and} \qquad 0 \in \mathscr{E}(\bar{p}, \bar{E});$$

$(\bar{p}, \bar{E})$ is the *general equilibrium*. The conditions sufficient for its existence are deduced in the situation in Lemma 14.

16 Lemma *If*

(i) $\mathscr{E}(p, E)$ *and* $\phi(p, E)$ *have zero Vietoris homology groups (or are convex) and are upper semicontinuous,* $p \in \mathscr{S}^{n-1}$, *and map into a compact set* $\mathscr{C}$,
(iii) $p\mathscr{E}(p, E) = 0$,
(iv)   *there is an* i *such that* $\mathscr{E}_i(0, p_{\sim i}, E) > 0$ *for all* $p_{\sim i}$, E, *then there is a* $(\bar{p}, \bar{E}) \in \mathscr{S}^{n-1} \times \mathscr{X}$ *such that*

(a) $0 \in \mathscr{E}(\bar{p}, \bar{E})$,
(b) $\bar{E} \in \phi(\bar{p}, \bar{E})$,
(c) $\bar{p}_i \neq 0$.

Condition (iv) would be satisfied if there were a Renoir good, or if, for some individual, a good were desired in positive quantities and no one objected to holding it.

Proof   Evidently, $e_i = (0,..., 0,..., -e, 0,...)$, $e > 0$, is never taken by $\mathscr{E}(p)$, since otherwise

$$pe_i = -p_i e = 0,$$

whereupon $p_i = 0$ and $-e \in \mathscr{E}_i > 0$, which is a contradiction of (iv). There is a cone of points of distance $e\varepsilon$ from e_i, for $\varepsilon > 0$, denoted $\mathscr{N}_\varepsilon(-e_i)$, such that $x \in \mathscr{N}_\varepsilon(-e_i)$ is not taken by $\mathscr{E}$, since $\mathscr{E}$ maps the compact sets $\mathscr{S}^{n-1} \times \mathscr{X}$ into a compact set.

Let $\mathscr{P} = \mathscr{S}^{n-1} \sim \mathscr{N}_\varepsilon(p_i)$ for that positive multiple of e_i in $\mathscr{S}^{n-1}$. Let π identify $e \in (p, E)$ with ke if $ke \in \mathscr{P}$, $k > 0$, and with all of $\mathscr{P}$, otherwise. Then $\pi\mathscr{E}$ is upper semicontinuous (since upper semicontinous correspondences of upper semicontinuous correspondences into compact sets are upper semicontinuous). Also, $\pi\mathscr{E}(p, E)$ is a compact and acyclic (homeomorphic to a convex) set. (Had $\mathscr{N}_\varepsilon(-e_i)$ not been eliminated from $\mathscr{S}^{n-1}$, the origin would have to be mapped onto $\mathscr{S}^{n-1}$, which has a nonzero Vietoris group.)

Consider the compound mapping $(\phi, \pi\mathscr{E})$ mapping

$$\mathscr{X} \times \mathscr{P}$$
$$\phi \Big\downarrow \pi\mathscr{E}$$
$$\overline{\mathscr{X} \times \mathscr{P}}$$

Evidently, $\mathscr{P}$ is (homeomorphic to) a convex set, as is $\mathscr{X} \times \mathscr{P}$. Hence Eilenberg and Montgomery's [1946] theorem applies.

This gives a fixed point

$$(\bar{E}, \bar{e}) \in (\phi, \pi\mathscr{E})(\bar{E}, \bar{e}).$$

Now either $\bar{e} = 0$ or $k\bar{e} = \bar{p}$, $k > 0$, whereupon $\bar{e}\bar{p} = 0 = k\bar{e}\bar{e} \neq 0$, which is a contradiction. Since $p_i \neq 0$, we can choose $p_i > 0$.   q.e.d.

Lemma 16 leads to the main socioeconomic equilibrium existence theorem.

17 Theorem *Let all individuals satisfy the hypothesis of Theorem* 12 *and there is an i such that* $\mathscr{E}_i(0, p_{\sim i}, E) > 0$, *for all* $p_{\sim i}$, E. *Suppose voluntaristic transfers between consumers are continuous. If all Cournot or collusive oligopolists have industries with quasi-concave profit functions continuous in output and in noncontrolled prices and continuous rules for distribution of profits, then there is a general equilibrium with an infinite vector p.*

Proof Excess demands for the competitive sector have the appropriate properties. Cournot oligopolies maximize quasi-concave profit functions subject to the output of other firms, given by x. Evidently, the residual profit to a given firm is continuous in the outputs of the others. Hence, there results from profit maximization convex and upper semicontinuous correspondes of outputs. Since profits are continuous and are allocated continuously, consumer expenditures change continuously by owners of firms in these sectors.

Similarly, for bargaining sectors, payoffs are continuous functions of outputs and decisions elsewhere. Finally, if i is a Renoir good, $\mathscr{E}_i(p) > 0$ for $p_i = 0$. We apply Lemma 16 and proceed analogously to the proofs of Theorems 11 and 12.   q.e.d.

It remains to verify conditions under which industries have quasi-concave profit functions.

6. Competitive and Cournot Groups

To show existence of equilibrium under oligopoly, we must show continuity of supplies and demands by the oligopolists. Also, these supplies and demands should be convex valued or at least acyclic valued. For instance, negatively sloped demand curves will be required.

Given the competitive demand for goods, we can obtain theorems about industries with differing degrees of monopoly power and with different laws of profit division. Nevertheless, restrictions on competitive demand in the relevant industries is imperative. To see this, consider the standard Giffin good shown in Figure 8. At very high marginal costs, the monopolist would operate between 0 and q as illustrated by q_i. Of course, the monopolist would never operate near a point of elasticity less than or equal to 1 in absolute value, since

$$-1 \geqslant \epsilon = \left(\frac{mc}{p} - 1 \right) \qquad \text{implies} \qquad mc \leqslant 0.$$

In particular, at q

$$\epsilon = \frac{dp}{dd} \frac{d}{p} = -\infty,$$

so that output never comes near q. On the other hand, at low marginal costs, the monopolist might well operate in the region beyond q, especially if the area under dd above large outputs is infinite, but the area under dd below small outputs is finite. Of course, below q, the upper part of the demand curve represents more profits.

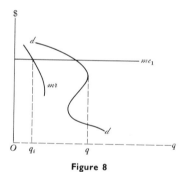

Figure 8

There are difficulties due to the determination of the equilibrium price and to a discontinuity in monopoly output as a function of costs. For example, one industry may take another (competitive) industry's price as given, where the other industry contributes to the one as a factor of production. As the factor price rises, the costs to the other industry increase and a discontinuous change in its outputs results. Clearly, community excess demand is not continuous in prices even though demand for the competitive sector alone is continuous. Here is a paradox. Monopolies allow industries to operate even if there are decreasing costs, a situation that makes competition impossible. However, monopolies find difficulty operating in a Giffen good market, a situation in which competition is possible. Generality gained in one direction is lost in another.

Should there be constant returns, it is sufficient for a unique profit-maximizing point that the marginal revenue curve be downward sloping, as in Figure 9a. Even if marginal cost is constant, as in Figure 9b, there

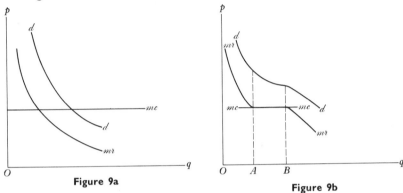

Figure 9a

Figure 9b

may be a convex set [A, B] of profit-maximizing points. In the case of increasing marginal costs, a nonupward-sloping marginal revenue curve is sufficient for a unique solution. For decreasing costs, the marginal revenue curve may intersect the marginal cost curve at several points, as in Figure 10, two of which represent (local) profit maxima:

$$\frac{dmr}{dq} = \frac{d^2p}{dq^2}q + 2\frac{dp}{dq}$$

is nonpositive whenever the demand curve is concave or if its convexity is not too extreme. Oddly enough, the extreme convexity of demand can exclude the concavity of revenues.

The general requirement is that the profit function must be concave, whereupon a convex set of quantities will be chosen by the monopoly.

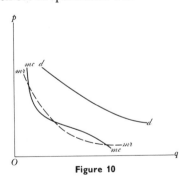

Figure 10

For one firm the solution of the paradox of nonconvexity (or discontinuity) of response is simple. The monopolist will discover that it is an impediment to equilibrium and that it does mightily influence the factor market (and all others) even though it appears to represent only a small portion of total demand. It is therefore constrained to choose among only those outputs that result in equilibrium.

The solution is more complicated with the existence of more than one monopolistic firm. There are outputs that the competitive sector can absorb, given by the solution of the equation

$$\mathcal{M} = \{y \mid y \in \mathcal{E}(p) \quad \text{for some} \quad p \in \mathcal{P}\}$$

where $\mathcal{M}$ is excess demand. The noncompetitive sector must negotiate equilibrium unless $\mathcal{M}$ is separable into *Cournot sectors*:

$$\mathcal{M}_i = \left\{ y_i \mid y_i + \sum_{j \neq i} y_i \in \mathcal{E}_{\mathcal{J}_i}(p) \quad \text{for some} \quad p \text{ in } \mathcal{P} \right\}.$$

Each Cournot sector, which may itself be a negotiated solution of several firms, chooses that point in $\mathcal{M}_i(y)$ which best suits its purposes, and allocates the "profits" to trader j by the (continuous) law $H_{ij}(\mathcal{M}_i(y))$. In particular, there is included the case of contractual duopoly with or without profit transfers, which operates like a monopoly. Of course, this decision is reflected in the competitive market, but presumably the Cournot sector has already accounted for that, so that there is the implicit relationship

$$\mathcal{M}_i(y) = \left\{ y_i \mid y_i + \sum_{j \neq i} y_i \in \mathcal{J}_i(p, y) \quad \text{for some} \quad p \in \mathcal{S} \right\}.$$

The Cournot "group" chooses from $\mathcal{M}_i(y)$ that which is best for it.

If y is chosen by the ordering $\mathcal{R}_i$ and

$$y \in \mathcal{M}(y),$$

then there is a *general Cournot equilibrium*. For this we must show that the y's are chosen in a convex and upper semicontinuous fashion. Several difficulties arise. First $\mathcal{E}(p, y)$ is not generally continuous unless $\mathcal{E}$ is single valued. Consequently, choice from $\mathcal{E}$ generally will not be upper semicontinuous. Therefore, the preferences and production of the competitive sector must be strictly convex. Actually, these conditions can be weakened on the production side. Second, if there are two

$$\mathcal{E}(p, y) = \mathcal{E}(\bar{p}, y), \qquad p \neq \bar{p},$$

then choice will be from a nonconvex set and the y's chosen will not constitute a convex set. Therefore, it appears necessary to assume a single Cournot solution, which results whenever the profit to Cournot firms is quasi concave.

Theorem 17 gives the conditions for the existence of Cournot equilibrium.

18 Corollary *If preferences are $\geqslant$-continuous, regular, strictly convex, and quasi transferable, production is closed, strongly convex, and there are limits to the returns to scale, all Cournot sectors have quasi-concave profit functions, and either*

  (i) *production is strictly convex, or*
  (ii) *there is a Renoir good that is not unproductive, and either*

    (a) *the Renoir good can be used in a nonproduction manner, or*
    (b) *factors are not unproductive and preferences are weakly monotonic in all producible goods,*

then there is a general Cournot equilibrium.

The case of monopoly is that where industries are separated and little account need be made by the monopolist of the price of one good upon the demand for another. Then, other prices are taken to be virtually fixed. This contradicts the obvious fact that the monopolist must influence other (factor) markets. Then the Cournot solution above becomes effectively an oligopoly solution with a single price under control. This will lead to a sharper analysis of Cournot sectors, as should be apparent from the next section.

19 Theorem *Let preferences for competitive traders be weakly convex, locally unsaturated, strongly quasi transferable, and continuous on straight lines. If each market $i \in \mathscr{I}$ is dominated by a Cournot group and if for all other markets, $\sim\mathscr{I}$, there is nondiscrimination and at least one trader with directional dense preferences, then in a Cournot equilibrium the $\sim\mathscr{I}$ markets are competitive, and to the extent that the group constitutes a small proportion of demand in $\sim\mathscr{I}$, the group sets prices only with regard to its influence on the prices of the goods it sells.*

Proof That the $\sim\mathscr{I}$ markets are competitive is argued simply by observing that each Cournot group buys and sells on that market to the directional dense competitors on their terms.

Let x be total sales, y be outputs listed firm by firm, and p be prices. Then the group maximizes a continuous payoff function $\pi(x, y, p)$ subject to

$$x \in \mathscr{E}_{\mathscr{I}}(p) + \epsilon \mathscr{F}_{\mathscr{I}}(p).$$

It is assumed that for equilibrium $\bar{p} \in \mathscr{E}(p)$, $\bar{p}_{\sim\mathscr{I}}$ is independent of $\mathscr{E}_{\mathscr{I}}(p)$.

Then the admissible x and p form a closed set that is a continuous correspondence in ϵ. From this it can be shown that the maximizers x, y, and p are upper semi-continuous in ϵ. Therefore for ϵ, small π, x, y, and p are nearly equal to one of their values when $\epsilon = 0$. q.e.d.

20 Corollary *Under the hypothesis of Theorem 19, if the group is nearly a monopoly, there is nearly monopoly profit and therefore nearly monopoly output.*

21 Corollary *If the group is a Cournot oligopoly with concentration ratio ℓ, then the degree of monopoly power is nearly ℓ.*

Evidently, the necessities are quite substantial for establishing a theory of monopoly or Cournot oligopoly at the level of the general economy. The nonbargaining world does not allow a very wide divergence of environmental conditions except for the case of large numbers of all kinds of individuals.

PROBLEM

G. General Equilibrium

Let a certain subset of commodities, $\mathscr{I}$ be such that consumer demand satisfies

$$\liminf \mathscr{E}_i(p_{ii}, p_i n) \geqslant 0 \qquad \text{whenever} \quad p_i^n \to 0.$$

(i) Show that general equilibrium exists with $p \geqslant 0$ and $p_i > 0$ whenever $\liminf \mathscr{E}_i(p_i, p_i^n) > 0$. (Hint: Choose $\mathscr{P} = \mathscr{S}_{\sim \mathscr{I}} \times \Delta_{\mathscr{I}}$ where Δ is the unit simplex given by $pw \geqslant 0$ and $\sum_{i \in \mathscr{I}} |p_i| = 1$. Show that $p_i \neq 0$, $i \in \mathscr{I}$, p_i in the proof of Theorem 17 and $\mathscr{E}_i = 0$ whenever $p_i > 0$.)

(ii) Weaker $p\mathscr{E} = 0$ to $p\mathscr{E} \leqslant 0$ by using $\liminf \mathscr{E}_i(p_{\sim i}, p_i^n) \geqslant 0$, $p_i^n \to 0$.

(iii) Show that for every $p \in \mathscr{P}$, there is a $t > 0$ such that

$$p + t\mathscr{E}(p) \subset \mathscr{P}$$

(we say that $\mathscr{E}(p)$ points *inward* on $\mathscr{P}$).

For market economies (see Chapter 5), this problem was solved by Arrow and Debreu [1954] and McKenzie [1959].

7. A Theory of Cournot Oligopoly

For Cournot oligopoly, properties of excess demand remain to be proved. In Section 6, we *assumed* profit functions to be quasi concave in order to obtain continuous and convex-valued excess demand. Here, we elaborate the ideas of the existence of Cournot equilibrium to obtain the case where we neeed only have the downward sloping of certain demand curves. Cournot groups or "combines" of various types are assumed to have demands resulting from competitors or from other combines. Excess demand is shown to be continuous and convex valued.

Let there be at most one (noncompetitive) combine in each industry, and let $\mathscr{I}$ be the set of industries with noncompetitive firms. Let x_j^i be the output of goods of type j to the ith "oligopolistic" combine. For $i \neq j$,

$$x_i^j \leqslant 0,$$

$$x_i^j = 0.$$

Whatever j's estimation of what the other combines will do,

$$x_j^j = \sum_{i \neq j} x_j^i + \mathscr{E}_j(p), \qquad j \in \mathscr{I}$$

where $\mathscr{E}_j(p)$ is the competitive demand.

Each combine assumes other prices as given and only considers the effect of its price. Let there be constant returns to scale in the input used in the case of intermediate products; then for a given set of of other prices, the ratio of inputs is constant whatever the level of output. Therefore,

$$x_j^j = \sum_{i \neq j} c_{ij} x_i^i + \mathscr{E}_j(p)$$

for c_{ij} the ratio of x_j^i to x_i^i. This is an input–output system of the Leontief type and can be uniquely solved for x_j^j as

$$(x_j^j) = (I - c)^{-1} \mathscr{E}_{\mathscr{I}}(p) \qquad \text{where} \quad c = (c_{ij}).$$

Hence, the combine can deduce the response of other combines provided that it assumes all other prices are going to remain constant.

Each combine has profits

$$p_j x_j^i + \sum_{i \neq j} p_i x_i^j$$

with which it must attempt to obtain $mc = (1 - t)p + mi$, subject to

$$x_j^j = (I - c)_j^{-1} \mathscr{E}_{\mathscr{I}}(p)$$

where $(I - c)_j^{-1}$ is the jth row of $(I - c)^{-1}$. Of course,

$$x_i^j = c_j x_j^j \,,$$

so that the combine has profits

$$\left(p_j + \sum_{i \neq j} p_i c_{ji} \right) x_j^j$$

subject to

$$x_j^j = (I - c)_j^{-1} \mathscr{E}_{\mathscr{I}}(p).$$

$(I - c)^{-1}$ is nonnegative, provided every industry can simultaneously operate at a positive level. Also, if there is the possibility of nonnegative profit,

$$p_j + \sum_{i \neq j} p_i c_{ji} = 0.$$

22 Theorem *The combines have outputs upper semicontinuous whenever*

(1) $\mathscr{E}(p)$ *is continuous and convex,*
(2) $(I - c)_j^{-1} \mathscr{E}_{\mathscr{I}}(p)$ *is downward sloping in p_i ,*
(3) *production sets are closed and convex.*

Note that condition (2) is easy to satisfy when j is used as an input into other goods that lower the sales of i. In fact, it was shown in Chapter 10 of the companion volume that a higher p_j causes a cut in the use of j, both because of a decrease in the output of the other monopolized goods and because of a decrease in its use for a given output.

PROBLEM

H. Perceived Demand Curves

Suppose that demands are thought to be linear given other prices and continuous in prices and quantitative demand at current prices. When does an oligopolistic industry have continuous demand?

This problem was solved by Negishi [1961].

8. Local Uniqueness of Equilibrium

The local uniqueness of equilibrium can be shown whenever excess demands define a differentiable function. This establishes the determinacy of equilibrium theory in the small. Potentially, the result could cover competitors, monopolists, oligopolists, etc. In this section we set forth the relevant mathematical conditions. In Section 9, these conditions are verified for competition only. The question of local uniqueness for monopoly, oligopoly, and the like is left open.

Several uniqueness results appear in the problems of the next chapter. This section is devoted to one very general result of Debreu [1970] that for almost all wealth distributions, equilibrium is locally unique. Here it is extended to excess demand functions satisfying the *Lipschitz condition*, $|f(x) - f(y)| \leqslant K |x - y|$, or more generally even to *absolutely continuous* functions. These are defined as functions that are continuous and almost everywhere differentiable, and that satisfy condition (N); that is to say, the function maps sets of measure zero into sets of measure zero. In Section 9, we show absolute continuity of demand from properties on preferences.

Let $\mathscr{D}(c) = \{x \mid f(x) = c\}$ be the prices with excess demand c and $\mathscr{C} = \{c \mid \mathscr{D}(c)$ is a discrete set$\}$. A set contained in a countable union of closed sets of measure zero has measure zero and is also "first category" and therefore *very small*. Lemma 23 shows $\sim\mathscr{C}$ to be very small.

23 Lemma   *Let f be absolutely continuous on an open subset of $\mathscr{E}^n$ mapping into $\mathscr{E}^n$. Then $\sim\mathscr{C}$ is of measure zero. If also f is continuously differentiable with a domain equal to a countable union of compact sets, then $\sim\mathscr{C}$ is very small.*

Proof   Let $\mathscr{Y}$ be the set of points at which f is differentiable. Let $\mathscr{X} = \{x \mid \det \partial f / \partial x = 0, x \in \mathscr{Y}\}$. Then $f(\mathscr{X})$ has measure zero (*Sard's lemma* [1958]). Also, $\sim\mathscr{Y}$ is of measure zero by condition (N). $\sim\mathscr{C} \subset f(\mathscr{X}) \cup f(\sim\mathscr{Y})$ since $x^n \to x$ and $f(x^n) = f(x)$ implies $|f(x^n) - f(x)|/|x^n - x| \to 0$ implies $\det \partial f / \partial x = 0$, whenever x is in $\mathscr{Y}$.

If f is continuously differentiable, $\mathscr{X}$ is closed. Let $\mathscr{X}_n$ be $\mathscr{X}$ intersected with the nth of the compact sets whose union is the domain. $f(\mathscr{X}_n)$ is compact and of measure zero. Hence, $f(\mathscr{X}) = \bigcup_{n=1}^{\infty} f(\mathscr{X}_n) \supset \sim\mathscr{C}$, which is the contable union of compact sets of measure zero.   q.e.d.

Our main result, Theorem 24, shows the uniqueness of equilibrium except for a small set of wealths. With differentiability of excess demand, the exceptional set is very small.

24 Theorem *Let excess demand be absolutely continuous (be continuously differentiable) in a finite number of prices for consumers other than i. For a competitive consumer i with a separation of production and consumption, let equilibrium exist for all positive wealths of i. Then except for a (very small) set of nonnegative wealths of i, of measure zero, equilibrium is locally unique and the number of equilibria is finite in any closed subset of the domain of excess demands $\mathscr{A}$.*

The existence theorems 11, 12, and 17 give conditions to which Theorem 24 applies (see also Problem G).

Proof Let w^i be the wealth of i. Define $\mathscr{F}^i = \mathscr{E}^i - w^i$. $\mathscr{F}^i$ can be regarded as a function on $\mathscr{S}^{n-1}$ and $\theta = pw/|p|$ (separation of production and consumption). Therefore, $\mathscr{F}^i$ is defined on an open subset of $\mathscr{S}^{n-1} \times (0, \infty)$, which is n-dimensional, and $\mathscr{F}^i$ maps onto Int $\Omega \subset \mathscr{E}^n$. Equilibrium occurs if

$$\mathscr{G}^i(p) \equiv \sum_{j \neq i} \mathscr{E}^i(p) + \mathscr{F}^i \in w \qquad \text{and} \qquad pw^i = \theta.$$

$\mathscr{G}^i$ is absolutely continuous as a translate of absolutely continuous function. Lemma 23 applies for almost all $w^i \in$ Int $\Omega : \mathscr{G}^i$ has locally unique solutions of $\mathscr{G}^i(p, \theta) = w^i$, so that also the (p, θ) for which $\mathscr{G}^i(p, \theta) = w^i$ and $\theta = pw^i$ are locally unique and equilibrium prices are locally unique.

For a given w^i, pw^i is bounded by b and hence, closed subsets $\mathscr{A} \subset \mathscr{S}^{n-1}$ are extendable to compact subsets $\mathscr{A} \times [\varepsilon, b]$ in $\mathscr{S}^{n-1} \times (0, \theta)$, $\varepsilon > 0$. There, equilibrium is finite by local uniqueness and the finite cover property of compact sets.   q.e.d.

Under conditions such as in Problem G, the equilibria are bounded away from the boundary of the domain of excess demand, since as prices tend to the boundary, excess demand by some consumer for some good tends to infinity, whereas that for others is bounded from below (see Debreu [1970]). This gives finiteness of the equilibrium price set.

By modifying the foregoing arguments, we can show

$$\det \partial \mathscr{E}_{\sim n}/\partial p_{\sim n} \neq 0$$

for almost all wealths. This result will be useful in the next chapter.

25 Remark If $\sum_{j \neq i} \mathscr{E}^j$ and $\mathscr{E}^i$ satisfy a Lipschitz condition (are continuously differentiable), then for all except a (very small) set of $\bar{w}^i_{\sim n}$, $\det \partial \mathscr{E}_{\sim n}/\partial \bar{p}_{\sim n} \neq 0$ at equilibrium $\bar{p}$.

Proof   Consider

$$\mathscr{F}^i_{\sim n} = \mathscr{E}^i_{\sim n} - w^i_{-n} .$$

Then

$$\mathscr{G}_{\sim n}(p_{\sim n}) = \mathscr{F}^i_{\sim n}(p_{\sim n}) + \sum_{j=1}^{n} \mathscr{E}^j_{\sim n}(p_{\sim n})$$

satisfies a Lipschitz conditions (is continuously differentiable). As in Theorem 24,

$$\det \frac{\partial \mathscr{G}_{\sim n}}{\partial p_{\sim n}} = \det \frac{\partial \mathscr{E}_{\sim n}}{\partial p_{\sim n}} \neq 0$$

except for a set of $w_{\sim n} = \mathscr{G}_{\sim n}(p_{\sim n})$ of measure zero. Clearly, if $\bar{p}_{\sim n}$ is an equilibrium, then $\mathscr{G}_{\sim n}(p_{\sim n}) = w_{\sim n}$. (Of course, the converse does not necessarily hold unless we invoke Walras' law.)   q.e.d.

9. Absolute Continuity of Excess Demand

This section is concerned with showing absolute continuity of excess demand functions. We assume that the excess demand function is defined, either because preferences are regular and strictly convex, or simply because preferences are regular and one point has been chosen from each value of the excess demand correspondences. Therefore, we have a function $e(p) \in \mathscr{E}(p)$ for which we seek to show differentiability almost everywhere (a.e.) and condition (N). This is done only for those prices which are strictly positive.

By making assumptions on utility, it is easy to show differentiability a.e. However, it is not known that demand will satisfy condition (N). Also, we wish to put conditions on preferences rather than utility, which is an artificial construct. Therefore, we must develop a deeper analysis. Along this line, we show how differentiability results from maximization. Application is made to homothetic preferences to show differentiability of demand a.e. Then we present an example of concave, homogeneous, everywhere continuously differentiable utility that implies a demand function differentiable a.e. but not satisfying condition (N). This necessitates the introduction of restrictions on prices associated with points in indifference curves to show both differentiability a.e. and condition (N). The specific property required is that along any given indifference curve the ratio of changes in price to changes in quantity is bounded from zero. Under conditions in some respects weaker, related methods will be used to show differentiability a.e. but without condition (N).

First, we make a brief excursion into demand derived from utility functions. The main purpose of this is to show how stringent conditions on utility must be to prove demand differentiable a.e. by known mathematical techniques. No measure theoretic properties are considered, and it remains a doubtful conjecture that the conditions cited in Theorem 26 are sufficient for condition (N).

26 Theorem *Demand is almost everywhere differentiable in prices in the open set $\mathscr{P}$ if the marginal rates of substitution are differentiable in consumption, as would be the case if utility were quasi concave, twice differentiable, and $\partial u / \partial x_k \neq 0$ for all i except possibly $i = 0$.*

Proof Let (x_0, x) be consumption, (p_0, p) price. Let $m(x_0, x)$ be the marginal rates of substitution in terms of good 0. If u is differentiable,

$$m_i(x_0, x) = \frac{\partial u / \partial x_0}{\partial u / \partial u_i}.$$

Then the first-order condition for preference optimization is $m(x_0, x) = p/p_0$ (Gossen's law). Therefore,

$$p_0(1, m)(x_0, x) = \theta$$

is the budget constraint or

$$p_0 = \frac{\theta}{(1, m)(x_0, y)}$$

is differentiable in (x_0, x) whenever m is differentiable. Hence, (p_0, p) is differentiable in (x_0, x). By Sard's [1958] lemma,

$$\det \frac{\partial(p_0, p)}{\partial(x_0, x)} \neq 0$$

for almost all (p_0, p). At such an (x_0, x), (p_0, p) is locally 1–1 and by quasiconcavity no other (x_0, x) maps onto (p_0, p). A simple compuputation shows that in such cases (x_0, x) is differentiable and $\partial(x_0, x)/\partial(p_0, p) = [\partial(p_0, p)/\partial(x_0, x)]^{-1}$. Hence, demand is differentiable almost everywhere. q.e.d.

In Theorem 24, it was required that the community excess demand function be absolutely continuous. However, we cannot merely show that the individual excess demand functions are absolutely continuous, since the sum of absolutely continuous functions may fail to be absolutely continuous. (Any continuous, almost everywhere differentiable function f is the sum of absolutely continuous functions, namely, the sum of functions of $f^i(x) = (0,..., 0, f_i(x), 0,..., 0)$.) Therefore, a stronger property will be sought: a function is *pointwise Lipschitz* at x if there is some neighborhood $\mathcal{N}$ of x such that for all y in $\mathcal{N}$

$$|f(x) - f(y)| \leqslant K|x - y|.$$

Equivalently,

$$\limsup_{\substack{k \to k}} \frac{|f(x) - f(y)|}{|x - y|} \leqslant K.$$

K is the *Lipschitz constant*. The function f is *locally Lipschitz* at x if there is a K and a neighborhood $\mathcal{N}$ of x such that for all $y, z \in \mathcal{N}$,

$$|f(y) - f(z)| \leqslant K|y - z|.$$

Functions pointwise Lipschitz on all points on an open set are known to be absolutely continuous (Federer [1969, p. 218] and Rado and Reichelderfer [1955, pp 201, 338–339]). Also, an easy computation shows that the sum of pointwise Lipschitz functions is pointwise Lipschitz.

We will take a rather involuted route in showing that demand functions are pointwise Lipschitz or differentiable a.e. Special attention will be given the *compensated income* function

$$M(p, x) = \inf\{\theta \mid \theta \geqslant py, \quad y \in \mathcal{R}(x)\}.$$

We will choose $y(p, x)$ to be a vector for which $y \mathcal{R} x$, $M(p, x) = py$. When there is no ambiguity, we sometimes write $y(p)$ for $y(p, x)$ and $d(p)$ for $d(p, \theta)$. Let d be the consumer *demand function*, $d(p, \theta)$ where p is price and θ is income. If preferences are locally unsaturated, $pd(p, \theta) = \theta$ must hold. Then an admissible choice for $y(p, x)$ is

$$d(p, M(p, x)) = y(p, x),$$

which is the choice assumed; y is then *compensated demand*.

The compensated income function is an example of a problem of constrained minimization. A general problem of Lagrange is to maximize $f : \mathcal{P} \times \mathcal{X} \subset \mathcal{E}^{n+m} \to \mathcal{E}^1$. We have x constrained to a set $\mathcal{X}$, and p a parameter. For example, a consumer maximizes $u(x)$, subject to x in a budget set that is dependent on prices and income: $px < \theta$. This can be reformulated for some real λ as the maximization of $u(x) - \lambda(px - \theta)$ subject to $x \geqslant 0$. The parameters p and λ are varied to obtain demand.

Let $\phi(p) = \max_{x \in \mathcal{X}} f(p, x)$ exist for $p \in \mathcal{P}$. Let $x(p)$ be an x maximizing $f(p, x)$ on $\mathcal{X}$. The following theorem will be applied to obtain differentiablity of appropriate functions.

27 Theorem *Let f and φ be defined as above.*

(i) *φ is concave whenever f is concave. If f is convex in p alone, φ is convex.*

(ii) *φ is Lipschitz whenever f is uniformly Lipschitz in p alone.*

(iii) *If f and φ are differentiable and p is interior to its domain, then $\partial\phi/\partial p = \partial f/\partial p$ where $\partial f/\partial p$ is evaluated at $(p, x(p))$.*

(iv) *If $\partial f/\partial p$ in x and p, f is continuous and x(p) is continuous, then φ is continuously differentiable with $\partial\phi/\partial p = \partial f/\partial p$ evaluated at $(p, x(p))$.*

Proof   Let $x = x(\bar p)$, $\bar x = x(\bar p)$, $\bar x = x(tp + (1 - x)\bar p)$.

(i)   For concavity,

$$\phi(tp + (1 - t)\bar p) = f(tp + (1 - t)\bar p, \bar x)$$
$$\geqslant f(tp + (1 - t)\bar p, tx + (1 - t)\bar x)$$
$$\geqslant tf(p, x) + (1 - t)f(\bar p, \bar x)$$
$$= t\phi(p) + (1 - t)\phi(\bar p).$$

For convexity,

$$\phi(tp + (1 - t)\bar p) = f(tp + (1 - t)\bar p, \bar x)$$
$$\leqslant tf(p, \bar x) + (1 - t)f(\bar p, \bar x)$$
$$\leqslant tf(p, x) + (1 - t)f(\bar p, \bar x)$$
$$= t\phi(p) + (1 - t) + (\bar p).$$

(ii) $\phi(p) - \phi(\bar p) = f(p, x) - f(\bar p, \bar x)$
$$\leqslant f(p, x) - f(\bar p, x).$$

Without loss of generality, let $\phi(p) - \phi(\bar p) \geqslant 0$. Then

$$|\phi(p) - \phi(\bar p)| \equiv \phi(p) - \phi(\bar p) = f(p, x) - f(\bar p, \bar x)$$
$$\leqslant f(p, x) - f(\bar p, x) = |f(p, x) - f(\bar p, x)|$$
$$\leqslant K|p - \bar p|.$$

(iii)   By maximization,

$$\frac{f(p, x) - f(\bar p, x)}{|p - \bar p|} \geqslant \frac{\phi(p) - \phi(\bar p)}{|p - \bar p|}.$$

In the limit, as $p \to \bar{p}$, by the definition of differentiability,

$$\frac{\partial f}{\partial p} \lim \frac{p - \bar{p}}{|p - \bar{p}|} \geqslant \frac{\partial \phi}{\partial p} \lim \frac{p - \bar{p}}{|p - \bar{p}|}$$

which is possible for all $p \to \bar{p}$ only if

$$\frac{\partial f}{\partial p} = \frac{\partial \phi}{\partial p}$$

(iv)   By maximization

$$\frac{f(p, x) - f(\bar{p}, x)}{|p - \bar{p}|} \geqslant \frac{\phi(p) - \phi(\bar{p})}{|p - \bar{p}|}$$

$$\geqslant \frac{f(p, \bar{x}) - f(\bar{p}, \bar{x})}{|p - \bar{p}|} .$$

Taking limits as in (iii) and noting that $\bar{x} \to x$ as $\bar{p} \to p$, we have

$$\frac{\partial f}{\partial p} \lim \frac{p - \bar{p}}{|p - \bar{p}|} \geqslant \lim \frac{\phi(p) - \phi(\bar{p})}{|p - \bar{p}|}$$

$$\geqslant \frac{\partial f}{\partial p} \lim \frac{p - \bar{p}}{|p - \bar{p}|} .$$

(The last inequality can be argued from the mean value theorem or by the uniform convergence of the continuous function

$$\frac{f(p) - f(\bar{p})}{|p - \bar{p}|}$$

converging to the continuous function

$$\frac{\partial f}{\partial p} \lim \frac{p - \bar{p}}{|p - \bar{p}|} .)$$

Hence,

$$\lim \frac{\phi(p) - \phi(\bar{p})}{|p - \bar{p}|} = \frac{\partial f}{\partial p} \lim \frac{p - \bar{p}}{|p - \bar{p}|} . \qquad \text{q.e.d.}$$

Note that the proof in (iv) cannot be extended to the case covered in (iii). The reason is that

$$\frac{f(p, \bar{x}) - f(\bar{p}, \bar{x})}{|p - \bar{p}|}$$

may not tend to

$$\frac{\partial f}{\partial p} \lim \frac{p - \bar{p}}{|p - \bar{p}|}$$

because $\partial f/\partial p$ evaluated at $(p, \bar{x})$ does not tend to $\partial f/\partial p$ evaluated at (p, x) as $x \to \bar{x}$. Therefore, in the absence of continuous differentiability of f, we must have independent knowledge about the differentiability of ϕ.

Let $y(p, x)$ be a point in the closed convex hull of $R(x)$ for which $M(p, x) = py(p, x)$.

28 Corollary *The compensation function $M(p, x)$ is concave in p and twice differentiable a.e. in p with*

$$\frac{\partial M}{\partial p} = y(p) \quad and \quad \frac{\partial^2 M}{\partial p^2} = \frac{\partial y}{\partial p}.$$

Evidently, for almost all p, $y(p)$ is uniquely determined.

Proof $M(p, x)$ maximizes $-px$ on $\mathscr{R}(x)$. Clearly px is convex in p. By Theorem 27(i), $-M(p, x)$ is convex, that is $M(p, x)$ is concave. By a theorem of Alexandroff [1939], a concave function, and therefore M, is twice differentiable a.e. in p. Also, $\partial py/\partial p = y$, so that Theorem 27(iii) applies to give $\partial M/\partial p = y(p)$.   q.e.d.

Now we show how McKenzie's [1957] construction yields differentiability a.e. for homothetic preferences where indifference hypersurfaces have the same slope or gradient along rays through the origin. It is appropriate to start here since the homothetic case admits the easiest adaptation of McKenzie's argument. Also, a concave, homogeneous utility function is studied for which demand is differentiable a.e. but that does not satisfy condition (N). Therefore, the homotheticity assumption is sufficient for differentiability a.e. but is not enough for our purposes.

The proof of the theorem following depends on viewing a change in demand as the sum of an income and a substitution term. The derivative of the substitution term exists by the fact that it is the second derivative of the compensating income function (Corollary 28). The income term is well behaved by virtue of the continuous differentiability of the compensated income function and the special properties of homothetic demand where multiplying income by a proportional k multiplies each demand by k.

29 Theorem *If d is defined on the open cone $\mathscr{P} \subset \Omega$ and preferences are homothetic, regular, and locally unsaturated, then almost everywhere in $\mathscr{P}$, d is differentiable with the Slutsky equation,*

$$\frac{\partial d}{\partial p} = \frac{\partial y}{\partial p} - \frac{1}{\theta} d(p)\, d(p)' \qquad where \quad y(\hat{p}) = d(\hat{p}, M(p, d(p, \theta))).$$

Note that since d is not necessarily continuous, demand need not be unique and preferences need not be strictly convex.

Proof   According to Corollary 28, for a given indifference curve and for almost all p, $y(p)$ is the derivative of M with respect to p and $\partial y/\partial p$ exists. Evidently, the choice of $y(p)$ is unique. Also, from homotheticity, it is easily shown that

$$d(tp, \theta) = \frac{1}{t}\, d(p, \theta).$$

Therefore, $\partial y/\partial p$ exists at p for $y(p, \bar{x})$ implies $\partial y/\partial p$ exists at tp and $y(p, x)$ for all $t > 0$ and all x. It follows that for almost all rays, and therefore for almost all prices p, $\partial y/\partial p$ exists at $y(p, d(p, \theta))$.

Let p be a price for which $\partial y/\partial p$ exists at $y(p, d(p, \theta))$. Also note that M is continuously differentiable for all p, with derivative $y(p, x)$. We show derivatives a.e. for d. The method will be repetitious of the chain rule of differential calculus, but it seems advisable to proceesd as carefully as possible.

Consider $\bar{p}$ tending to p. Without loss of generality and for $x = d(p, \theta)$, either $M(\bar{p}, x) = \theta$ for all $\bar{p}$ or $M(\bar{p}, x) \neq \theta$ for all $\bar{p}$. In the latter case $y(\bar{p}) = d(\bar{p}, M(\bar{p}, x)) = d(\bar{p}, \theta)$. Therefore

$$\frac{d(p) - d(\bar{p})}{|p - \bar{p}|} = \frac{y(p) - y(p)}{|p - \bar{p}|} \to \frac{\partial y}{\partial p} \frac{p - \bar{p}}{|p - \bar{p}|},$$

As $\bar{p} \to$, $y(\bar{p}) \to y(p)$. Also, we have $\bar{p}y(\bar{p}) \leqslant \bar{p}y(p)$ and $py(p) \leqslant py(\bar{p})$, which implies

$$\frac{(\bar{p} - p)y(\bar{p})}{|\bar{p} - p|} \leqslant - \frac{(\bar{p} - p)y(p)}{|\bar{p} - p|}$$

or in the limit

$$\lim \frac{(\bar{p} - p)}{|\bar{p} - p|} y(p) = -\lim \frac{(\bar{p} - p)}{|\bar{p} - p|} y(p) = 0.$$

Therefore

$$\frac{1}{\theta} d(p) \, d(p)' \lim \frac{\bar{p} - p}{|\bar{p} - p|} = 0$$

and the Slutsky equation is satisfied.

We finally consider the case in which $M(\bar{p}, x) \neq 0$. Again we note the continuous differentiability of M in p.

$$
\begin{aligned}
\frac{d(p) - d(\bar{p})}{|p - \bar{p}|} &= \frac{y(p) - d(\bar{p})}{|p - \bar{p}|} \\[2mm]
&= \frac{y(p) - y(\bar{p})}{|p - \bar{p}|} + \frac{y(\bar{p}) - d(\bar{p})}{|p - \bar{p}|} \\[2mm]
&= \frac{y(p) - y(\bar{p})}{|p - \bar{p}|} + \frac{y(\bar{p}) - d(\bar{p})}{M(\bar{p}, x) - \theta} \frac{M(\bar{p}, x) - \theta}{|p - \bar{p}|} \\[2mm]
&\equiv \frac{y(p) - y(\bar{p})}{|p - \bar{p}|} - \frac{\partial d}{\partial \hat{\theta}}\bigg|_{\substack{\bar{p}, \hat{\theta} = t, \theta + (1-t)M(\bar{p},x) \\ 0 < t < 1}} \frac{M(\bar{p}, x) - \theta}{|p - \bar{p}|}
\end{aligned}
$$

(mean value theorem)

$$
\begin{aligned}
&= \frac{y(p) - y(\bar{p})}{p - \bar{p}} + \frac{1}{\theta} d(\bar{p}) \frac{M(\bar{p}, x) - \theta}{|p - \bar{p}|} \quad \text{(homotheticity)} \\[2mm]
&\rightarrow \frac{\partial y}{\partial p} \frac{p - \bar{p}}{|p - \bar{p}|} - \frac{1}{\theta} d(p) \, y(p) \frac{p - \bar{p}}{|p - \bar{p}|} \,.
\end{aligned}
$$

The theorem follows.   q.e.d.

It will be seen that for a certain differentiable, concave utility function, the Slutsky substitution matrix is zero. It follows that most change in demand takes place on a small set of prices where the Slutsky equations are not defined and demand is not differentiable. Observations on a consumer with such utility would reveal a paradox. From a typical price system, ever smaller changes in price would reveal only an income effect, whereas from an exceptional price, the substitution effect would grow to infinity. Most of the change in demand would occur at prices that are sampled with probability zero. Furthermore, the exact magnitude of the change could hardly be deduced from an infinite Slutsky substitution effect, $\partial y / \partial p$.

To construct the example, let an indifference curve be defined by $x_2 = f(x_1)$ and

$$f' = \frac{df}{dx_1} = q(x_1) < 0$$

where q is continuous and monotone decreasing. Such an indifference curve will be monotonic decreasing and strictly convex to the origin. This can be done so that for almost all q,

$$\frac{dx_1}{dq} = \frac{dq^{-1}}{dq} = 0$$

(Riesz–Sz-Nagy [1955, p. 48]). Evidently, most of the change in x takes place on a set of q's of measure zero. Preferences are then to be generated by taking rays through the origin and projecting the original indifference curve equiproportionally along the rays. Resulting preferences are homothetic and are representable by the utility function $u(x) = 1/k$ if $kx_2 = f(kx_1)$. Clearly, u is strictly quasi concave, increasing in both goods, and homogeneous of degree one. Therefore, it is concave (Theorem 14 of Chapter 6 of the companion volume). Indeed, u^α is homogeneous of degree α and is strictly concave for $0 < \alpha < 1$. It is easy to prove that u is continuously differentiable.

30 Remark The foregoing utility function u is a continuously differentiable function of x_1 and x_2.

Proof Let u equal $1/k$ at x if k solves $k = (1/x_2)f(kx_1)$. Since u is concave, it is differentiable almost everywhere. The derivatives are continuous by the equations

$$\frac{\partial k}{\partial x_2}\left(1 + f'\,\frac{x_1}{x_2}\right) = -\frac{1}{x_2^2}f(kx_1) \quad \text{or} \quad \frac{\partial k}{\partial x_2} = -\frac{1}{1 - q(x_1/x_2)}\,\frac{1}{x_2^2}f(kx_1)$$

and

$$\frac{\partial k}{\partial x_1}(x_2 + f'x_1) = f'k \quad \text{or} \quad \frac{\partial k}{\partial x_1} = \frac{qk}{x_2 + x_1 q}.$$

Hence u is differentiable everywhere.   q.e.d.

31 Remark Almost everywhere, the demand curve derived from the forgoing concave utility u has derivative

$$\frac{\partial d_i}{\partial p_j} = -\frac{x_i x_j}{\theta}$$

where $px = \theta$. Therefore the substitution effect is zero almost everywhere. Also, u does not satisfy condition (N) and the set of all points where u is differentiable is a set of measure zero.

Proof By Theorem 29, u is differentiable almost everywhere. Let $r = p_2/p_1$. By construction,

$$\frac{\partial y_2}{\partial p_j} = \frac{dy_2}{dy_1} \frac{dy_1}{dr} \frac{dr}{dp_j} = 0$$

for almost all r. Also,

$$\frac{\partial y_1}{\partial p_j} = \frac{dy_1}{dr} \frac{dr}{dp_j} = 0$$

for almost all r. Evidently, $\partial y/\partial p = 0$ for alsmost all rays through the origin. Also, $d(tp) = (1/t)\, d(p)$ by homotheticity and hence for almost all rays through the origin

$$\frac{\partial d}{\partial p} = \frac{1}{\theta} d(p)\, y(p);$$

that is, for almost all p,

$$\frac{\partial d}{\partial p} = -\frac{1}{\theta} d(p)\, d(p)'.$$

Here $\mathscr{P} = \text{Int } \Omega$. Let $\mathscr{S}$ be the set of points where $\det \partial d/\partial p = 0$. Note that $\det \partial d/\partial p = \det - d(p)\, d(p)'/\theta = 0$. Let μ be (Lebesgue) measure in $\mathscr{E}^2$. Then, $\mu(\text{Int } \Omega \sim \mathscr{S}) = 0$. On the other hand, by concavity of utility and desirability of both goods, $d(\text{Int } \Omega) = \text{Int } \Omega$. A set of measure zero, $\text{Int } \Omega \sim \mathscr{S}$, is mapped into a set of positive measure —indeed, into a set with all measures of Ω. q.e.d.

At last we show how Lipschitz conditions on preferences and demand can be used to obtain differentiablity a.e. In some strong cases, demand is shown to be pointwise Lipschitz, so that both differentiability a.e. and condition (N) are verified. Because the proofs are simpler, we take up these cases first. Then we introduce weaker assumptions that are sufficient only for differentiability a.e.

The function d is *uniformly locally Lipschitz* in θ at (p, θ) if for a some neighborhood $\mathscr{N}$ of (p, θ) there is a K such that for all $(\bar{p}, \bar{\theta})(\bar{p}, \bar{\bar{\theta}}) \in \mathscr{N}$,

$$|d(\bar{p}, \bar{\theta}) - d(\bar{p}, \bar{\bar{\theta}})| < K|\bar{\theta} - \bar{\bar{\theta}}|.$$

Demand is a uniformly locally Lipschitz in income on a set $\mathscr{U}$ if it is a uniformly locally Lipschitz function of income at each point of $\mathscr{U}$. Goods are *normal* if increases in income do not decrease their consumption. If demand is nonnegative valued, homothetic, and single valued, then it is easily shown that it is normal. If demand is normal, then demand is uniformly Lipschitz in income (Uzawa [1960]). To see this, let $\Delta d = d(p, \theta) - d(p, \theta)$. Then $p \, \Delta d = \Delta p d = \Delta \theta$. Also, by $p_i > 0$, $\Delta d_i > 0$, for all i,

$$p_i \, \Delta d_i \leqslant p \, \Delta d = \Delta \theta \qquad \text{or} \qquad \Delta d_i \leqslant \frac{\Delta \theta}{p_i}.$$

Throughout the rest of this section, we assume a Lipschitz condition in income that is assured by normality of demand in income. The other Lipschitz conditions are not likely to be derivable from normal demand behavior but rather relate to the properties of the indifference surfaces.

The theorem following shows differentiability a.e. and condition (N) even if several prices are compatible with given demand. The result reduces the problem to finding separately a Lipschitz condition of demand in income and along an indifference surface of demand in prices. Variants of these Lipschitz conditions lead to different versions of nice demand.

Theorem 32 is the foundation for our applications to general equilibrium in Section 8.

32 Theorem *Let demand be continuous on an open cone $\mathscr{P} \subset \text{Int } \Omega$ and let it satisfy a uniform Lipschitz condition in income (as in the case of normal demand). Let preferences be regular and locally unsaturated.*

(i) Individual demand is differentiable for almost all values in $d(\mathscr{P})$ and satisfies condition (N) if, excluding a set of consumptions of measure zero, on any indifference set $\mathscr{I}(x)$ there is $k_x > 0$ such that $| \Delta p \, | / | \, \Delta y \, | > k_x$ for $y, \bar{y}$ in $\mathscr{I}(x)$.

(ii) Community demand is pointwise Lipschitz and therefore differentiable a.e. and satisfies condition (N) whenever on any indifference set $\mathscr{I}(x)$ there is a $k_x > 0$ such that $| \Delta p \, | / | \, \Delta y \, | > k_x$ for $y, \bar{y}$ in $\mathscr{I}(x)$.

(iii) Individual and community demand satisfies a local Lipschitz condition on $\mathscr{P} \subset \text{Int } \Omega$ if for any individual there is a k such that for every y near $\bar{y}$ and $y, \bar{y}$ in $\mathscr{I}(x)$, $| \Delta p \, | / | \, \Delta y \, | > k$.

In all three cases, individual demand has derivatives a.e. evaluated by the Slutsky equation

$$\frac{\partial d}{\partial p} = \frac{\partial y}{\partial p} = \frac{\partial d}{\partial \theta} \, d'$$

where $y(p) = d(p, \theta)$.

The following corollary is the final payoff for our analysis.

33 Corollary *Under the hypothesis of* (ii) *of Theorem* 32 *with* $\mathscr{P} = \text{Int } \Omega$, *for almost all wealths, equilibrium is locally unique and* $\det \partial e/\partial p \neq 0$.

Proof   Theorem 32 gives that d is pointwise Lipschitz and absolutely continuous, as must be its translate, $f(p) = d(p) - \sum_{j \neq i} w^j$. Apply Theorem 24.   q.e.d.

To see the need for Lipschitz conditions to get condition (N), consider a function p that is differentiable and 1–1. Its inverse takes sets of measure zero into sets of measure zero if and only if $\det \partial p/\partial d \neq 0$ for almost all d. In effect, almost everywhere in the range and domain of f, $(\partial d/\partial p)^{-1} = \partial d^{-1}/\partial d$. It is not enough merely to have d and d^{-1} differentiable almost everywhere, since most of the change may take place at points at which $\det \partial p/\partial d = 0$ and $\partial d/\partial p$ is "infinite." By Sard's [1958] lemma, such points are of measure zero in the range space of d^{-1} but possibly not in the domain of d^{-1}. Hence, d would take the sets where $\det \partial d^{-1}/\partial p = 0$ onto a set of positive measure.

Proof   Since d is continuous, $M(p, x)$ is continuously differentiable (Corollary 28). As in the proof of Theorem 29, we can break the change into income and substitution terms. Either

$$\frac{|d(p) - d(\bar{p})|}{|p - \bar{p}|} = \frac{|y(p) - y(\bar{p})|}{|p - \bar{p}|} \leq \frac{1}{k_x}$$

or

$$\frac{|d(p) - d(\bar{p})|}{|p - \bar{p}|} \leq \frac{|y(p) - y(\bar{p})|}{|p - \bar{p}|} + \frac{|y(\bar{p}) - d(p)|}{|M(\bar{p}, x) - \theta|} \frac{|M(\bar{p}, x) - \theta|}{|p - \bar{p}|}$$

$$< \frac{1}{k_x} + LK.$$

Setting $k_x = k$ gives part (iii).

For (i), let $\mathscr{Y}$ be the set of points $x = d(p)$ such that d is pointwise Lipschitz. Evidently $d(\mathscr{P}) \sim \mathscr{Y}$ is of measure zero. Also, on the set $\mathscr{Z} \equiv d^{-1}(d(\mathscr{P}) \sim \mathscr{Y})$, d satisfies condition (N) by the pointwise Lipschitz property. Since a set of measure zero $\mathscr{W} \subset \mathscr{P}$ is the union of two sets of measure zero $\mathscr{W} \cap \mathscr{Z}$ and $\mathscr{W} \cap (\mathscr{P} \sim \mathscr{Z})$, both of which are sent into sets of measure zero, d satisfies condition (N).

For (ii), we observe that for all $p \in \mathscr{P}$ individual demand is pointwise Lipschitz. Therefore, the sum of individual demands equals community demand is pointwise Lipschitz at all $p \in \mathscr{P}$. Therefore, individual and community demand is almost everywhere differentiable and satisfies condition (N).

We turn to the Slutsky equation. Let $\mathcal{Y}$ be the set of values $x = d(p)$ at which d and y are pointwise Lipschitz. For the individual consumer we have in each case (i)–(iii) a local Lipschitz condition on $y(p)$ and on demand in income. Therefore y is differentiable in price at $y(p, d(p))$ and d is differentiable in price almost everywhere in $d^{-1}(\mathcal{Y})$. The derivative for income $\theta = pd$ is computable as follows.

Since $d(p, t\theta) = d((1/t)p, \theta)$,

$$\frac{\partial d}{\partial t} = \frac{\partial d}{\partial (1/t)p} \frac{\partial (1/t)p}{\partial t} = -\frac{1}{t^2} \frac{\partial d}{\partial (1/t)p} p.$$

Since $dt\,\theta/dt = \theta$, we have $dt/dt\,\theta = 1/\theta$. Therefore,

$$\frac{\partial d}{\partial t\,\theta} = \frac{\partial d}{\partial t} \frac{dt}{dt\,\theta} = -\frac{1}{t^2\theta} \frac{\partial d}{\partial (1/t)p}.$$

Evaluating at $t = 1$ gives

$$\frac{\partial d}{\partial \theta} = -\frac{1}{\theta} \frac{\partial d}{\partial p} p.$$

Therefore differentiability in price implies differentiability in income. Now for p at which the derivatives of d and y exist for all $x = d(p, \theta)$, we write

$$d(p) = y(p) - (y(p) - d(p))$$
$$= y(p) - (d(p, M(p, x)) - d(p, \theta)) \qquad \text{where} \quad y(p) = y(p, x).$$

Differentiating with respect to p and applying the addition and chain rules of calculus, we have

$$\frac{\partial d}{\partial p} = \frac{\partial y}{\partial p} = \frac{\partial d}{\partial p}\bigg|_{M(p,x)} - \frac{\partial d}{\partial \theta} \frac{\partial M}{\partial p} + \frac{\partial d}{\partial p}\bigg|_\theta$$

$$= \frac{\partial y}{\partial p} - \frac{\partial d}{\partial \theta} d' - \frac{\partial d}{\partial p}\bigg|_{M(p,x)} - \frac{\partial d}{\partial p}\bigg|_\theta.$$

Evaluating at $x = d(p)$, we have

$$\frac{\partial d}{\partial p} = \frac{\partial y}{\partial p} - \frac{\partial d}{\partial \theta} d'.$$

For the community, demand is the sum of individual demands. Therefore the community derivatives are the sums of individual demand derivatives whenever they all exist. The individual demand functions are all differentiable except for the finite union of sets where any one individual may not have differentiable demand. Each individual's set of non-differentiability is of measure zero and therefore the union of these sets is of measure zero. Almost everywhere in $\mathscr{P}$, community demand is differentiable and its derivative is the sum of the individual demands that are given by the Slutsky formula.   q.e.d.

We now consider a proof of differentiability a.e. only. Perhaps at some future date, conditions alternative to those in Theorem 32 can be added to show condition (N).

In Theorem 34 following, we need a substitute for the Lipschitz condition on prices in Theorem 32. One substitute is provided by the assumption of concave utility. Homothetic preferences are included since they are known to be representable by concave utility (Corollary 15 of Chapter 6 of the companion volume).

Unfortunately, concave utility functions may exclude many applications and we need alternative assumptions. As will be seen, a substitute is to assume that the compensated demand function y satisfies a uniform Lipschitz condition in x:

$$| y(p, x) - y(p, \bar{x})| \leqslant K(x - \bar{x}).$$

We shall formulate this in a slightly more intuitive way. Let

$$\delta(\mathscr{X}, \mathscr{Y}) = \inf\{| x - y | \mid x \in \mathscr{X}, \quad y \in \mathscr{Y} |\}$$

be the Euclidean distance between the sets $\mathscr{X}$ and $\mathscr{Y}$. Indifference curves are *Lipschitz related* if for any x there is a neighborhood $\mathscr{N}$ of x and a $K > 0$ such that for all $\bar{x} \in \mathscr{N}$,

$$| y(p, x) - y(p, \bar{x})| \leqslant K\delta(\mathscr{I}(x), \mathscr{I}(\bar{x}))$$

for all $p \in \mathscr{P}$. To see that the Lipschitz condition of y in x implies that indifference curves are Lipschitz related, we observe that for all $z \in \mathscr{I}(x)$, $\bar{z} \in \mathscr{I}(\bar{x})$, we have

$$| y(p, x) - y(p, \bar{x})| = | y(p, z) - y(p, \bar{z})| \leqslant K | z - \bar{z} |.$$

Therefore

$$| y(p, x) - y(p, \bar{x})| \leqslant \inf K | z - \bar{z} |.$$

In the proof of Theorem 34, we will see that Lipschitz related indifference curves imply a locally uniform Lipschitz condition on the compensated demand function, and therefore the two concepts are equivalent.

The basic idea in Theorem 34 is as follows. A change in demand is the sum of an income term and a substitution term. The income term is itself a product of two terms, one of which can be shown to be locally Lipschitz and the other of which is assumed to be locally Lipschitz. The substitution term is seen to be the derivative of the compensation function and therefor it is pointwise Lipschitz for almost all prices along the surface of the upper contour sets. Since the surfaces of the upper contour sets form $(n - 1)$-dimensional subspaces of Euclidean n-space, it follows that the points at which the substitution term is pointwise Lipschitz are of full measure. That is to say, by *Fubini's theorem* the converse set is of measure zero, since its intersection with all the $(n - 1)$-dimensional indifference surfaces is of measure zero. Taking the income terms and substitution term together, demand is pointwise Lipschitz as the sum of two pointwise Lipschitz functions.

34 Theorem *Suppose that either indifference surfaces are Lipschitz related or preferences are represented by concave utility, preferences are regular and locally unsaturated, and demand is continuous and satisfies a uniform local Lipschitz condition in income in a locale of prices and income in an open cone of prices $\mathscr{P} \subset \Omega$. Then for almost all prices in $\mathscr{P}$, demand is differentiable and $\partial d / \partial p = A(p) - (\partial d / \partial \theta) d'$ where $A(p)$ is the negative semidefinite substitution matrix.*

In view of the foregoing discussion of homothetic preferences, Theorem 34 implies Theorem 29.

Proof We first show how the prices associated with indifference curves can be straightened out to allow application of Fubini's theorem. We consider a neighborhood $\mathscr{N}$ of p. Choose $\hat{p} = pk$ such that $\hat{p}\hat{p} = 1$. Define $x\lambda = d(\lambda\hat{p})$, $\lambda > 0$. Let $\lambda(p) = \theta/p\hat{p}$ and $\mathscr{S}_\lambda = \{p \mid \lambda p\hat{p} = \theta\}$.
   Let

$$f(p) = p \, \frac{\theta}{M(p, \, x_{\lambda(p)})} \, .$$

Then $M(f(p), x_{\lambda(p)}) = \theta$, so that $f(p)$ is the price proportional to p that gives a demand in $\mathscr{I}(x_{\lambda(p)})$. Since $\lambda(p) = \lambda$ on $\mathscr{S}_\lambda$, f maps $\mathscr{S}_\lambda$ onto the prices associated with $\mathscr{I}(x_\lambda)$.
   We know from Corollary 28 that the derivative of the substitution term exists for almost all p in $\mathscr{S}_\lambda$, since each such p is associated under f with points in the same indifference curve. By Fubini's theorem, the set $\mathscr{Q}$ for which the substitution term is not differentiable is of measure zero. If only f satisfies condition (N), we will have that $\mathscr{P}_0 = f(\mathscr{Q})$

is a set of measure zero. To show this, we need that f is pointwise Lipschitz.

First, we must show that M is uniformly locally Lipschitz in x. Since M is concave on $\mathscr{S}_\lambda$, it is well known that $f(p)$ is locally Lipschitz on $\mathscr{S}_\lambda$. Also we show M uniformly locally Lipschitz in λ.

For the case where preferences are representable by a concave utility function, we consider that $M(p, x)$ is the maximum of $-py$ subject to $u(y) \geqslant u(x)$. As in Karlin [1959, p. 201] or Problem B of Chapter 2 of the companion volume, there is a $\lambda > 0$ such that $-M(p, x)$ is the unconstrained maximum with respect to x of the Lagrangian form $L(p, y, x, \lambda) = -py + \lambda(u(y) - u(x))$ and the minimum of L with respect to λ. (The necessary Slater condition is easily verified.) Also, we note on a compact subset of the domain of the commodity space, the concave utility function u satisfies a Lipschitz condition. We use this to show a Lipschitz condition on $M(p, x)$ related to u that will therefore be independent of p. Let λ be the Lagrangian multiplier for $M(p, x)$ and $\bar\lambda$ be the one for $M(p, \bar{x})$. Let $y = y(p, x)$, $\bar{y} = y(p, \bar{x})$. Without loss of generality, let $M(p, \bar{x}) \leqslant M(p, x)$. Then

$$0 \leqslant |M(p, x) - M(p, \bar{x})| = M(p, x) - M(p, \bar{x})$$

$$= -L(p, y, x, \lambda) + L(p, \bar{y}, \bar{x}, \lambda) \quad \text{(by } u(y) = u(x) \text{ and } u(\bar{y}) = u(\bar{x}))$$

$$\leqslant -L(p, y, x, \lambda) + L(p, \bar{y}, \bar{x}, \bar\lambda) \quad \text{(minimization with respect to } \lambda\text{)}.$$

$$\leqslant -L(p, \bar{y}, x, \lambda) + L(p, \bar{y}, \bar{x}, \bar\lambda) \quad \text{(maximization with respect to } y\text{)}$$

$$= -p\bar{y} + \lambda(u(\bar{y}) - u(x)) + p\bar{y} - \lambda(u(\bar{y}) - u(\bar{x}))$$

$$= \lambda(u(\bar{x}) - u(x))$$

$$= \lambda|u(\bar{x}) - u(x)|$$

$$\leqslant \lambda K|\bar{x} - x|.$$

Therefore, the Lipschitz constant is λK, where K is the Lipschitz constant for u.

If we can show that the admissible $\lambda(p)$ are bounded, then the Lipschitz constant will be bounded from infinity and a uniform Lipschitz condition will follow immediately. By maximization of L with respect to y,

$$-py + \lambda(u(y) - u(x)) \geqslant -p\hat{y} + \lambda(u(\hat{y}) - u(x))$$

or

$$-p(y - \hat{y}) \geqslant -\lambda(u(y) - u(\hat{y}))$$

for all admissible $\hat{y}$. Choose $u(\hat{y}) > u(y)$. By continuity of u in the interior of its domain, as $y \to \bar{y}$, $p \to \bar{p}$, for some $\varepsilon > 0$ we can choose $u(\hat{y}) > u(y) + \varepsilon$ for all y. Also, if $\lambda \to \infty$, then $-\lambda(u(y) - u(\hat{y})) \to \infty$ and $-p(y - \hat{y}) \to \infty$. This contradicts $-p(y - \hat{y}) \to -\bar{p}(\bar{y} - y)$, so that λ must be bounded.

This completes our proof of the uniform, local Lipschitz condition of M in x whenever utility is concave.

Alternatively, we consider the Lipschitz condition on indifference surfaces. Here we have

$$
\begin{aligned}
| M(p, x_\lambda) - M(p, x_{\bar{\lambda}})| &= | py(p, x_\lambda) - py(p, x_{\bar{\lambda}})| \\
&\leqslant | p | | y(p, x_\lambda) - y(p, x_{\bar{\lambda}})| \\
&\leqslant | p | K\delta(I(x_\lambda), I(x_{\bar{\lambda}}))| \\
&\leqslant | p | K | x_\lambda - \bar{x}_{\bar{\lambda}} |.
\end{aligned}
$$

The uniform Lipschitz constant is then $L = \sup | p | K$.

Now we can show that f is pointwise Lipschitz. For $\bar{p}$ near p

$$
|f(p) - f(\bar{p})| \leqslant \left| f(p) - f\left(\frac{p\hat{p}}{\bar{p}\hat{p}} p\right)\right| + \left| f\left(\frac{p\hat{p}}{\bar{p}\hat{p}} \bar{p}\right) - f(\bar{p})\right|
$$

$$
\leqslant K_\lambda \left| p - \frac{p\hat{p}}{\bar{p}\hat{p}} \bar{p}\right| + L \left| \frac{p\hat{p}}{\bar{p}\hat{p}} - 1\right|
$$

(Lipschitz conditions in $f(p)$, $M(p, x_\lambda)$ in x, and x_λ in λ).

$$
\leqslant K_\lambda | p - \bar{p} | + (K_\lambda + L)M| p - \bar{p} |
$$

$$
\left(\text{Lipschitz condition for } 1 - \frac{p\hat{p}}{\bar{p}\hat{p}}\right)
$$

$$
= (K_\lambda + (K_\lambda + L)M) | p - \bar{p} |.
$$

Therefore, f is pointwise Lipschitz at p. Therefore f satisfies condition (N) on $\mathscr{P}$ and f^{-1} takes measurable sets into measurable sets.

As in the proof of Theorem 29, $y(p)$ is differentiable almost everywhere and the derivative of $M_x(p)$ is $y(p)$ whenever it exists (Theorem 27(iii)), which is almost everywhere.

For $\bar{p}$ near p,

$$
\frac{d(p) - d(\bar{p})}{| p - \bar{p} |} = \frac{y(p) - y(\bar{p})}{| p - \bar{p} |} + \frac{y(\bar{p}) - d(\bar{p})}{M(\bar{p}, x) - \theta} \frac{M(\bar{p}, x) - \theta}{| p - \bar{p} |},
$$

every term of which is bounded for p giving demand in $\mathscr{I}(x)$.) except for rays of prices of measure zero where $y(p)$ is not differentiable. The set $\mathscr{P}_0$ of prices p, at which $|\Delta d|/|\Delta p|$ is unbounded for $\bar{p}$ near p, is measurable and $\mathscr{Q} = f^{-1}(\mathscr{P}_0)$ is measurable. The exceptional rays intersect $\mathscr{S}_y$ in a set of $n - 1$ measure zero, that is, $\mathscr{P}_0$ has measure zero (Fubini's theorem). Therefore, $f(\mathscr{Q}) = \mathscr{P}_0$ is measure zero (Riesz–Sz.- Nagy [1955, p. 84]). For almost all p in $\mathscr{P}$, $\lim |\Delta d|/|\Delta p|$ is not infinite. By Stepanoff's theorem (Federer [1969, p. 218]), d is differentiable almost everywhere.

As in the conclusion of the proof of Theorem 29, we have the derivative of d in income and M in p whenever d is differentiable in p. The Slutsky equation follows.   q.e.d.

5

Macrostatics

Within the framework of any system the relationships between variables are strictly those of mutual interdependence. It is sterile and misleading to speak of one variable as causing or determining another. Once the conditions of equilibrium are imposed, all variables are simultaneously determined. Indeed, from the standpoint of comparative statics equilibrium is not something which is attained; it is something which, if attained, displays certain properties.

Paul Samuelson
in FOUNDATION OF ECONOMIC ANALYSIS, 1947

1. The Correspondence Principle

Much of economic analysis as applied to empirical studies is macro-comparative statics, whereby assertions are made about the effects of a change in one or more economic variables on the equilibrium values of other economic variables. Given the breadth of the subject, we cannot hope to cover every relevant principle. Instead, we study that part of macrostatics which is most thoroughly developed.

Three main topics are considered in this chapter. First, there is a presumption that we observe a stable equilibrium. In this case certain microproperties must follow. The study of the static implications of stable equilibrium constitutes the correspondence principle, which is the subject of this section.

Second, there are laws governing the response of supplies of goods to changes in prices of goods and quantities of factors of production. These laws, many of which traditionally have been studied only in the theory of international trade, are outlined in Sections 3–5. Typical results that can be established to a high level of generality are that increasing the price of a good increases its supply, and to increase only its supply, we must increase its price. Under somewhat restrictive conditions, changes in factor endowments do not change factor prices.

Third, in Sections 6–8 we study the effect on prices of changes in supplies or demands. A major theorem studied is that an increase in the demand for a good increases its price. Although the theorem is one of the cornerstones of applied economics, it is surprising how restrictive are the assumptions required for a proof. Even harder to get are results, such as that the prices of other substitutable goods rise along with the price of the good in greater demand. The theory in these later sections will be applied in Chapter 7 to show dynamic stability of equilibrium.

There is a question as to the best way to approach statics. Some formulate the microfoundations, such as profit maximization or consumer choice, and then prove theorems about the way the whole system works. Others postulate the macrofoundations, such as stability and equilibrium of the system. In this section, we start with macroproperties and prove microtheorems from which other macrotheorems will follow. This will be seen to yield only weak results. To obtain more powerful theorems, the rest of the chapter moves from microproperties to macrotheorems.

Perhaps the most ambitious effort to use macroanalysis to obtain microtheorems was the correspondence principle proposed by Samuelson [1947]. According to this principle, we consider the implications of the stability of a dynamic economic system. The idea is that any observed equilibrium is highly likely to have evolved from a disequilibrium state and hence represents a limiting equilibrium. Furthermore, there will be ample opportunity for more disturbance to nearby disequilibrium states, so that it must be the limit point of all nearby states. We consider the Walrasian price adjustment system

$$\frac{dp_i}{dt} = d_{ii}\mathscr{E}_i(p), \qquad d_{ii} > 0,$$

where d_{ii} is the rate of adjustment. In vector terms,

$$\frac{dp}{dt} = D\mathscr{E}(p);$$

D is a diagonal matrix. Note that $0 = \mathscr{E}(p)$ is the equilibrium condition. For a change in excess demand to $\mathscr{E}(p) + \varepsilon e(p)$, $0 \leqslant \varepsilon \leqslant 1$ is the intensity of the change. Whenever $\partial(\mathscr{E} + \varepsilon e)/\partial p$ is nonsingular, we have

$$\frac{\partial \mathscr{E} + \varepsilon e}{\partial p} \frac{dp}{d\varepsilon} + e(p) = 0 \qquad \text{or} \qquad \frac{dp}{d\varepsilon} = -\left(\frac{\partial \mathscr{E} + \varepsilon e}{\partial p}\right)^{-1} e(p).$$

Therefore, comparative of prices from quality changes depend on the study of the inverse matrix of $\partial \mathscr{E} + \varepsilon e/\partial p$.

Ordinarily, a proportional increase in *all* prices leaves demand unchanged, and it is easy to see from Euler's theorem that $(\partial \mathscr{E}/\partial p)$ $p = 0$. Therefore, we can expect $\partial \mathscr{E}/\partial p$ to have an inverse only if we restrict ourselves to one less than the totality of goods. From the outset, one good is denoted the *numéraire* and its price must be constant. The system now reads

$$\frac{dp_0}{dt} = 0, \qquad \frac{dp_i}{dt} = d_{ii}\mathscr{E}_i(p), \qquad i > 0, \quad d_{ii} > 0.$$

Much more about this system will be recorded in Chapters 7 and 8. For present purposes, however, we consider only an equilibrium $\bar{p}$ that is *locally stable*, that is, for initial $p(0) = p$ near to $\bar{p}$, the solution of the differential equation system from p tends to $\bar{p}$. The correspondence principle consists of assuming information about $\bar{p}$, namely, that it is locally stable, and then deducing the signs of $\partial \mathscr{E}_i/\partial p_j$ and of $((\partial \mathscr{E}/\partial p)^{-1})_{ij}$.

First, we deal with the n-dimensional case, where little information is forthcoming. Then we study the two-dimensional case, where there are three goods, one of which is the *numéraire*. There emerges a classification of the signs of $\partial \mathscr{E}_i/\partial p_j$ and consequent theorems about the influence of changes in excess demand on prices. Therefore, macro-information yields microtheorems, which give still other macrotheorems. This case shows the most that can be expected from the correspondence principle.

To begin with, we see that dynamic stability is a matter of the signs of the real parts of the roots of $\partial \mathscr{E}/\partial p$ at equilibrium.

1 Lemma *The dynamic system $dp/dt = D\mathscr{E}(p)$ is locally stable at $\bar{p}$ if (only if) $D \, \partial \mathscr{E}/\partial \bar{p}$ has all roots with negative (nonpositive) real parts* (Coddington and Levinson [1955]).

Often the analysis of D is lacking, so that stability is considered for different D. If for all positive diagonals D, the differential equation system is locally stable at $\bar{p}$, then $\bar{p}$ is *always (locally) stable*. (It is also said that $\bar{p}$ is P-stable.) If for some positive diagonal D, $\bar{p}$ is locally stable, then $\bar{p}$ is *sometimes (locally) stable*.

One illustration of the correspondence principle is the case in which $\partial \mathscr{E}_i / \partial p_j \geqslant 0$, $i \neq j$, the so-called *weak gross substitution* of excess demand. Here we conclude that always stable and sometimes stable are equivalent. Also, an increase in the demand for a good i (at the expense of the *numéraire*) increases the price of good j.

2 Theorem *If $\partial \mathscr{E}_i / \partial p_j \geqslant 0$, $i \neq j$, and $(\partial \mathscr{E}_i / \partial p_j)^{-1}$ exists, then $\bar{p}$ is always stable if and only if it is sometimes stable if and only if $(\partial \mathscr{E} / \partial p)^{-1}$ is non-positive and nonsingular. If $(\partial \mathscr{E} / \partial \bar{p})$ is also indecomposable, then $\bar{p}$ is stable if and only if $(\partial \mathscr{E} / \partial \bar{p})^{-1}$ is strictly positive.*

Proof The infinite case appears in Problem K of Chapter 10 of the companion volume. Every such matrix $D \, \partial \mathscr{E} / \partial \bar{p}$ can be represented as

$$c(A - I) \quad \text{for} \quad c = \max d_{ii} \, \partial \mathscr{E}_i / \partial \bar{p}_i > 0, \quad A \geqslant 0.$$

The Frobenius theorem gives that a nonnegative matrix has a nonnegative characteristic vector x, with a real root of largest real part (Gantmacher [1959, Volume II, pp. 53–62] and Problem K of Chapter 10 of the companion volume).

Evidently, $x(A - I) = (\lambda - 1)x$ or since $(\lambda - 1) < 0$, we have $xA \ll x$, as in the case of Theorem 15, Chapter 4 of the companion volume,

$$c(A - I)^{-1} = -\frac{1}{c}(I + A + A^2 + \cdots).$$

Therefore, $(\partial \mathscr{E} / \partial \bar{p})^{-1} = (D \, \partial \mathscr{E} / \partial p)^{-1} D$ has the same signs as $(D \, \partial \mathscr{E} / \partial \bar{p})^{-1}$.

On the other hand, if $(\partial \mathscr{E} / \partial \bar{p})^{-1}$ is nonnegative, then so is $(D \, \partial \mathscr{E} / \partial \bar{p})^{-1}$, and there is nonnegative characteristic vector x for which

$$\left(D \frac{\partial \mathscr{E}}{\partial \bar{p}}\right)^{-1} x = \lambda x, \quad \lambda \text{ real and negative}$$

$$\frac{1}{\lambda} x = \left(D \frac{\partial \mathscr{E}}{\partial \bar{p}}\right) x \quad \text{or} \quad \frac{1}{\lambda} x = c(A - I)x \quad \text{or} \quad 0 \geqslant (A - I)x.$$

Applying Lemma 16 of Chapter 4 of the companion volume, we find that the roots of $(A - I)$ are negative in real part and hence so are those of $D \, \partial \mathscr{E} / \partial \bar{p}$. q.e.d.

Note that in Theorem 2 microinformation, namely, that an increase in the ith price increases the excess demand for the jth good, is combined with macroinformation, namely, stability, to obtain comparative statics theorems. The argument of Samuelson was that only stable equilibria are observed and therefore the use of the macroinformation is valid.

In the particular instance of Theorem 2, the comparative statics results can be obtained without the macroassumptions (by using Walras' law or the no-money illusion instead). The correspondence principle is not especially powerful here, and therefore its advocates have turned to other techniques. To consider the most powerful results available and then special cases, some definitions are needed. A matrix A is *negative definite* if $xAx < 0$ for all x and if A is symmetric. If only $xAx < 0$, then A is *negative quasi definite*. A is *positive (quasi) definite* if $-A$ is *negative (quasi) definite*. We now list three criteria for stability.

3 Lemma (Lyapunov)   *A has roots with negative real parts if and only if there is a positive definite matrix S such that SA is negative quasi definite* (Gantmacher [1959] Volume II, p. 187).

4 Lemma   *Let λ_i be roots of A. Then*

(i) $\sum \lambda_i = \sum a_{ii}$,
(ii) $\prod \lambda_i = \det A$ (Gantmacher [1959], Volume I, pp. 72–74).

Let $A_{\mathcal{I}}$ be the $(a_{ij} \mid i, j \in \mathcal{I})$. Let $\Delta_i = \sum_{\mathcal{I} \subset \{1\} \cup \dots \cup \{n\}},\ \mathcal{I}$ has i members $\det A_{\mathcal{I}}$, and $k_i = \Delta_i(-1)^i$.

5 Lemma (Routh-Hurwicz)   *A has roots with negative real parts if and only if*

(i) $k_i > 0$,

(ii) $\begin{vmatrix} k_1 & k_3 \\ 1 & k_2 \end{vmatrix} > 0,\quad \begin{vmatrix} k_1 & k_3 & k_5 \\ 1 & k_2 & k_4 \\ 0 & k_1 & k_3 \end{vmatrix} > 0,\dots,\ \begin{vmatrix} k_1 & k_3 & \cdots & 0 \\ 1 & k_2 & \cdots & 0 \\ 0 & k_1 & \cdots & 0 \\ \vdots & & & \vdots \\ 0 & & \cdots & k_n \end{vmatrix} > 0$

(Gantmacher [1959], Volume II, pp. 190–195).

If A has roots with negative real parts, then so does A^{-1}

$$(xA = \lambda x \quad \text{implies} \quad x\frac{1}{\lambda} = A^{-1}x)$$

and

$$\lambda = \rho + i\mu \qquad \text{implies} \qquad \frac{1}{\lambda} = \frac{1}{\rho + i\mu} = \frac{\rho - i\mu}{\rho^2 + \mu^2} = \frac{\rho}{\rho^2 + \mu^2} - \frac{i\mu}{\rho^2 + \mu^2} \Big) \, .$$

The theorem following lists some implications of always stability.

6 Theorem *If p is always stable, then*

$$\left(\frac{\partial \mathscr{E}}{\partial p} \right)^{-1}_{ii} \leqslant 0 \qquad \text{for all } i$$

and

$$\left(\frac{\partial \mathscr{E}}{\partial p} \right)^{-1}_{ii} < 0 \qquad \text{for some } i,$$

If p is only sometimes stable, then

$$\left(\frac{\partial \mathscr{E}}{\partial p} \right)^{-1}_{ii} < 0 \qquad \text{for some } i.$$

Proof   Apply Lemma 5, part (i).   q.e.d.

There is a sense in which Theorem 6 is the best general result possible. Hence, in general the correspondence principle does not appear to be very powerful. On the other hand, if we make some reasonable, yet undiscovered, restrictions that are less strong than gross substitutability then better results may be forthcoming.

In two dimensions, we here present a better theory. Lemma 5 refers to roots with negative real parts if and only if

(i) $\lambda_1 + \lambda_2 = a_{11} + a_{22}$,
(ii) $\lambda_1\lambda_2 = \det A = a_{11}a_{22} - a_{21}a_{12}$.

7 Lemma *A has roots with negative real parts for some positive diagonal D if and only if*

(i) $a_{11} + a_{22} < 0$,
(ii) $\det A > 0$.

Proof   *Necessity*

$$\lambda_j = \rho_j + \mu_j i, \rho_j, \mu_j \text{ real}, \quad j = 1, 2,$$

and

$$\mu_1 = -\mu_2 \, .$$

Therefore, $\lambda_1 + \lambda_2$ is negative for roots with negative real parts, and

$$a_{11} + a_{22} < 0.$$

Also,

$$\lambda_1\lambda_2 = \rho_1\rho_2 + \mu_1^2,$$

which is positive if both ρ_1 and ρ_2 are negative. Therefore $\det A > 0$.

Sufficiency Evidently, one of the real parts is negative. If there are complex roots, the other is automatically negative in real part, otherwise

$$\det A = \lambda_1\lambda_2 > 0,$$

only if the other root is negative.   q.e.d.

A criterion for sometimes stability is as follows.

8 Corollary *DA has roots with negative real parts for some positive diagonal D if and only if*

(i) $a_{ii} < 0$ *for some i,*
(ii) $\det A > 0$.

Proof $\det DA = \det D \det A$ is positive if and only if $\det A > 0$.

If $a_{ii} < 0$, then for d_{ii} sufficiently large relative to a_{jj}, we have $d_{ii}a_{ii} + d_{jj}a_{jj} < 0$.

Apply the previous lemma to DA. Also, if DA has roots with negative real parts, then

$$d_{11}a_{11} + d_{22}a_{22} < 0,$$

so that $a_{ii} < 0$ for at least one i.   q.e.d.

Recall that a *Giffen good* is one for which $a_{ii} > 0$. Corollary 9 applies to an always stable equilibrium.

9 Corollary *DA has roots with negative real parts for all positive diagonals D if and only if*

(i) $a_{11} \leqslant 0$, $a_{22} \leqslant 0$, $a_{11} + a_{22} < 0$,
(ii) $\det A > 0$.

Hence, if there are no Giffen goods, sometimes stable implies always stable.

Proof Observe that if $a_{ii} > 0$, then for d_{ii} large, $a_{11}d_{11} + a_{22}d_{22} > 0$, while $\det DA = \det D \det A > 0$, so that DA has at least one root with positive real parts. On the other hand, $a_{11}d_{11} + a_{22}d_{22} < 0$ for all $d_{ii} > 0$ whenever $a_{ii} \leqslant 0$ and $a_{11} + a_{22} < 0$. It follows that both roots have negative real parts.

The analysis in Corollary 9 can be further refined.

10 Theorem *DA has roots with negative real parts for all positive diagonals D if and only if*

(i) $a_{ii} \leqslant 0$, $a_{22} \leqslant 0$, $a_{11} + a_{22} < 0$, and
(ii) *either* (a) $a_{12}a_{21} < 0$ *or*
(b) *there are $k_1 > 0$, $k_2 = 1/k_1$ for which $k_1 | a_{11} | > | a_{12} |$, $k_2 | a_{22} | > | a_{21} |$.*

For example, condition (ii)b can be modified by setting $k_i = p_i/p_j$, and we obtain $| a_{ii} | p_i > | a_{ij} | p_j$. At equilibrium, elasticity of excess demand is undefined (since $\mathscr{E}_i$ is zero) but nearby elasticity is defined, and by continuity of partial derivatives, (ii)b modified gives that it is greater for the own price than for the other.

More generally, condition (ii)b is McKenzie's [1960a] dominant diagonal, whereas (ii)a is the qualitative theory that one direction of interrelationship is complementary whereas the other is substitutable (Lancaster [1962], Gorman [1964], and Quirk and Ruppert [1965]). The analysis of symmetric A due to Hicks [1938] is an example of economic assumptions (homothetic preferences) leading to dominant diagonal, as is the gross substitutability of excess demand analyzed by Arrow and Hurwicz [1958].

Proof Case (a) is immediate. For case (b),

$$a_{12}a_{21} \geqslant 0, \qquad k_i | a_{ii} | > | a_{ij} |,$$

then

$$| a_{ii} | | a_{jj} | > | a_{ij} | | a_{ji} | \qquad \text{or} \qquad \det A = | a_{ii}a_{jj} | - | a_{ij}a_{ji} | > 0.$$

Evidently, if $\det A > 0$ and $a_{12}a_{21} > 0$, we can choose $\varepsilon > 0$ so that $(| a_{ii} | | a_{jj} |/| a_{ij} | | a_{ji} |)(1 - \varepsilon) > 1$. Set $(| a_{jj} |/| a_{ji} |)(1 - \varepsilon) = k_i$, $k_j = 1/k_i$ to obtain (ii)b from

$$| a_{ii} | | a_{jj} | > | a_{ij} | | a_{ji} | . \qquad \text{q.e.d.}$$

For the sometimes stable equilibrium we must add one possibility to the list in Theorem 10, namely, the case in which there is a Giffen good.

11 Theorem *DA has negative roots for some positive diagonal D if and only if either DA has negative roots for all positive diagonals D or*

(i) $a_{12}a_{21} < 0$, *and*
(ii) *there are* $k_1 > 0$, $k_2 = 1/k_1$ *for* *which* $k_1 | a_{11} | < | a_{12} |$, $k_2 | a_{11} | < | a_{21} |$.[1]

In the case of a Giffen good, $a_{jj} > 0$ for some j, we must have one complementarity and one substitutability relationship.

Proof If $a_{jj} > 0$, then $a_{ii}a_{jj} < 0$, so that $\det A < 0$ if and only if

(i) $a_{ij}a_{ji} < 0$,
(ii) $| a_{ij} | | a_{ji} | > | a_{ii} | | a_{jj} |$.

Evidently, if $k_i | a_{ii} | < | a_{ij} |$, (ii) is satisfied. If (ii) is satisfied, then set $k_i = | a_{jj} |/| a_{ij} | (1 - \varepsilon)$ as in the proof of Theorem 10.   q.e.d.

Since

$$\frac{d\bar{p}}{d\epsilon} = -\left\{\frac{\partial \mathscr{E} + \epsilon e}{\partial \bar{p}}\right\} e(\bar{p}),$$

and in two dimensions,

$$A^{-1} = \frac{1}{\det A} \begin{bmatrix} a_{22} & -a_{12} \\ -a_{21} & a_{11} \end{bmatrix},$$

we have

$$\frac{d\bar{p}_i}{d\epsilon} = \frac{a_{jj}e_i - a_{ij}e_j}{\det A}.$$

Since the sign pattern of $a_{,j}$, $i \neq j$, is not determined, we can speak only of the effects on the own good.

12 Corollary *If an equilibrium is always stable, then an increase in the ith excess demand never reduces by a large amount the equilibrium price*

---

[1] Actually, a theorem of Olech [1963] shows that global stability is ensured if the conditions hold for all prices and if also either $| a_{11}a_{22} | \neq 0$ for all prices or $| a_{12}a_{21} | \neq 0$ for all prices. For example, equilibrium is always globally stable if

(i) both goods are always normal, and
(ii) at any given price, either there are dominant diagonals or there are both complementarity and substitutability relationships.

for i.[2] If DA has roots with negative real parts, for at least one commodity i, there is an increase in the equilibrium price for i.

13 Corollary   *If an equilibrium is sometimes but not always stable, there is one commodity whose equilibrium price will increase when its excess demand is increased and another whose equilibrium price will decrease when its excess demand is increased. If the increase in the excess demand for one commodity leads to an increase in the equilibrium price of the other, then an increase in the excess demand for the other would lead to a decrease in the equilibrium price of the one.*

Oddly enough, the case that is only sometimes stable leads to the best comparative statics results.

Note that in the foregoing analysis no allowance has been made for Walras' law or zero homogeneity. Recent unpublished research of Sonnenschein indicates that these laws of markets are compatible with virtually any continuous function of two variables acting as excess demands for those two variables as prices plus a third price for a *numériare*. Therefore, it seems appropriate to assume that $\mathscr{E}(p)$ can be any continuous (or differentiable) function. If such an assumption is warranted, the results above are the best that can be obtained.

Incidentally, the market laws have been used with substantive conclusions only for the gross substitutability case in which an increase in the price of one commodity leads to an increase in the demand for the others, including the *numériare*. As was seen in Chapter 10 of the companion volume, there is nothing natural about gross substitutability in the general equilibrium framework.

PROBLEM

A. Keynesian System I

The work of Keynes [1936] is often interpreted as a four-commodity model with money, bonds, labor, and goods (Patinkin [1956]). The price of money and labor are assumed fixed. "Equilibrium" occurs whenever the other markets are in equilibrium. Although in the short run, the supply of goods does not depend on the rate of interest (equals the reciprocal of the price of bonds), their demand does; and similarly, the demand for bonds depends on the (current) price of goods. Let output

---

[2] Indeed, $\lim[x_i(\epsilon) - x_i(0)]/\epsilon \geqslant 0$ as $\epsilon \to 0$.

be a function of labor input (other factors fixed), and let firms maximize current profits. Suppose high interest rates discourage demand for goods.

(i) When is "equilibrium" sometimes stable?

(ii) If "equilibrium" is always stable, what can be said about the effect of an increase in government spending or purchase of bonds on the demand of labor?

(iii) Suppose "equilibrium" were only sometimes stable; what would happen to unemployment if the government were only to buy bonds? To interest rates if the government were to buy goods?

(iv) If in (iii) the Giffen effect was attributed to goods, what would happen to employment as the government bought goods and bonds? What if the Giffin good were bonds and the government bought goods with the proceeds of sales of bonds?

2. A Small Country in International Trade

In this section we show the existence of nonnegative wages of factors and prices of goods. Continuity and convexity properties are proved for wages and outputs resulting from factor supplies and goods prices and for factor quantities and prices associated with given future wages and outputs of goods. It is shown that factor wages are dependent only on goods prices and factor endowments (Theorem 18). Under more restrictive conditions, given factor endowments, wages are 1–1 in goods prices (Theorem 19). The rest of the section proves mathematical conditions such as directional density of production and the invertibility of the factor utilization matrix (to be defined). All these theorems form a basis from which other statical theorems are proved in Sections 3 and 4.

The statics of supply are especially appropriate for a small country in international trade, since there the price of consumer goods is taken as a given. As an orientation it is appropriate to take this as one possible interpretation of what follows. We emphasize, however, that any comparative statics analysis should have a supply theory identical with that in international trade theory, such as presented by Rader [1968a].

Consider a country that produces n goods from m factors. The n goods are subject to the international price system

$$p = (p_1, ..., p_n)$$

and a home wage system

$$w = (w_1, ..., w_m).$$

Normally, w is determined by home conditions, namely, the demand and supply for factors. These factors are denoted y,

$$y = (y_1, ..., y_n),$$

whose supply is assumed to be invariant to changes in prices or wages.

Production is assumed to proceed according to the laws stated in the *production possibility set* $\mathscr{Y}$, whose elements are *input–output vectors* (y, x) where

$$x = (x_1, ..., x_n)$$

gives quantities of goods q producible from the factors

$$y = (y_1, ..., y_m).$$

Therefore, $\mathscr{Y}$ is representable in Euclidean $(n + m)$-space. If each industry is independent, then each industry has a production possibility set $\mathscr{Y}_i$ in Euclidean $(m + n)$-space. Presumably, for (y^i, x^i) in $\mathscr{Y}_i$, the output of i is positive,

$$x^i_i > 0,$$

whereas the other goods are at most used as intermediate products,

$$x^i_j \leqslant 0.$$

The community production possibility set is then

$$\mathscr{Y} = \sum_{i=1}^{n} \mathscr{Y}_i.$$

The industry takes the price of goods and the wage of factors as given, whereas from the social viewpoint, the price of goods and the quantity of factors are given.

It is assumed that each industry, and therefore the community, maximizes profits, which are computed to be the value of output minus the cost of factors:

$$px - wy = \sum_{i=1}^{n} p_i x_i - \sum_{j=1}^{m} -w_j y_j.$$

The relationship between the profits of subparts and the whole system is that the whole system maximizes profits if and only if each subpart does. This is the additivity theorem of Chapter 1 and applies whenever the subparts operate independently of each other. In summary:

1. p is determined in the international market.
2. Given w and p, (y, x) is chosen from $\mathscr{Y}$ in order to maximize the profits.
3. Consequently, w must be such that a y is chosen that is equal to the actual factor supplies.
4. Modification in this structure may be made by the state by adopting tariff or tax policies, thereby changing the effective home price system to p. However, internal changes are assumed to affect in no way the international market beyond the country's boundaries. Therefore, the international price at which the country can sell remains fixed.

The main theorems already relating to the foregoing system appear in Chapters 1 and 2. In many cases, m and/or n may be countable infinity; exceptions to this are specified as $m < \infty$ or $n < \infty$.

From the viewpoint of the theory of international trade, the important dichotomy is not (y, x) on the one hand and (w, p) on the other, as studied in Chapter 1, Section 10. Rather, it is that between the given (y, p) and the derived quantities (w, x). Therefore, we must analyze the wage–output correspondence $\eta(y, p)$ and its inverse, the input–price correspondence

$$\eta^{-1}(w, x) = \{(y, p) \mid (w, x) \in \eta(y, p)\}.$$

If it can be shown that the domain of η covers virtually all international price systems and factor endownments, then we can be assured that the assumption that the country does not influence the international price system is not nonsense.

14 Theorem

(i)   *If $\mathscr{Y}$ does not allow arbitrarily large output from given input y,*
(ii) *$\mathscr{Y}$ is closed and convex,*
(iii) *$\mathscr{Y}$ allows some degree of free disposal on its upper boundary, so that it has a nonempty interior,*

then for every nonnegative, nonzero p and y, y variable in any direction, $\eta(p, y)$ is nonempty, $w \neq 0$. If factors are not negatively productive, then

$$w > 0.$$

If factors are productive and if p_i is positive for every good, then w_j is positive for every factor j.

This theorem gives the set of outputs and factor prices observable in a small country. Said differently, it specifies the domain of the supply correspondence and deduces that its range is restricted to nonnegative factor prices.

Proof   Consider the set

$$\hat{\mathcal{Y}} = \{(y, px) \mid (y, x) \text{ is in } \mathcal{Y}\}.$$

It is possible to choose (y, px) in the boundary of $\hat{\mathcal{Y}}$ if px has an upper bound, and if y is closed so that the least upper bound is taken. The closedness of $\hat{\mathcal{Y}}$ and the boundedness of px follow whenever $\mathcal{Y}$ is closed and the set of x's producible from y are bounded from above.

If $\mathcal{Y}$ is convex, then so is $\hat{\mathcal{Y}}$, and therefore there exists $(-w, k)$ such that

$$(-\bar{w}, k)(y, px) = -\bar{w} + kpx \geqslant -\overline{wy} + kp\bar{x}$$

for all other $(\bar{y}, p\bar{x})$ in $\mathcal{Y}$. This is simply the Minkowski theorem, which says that every point on the boundary of a convex set can be separated from the convex set by a bounding hyperplane.

If $k = 0$, then a small change in x will give $\bar{x}$ for which $\bar{w}x$ is larger. This gives a higher profit, which is impossible. Therefore $k \neq 0$. Also, if $k < 0$ and if there is the slightest degree of free disposal, so that px can be reduced to $p\bar{x}$ with changing y, $px > p\bar{x}$, then

$$-wy + kpx < -wy + kp\bar{x},$$

which cannot be. Therefore $k > 0$, and

$$-(w/k)y + px \geqslant -(\bar{w}/k)\bar{y} + p\bar{x}$$

for all $(\bar{y}, \bar{x})$ in $\mathcal{Y}$.

Let $w = \bar{w}/k$ be the wage vector; w is nonnegative whenever all factors are not unproductive and p is nonnegative, since otherwise an increase in y_j for which $w_j > 0$ would not decrease px and therefore would increase profits. If p is positive in every component, an increase in y_j for $w_j = 0$ would actually increase px whenever y is productive and would not decrease wy, whereupon profits would increase. Therefore if p is positive in every component, so is w.   q.e.d.

Next, consider the range of η.

15 Theorem   *Let $\mathcal{Y}$ be convex and closed, and let every nonnegative output be producible. If factors are not negatively productive, then for nonzero*

$(w, x) \geqslant 0$, x *an internal point among those outputs producible according to* $\mathcal{Y}$, *there is a pair* (y, p) *for which* (w, x) *is in* $\eta(y, p)$. *If there is some degree of free disposal, so that a decrease in* x *can be obtained with no change in* y, *then* p *must be nonnegative. If* $\mathcal{Y}$ *allows some degree of free disposal at* (y, p),

$$p_i \geqslant 0$$

for whatever good the free disposal is allowed.

The theorem says that the observable (w, x) for different (y, p) are so broad as to include all of the nonnegative vectors.

Proof   If $x \geqslant 0$, then there is a $y \geqslant 0$ such that (y, x) is in $\mathcal{Y}$. Consider

$$\underset{\vee}{\mathcal{Y}} = \{(-wy, x) \mid (y, x) \in \mathcal{Y}\}.$$

Let y be chosen so as to minimize wy, given that (y, x) is in $\mathcal{Y}$. This is possible if $\mathcal{Y}$ is closed and if for every output, the set of inputs giving this output is bounded from below, that is, if a minimum input (zero) is needed to obtain a given output. Clearly, $(-wy, x)$ is in the boundary of $\underset{\vee}{\mathcal{Y}}$. Therefore, apply Minkowski's theorem again: there is a vector $(k, \underset{\vee}{\bar{p}})$ such that

$$(k, \bar{p})(wy, x) = -kwy + \bar{p}x \geqslant -kw\bar{y} + \overline{px}$$

for all other $(w\bar{y}, \bar{x})$ in $\underset{\vee}{\mathcal{Y}}$, or alternatively, for all other $(\bar{y}, \bar{x})$ in $\mathcal{Y}$.

As before, k cannot be zero, since otherwise a larger profit would be obtained by changing wy without reducing revenues. Also, if there is some degree of free disposal, k cannot be negative, since then an increase in y would not decrease output and revenue but would decrease costs. Therefore, as before,

$$\frac{\bar{p}}{k} x - wy \geqslant \frac{\bar{p}}{k} \bar{x} - w\bar{y}$$

for all $(\bar{y}, \bar{x})$ in $\mathcal{Y}$

To conclude, if $\mathcal{Y}$ is convex and closed, if every nonnegative output is producible, and if factors are not negatively productive, then for nonnegative, nonzero (w, x) there is a pair (y, p) for which (w, x) is in $\eta(y, p)$.

If there is some degree of free disposal in the ith component, then p must be nonnegative in that component.   q.e.d.

Some properties of η and η^{-1} are listed.

16 Theorem

(i) *Both $\eta^{-1}(w, x)$ and $\eta(y, p)$ are convex sets whenever $\mathcal{Y}$ is convex.*

(ii) *If there are constant returns to scale, multiplication of p (or y) by a positive constant leads to a multiplication of w (or x) by the same positive constant.*

(iii) *If there are constant returns to scale, wy and px are constant in both $\eta(y, p)$ and $\eta^{-1}(w, x)$.*

(iv) $\eta(y, p) = (\eta_1(y, p), \eta_2(y, p))$

$$(\eta_1 : \mathscr{E}^{n+m} \to \mathscr{E}^m, \eta_2 : \mathscr{E}^{n+m} \to \mathscr{E}^n)$$

and

$$\eta^{-1}(w, x) = ((\eta^{-1})_1(w, x), (\eta^{-1})_2(w, x)),$$

$$((\eta^{-1})_1 : \mathscr{E}^{n+m} \to \mathscr{E}^m, (\eta^{-1})_2 : \mathscr{E}^{n+m} \to \mathscr{E}^n).$$

The dimension of variation in each $\eta_i((\eta^{-1})_1)$ is equal to one less than the number of linearly independent vectors in $\eta_i((\eta^{-1})_i)$.

(v) *η and η^{-1} are upper semicontinuous whenever $\mathcal{Y}$ is closed.*

Parts (iv) and (v) are particularly noteworthy. In effect, there is no functional interaction between x and w or between y and p. For example, observation of w and x can be used to derive the factor endownments, independently of the international price system. A computation of cost-minimizing industry inputs follows from w and the number of (profitable) industries needed to produce x. Also, sequential and convergent changes in independent variables lead to dependent variables which in the limit equilibrate the factor markets vis-à-vis the limiting values of the dependent variables.

Proof (iii) For (w, x), $(\bar{w}, \bar{x})$ in $\eta(y, p)$.

$$px - wy \geqslant p\bar{x} - wy, \qquad p\bar{x} - \bar{w}y \geqslant px - \bar{w}y,$$

or

$$px \geqslant p\bar{x}, \qquad p\bar{x} \geqslant px,$$

whereupon

$$px = px.$$

For (y, p), $(\bar{y}, \bar{x})$ in $\eta^{-1}(w, x)$,

$$px - wy \geqslant px - w\bar{y}, \qquad p\bar{x} - w\bar{y} \geqslant \bar{p}x - wy,$$

or

$$\bar{w}y \geqslant wy, \qquad w\bar{y} \geqslant \bar{w}y,$$

whereupon

$$\bar{w}y = wy.$$

(iv) Since $pw = p\bar{x}$, x and $\bar{x}$ producible from y may be permuted to obtain the same profit. Since

$$wy = w\bar{y},$$

w may be permuted with $\bar{w}$ to obtain the same profit. Also, the dimension of a convex set that is nowhere dense is equal to one less than the number of its linearly independent vectors.

(v) $y^n \rightarrow y$,
$p^n \rightarrow p$,
$w^n \rightarrow w$
$x^n \rightarrow x$,
$p^n x^n = w^n y^n \geqslant p^n \tilde{x} - w^n \tilde{y}$

for all $(\tilde{y}, \tilde{x})$ in y implies that

$$px - wy \geqslant p\tilde{x} - w\tilde{y}$$

for all $(\tilde{y}, \tilde{x})$ in $\mathscr{Y}$. q.e.d.

Let f^i be the production function describing the boundary of industry i's production set.

17 Remark If under a Leontief technology f^i is strictly quasiconcave and linear homogeneous, then given p and w, y^i is uniquely determined.

Proof If $(y^i, f^i(y^i))$, $(\bar{y}^i, f^i(\bar{y}^i))$ gives a zero profit, then so does $(k\bar{y}^i, f^i(k\bar{y}^i)) = k(\bar{y}, f^i(\bar{y}^i))$ where $k\bar{y}^i = y^i$. Then, for $0 < s < 1$, $f^i(sy^i + (1 - s)\bar{y}^i k) > (sf^i(y^i) + (1 - s)kf^i(y^i))$ gives a positive profit whenever $wy \neq 0$. q.e.d.

An important consequence of Theorem 16 is that the wage rate is uniquely determined by p and y alone.[3] Under conditions listed in Theorem 18, part (ii), we also have a unique determination of output.

---

[3] The uniqueness of w can be proved without using differentiability of f^i, provided that there are m linearly independent y^i (McKenzie [1955]). Using the notation developed for the Leontief technology for these industries, and recalling from the proof of Theorem 16 that given that (y^i, x^i) is profitable under one (w, p), it is profitable under another, $w = pX(w)Y^{-1}$, $y = Y\xi$. (Of course, X is not necessarily invertible or even square.) Therefore, for any p, η_1 is determined to be w computed above.

18 Theorem

(i) *If f^i is differentiable, and satisfies constant returns to scale, for all industries, $i = 1,..., k$, and if y_j is strictly positive for all factors, $j = 1,..., m$, then $\eta_1(y, p)$ is a continuous function.*

(ii) *If also there is a Leontief technology, f^i strictly quasi concave, and if Y^{-1} exists (so that $m = n$), then η_2 is a continuous function also.*

According to the second sentence of (i) in Theorem 18, small changes in international prices and factor endowments lead to small changes in factor wages.

Proof (i) Given (w, x), $(\bar{w}, \bar{x})$ in $\eta(y, p)$, $(\bar{w}, x)$ is in $\eta(y, p)$ (Theorem 16(iv)). Therefore, $w = \bar{w}$ (Theorem 28 of Chapter I).

An upper semicontinuous correspondence is a continuous function whenever it is single valued and it takes bounded sets into bounded sets. By the continuity of the production functions, x is bounded, given y, and therefore,

$$wy = xp$$

forces w to be bounded, given p and a strictly positive y.

(ii) Since

$$y = Y\xi, \qquad \text{and} \qquad x = X\xi,$$

$$Y^{-1}y = \xi, \qquad \text{and} \qquad x = X\xi, \qquad \text{or} \qquad x = XY^{-1}y. \qquad \text{q.e.d.}$$

In Theorem 19, factor endowments are seen to be uniquely determined by outputs and wages, whereas under more restrictive assumptions, prices are 1–1 in wages.

19 Theorem

(i) *If technology is Leontief, $(\eta^{-1})_2$ is a continuous function.*

(ii) *Let there be m profitable industries with linearly independent x^i, constant returns to scale, and differentiable production as in the Leontief technology. Then $(\eta^{-1})_1$ is a continuous function of w alone. Given the factor endowment y, w is 1–1 in p.*

According to (i), changes in y are uniquely related to changes in w. According to (ii), for almost all outputs, price is dependent on factor wages alone. Given wages, we can immediately compute prices. This gives an alternative proof of the unique wage theorem (Theorem 16), since given two prices and the same wage, there must be only one price implies by the wage—a contradiction.

Proof

(i) $x = X\xi$, or $\xi = xX^{-1}$, so that $y = Y\xi$, $\xi = YX^{-1}x$. Y is continuous in w.

(ii) Apply $p = wYX^{-1}$. Y is continuous in w since it is the unique maximizer of a continuous profit function (it is an upper semicontinuous correspondence and it takes compact sets into compact sets)—of course, given y, w is a function of p (Theorem 27 of Chapter 1).   q.e.d.

Theorems 18 and 19 give conditions under which w and p are uniquely determined by each other, given x and y, respectively. Nevertheless, $\mathcal{Y}$ might not be directional dense at (y, x), since there may exist $\bar{w}$ and $\bar{p}$ mutually determining each other and still having (y, x) as a profit-maximizing input–output vector. This turns out to be impossible.

20 Theorem

(i) *Let $\mathcal{Y}_i$ be convex, $i = 1,..., k < \infty$.*

(ii) *Let the technology be Leontief with only one positive output for each industry $(m = n < \infty)$.*

(iii) *Let f^i be differentiable and satisfy constant returns to scale and a strong concavity assumption. Then at strictly positive y and x, $\mathcal{Y}$ is directional dense.*

Proof   Since

$$x \gg 0, \qquad x = X\xi, \qquad X^{-1} \geqslant 0,$$

there must be

$$\xi = X^{-1}x \gg 0, \qquad X\xi = x,$$

so that $\xi = X^{-1}x$. Therefore, industries are always operated at the intensities ξ. Combining y and $\bar{y}$ convexly, each of which produces x, increases the scale of output in each industry. Therefore, ξ is multiplied by a diagonal matrix D where $d_{ii} > 1$ is the scale of operation of the ith industry. Combine $d_{ii}x^i$ with the inefficient production x^i (convexity) to reduce scale in all industries except where d_{ii} is minimal. Then $\min(d_{ii}) x\xi$ is the new output, which yields a positive profit, whether (w, p) or $(\bar{w}, \bar{p})$ is the price system.   q.e.d.

The following theorem shows that for most prices, wages are differentiable functions of prices.

21 Theorem   *In a Leontief technology, with constant returns to scale and strictly quasi-concave production functions, p is continuously differentiable in w with derivative YX^{-1}. Also, $\partial w/\partial p = XY^{-1}$ and Y^{-1} exists for all p that allow the production of all goods, except those in a closed, very small set of prices.*

Proof   Given y, $pX = wY$. Therefore,

$$
\begin{aligned}
pX - \bar{p}X &= wY(w) - \bar{w}Y(\bar{w}) \\
&= wY(w) - \bar{w}Y(w) + \bar{w}[Y(w) - Y(\bar{w})] \\
&\geqslant (w - \bar{w})Y(w)
\end{aligned}
$$

and

$$
\begin{aligned}
pX - \bar{p}X &= wY(w) - wY(\bar{w}) + (w - \bar{w})Y(\bar{w}) \\
&\leqslant (w - \bar{w})Y(\bar{w}).
\end{aligned}
$$

Taking limits, we obtain

$$
\lim_{\bar{w} \to w} \frac{(p - \bar{p})}{|p - \bar{p}|} X = \frac{(w - \bar{w})}{|w - w|} Y(w)
$$

or pX is continuously differentiable in w (continuity of $Y(w)$). Applying Sard's lemma (as in Section 8 of Chapter 4), we get, except for a very small set of prices, $\det \partial p/\partial w \neq 0$. Also $\partial p/\partial w \, X = Y$ or

$$
\det \partial p/\partial w \, \det X = \det Y \neq 0.
$$

Also, if $w^n \to w$, $p^n = w^n YX^{-1}$, then p^n remains bounded, since $p^n x^n = p^n X \xi^n = w^n Y \xi^n = w^n y$ is bounded, as is ξ^n and $x^n \gg 0$, and therefore p^n. Hence, $p^{n_k} \to p$ and $p = wYX^{-1}$ by continuity, so that closed sets in wage space are mapped into closed sets in factor space. Evidently, $\{x \mid \det \partial f/\partial x = 0\}$ is closed.   q.e.d.

PROBLEMS

B. Welfare Cost of Monopoly

Assume that there is a tariff sufficiently high to permit a monopoly producing only for the home market of a small country in international trade. What is the effect on national income in terms of international prices? Is this effect the only one in determining consumer welfare? (Hint: Assume the state can redistribute income without welfare loss, and see Section 7 of Chapter 6 of the companion volume.)

The problem appears in Rader [1971].

C. Optimal Tariffs II

For a "quasi" small country with a monopoly power in only one good, when would it pay to apply a tariff on the other commodities? To what extent? How would the tariff system compare with an excise tax? Would the tariff involve any loss of efficiency? (Hint: Make home prices equal to world marginal revenues.)

The problem appears in Rader [1971].

3. Comparative Statics of Supply

In the k-industry case, Theorems 16, 18, and 19 give some information about changes in η and η^{-1} in response to changes in the independent variables. This is the subject of comparative statics, and it is well to develop it more extensively. Emphasis is placed on the k-industry case, which is of special interest in international trade and development theory.

In this section, it is shown that increases in one factor only would decrease its wage, and increases in one product can result only with an increase in its price (Theorem 22). Symmetrically, increases in a wage must decrease the utilization of the factor, and increases in a price must increase the output of the good (Theorem 22). Under more restrictive conditions, increases in wages unambiguously increase prices (Theorem 23). For two goods and two factors only, an increase in a product price increases the wage of the factor used relatively intensely in that product (Theorem 24).

22 Theorem   *Let there be constant returns to scale.*

(i)   *For* $(w, x) \in \eta(y, p)$, $(\bar{w}, \bar{x}) \in \eta(\bar{y}, p)$,

$$0 \geqslant \Delta w \, \Delta y.$$

If y_i alone increases, w_i must not increase. Strict inequality holds under the hypothesis of Theorem 18, part (i).

(ii)   *For* $(y, p) \in \eta^{-1}(w, x)$, $(\bar{y}, \bar{p}) \in \eta^{-1}(w, \bar{x})$,

$$0 \leqslant \Delta p \, \Delta x.$$

If x_i alone increases, p_i must not decrease. Strict inequality holds under the hypothesis of Theorem 19, part (ii).

(iii)   *For* $(w, x) \in \eta(y, p)$, $(\bar{w}, \bar{x}) \in \eta(y, \bar{p})$,

$$0 \geqslant \Delta p \, \Delta x.$$

If p_i alone increases, x_i must not decrease. Strict inequality holds under the hypothesis of Theorem 18, part (ii).
    (iv) *For* $(y, p) \in \eta^{-1}(w, x)$, $(\bar{y}, \bar{p}) \in \eta^{-1}(\bar{w}, x)$,

$$0 \geqslant \Delta w \, \Delta y.$$

If w_i increases, y_i must not increase. Strict inequality holds under the hypothesis of Theorem 19, part (i).

The theorem gives some simple rules of change in values. They are analogous to results of Samuelson [1947, Chapter 4].

Proof (i) Let y change, p fixed. Then

$$0 = p\bar{x} - \bar{w}\bar{y} \geqslant px - \bar{w}y \quad \text{and} \quad 0 = px - wy \geqslant p\bar{x} - \bar{w}\bar{y},$$

or

$$\bar{w}y \geqslant \bar{w}\bar{y} \quad \text{and} \quad \bar{w}y \geqslant wy,$$

or

$$0 \geqslant -(w - w)\,\bar{y} + (\bar{w} - w)\,y = (\bar{w} - w)(\bar{y} - y).$$

Strict inequality holds whenever w is determined by y and p, since then

$$\bar{w}y = wy,$$

given p, implies

$$px - \bar{w}y = px - wy = 0.$$

This condition is assured by Theorem 18, part (i). If w changes at all, then strict inequality holds above and w_i actually decreases.
    (ii) Let x change, w fixed. Then

$$0 = \bar{p}\bar{x} - \bar{w}\bar{y} \geqslant \bar{p}x - wy \quad \text{and} \quad 0 = px - wy \geqslant p\bar{x} - w\bar{y},$$

or

$$\bar{p}\bar{x} \geqslant p\bar{x} \quad \text{and} \quad px \geqslant \bar{p}x,$$

or

$$0 < (\bar{p} - p)\bar{x} - (\bar{p} - p)x = (\bar{p} - p)(\bar{x} - x).$$

Strict inequality holds whenever $\bar{p}$ is uniquely determined by w and y (Theorem 19, part (ii)).
    (iii) Let p change, y fixed. Then

$$\bar{p}\bar{x} \geqslant \bar{p}x \quad \text{and} \quad px \geqslant p\bar{x},$$

so that

$$0 \leqslant \bar{p}(\bar{x} - x)pp(\bar{x} - x) = (\bar{p} - p)(\bar{x} - x).$$

Strict inequality holds whenever x is uniquely determined by $\bar{p}$ and y (Theorem 18, part (ii)). Since w is uniquely determined by x and $\bar{x}$ in the k-industry case, strict inequality holds for that initial price system maximizing the number of profitable industries. Therefore, an increase in p_i increases x_i .

(iv) Similarly, if w changes, x fixed, then

$$\bar{w}\bar{y} \leqslant \bar{w}y \quad \text{and} \quad wy \leqslant w\bar{y},$$

or

$$0 \geqslant \bar{w}(\bar{y} - y) - w(\bar{y} - y) = (\bar{w} - w)(\bar{y} - y).$$

Strict inequality holds whenever y is uniquely determined by w and x (Theorem 19, part (ii)).

23 Theorem *If the technology is Leontief with only one positive output from each industry, then an increase in w increases the p, allowing all industries to operate. If w is positive, each price increases.*

Proof

$$pX = wY,$$

or

$$p = wYX^{-1}, \quad Y \geqslant 0, \quad X^{-1} \geqslant 0,$$

so that

$$\Delta p = \Delta w \, YX^{-1} + w\Delta \, YX^{-1}$$

and since $w \, \Delta Y = wY(\bar{w}) - wY \geqslant 0$,

$$\Delta p \geqslant \Delta w \, YX^{-1}.$$

Therefore,

$$p \geqslant 0 \quad \text{whenever} \quad w \geqslant 0.$$

Generally, $\Delta w \, YX^{-1}$ is positive and Δp is strictly positive.   q.e.d.

It might be added that an increase in w need not lead to an increase in p since YX^{-1} need not be nonnegative.

A final result, due to Stolper and Samuelson [1941], shows that the wage of the factor used relatively intensely in the industry producing a good whose price has increased also increases.

24 Theorem *Suppose*

$$m = 2, \qquad n = 2.$$

Both industries are profitable. Then as p_i increases, w increases in that component which is less intensively used in industry i.

As Chipman [1966] has pointed out, the theorem does not readily generalize to the m-factor case,

$$m > 2,$$

if for no other reason than that there is no 1–1 relationship between industries and intensity of use of each factor.

In order to avoid differentiability assumptions, a proof longer than that of Stolper and Samuelson is required.

Proof Let there be only two factors of production, and suppose that a change in p does increase the revenues of industry i but does not increase revenues of j. Then the costs of industry i must increase and those of j must not increase:

$$\bar{w}y^i > wy^i, \qquad \bar{w}y^j \leqslant wy^j,$$

or

$$(\bar{w} - w)y^i + \bar{w}(\bar{y}^i - y^i) > 0, \qquad (\bar{w} - w)\bar{y}^j + w(\bar{y}^j - y^j) \leqslant 0.$$

Since profits are a maximum at $(\bar{y}^i, x^i)$ and (y^i, x^i), respectively,

$$\bar{w}(\bar{y}^i - y^i) \leqslant 0 \qquad \text{and} \qquad w(\bar{y}^j - y^j) \geqslant 0.$$

Therefore,

$$(\bar{w} - w)y^i > 0, \qquad (\bar{w} - w)\bar{y}^j \leqslant 0.$$

This can be written

$$\Delta w_1 y_1^i + \Delta w_2 y_2^i \geqslant 0, \qquad \Delta w_1 y_1^j + \Delta w_2 y_2^j < 0.$$

Suppose $\Delta w_1 > 0$. Then

$$\frac{y_1^i}{y_2^i} \geqslant -\frac{\Delta w_2}{\Delta w_1}, \qquad \text{and} \qquad \frac{y_1^j}{y_2^j} < -\frac{\Delta w_2}{\Delta w_1},$$

so that

$$\frac{y_1^i}{y_2^i} > \frac{y_1^j}{y_2^j}.$$

Similarly, if $\Delta w_2 > 0$,

$$\frac{y_2^i}{y_1^i} > \frac{y_2^i}{y_1^j}.$$

Therefore w increases in that component corresponding to the factor that is more intensively used in the industry with a revenue gain.   q.e.d.

4. Factor Price Equalization

The modern theory of international trade is concerned with the influence of changes in outputs y and prices p on wages w. It is presumed that there are two or more countries trading at the same prices. If there are a sufficient number of profitable industries, it will be seen that small changes in factor endowments do not change factor prices. When such a situation exists, it is said that there is *factor price equalization*. The international trade application is that nations that have appropriate factor endowments have equal factor prices. There is no incentive for factor movement, and therefore, trade substitutes for factor migration.

25 Remark Let there be k production functions, continuously differentiable, satisfying a strict concavity production, and subject to constant returns to scale. Then the set of strictly positive factor endowments, small changes in which lead to no change in factor prices, is open. Also, the subsets of those endowments with factor price w has closure disjoint from any other such closure.

Proof Clearly, the sets of factor price equalization are open. The closures are disjoint, since factor prices are the same on a closure of a set of factor endowments with factor price equalization and different factors result from different factor endowments (Theorem 18(i)). Therefore, the closures of sets of factor price equalization for a given factor price are disjoint.   q.e.d.

Heckscher and Ohlin conjectured, and Samuelson [1949] was the first to show, that in the two-industry, two-factor case, with constant returns to scale, there is factor price equalization provided

(1) all industries are profitable at some w,
(2) for all w, one industry uses one factor more intensely than the other.

These two assumptions are needed. If (2) does not hold, the w for which all industries are profitable may not be one satisfying the factor intensity assumption, so that $Y(w)$ is singular. If (1) does not hold, one industry may not be profitable for any f, as is illustrated in Figure 1. In Figure 1, isorevenue curves, $px^i = 1$, $i = 1, 2$, are drawn. The curves are constructed to be vertically parallel. It can be seen that the ratio of y_2 to y_1 utilized in industry 1 always exceeds that utilized in industry 2. This is assumption (2). Nevertheless, there is not factor price equalization, since industy 1 is never profitable.

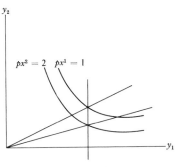

Figure 1

Questions arise as to how Samuelson's basic results can be extended. First, does an increase in the number of industries increase or decrease the likelihood of factor price equalization; second, is there factor price equalization when the number of factors exceeds two? In response to the second question, it must be noted that factor price equalization cannot be expected for

$$m > n,$$

since

$$y = Y\xi$$

does not map ξ onto an m-dimensional space of y's, and hence the strictly positive orthant of ξ's cannot map onto an open set of y's. Therefore, $m \geqslant n$ is necessary.

Beyond these generalizations, elimination of Samuelson's condition (1) leads to two versions of factor price equalization. First, given w, there exists p such that for some y there is factor price equalization. Second, given p, there exists w such that for some y there is factor price equalization. Each of these theorems is itself divided into two parts, first, that m industries operate, and second, that they have independent y^i.

26 Theorem *If w is strictly positive in every component and if the technology is Leontief, then there is a price system p at which every industry* *is profitable. If the y^i are also linearly independent, then there is factor price equalization.*

The theorem is that of McKenzie [1955] and is the generalization of Samuelson's result vis-a-vis the number of industries and factors.

Proof   For given w, choose a ratio Y and solve

$$pX = wY \quad \text{or} \quad p = wYX^{-1}. \quad \text{q.e.d.}$$

The more difficult theorem is that given p, there is a w that allows factor price equalization. Considering $p(w)$, an m-dimensional space is mapped into an n-dimensional space,

$$n > m.$$

In general, we should not expect $p(w)$ to lead to the profitability of all industries. For factor price equalization, however, all that is required is that m industries be operable. Nevertheless, the excess of the number of industries over the number of factors complicates matters insofar as zero profitability in n industries does not ensure nonpositive profitability in the remaining industries.

27 Theorem   *Let there be a Leontief technology and let f^i be continuously differentiable and strictly quasi concave. If given p, there are exactly m profitable industries, and there is factor price equalization for some w, then for all nearby p, there is factor price equalization.*

Proof   1.   There is factor price equalization at (p, w) if and only if there are m profitable industries with linearly independent y^i. This follows since no change in w implies no change in the function $y^i(w)$. Therefore, absorption of an open set of factor endowments requires linearly independent factor utilization vectors y^i.

2.   For nearby p, no industries formerly unprofitable become profitable, since small changes in p lead to small changes in w, and therefore lead to small changes in profits.

3.   Restricting attention to m industries with linearly independent y^i, we have

$$pX = wY \quad \text{or} \quad \frac{\partial w}{\partial p} = XY^{-1},$$

since

$$w \frac{\partial Y}{\partial w_i} = 0$$

by cost minimization. The differential equation may be solved for small changes in p, since Y is continuous in w.

4. Since $Y(w)$ is continuous, for small changes in w, $Y(w)$ has the same m linearly independent columns. Applying 1 gives the theorem.

q.e.d.

There are results more general in terms of the goods price space. First, in the two-factor case, a quite general theorem can be obtained with a definite answer to question 1. There is also a generalization of Samuelson's condition (1).

28 Theorem   *Given*

   (i)   *k industries are separately profitable at factor prices w_i, $i = 1,..., k < \infty$,*
   (ii)   *two factors,*
   (iii) $k \geqslant 2$,
   (iv) f^i *continuous and satisfies constant returns to scale, then for each industry i, there is another industry j such that both i and j are operated simultaneously. Therefore, if there is any industry i that has y^i linearly independent of all other j, there is factor price equalization. If, also the f^i are continuously differentiable, then for all p except in a very small set, there is factor price equalization.*

That y^i is independent of y^j and y^k does not preclude the possibility that y^k and y^j are linearly dependent. In effect, i can be chosen as one of the (somewhere) profitable industries, and it need not be the case that all y^i and y^j are linearly independent, as in the Samuelson theorem. Therefore, an increase in the number of industries is seen to make factor price equalization more likely. The view of Samuelson [1949] is confirmed.

Proof   Let $\mathscr{S}_i$ be the set of strictly positive factor endowments that lead to w for which industry i is profitable. $\mathscr{S}_i$ is closed, since

$$0 = pf^i(y^i(w)) - w y^i(w)$$

is zero in the limit, as $w \to \bar{w}$, $y^i(w) \to y^i(\bar{w})$. Therefore,

$$\bigcup_{j \neq i} \mathscr{S}_i$$

is closed relative to the positive y. Also,

$$\bigcup_i \mathscr{S}_i$$

equals the set of strictly positive factor endowments, a connected set. A connected set cannot be disjointed into two closed sets, whereupon for each i,

$$\mathscr{S}_i \cap \left(\bigcup_{j \neq i} \mathscr{S}_j \right)$$

is nonempty; that is, there exists a y leading to w for which i is profitable and to $\bar{w}$ for which j is profitable. Simply observe that whenever i is profitable for w in $\eta(y, p)$, j for $\bar{w}$ in $\eta(y, p)$, both i and j are profitable for w (Theorem 16).

If y^i and y^j are independent, there is factor price equalization at

$$y = \xi_i y^i + \xi_j y^j, \qquad \xi_i > 0, \quad \xi_j > 0.$$

For the rest of the theorem, apply Theorem 21. For each i, j, det $Y = 0$ only on a very small set of prices. Therefore, for every p allowing i, j to operate, det $Y = 0$ only on a finite sum of closed, very small sets that is closed and very small.   q.e.d.

In the m-factor case, Chipman [1966] has generalized a result of Kuhn [1959] that gives conditions ensuring factor price equalization. In two dimensions, it appears that Kuhn's conditions require that factor inputs be used in fixed proportions except for a bounded set of factor utilizations. For Robinson [1956] and Kaldor [1957], this may be well enough, but economists are usually interested in a larger variety of production functions. Hence, other conditions on production should be allowed. It will be seen that the domain of p for which factor price equalization results can be specified. In the two-dimensional case, factor price equalization holds up to the point where Samuelson's factor intensity assumption fails.

29 Theorem   *Suppose*

(i)   *there is a Leontief technology,*
(ii) f^i *is continously differentiable and strictly quasi concave,*
$i = 1,..., n,$
(iii)   *for each factor i, either*

    (a)   *there is some good for which a minimum quantity of i is needed in order to produce a minimum quantity of the good, or*

(b) $y^i \to 0$ *implies $\partial f^j / \partial x_i^j$ is bounded, for all j,*

(iv) *either*

(a) *an infinite amount of one factor j combined with a nonzero zero amount of the other factors leads to an infinite output in some industry, or*

(b) *$y^i(w)$ is bounded for all i,*

(v) *$m = n$,*

(vi) *all $y^i(w)$ are linearly independent so long as all industries are profitable, for p in a differentiable arc $\mathscr{L}$ allowing factor price equalization.*

Then for all p allowing positive revenues in each industry, there is factor price equalization.

Supposition (iii)a amounts to saying that for each factor i there is at least one industry j such that the production isoquant for other factors is asymptotic to hyperplanes

$$y_i^j = \text{constant}.$$

(iii)a and (iv)a together must refer to the same pairing of factors and industries, insofar as an industry j for which (iii)a holds vis-à-vis factor i automatically does not satisfy (iv)a for the other factors. Therefore, in order for there to be enough industries to satisfy by (iii)a and (iv)a, i and j are uniquely associated.

Counterexamples appear in Figure 1, where minimum inputs of a given factor are not needed for any goods, and in Figure 2a, where both industries operate but the y^i are not linearly independent, contradicting (vi). Supposition (iii)b covers the case where isoproduct curves intersect the $\sim i$ axis(es), whereupon the marginal rate of transformation of $\sim i$ for i is bounded. There is factor price equalization in Figure 2b, which is Figure 2a when revenues in industry 2 are decreased. Wages are

$$w_1 = \frac{1}{\bar{y}_1}, \qquad w_2 = \frac{1}{\bar{y}_2}.$$

For revenues in industry 2 still higher than in Figure 2b, there is factor price equalization. For smaller revenues in industry 2, as in Figure 2a, both industries may operate but there is not factor price equalization. For still smaller revenues, only one industry is operated.

Supposition (iv)b is a quasi-Leontief assumption in that substitution is limited. It appears that (iii)a and (iv)b are the assumptions used by

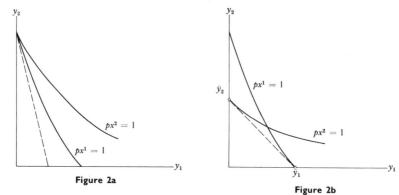

Figure 2a

Figure 2b

Kuhn [1959] and Chipman [1966]. For example, if factors could be so renumbered that Y is diagonalized,

$$
Y = \begin{bmatrix} y_{11} & & & 0 \\ & y_{22} & & \\ & & \cdot & \\ & & & \cdot \\ & & & & \cdot \\ y_{m1} & & \cdots & & y_{nm} \end{bmatrix},
$$

then (iii)a is satisfied. In a Colin Clark type scheme, land, capital, and labor are used in extraction; capital and labor are used in manufacturing; only labor is used in servicing. Supposition (vi) is a generalization of Samuelson's two-dimensional assumption of no factor reversal. In two dimensions, the y^i are independent for all w if and only if the factor ratios remain different for all w. Since these factor ratios are continuous in w, they cannot be reversed. The diagonalized Y is an example of the n-dimensional case, $n > 2$.

Proof   Apply Theorem 26 to obtain $\bar{p}$, for which w is strictly positive and therefore $\bar{p}X$ is nonnegative and for which there is factor price equalization. As p changes, simply solve for w as

$$
\frac{\partial w}{\partial p} = XY^{-1},
$$

which is possible so long as Y is bounded. So long as w is bounded, both from infinity and from zero, $(Y(w))^{-1}$ is continuous in w and bounded. Therefore

$$
w(p) = \int_{\mathscr{L}} \frac{\partial w}{\partial p}\, dp,
$$

$\mathscr{L}$ a continuously differentiable arc between p and $\bar{p}$, gives a solution of w for p that makes all m industries zero profitable.

Now consider a fixed ξ so that

$$x = X\xi$$

is fixed. Then

$$wY = pX$$

is fixed, so that

$$w_i \to \infty \quad \text{implies} \quad Y_i \to 0.$$

In case (iii)a, this is impossible if ξ is to be produced. In case (iii)b,

$$y_i \to 0$$

implies $F_i \equiv (\partial f^j / \partial y_i^j)$ bounded, so that eventually

$$w_i > pF_i$$

and y_i is identically zero. This contradicts the linear independence of the y^j.

On the other hand, if

$$w_i \to 0,$$

(iv)a applies, so that industry j can use y_j intensely to obtain a virtually zero cost and therefore a positive profit (for pX strictly positive). Therefore, it cannot be that

$$w_i \to 0.$$

In the absence of (iv)a, (iv)b ensures that Y is continuous as

$$w_i \to 0.$$

It remains to verify that zero profitable industries at $Y(w)$ necessarily have nonpositive profits for other factor combinations. This follows from the concavity of pf^i, for

$$p > 0,$$

whereby

$$p\tilde{x}^i - px^i = pf^i(y^i) - pf^i(\tilde{y}^i) \geqslant pF^i(y^i - \tilde{y}^i)$$
$$= wy^i - w\tilde{y}^i$$

(Problem C of Chapter 2 of the companion volume.) Therefore, other factor utilizations producing x^i are no more profitable.   q.e.d.

UNSOLVED PROBLEM

D. Factor Price Equalization I

Prove the factor price equalization Theorem 28 for $n \geqslant m$, $m > 2$.

5. Conservation Laws and Gross Substitution

The balance of this chapter shows the effect of changes in excess demands on prices and wages. Laws of conservation of value are presented in this section but are used throughout. The rest of this section is concerned with the very special case of gross substitutes. The basic result, true only for the gross substitutes, is that increases in one excess demand at the expense of another decrease all prices relative to the good whose demand increased. Weaker laws applicable to more realistic economies are considered in Sections 6 and 7.

As has been shown, competitive systems normally have equilibria as do monopolistic systems under the conditions discussed in Chapter 4. These equilibria are the result of two different properties. An economic system with excess demand $\mathscr{E}$ is an *exchange system* if

$$p(\mathscr{E}(p)) = 0,$$

which is Walras' law. A constant θ may be substituted for 0, representing the value of the exchanges of extraeconomic units (for example, the state). It is a *market system* if there is no *money illusion*,

$$\mathscr{E}(kp) = \mathscr{E}(p) \qquad \text{for} \quad k \neq 0,$$

that is, only relative prices are of importance. As usual, equilibrium occurs whenever

$$0 \in \mathscr{E}(\bar{p}).$$

(Note that equilibrium is possible only if $\theta = 0$.) These two laws are conservation laws, analogous to those in physical systems. Differentiation yields the equations

$$p \, \frac{\partial \mathscr{E}}{\partial p} + \mathscr{E}(p) = 0,$$

$$p \, \frac{\partial \mathscr{E}}{\partial \bar{p}} = 0,$$

and by Euler's theorem for homogeneous functions

$$\frac{\partial \mathscr{E}}{\partial p}\, p = 0,$$

which put restrictions on the matrices, $\partial \mathscr{E}/\partial p$.

Recall that commodities are *normal* if an increase in p_i increases $\mathscr{E}_i$, and commodities are *(weak) i–j gross substitutes* if an increase in p_i (does not increase) increases $\mathscr{E}_j$, $j \neq i$.

30 Remark If there are two commodities in an exchange system, then i is (not a Giffen good) normal at positive equilibrium prices if and only if the goods are (weak) i–j gross substitutes.

Proof Let $\Delta p_i = \bar{p}_i - p_i$. From Walras' law, $\Delta \mathscr{E}_i < 0$ whenever $\Delta p_i > 0$ if and only if

$$\Delta \mathscr{E}_j = \frac{1}{p_j}\,(-\bar{p}_i\,\Delta \mathscr{E}_i - \Delta p_i\,\mathscr{E}_i)$$

$$= -\frac{\bar{p}_i}{p_j}\,\Delta \mathscr{E}_i \qquad (\mathscr{E}_i = 0)$$

$$> 0. \qquad \text{q.e.d.}$$

31 Remark If there are two commodities in a market system, then j is (not a Giffen good) normal if and only if the goods are (weak) i–j gross substitutes.

Proof Increasing p_i, p_j constant, is equivalent to decreasing p_j, p_i constant, whereupon increasing p_i increases $\mathscr{E}_j$ if and only if decreasing p_j increases $\mathscr{E}_j$. q.e.d.

32 Remark If there are two commodities in a market–exchange system, then at equilibrium prices, all goods are (not Giffen goods) normal and (weak) gross substitutes if and only if one good is (not a Giffen good) normal or a (weak) gross substitute for the other.

The more general case, $n > 2$, is due to Arrow and Hurwicz [1958]. Among other results, we can show the impossibility of the Giffen effect, either for a single good or for aggregates of goods.

33 Theorem *If there is (weak) i–j gross substitution in an exchange economy at strictly positive equilibrium prices, all $i \in \mathscr{I}$, $j \in \sim\mathscr{I}$, then*

$$\sum_{i \in \mathscr{I}} \bar{p}_i\,\Delta \mathscr{E}_i < (\leqslant)\, 0$$

whenever the price of one or more $i \in \mathscr{I}$ *is increased from* p_i *to* $\bar{p}_i$ *. If*

$$\sum_{i \in \mathscr{I}} \bar{p}_i \, \varDelta \mathscr{E}_i \, (\leqslant) < 0$$

whenever one or more p_i *is increased from* p_i *to* $\bar{p}_i$ *,* $i \in \mathscr{I}$ *, then*

$$\sum_{i \in \sim \mathscr{I}} p_i \, \varDelta \mathscr{E}_i \, (\geqslant) > 0.$$

If there is i–j *(weak) gross substitution for all* j, *then* i *is (not a Giffen good) normal. If* i *is (not a Giffen good) normal, then there is at least one* j *displaying* i–j *(weak) gross substitution, and if in this case there is no* i–j *gross substituion, then there is* i–j *(weak) gross substitution for all* j.

34 Theorem   *If there is (weak)* i–j *gross substitution in a market economy, for all* i, *all* $j \in \mathscr{J}$, *then a proportional increase in* $p_{\mathscr{J}_0}$, $\mathscr{J}_0 \subset \mathscr{J}$, *leads to (no increase) a decrease in the demand for all goods* j *in* $\mathscr{J}_0$ *. If a proportional decrease in* $p_{\mathscr{J}_0}$, $\mathscr{J}_0 \subset \mathscr{J}$, *leads to (no increase) a decrease in the demand for each good in* $\mathscr{J}_0$, *then for every* $j \in \mathscr{J} \sim \mathscr{J}_0$ *there is (weak)* i–j *gross substitution for some* $i \in \mathscr{J}_0$.

All goods are (weak) gross substitutes if and only if subaggregates of commodities are (not Giffen) normal goods.

The proof of Theorem 33 follows simply from the fact that for $\varDelta x \equiv \bar{x} - x$, $\varDelta y \equiv \bar{y} - y$, we have

$$\varDelta \left(\sum_i x_i \right) = \sum_i \varDelta x_i \qquad \text{and} \qquad \varDelta xy = x \, \varDelta y + \bar{y} \, \varDelta x.$$

The proof of Theorem 34 is by direct application of the appropriate definitions. Evidently, conservation laws put restrictions on the relationships between changes in price and changes in quantities. It will be shown how more substantive statics theorems can be so deduced.

The first comparative statics laws to be considered are those of Hicks [1938], Mosak [1944], and Morishima [1964]. Some generalizations appear, mainly with regard to allowing an infinite number of commodities.

Under weak gross substitutability, there is *indecomposability* if for all sets of commodities $\mathscr{I}$ increases in all prices in $\mathscr{I}$ necessarily increase at least one excess demand in $\sim \mathscr{I}$. An increase in excess demand for one commodity is paired with a decrease in the excess demand for another. By virtue of Walras' law, an increase in one alone would not be possible.

The following theorem shows that an increase in the demand for a good increases its price relative to all other goods.

35 Theorem *If there is weak gross substitution and indecomposability in an exchange system, if an increase in the excess demand for i_0 together with a decrease in the excess demand for i_1 leads to a strictly positive equilibrium price system, $\bar{p} \neq p$, where $\bar{p}_{i_1} = p_{i_1}$, then $\bar{p} \geqslant p$ and $\bar{p}_{i_0} > p_{i_0}$. If instead $p_{i_0} = \bar{p}_{i_0}$ and $p \neq \bar{p}$, then $p \geqslant \bar{p}, p_{i_1} \geqslant \bar{p}_{i_1}$.*

Proof Let $\mathscr{J} = \{j \mid \bar{p}_j < p_j\}$. A change from $(p_{\mathscr{J}}, p_{\mathscr{J}})$ to $p_{\mathscr{J}}, \bar{p}_{\sim\mathscr{J}})$ decreases neither $\mathscr{E}_{\mathscr{J}}$ nor $\sum_{j\in\mathscr{J}} p_j \mathscr{E}_j$. A change from $(p_{\mathscr{J}}, \bar{p}_{\sim\mathscr{J}})$ to $(\bar{p}_{\mathscr{J}}, \bar{p}_{\sim\mathscr{J}})$ does not increase $\mathscr{E}_{\sim\mathscr{J}}$. By virtue of indecomposability, one $\mathscr{E}_j$ decreases for $j \in \sim\mathscr{J}$, so that $\sum_{j\in\sim\mathscr{J}} p_j \mathscr{E}_j$ decreases and $\sum_{j\in\mathscr{J}} p_j \mathscr{E}_j$ increases, $\mathscr{J} \neq \varnothing$. Therefore, a change from p to $\bar{p}$ increases $\sum_{j\in\mathscr{J}} p_j \mathscr{E}_j$ from its former value of zero (where $0 \in \mathscr{E}_j$ for all j). This is contrary to $\Delta\mathscr{E}_{i_0} < 0$, $\Delta\mathscr{E}_j = 0$ for $j \neq i_0, i_1$. Hence $\mathscr{J} = \varnothing$.

Let $\mathscr{J} = \{j \mid \bar{p}_j = p_j\}$. $\sim\mathscr{J}$ is nonempty since $p \neq \bar{p}$. A change from $(p_{\mathscr{J}}, p_{\sim\mathscr{J}})$ to $(p_{\mathscr{J}}, \bar{p}_{\sim\mathscr{J}})$ decreases $\sum_{i\in\sim\mathscr{J}} p_i \mathscr{E}_i$, which is possible only if $i_0 \in \sim\mathscr{J}$. q.e.d.

36 Remark Under the conditions of Theorem 35, $p \neq \bar{p}$ for a change in excess demand whenever $\mathscr{E}$ is single valued.

We can deduce the Hicksian laws: The good whose relative price increases most is the one whose demand increases. First we consider the system that is both a market and exchange economy.

37 Corollary *If there is weak gross substitution and indecomposability in a market–exchange economy and there is an increase in the excess demand for i_0 at the expense of i_1 that gives a change in equilibrium price from p to $\bar{p} \gg 0$, then*

$$\frac{\bar{p}_{i_0}}{p_{i_0}} \geqslant \frac{\bar{p}_j}{p_j} \geqslant \frac{\bar{p}_{i_1}}{p_{i_1}} \quad \text{for all } j,$$

and

$$\frac{\bar{p}_{i_0}}{p_{i_0}} > \frac{\bar{p}_{i_1}}{p_{i_1}}.$$

If an increase in either p_{i_1} or p_{i_0} increases all other excess demands, then

$$\frac{\bar{p}_{i_0}}{p_{i_0}} > \frac{\bar{p}_j}{p_j} > \frac{\bar{p}_{i_1}}{p_{i_1}} \quad \text{for all } j \neq i_1, i_0.$$

Proof Multiply $\bar{p}$ by a positive constant so that $p_{i_1} = \bar{p}_{i_1}$. From Theorem 35, $p_{i_0} \leqslant \bar{p}_{i_0}$ and $pj \leqslant \bar{p}j$. Dividing to obtain p gives the first sentence of Theorem 37. For the second sentence, after multiplication to get $p_{i_1} = \bar{p}_{i_1}$, note that $\mathscr{E}_j$ actually increases for any $p_j = \bar{p}_j$, whereupon $\mathscr{E}_j(\bar{p}) > 0$ contrary to equilibrium. Therefore, $\bar{p}_j > p_j$. Similarly, letting $p_{i_0} = \bar{p}_{i_0}$ for $j \neq i_0$, we get $p_j < \bar{p}_j$.   q.e.d.

In Theorem 38, the Hicksian laws are stated for a market economy, where most of the laws take the form of weak inequalities.

38 Theorem *Let there be a finite number of commodities, weak gross substitution, and indecomposability in a market system with a strictly positive equilibrium price system. If an increase in the excess demand for i_0 together with a decrease in the demand for i_1 leads to $p \neq \bar{p}$, then*

$$\frac{\bar{p}_{i_0}}{p_{i_0}} \geqslant \frac{\bar{p}_j}{p_j} \geqslant \frac{\bar{p}_{i_1}}{p_{i_1}} \qquad \text{for all } j$$

and

$$\frac{\bar{p}_{i_0}}{p_{i_0}} > \frac{\bar{p}_{i_1}}{p_{i_1}}.$$

Proof $\mathscr{E}_{i_0}(\bar{p}) < 0$ and $\mathscr{E}_{i_1}(\bar{p}) > 0$, $\mathscr{E}_j(\bar{p}) = 0$ for all other j. Let

$$\mathscr{J} = \left\{ j \,\Big|\, \frac{p_j}{\bar{p}_j} \geqslant \frac{p_i}{\bar{p}_i} \text{ for all } i \right\}, \qquad \mathscr{K} = \left\{ j \,\Big|\, \frac{p_j}{\bar{p}_j} \leqslant \frac{p_i}{\bar{p}_i} \text{ for all } i \right\}.$$

Then

$$\mathscr{K} \cap \mathscr{J} = \phi \qquad \text{by } p \neq \bar{p}.$$

Since

$$\mathscr{E}(p) = \mathscr{E}(kp), \qquad k = \max \frac{p_j}{\bar{p}_j} \quad \text{or} \quad k = \min \frac{p_j}{\bar{p}_j},$$

gross substitution gives

$$\mathscr{E}_{\mathscr{J}} \leqslant 0 \text{ (decreasing prices in } \sim\!\mathscr{J}) \quad \text{and} \quad \mathscr{E}_{\mathscr{K}} \geqslant 0 \text{ (increasing prices in } \sim\!\mathscr{K}).$$

Therefore, $i_1 \in \sim\!\mathscr{J}$ and $i_0 \in \sim\!\mathscr{K}$. Also, there is by indecomposability one $j \in \mathscr{J}$ for which $\mathscr{E}_j < 0$, which must be i_0. Similarly, there is one $j \in \mathscr{J}$ for which $\mathscr{E}_j > 0$, that is, $i_1 \in \mathscr{K}$.   q.e.d.

Conditions in market economies for Hicksian laws that are strict inequalities follow.

39 Corollary *If there are a finite number of commodities, weak gross substitution, and indecomposability in a market system for equilibrium*

$p \gg 0$, and if $\mathscr{E}_j$ is increased by either an increase in p_{i_0} or an increase in p_{i_0}, then an increase in the excess demand for i_0 and a decrease in that of i_1 leads to equilibrium $\bar{p}$ for which

$$\frac{\bar{p}_{i_0}}{p_{i_0}} > \frac{\bar{p}_j}{p_j} > \frac{\bar{p}_{i_1}}{p_{i_1}}, \qquad \text{for all} \quad ij = i_1, i_0. \qquad \text{q.e.d.}$$

For the infinite-commodity case, see Problem H.

Gross substitution under competition was discussed in Chapter 8 (on demand) in the companion volume, and it will be considered further in the balance of this chapter. However, we will not hereafter consider the case of monopolists. Therefore a brief comment is in order.

To verify gross substitution for monopolists, consider that if the price of another substitutable good rises, the demand for the monopolist's good increases. Hence, output increases and the monopolist's "demand" from its "competitive" firm increases. However, the monopolist also supplies more to the market at large. The effect on excess demand depends on whether the monopolist provides more or less than the increased demand. If the new demand is more inelastic than the old one, the monopolist provides less, so that excess demand increases, which is the gross substitution case. In Section 10 of Chapter 7 of the companion volume, especially Theorem 41, there are conditions sufficient for an economy with a monopolist to have gross substitution.

6. Comparative Statics under Competition I

As seen in Chapter 10 of the companion volume, the economy in pure competition does not normally display the gross substituion property whenever there are more than one factors of production. Hence, further efforts are required to produce a theory of comparative statics.

The condition

$$\Delta\mathscr{E} \, \Delta p < 0$$

is one of the weakest of comparative statics laws. For example, if we perturb demand to $\mathscr{E} + e$, at the new equilibrium, $\mathscr{E} = -e$ and $0 > \Delta\mathscr{E} \, \Delta p = -e \, \Delta p$. If e increases the demand for good i only, e is zero except in the ith component and $\Delta p_i > 0$. Laws intermediate between this and the Hicksian laws of Section 5 require more assumptions and are put off to the next section. The key condition needed here is that consumers have gross substitution only on the side of demand.

Let d^i be the excess demand for the ith consumer. Preferences are *homothetic* if changes in income lead to equiproportional changes in demand. A parenthetical result is as follows.

40 Remark If a consumer has convex, directional dense, homothetic preferences, then $\Delta d^i \, \Delta p \leqslant 0$.

Proof By virtue of Lemma 12 of Chapter 6 of the companion volume, $\partial d^i / \partial p$ is negative semidefinite. Hence,

$$\Delta d^i \, \Delta p = \Delta p \, \frac{\partial d^i}{\partial \bar{p}} \bigg|_{\bar{p} = tp + (1-t)\bar{p}} \Delta p \leqslant 0 \qquad \text{(mean value theorem).} \qquad \text{q.e.d.}$$

The following is the basic result applied in Chapter 7 to show dynamic stability of equilibrium.

41 Theorem *In a market–exchange system, with a finite number of commodities, suppose*

(i) *the excess demand* $-s$ *of the traders who are competitive firms is a continuously differentiable function of prices that is derived from continuously differentiable and strictly concave production functions,*

(ii) *summed excess demands d of traders who are not competitive firms are differentiable, and for them, commodities are weak gross substitutes at equilibrium,*

(iii) *for some i,*

$$\frac{\partial d_j}{\partial p_i} + \frac{\partial d_i}{\partial p_j} > 0 \qquad \text{for all} \ \ j \neq i$$

that are in variable demand, which includes all nonfactors. Then $0 > \Delta(p, w) \, \Delta(d - s) = (\bar{p}, \bar{w})(d - s)$ *whenever* (p, w) *is sufficiently near equilibrium and* $(\bar{p}, \bar{w})$ *and* (p, w) *is not proportional to* $(\bar{p}, \bar{w})$.

It should be noted that shares of firms will be owned by consumers. Hence, for consumer i with wealth ϕ^i,

$$\frac{\partial d^i}{\partial p} = \frac{\partial d^i}{\partial p} \bigg|_{\phi^i} + \frac{\partial d^i}{\partial \phi^i} \bigg|_p \frac{\partial \phi^i}{\partial p} \, .$$

If goods are not inferior, $\partial d^i / \partial \phi \geqslant 0$. If i's shares of firms are such that no lower profits occur whenever p_j increases, the second term on the left is always nonnegative. Hence, there is a tendency for gross substitution above and beyond ordinary demand.

Proof From equilibrium $(\bar{p}, \bar{w})$,

$$\varDelta(p, w)\, \varDelta(d - s) = [(\bar{p}, \bar{w}) - (p, w)][\bar{d} - \bar{s} - (d - s)]$$
$$= [(\bar{p}, \bar{w}) - (p, w)](s - d) \quad (\bar{d} - \bar{s} = 0)$$
$$= (\bar{p}, \bar{w})(s - d) \quad \text{(Walras' law)}.$$

Since $s - d$ is zero homogeneous, we can consider only the case in which p_i is constant.

The conservation laws give

$$0 = (\bar{p}, \bar{w}) \frac{\partial d - s}{\partial(\bar{p}, \bar{w})} = (\bar{p}, \bar{w}) \frac{\partial d}{\partial(\bar{p}, \bar{w})} - (\bar{p}, \bar{w}) \frac{\partial s}{\partial(\bar{p}, \bar{w})}$$

and

$$(\bar{p}, \bar{w}) \frac{\partial s}{\partial(\bar{p}, \bar{w})} = 0$$

by profit maximization. Therefore,

$$0 = (\bar{p}, \bar{w}) \frac{\partial d}{\partial(\bar{p}, \bar{w})}.$$

Similarly,

$$\frac{\partial d}{\partial(\bar{p}, \bar{w})} (\bar{p}, \bar{w}) = 0.$$

Therefore, for $p_i = 1$,

$$\left(\frac{\partial d_{\sim i}}{\partial(\bar{p}_{\sim i}, \bar{w})} + \frac{\partial d_{\sim i}}{\partial(\bar{p}_{\sim i}, \bar{w})} \right)' (p, w) = - \frac{\partial d}{\partial(\bar{p}_i, \bar{w})} + \left(\frac{\partial d_i}{\partial(\bar{p}_i, \bar{w})} \right)' \leqslant 0,$$

which implies that the roots of the Metzler–Mosak matrix

$$\left(\frac{\partial d_{\sim i}}{\partial(\bar{p}_{\sim i}, \bar{w})} + \left(\frac{\partial d_{\sim i}}{\partial(\bar{p}_{\sim i}, \bar{w})} \right)' \right)$$

are nonpositive; hence, the matrix is negative quasi semidefinite.

In the event that $d_{\sim \mathscr{J} \sim i}$ is fixed, $\sim \mathscr{J} \sim i$ including only factors, then $\partial d_\mathscr{J} / \partial \bar{w} \geqslant 0$ and $p\, \partial d_\mathscr{J} / \partial \bar{w} = 0$ (Walras' law), so that $\partial d_\mathscr{J} / \partial \bar{w} = 0$. Hence,

$$\frac{\partial d}{\partial(\bar{p}, \bar{w})} = \begin{pmatrix} \partial d_\mathscr{J} / \partial \bar{p} & 0 \\ 0 & 0 \end{pmatrix}$$

where $\partial d_\mathscr{J} / \partial \bar{p}$ is negative quasi definite.

By profit maximization,

$$(p, w)s \leqslant (p, w)\bar{s} \quad \text{and} \quad (\bar{p}, \bar{w})s \leqslant (\bar{p}, \bar{w})\bar{s}$$

or

$$(p, w)(s - \bar{s}) + (\bar{p}, \bar{w})(\bar{s} - s) \geqslant 0 \quad \text{or} \quad \Delta p\, \Delta s = [(\bar{p}, \bar{w}) - (p, w)][s - \bar{s}] \geqslant 0$$

By the mean value theorem, for (p, w) near $(\bar{p}, \bar{w})$,

$$\Delta p\, \Delta s \equiv \Delta p\, \frac{\partial s}{\partial(\bar{p}, \bar{w})}\Bigg|_{\substack{\bar{\bar{p}}=tp+(1-t)\bar{p} \\ \bar{\bar{w}}=tw+(1-t)\bar{w}}} \Delta p \leqslant 0$$

or letting $(p, \bar{w}) \to (\bar{p}, \mathrm{E})$, for all $x = \Delta(p, w)/|\Delta(p, w)|$, we get

$$x\, \frac{\partial s}{\partial p}\, x' \leqslant 0.$$

Hence, $\partial s/\partial(\bar{p}, \bar{w})$ is positive quasi semidefinite and

$$\partial d_{\sim i}/\partial(\bar{p}_{\sim i}, \bar{w}) - \partial s/\partial(\bar{p}_{\sim i}, \bar{w})$$

is negative quasi semidefinite.

Next we see when the derivative of $s_{\mathcal{J}}$ with respect to w is defined. Define $S = \partial s_{\mathcal{J}}/\partial w$. Note that whenever $S^i = \partial s^i_{\mathcal{J}}/\partial w$ exists for the ith firm, $S = \sum_i S^i$. On the other hand, if for some j, S^j does not exist, we have $y(\partial^2 f^j/\partial y_k\, \partial y_1)\, y = 0$ for some $y = \Delta w/|\Delta w|$, then

$$\frac{\Delta w\, \Delta s^j_{\mathcal{J}}}{|\Delta w|^2} \to \infty \quad \text{as} \quad \Delta w \to 0, \quad \frac{\Delta w}{|\Delta w|} = y.$$

Also, by cost minimization, $\Delta w\, \Delta s^i_{\mathcal{J}} \geqslant 0$ for all i and

$$\frac{\Delta w\, \Delta s_{\mathcal{J}}}{|\Delta w|^2} = \sum \frac{\Delta w\, \Delta s^i_{\mathcal{J}}}{|\Delta w|^2} \to \infty.$$

The existence of S would give

$$\frac{\Delta w\, \Delta s_{\mathcal{J}}}{|\Delta w|^2} \to \frac{\Delta w}{|\Delta w|}\, S\, \frac{\Delta w}{|\Delta w|},$$

which must be finite. We have a contradiction, so that the derivative S cannot exist whenever the derivative S^i does not exist. Therefore, S is defined if and only if $S = \sum S^i$ and each S^i is defined.

To show $\partial \mathscr{E}_{\sim i}/\partial(\bar{p}_{\sim i}, \bar{w})$ negative quasi definite, we consider two cases. If x is nonzero in the $\mathscr{J}$ components,

$$x \frac{\partial(d-s)_{\sim i}}{\partial(p_{\sim i}, w)} x' \leqslant x \frac{\partial d_{\sim i}}{\partial(\bar{p}_{\sim i}, \bar{w})} x'$$

$$= x_{\mathscr{J}} \frac{\partial d_{\mathscr{J}}}{\partial \bar{p}} x'_{\mathscr{J}} < 0.$$

Otherwise, if $x(\partial d_{\mathscr{J}}/\partial \bar{p}_{\sim i}) x' = 0$,

$$x = (0, x_{\sim \mathscr{J} \sim i})$$

or

$$\frac{x(\partial(d-s)_{\sim i}}{\partial(\bar{p}_{\sim i}, \bar{w})} x' = (0, x_{\sim \mathscr{J} \sim i}) \begin{pmatrix} \dfrac{\partial(d-s)_{\mathscr{J}}}{\partial \bar{p}_{\sim i}} & \dfrac{\partial(d-s)_{\mathscr{J}}}{\partial \bar{w}} \\ \dfrac{\partial(d-s)_{\sim \mathscr{J} \sim i}}{\partial \bar{p}_{\sim i}} & \dfrac{\partial(d-s)_{\sim \mathscr{J} \sim i}}{\partial \bar{w}} \end{pmatrix} \begin{pmatrix} 0 \\ x'_{\sim \mathscr{J} \sim i} \end{pmatrix}$$

$$= x_{\sim \mathscr{J} \sim i} \frac{\partial - s_{\sim \mathscr{J} \sim i}}{\partial \bar{w}} x'_{\sim \mathscr{J} \sim i} < 0$$

(by Theorem 14 of Chapter 10 of the companion volume). Hence, $\partial(d-s)_{\sim i}/\partial(\bar{p}_{\sim i}, \bar{w})$ is negative quasi definite. Fixing p_i, we get

$$0 > \varDelta(p, w) \varDelta(d-s) = \varDelta(p_{\sim i}, w) \varDelta(d-s)_{\sim i}$$

$$= \varDelta(p_{\sim i}, w) \frac{\partial(d-s)_{\sim i}}{\partial(p_{\sim i}, w)} \Bigg|_{(\bar{p}_{\sim i}, \bar{w}_{\sim}) \text{near} (\bar{p}_{\sim i}, \bar{w}_{\sim i})} \varDelta(p_{\sim i}, w)$$

q.e.d.

In the proof of Theorem 41, $\partial d_{\mathscr{J}}/\partial w = 0$ might be surprising, but the rationale is as follows.

Residual profits are $\pi = ps_{\mathscr{J}} + ws_{\sim \mathscr{J}}$. Total consumer income is $\pi + w(-d_{\sim \mathscr{J}}) = pd_{\mathscr{J}}$. Now

$$\frac{\partial pd_{\mathscr{J}}}{\partial w} = \frac{\partial \pi}{\partial w} - w \frac{\partial d_{\sim \mathscr{J}}}{\partial w} - d_{\sim \mathscr{J}}$$

$$= \frac{\partial \pi}{\partial w} - d_{\sim \mathscr{J}}$$

$$= p \frac{\partial s_{\mathscr{J}}}{\partial w} + s_{\sim \mathscr{J}} + w \frac{\partial s_{\sim \mathscr{J}}}{\partial w} - d_{\sim \mathscr{J}}$$

$$= p \frac{\partial s_{\mathscr{J}}}{\partial w} + w \frac{\partial s_{\sim \mathscr{J}}}{\partial w} = 0$$

by profit maximization. Hence, $\partial d_{\mathscr{J}}/\partial w = 0$ if there are no distribution effects on income to recipients or, alternatively, on demand from changes in income. More generally, since $\varDelta p \, \varDelta s > 0$, only $\partial d_{\mathscr{I}}/\partial w \simeq 0$ is required, where the approximation to zero is sufficient to keep

$$\max \frac{\varDelta p}{|\varDelta p|} \varDelta d < \min \frac{\varDelta p}{|\varDelta p|} \varDelta s.$$

In Theorem 41, constant returns to scale can be accounted if one factor is a residual income holder. Only the others have market prices. As before, monopoly can be introduced as a consumer with gross substitution of demand.

PROBLEMS

E. Uniqueness of Equilibrium I

Show that a distribution of wealth for which the zero trade is nearly an equilibrium has competitive equilibrium giving levels of preference to all participants nearly equal to that at their zero trade positions. (Hint: Use upper semicontinuity of $\mathscr{E}$.)

F. Uniqueness of Equilibrium II

Equilibrium is *locally unique* if there is no other equilibrium nearby. It is *globally unique* if there is but one equilibrium price system. Show that if $\det(\partial \mathscr{E}_{\sim i}/\partial p_{\sim i}) \neq 0$,

   (i)   Equilibrium is locally unique for $p_i = \bar{p}_i$. (Hint: Apply the mean value theorem of differential calculus.)

   (ii)   A distribution of wealth for which the zero trade is nearly an equilibrium has a globally unique equilibrium. Gale and Nikaido [1965] have shown that if $\det \partial \mathscr{E}_{\sim \mathscr{I}}/\partial p_{\sim \mathscr{I}}$ has sign equal to $(-1)^n$ where n is the number of elements in $\mathscr{I}$, for all nonempty $\mathscr{I}$ and for all $p > 0$, then equilibrium is globally unique. See also Pearce [1967].

G. Comparative Statics I

Let $\mathscr{E}_i$ be differentiable and fix p_n. Show that:

   (i)   If $\partial \mathscr{E}_{\sim n}/\partial p_{\sim n}$ in an exchange system is indecomposable and Metzler–Mosak, and if $\partial \mathscr{E}_n/\partial p_i > 0$ for all i, then an increase in one or more excess demands for $i \neq n$ (with a decrease in the excess demand for n) leads to an increase in all prices except for p_n.

   (ii)   If $\partial \mathscr{E}_{\sim n}/\partial p_{\sim n}$ in a market system is indecomposable and Metzler–Mosak and if $\partial \mathscr{E}_i/\partial p_n > 0$ for all $i \neq n$, then an increase in one or more excess demands for $i \neq n$ leads to an increase in all prices except for p_n.

(iii) If $\partial \mathscr{E}_{\sim n}/\partial p_{\sim n}$ in a market system is indecomposable, if the number of commodities is finite, and if $\partial \mathscr{E}_i/\partial p_n + \partial \mathscr{E}_n/\partial p_i > 0$, then $\partial \mathscr{E}_{\sim n}/\partial p_{\sim n}$ is negative quasi definite.

(iv) In (iii), equilibrium is locally unique. These results are analogous to those of Hicks [1938], Metzler [1945], Mosak [1944], and McKenzie [1960a].

H. *Uniqueness of Equilibrium III*

Show under weak gross substitution that:

(i) In an exchange system with two goods, for p_i fixed, equilibrium is globally unique if an increase in one price (not p_i) always changes the excess demand for one or more of the other goods.

(ii) In a market system with two goods, equilibrium is globally unique up to a multiplicative constant if an increase in one price always changes the excess demand for one or the other good.

(iii) In an exchange system with indecomposability, a strictly positive equilibrium price system for which p_i is fixed is globally unique. (Hint: Alter the proof of Theorem 35.)

(iv) In a market system with a finite number of commodities and indecomposability, a strictly positive equilibrium price system is unique up to a multiplicative constant.

UNSOLVED PROBLEM

I. *Comparative Statics II*

Generalize Theorem 41 to cover cases with a particular class of demand functions (for example, separable or Bergson), a Leontief technology, and an arbitrary distribution of factors.

7. Comparative Statics under Competition II

In Section 6, results were less powerful than under the gross substitution property of Section 5. To obtain stronger results, several difficulties must be surmounted.

First, increases in the price of factors may affect their supplies as well as demands, giving a virtually infinite variety of sign patterns for $\Delta \mathscr{E}_i/\Delta w_j$. In some applications, it must be assumed that factor supplies are fixed. In this case, we are restricted to short-term statics since in the long run, most factors are variable.

Second, changes in factor prices lead to a distribution of effects on various individuals. For owners of decreasing returns firms, profits are increased by the reduction of factor prices so that firm owners increase consumption, whereas the appropriate factor owners decrease consumption. Only in the case where there are constant returns to scale, and therefore zero profits, can this distribution effect be avoided. In the constant returns case, it is still true that differential changes in factor prices lead to differential effects on demand. One way out is to assume that all consumers have the same marginal propensities to consume out of income, so that changes in demand do not result from changes in factor prices which leave fixed total factor income wy. This is the *Keynes case* where, as Gorman [1953] has shown, the consumer sector acts as if it were a single representative consumer.

Recall that commodities i and j are *net substitutes* if in the Slutsky term, $a_{ij} > 0$, $j \neq i$, that is, if adjusting for changes in real income, an increase in the price of one good increases the purchases of another. Under pure competition and in the Keynes case, gross substitution follows from net substitution.

42 Theorem *If there is the Keynes case, with strictly convex (induced) preferences for all competitive traders,*

$$\frac{\partial \mathscr{E}_{\sim n}}{\partial p_{\sim n}} = \frac{1}{p_n} \sum_i a^i \equiv A$$

where a^i is the Slutsky substitution term (which is assumed to exist) for trader i, good n fixed in price. Therefore,

$$\Delta p \, \Delta \mathscr{E} < 0$$

for p not proportional to $\bar{p}$ and there is (weak) gross substitution if there is (weak) net substitution for each consumer.

For comparative statics, see Section 5.

Proof The Slutsky equations give

$$\frac{\partial \mathscr{E}_{\sim n}^i}{\partial p_{\sim n}} = \sum_i \frac{1}{p_n} a^i - \sum_i x_{\sim n}^i \frac{\partial x_{\sim n}^i}{\partial \theta}$$

$$= \sum_i \frac{1}{p_n} a^i - \left(\sum_i x_{\sim n}^i \right) \left(\frac{\partial x_{\sim n}}{\partial \theta} \right)$$

$$= \sum_i \frac{1}{p_n} a^i,$$

which are negative definite.   q.e.d.

It should be noted that Theorem 42 includes production separated from consumption, since shares in surplus profit specify ownership of (parts of) production sets, and increases in consumer incomes do not change their production decisions. However, comparative statics results beyond Theorem 42 follow from sign patterns of

$$\sum_i \frac{\partial \mathscr{E}^i_{\sim n}}{\partial p_{\sim n}}$$

that do not include the case of production from several factors.

Consumption is *Keynesian* if, there is the Keynes case, where

$$\frac{\partial x^i}{\partial \theta} = \frac{\partial x}{\partial \theta}$$

for all consumers i. Production is *strictly Leontief* if it is Leontief and the factor utilization matrix is fixed. We show that an increase in a factor decreases its price even after consequent changes in product prices.

43 Corollary *If production is strictly Leontief and consumption is Keynesian with all outputs consumed in positive quantities, then, fixing p_n, we have*

$$\frac{\partial p_{\sim n}}{\partial y} = -A^{-1}(XY^{-1})_{\sim n'}, \qquad A = \sum_i a^i\, p_n.$$

Factor price changes are given by

$$\frac{\partial w}{\partial y} = \frac{\partial w}{\partial p_{\sim n}}\, \frac{\partial p_{\sim n}}{\partial y} = -(X^{-1}Y)'_{\sim n} A^{-1}(YX^{-1})_{\sim n}$$

so that increasing y_i alone decreases its price.

Proof $\partial p/\partial y = (\partial p/\partial x)(\partial x/\partial y)$, the supply of goods is $x = XY^{-1}y$, and $w = pX^{-1}XY$.   q.e.d.

In the more general case, where Y is variable, supply changes by the law

$$0 = Y\frac{\partial \xi}{\partial w} + \sum \frac{\partial y^i}{\partial w}\, \xi^i,$$

$$\frac{\partial \xi}{\partial w} = -Y^{-1}\left(\sum \frac{\partial y^i}{\partial w}\, \xi^i\right),$$

$$\frac{\partial x}{\partial p} = -XY^{-1}\left(\sum \frac{\partial y^i}{\partial w}\, \xi^i\right)(XY^{-1})'.$$

It is hard to see what the signs of $\partial x/\partial p$ will be.

The following corollary shows the Hicksian laws restricted to final products only.

44 Corollary *If production is strictly Leontief and consumption is Keynesian with all outputs consumed in positive quantities, then, fixing p_n, we have*

$$\frac{\partial d_i}{\partial p_n} + \frac{\partial d_n}{\partial p_i} > 0 \quad \text{for all} \quad i \neq n,$$

and for a change in excess demand $\varepsilon\delta$, $\varepsilon > 0$,

$$\frac{\partial p_{\sim n}}{d\epsilon} = -(A^{-1})\,\delta, \qquad \frac{dw}{d\epsilon} = -(X^{-1}Y)'_{\sim n}A^{-1}\,\delta.$$

Therefore, with net substitution and indecomposability of A, an increase in one or more excess demands with a decrease in the excess demand of n increases all prices (relative to p_n), and an increase in demand that leads to increased use of factors j in $\mathscr{J}$ increases the price of j by at least one $j \in \mathscr{J}$.

Corollaries 43 and 44 might be thought to apply to the very short run when factors are not mobile between industries. Aside from these cases, and the weak laws of Section 6, comparative statics results for competitive economies do not appear to be very strong.

PROBLEMS

J. Uniqueness of Equilibrium IV

Show that

(i) Equilibrium is globally unique if $\partial \mathscr{E}_{\sim i}/\partial p_{\sim i}$ is negative quasi indefinite. (Hint: Let p, $\bar{p}$ be equilibria, $p^t = tp + i(1 - t)\,\bar{p}$, and show that

$$0 > \frac{d}{dt}\,\Delta\mathscr{E}\,\Delta p = \frac{d}{dt}\,(\mathscr{E}(tp + (1 - t)\bar{p}) - \mathscr{E}(p))((t - 1)p + (1 - t)\bar{p}).)$$

(ii) Equilibrium is globally unique whenever preferences are Hicksian or Keynesian.

The Hicksian case was solved by Hicks [1938].

K. Uniqueness of Equilibrium V

Show that if there are two goods that are normal, then equilibrium is unique.

This problem was solved by Arrow and Hurwicz [1958].

L. Leontief–Keynes Case

Let $\partial x^i / \partial \theta = c$ for all consumers i and assume a Leontief technology with a positive amount of each good produced. Let demand be $d(p, w(p))$ and show that $\partial d_{\sim n} / \partial p_{\sim n} = \sum_i a^i_{\sim n} / p_n$ where $a^i_{\sim n} / p_n$ is the Slutsky substitution effect.

M. Leontief Technologies I

(i)   Show that if there is a strict Leontief technology and if Y and X are simultaneously diagonalized,

$$
Y = \begin{pmatrix} y_{11} & & 0 \\ & \ddots & \\ X & & y_{nn} \end{pmatrix}, \qquad X = \begin{pmatrix} x_{11} & & 0 \\ & \ddots & \\ X & & x_{nn} \end{pmatrix},
$$

then increases in y^i increase x^i.

(ii)   Show that in (i) if there is only a Leontief technology with Y and X properly diagonalized, an increase in p_i increases w_i.

(iii)   In case (ii) show that increases in p_i leave w_j unchanged, $w_j > p_i$.

N. Leontief Technologies II

(i)   Show that changes in demand under a strict Leontief system with fixed factors of production can change relative prices.

(ii)   How do the consumers in (i) change demands if there is only one factor of production? What determines the rate of return on the factor? What is the degree of arbitrariness of the rate of return? (A contrary view is expressed by Schwartz [1961, pp. 252–254]).

Part (ii) is due to Georgescu–Roegen [1951] (see also articles by Samuelson, Koopmans, and Arrow in the same volume). It might correspond to a long-run situation where only one factor, say, natural resources, is in short supply. In the Marxian scheme, it would be labor.

O. *Excise Taxes II*

(i)   Assume constant returns to scale, one consumer, and no inferior goods. Returning to Problem Q of Chapter 4, show that two different levels of prices, $p^1 + t$, $p^2 + kt$, t and kt the respective tax rates, $k > 0$, lead to a decrease in the level of the consumers' preferences (whenever government expenditures are held constant). (Hint: Show that one and only one of $(p^1 + t)d^1 \geqslant (p^1 + t)d^2$ or $p^2d^2 \geqslant p^2d^1$ holds (using $p^1x^1 \geqslant p^1x^2$, $p^2x^2 \geqslant p^2x^1$ for outputs x^1 and x^2) and that $p^1d^1 > p^1d^2$ and $p^2d^2 > p^2d^1$ cannot both hold, since there is only one consumer. Next, for $k > 1$, show that $p^1d^1 \geqslant p^1d^2$, so that d^1 is revealed preferred to d^2. Use the fact that $p^1x^1 = p^1d^1$.)

(ii)   In (i) assume that there are two goods, none inferior, and one consumer, but not necessarily constant returns to scale. Show that one proportional increase in all taxes will decrease utility.

This problem was first solved by Foster and Sonnenschein [1970].

III

Dynamics

6

Classical Dynamics

Then you ought to have invested my money with the bankers, and at my coming I should have received what was my own with interest. So take the talent from him, and give it to him who has ten talents. For to every one who has will be given, but from him who has not, even what he has will be taken away.

MATTHEW, 25: 27–29 (RSV)

1. Dynamics for a Small Country in International Trade

Classical dynamics is usually viewed as analysis of the economy over time, assuming that the economy is always in equilibrium (Keynes [1937, Chapter 1]). Here, when possible, we try to assume only equilibrium conditions in commodity markets. If equilibrium conditions, including full employment of factors, hold most of the time, our dynamical analysis indicates the long-run tendencies of the economic system. For example, we give conditions showing the Malthusian theory whereby population expansion drives wages to the subsistence level. Another important topic concerns the foundations of the Ricardian steady state. We will make some efforts to establish conditions under which the economy tends to the kinds of limiting states postulated in long-run Ricardian analysis (Sections 3–5). Related to the Malthusian theory is the result that over time in an economy with Koopmans-type consumers, the families with the lowest rate of discount will eventually dominate (Section 2).

As will be seen, some powerful assumptions must be made in order to get theorems about dynamics in large countries. For small countries, however, some general points can be made without any special assumption except that international prices have a time path. In this section, we show that over time as capital accumulates factor prices will pass through regions of factor price nonequalization. Here tariffs may arrest the decline in capital returns and encourage growth.

Suppose a small country in international trade. Let a particular factor y_j increase in quantity. Let there be n factors of production.

1 Remark   So long as there are not m independent y^i, increases in y^j over time, given constant goods prices, will force changes in the factor wages, and in fact the wages for j will fall (Theorem 22 of Chapter 5). Whether or not there are m independent y^i, as y^j increases, eventually the wages w will pass through regions in which there are not m independent y^i (Theorems 26 and 27 of Chapter 5).

Whether total factor income will decrease or increase is a complex story depending on the extent to which other factor prices change and on the response of the share of the factor in the industries' outputs, which is determined by the elasticity of substitution in each industry to the change in factor endowments. In any case, the income of the changing factor can be improved by a government subsidy or by an appropriate tariff that allows the new factor endowment to be employed in a new industry, after a transfer of resources from other industries.

What is required is that there be an industry available to absorb the new factor supply and that it be possible to make this industry profitable without changing the factor prices. It would follow that the price of the growing factor would not fall. All this will occur if

(i)   there are exactly n industries with linearly independent outputs x^i, n the number of goods,

(ii)   of which m have linearly independent factor inputs $y^i(w)$, $m \leqslant n$,

(iii) $y = \sum_{\xi_i > 0} \xi_i y^i$.

In this case, for a time, increases in y_j can be absorbed simply by ensuring that all industries are profitable, which can be accomplished by an appropriate tariff system (Theorem 25 of Chapter 5). (The restriction to n industries prevents the situation where one industry must have positive profits in order for another to be profitable.)

For example, suppose a country has a sufficiently low capital/labor ratio to be below the range where factor price equalization occurs. To absorb the large labor force, it is necessary that the labor intensive industry be the only operating industry due to a high price of capital and a low price of labor. As capital accumulates, a tariff may be imposed to make the capital intensive industry profitable (Theorem 24 of Chapter 5). The new capital can then be absorbed without affecting factor prices. As capital continues to accumulate, the capital intensive industry eventually exhausts the labor force. Thereafter, the price of capital must fall to absorb great quantities of capital.

If such a policy is followed, a particular factor increases its income only in response to an increase in its quantity. That is to say, there is a tariff policy by which an increase in one factor (say, capital) gives no benefit to the other factors (say, labor). The remarks following are based on Section 12 of Chapter 2.

For example, consider a foreign investment in a new industry, with a protective tariff. If the profitability of other industries is not disturbed, there will be no benefits for the home country, since the investment will not increase the income of any other factors. In addition, the home country's consumers must pay the higher price, so that there is a potential loss. The tariff cannot raise enough revenues to subsidize the home producers by an amount equal to the added cost since tariff revenues $(\bar{p} - p)\bar{z}$ do not equal consumer costs $(\bar{p} - p)\bar{x}$. Therefore, consumers cannot be returned to their former position.

2 Remark A foreign investment made possible by a protective tariff involves a potential loss.

As a second example, capital accumulation leads to a decrease in the rate of return on capital.

3 Remark Outside the set of factor endowments where there is factor price equalization, the return to capital will fall with an increase in the supply of capital, international prices fixed. Assuming the accumulation of capital to depend positively on its price, this will lead to a slower accumulation of capital.

The likelihood is that very low income countries specializing in labor intensive goods, and very high income countries, specializing in capital intensive goods, will experience this effect. There may be some incentive to increase growth rates by raising tariffs. On the other hand, the real return to capital will fall to the extent that prices of consumer goods increase. The tariff will be inferior to a direct tax–subsidy scheme, but for an underdeveloped country the impossibility of an effective tax–subsidy system may make a tariff the best available stimulus for growth.

Theorems about the effects on the home economy of various changes in international prices can be deduced from the theorems in Section 4 of Chapter 5.

2. Consumer Choice over Time

In the dynamics of large countries, our first concern is the long-run fortunes of families, depending on their choice and preferences. As an example of the kinds of families considered, we sketch a theory of inter-generational utility. Suppose each generation of a family evaluates its own consumption by a utility function u. Let the welfare of the tth generation be defined by $\bar{U}_t$ where

$$\hat{U}_t = u(x^t) + \alpha \hat{U}_{t+1} .$$

Then we can easily show $\hat{U}_t = \sum_{s \geqslant t} u(x^t) \alpha^{s-t}$. Just as well, we could define $U_t = \sum_{s=1}^{\infty} u(x^s) \alpha^s$ since of course generation t has no power over and is not influenced by the first $t - 1$ consumptions, and therefore U_t is an increasing linear transformation of $\hat{U}_t$. Starting from preferences alone, if they are stationary and time separable, they are representable by the *simple Koopmans utilitary function*

$$\sum_{t=0}^{\infty} u(x^t) \alpha^t$$

(Theorem 13 of Chapter 6 of the companion volume). Even for more general preferences and utility functions it will be seen that the *discount rate* α is critical in determining the asymptotic consumptions of such consumers. The families with the highest α will end up with all the property.

Under increasingly stringent conditions, we show that per capita consumptions are bounded (Lemma 4); in the long run, a consistent rate of interest over time appears (Lemma 8), and that rate of interest is equal to the discount rate of the only surviving consumers, namely, those with the lowest rate of discount (Theorem 9). At the end of the section there are some remarks about the situation where several families have the same lowest rate of discount.

It is presumed that preferences are directly concerned with per capita stocks and reproductions. Let m be the labor good synonomous with population. Then, the evaluation of a stream of capital stocks is reduced to that of a stream of per capita capital stocks, denoted by

$$c(t) = \frac{y_{\sim m,t}}{y_{m,t}},$$

and the expansion in population or labor force,

$$l(t) = \frac{y_{m,t+1}}{y_{m,t}}.$$

Then the arguement of utility is $x(t) = (l(t), c(t))$.

We briefly sketch the theory of family choice for the simple Koopmans utility function: the simple Koopmans utility is now

$$\sum_{t=0}^{\infty} u(l(t), c(t)) \, \alpha^t.$$

A family has a budget constraint

$$\theta = \sum_{t=0}^{\infty} p(t) \, c(t) \prod_{s=0}^{t} l(s) \, y_{m,0}$$

where θ is the present value of all future capital or wage income available to the family. The first-order conditions of demand include

$$\frac{\dfrac{\partial u}{\partial c_i(t)} \, \alpha^t}{p_i(t) \prod_{s=0}^{t} l(s) \, y_{m,0}} = \frac{\dfrac{\partial u}{\partial c_i(t_0)} \, \alpha^{t_0}}{p_i(t_0) \prod_{s=0}^{t_0} l(s) \, y_{m,0}}$$

or

$$\frac{\dfrac{\partial u}{\partial c_i(t)}}{\dfrac{\partial u}{\partial c_i(t_0)}} = \frac{p_i(t)}{p_i(t_0)} \, \alpha^{t_0-t} \prod_{s=t_0+1}^{t} l(s),$$

whenever $c_i(t) > 0$, $c_i(t_0) > 0$. In words. the marginal rate of substitution equals the relative prices multiplied by a discount factor that is required by difference in time.

Utility u is *quasi concave* if $u(tx + (1 - t)y) \geqslant \min(u(x), u(y))$ for $0 < t < 1$.

If $c_i(t_k)$, $t_k \to \infty$, is bounded from zero, then by concavity of u, $\partial u / \partial c_i(t_k)$ is bounded from infinity, and for some subsequence of t_k, $\partial u / \partial c_i$ converges to c. Without loss of generality, let

$$\frac{\dfrac{\partial u}{\partial c_i(t_k)}}{\dfrac{\partial u}{\partial c_i(t_0)}} \to c.$$

Evidently,

$$\frac{p_i(t_k)}{p_i(t_0)} \, \alpha^{t_0 - t_k} \prod_{s=t_0+1}^{t_k} l(s) \to c$$

or

$$0 \geqslant \lim \frac{1}{t_k} \log \frac{p_i(t_k)}{p_i(t_0)} + \lim \frac{1}{t_k} \log \alpha^{t_0 - t_k} \prod_{s=t_0+1}^{t_k} l(s)$$

$$= \lim \frac{1}{t_k} \log \frac{p_i(t_k)}{p_i(t_0)} - \log \alpha + \lim \frac{1}{t_k} \log \prod_{s=t_0+1}^{t_k} l(s),$$

with equality if $c > 0$. If $c_i(t_k)$ is bounded from infinity, we would expect $c > 0$. Then letting

$$\lim \frac{1}{t_k} \log \prod_{s=t_0+1}^{t_k} l(s) \equiv \log l,$$

we have

$$\lim \frac{1}{t_k} \log \frac{p_i(t_k)}{p_i(t_0)} = \log \frac{\alpha}{l},$$

which can be so only for one value of α/l. Therefore, the consumers whose limiting consumption of i is neither zero nor infinity are members of a unique class having $\alpha^i / l^i = \alpha/l$. Other families have infinite consumption if $\alpha^i / l^i > \alpha/l$ and zero consumption if $\alpha^i / l^i < \alpha/l$. The reader can work this out from the foregoing analysis or read on to Remark 10, where a more general case is treated.

We now turn to more general kinds of preferences but less general kinds of consumption possibilities. Special interest accrues to the generalized Koopmans utility function that represents preferences that are τ-stationary and τ-separable (to be defined). In Chapter 6, Section 5 of the companion volume, the *Koopmans utility function* was presented as

$$\sum_{t=1}^{\infty} u\left(^{t-\tau+1}x^{t+\tau}\right)\alpha^t + \sum_{s=0}^{\tau-1} u\left(^1y^s,\, ^0x^{\tau-1-s}\right)\alpha^{t-1-s} \qquad \text{where} \quad {}^sx^t = (x_s,\, ...,\, x_t).$$

In this function, the evaluation of current consumption is influenced by memory and anticipation. Also, the relevant past of the consumer is given as y.

The strongest form of the following theory will require the boundedness of x^t. For this purpose, let m above be the population commodity. In most cases the mth good is not marketed (as an argument of the utility function). Define relative family size by

$$n^i(t) = \frac{y_{m,t}^i}{\sum_i y_{m,t}^i}.$$

From the general point of view, given $x^i(t)$ for each family and the family size $y_{m,t}^i$, total capital stock for each family is determined. Similarly, if $n^i(t)$ is known instead of $y_{m,t}^i$, then family capital stocks are determined up to a positive multiplicative constant.

We can imagine a family owning all of a durable factor, land, and always reducing its population. In such a case, the family's per capita wealth would tend to infinity. Hence, boundedness is not trivial to verify.

4 Lemma *If*

   (i)   *there are constant returns to scale,*

   (ii)   *for bounded capital per unit labor and expanding labor inputs, production possibilities per unit labor are bounded,*

   (iii)   *there is either free disposal or costless transferral to unproductive consumer goods,*

   (iv)   *every commodity is either substitutable in production or a universal capital good,*

   (v) $|c^i(t)| > b$ *implies that eventually for some $\varepsilon > 0$, $l^i(t) > \varepsilon + 1$, then there is a B such that $|c^i(t_j)| < B$ for some $t_j \to \infty$. If also*

   (vi) $l(t) > \delta > 0$,

then there is a B such that $|c^i(t)| < B$ for all t.

An application of (vi) would be the case where very large per capita consumption has very small marginal utility at very low rates of reproduction.

To prove Lemma 4, another lemma is required.

5 Lemma   *If no commodities are negatively productive, population is either substitutable in production or a universal capital good, and there are constant returns to scale, then it is possible to decrease only $l(t)$ and increase $c(s)$ for all $s > t$. If population is producible from other goods, then we can increase $l(s)$, $s > t$.*

Proof   We can increase $l(t)$ alone by decreasing $y_{m,t}$ and thereby increasing $c(t+1)$. Since there is more per capita capital, it is possible to produce more of each commodity per capita in the future (by virtue of the three hypotheses of the lemma).

If population is producible from other goods, part of the extra capital can be devoted to the production of more population in time $(t + 1)$ below its former level. Proceeding inductively, we can show that it is possible to increase $l(s)$ for all $s > t$.   q.e.d.

Proof of Lemma 4   Whenever $|c^i(t)| > b$, by (v) we have $|l_i(t)| > (1 + \varepsilon)$. By Lemma 5, we can lower $l_i(t)$ to $1 + \varepsilon$ and have $c^*(t) \geqslant c^i(t)$. By (ii), $|c^*(t)|$ is bounded by some k whenever $l^i(t) = 1 + \varepsilon$.

Assume $|c^i(t)| \to \infty$; then for any $b > 0$, eventually $|c^i(t)| > b$ for $s > t$. However, $|c^i(t)| < |c^*(t)| < k$ contrary to hypothesis. This gives the first conclusion of the theorem.

Let us construct a path $\hat{c}$ as follows. Let $\hat{c}(0) = c^i(0)$. If at time t $l_i(t) > (1 + \varepsilon)$, let $\hat{c}(t) \geqslant c^i(t)$ and $\hat{l}(t) = (1 + \varepsilon)$. If $l_i(t) < (1 + \varepsilon)$ (and therefore $|c^i(t)| \leqslant b$) but a choice $|\hat{c}(t)| > b$, $\hat{c}(t) \geqslant c^i(t)$ is possible, then increase $l(t)$ so long as $\hat{c}(t) \geqslant c^i(t)$, $l_i(t) \leqslant (1 + \varepsilon)$. The increase in $l_i(t)$ is halted only by $|c(t)| \leqslant b$ or $\hat{l}(t) = (1 + \varepsilon)$. Evidently, for every time period, either $|\hat{c}(t)| \leqslant b$ or $\hat{l}(t) = (1 + \varepsilon)$, but always $l(t) > \delta$ and $\hat{c}(t) \geqslant c^i(t)$. Therefore, either $\hat{c}(t)$ is derived from $|\hat{c}(t-1)| \leqslant b$ or $\hat{l}(t-1) \leqslant (1 + \varepsilon)$ leads to $\hat{c}(t)$ bounded by k.

We consider a possible $\hat{c}(t)$ unbounded by k. Evidently, $l(t-1) < (1 + \varepsilon)$ and $|\hat{c}(t-1)| < b$. It can be shown that output–input ratios are bounded. Also, $|y_m(t)| > \delta |y_m(t-1)|$, and we have for some $L > 0$

$$L \geqslant \frac{|y_{\sim m}(t)|}{|y_m(t-1)| + |y_{\sim m}(t-1)|} = \frac{|y_{\sim m}(t)|}{|\delta^{-1}y_m(t)| + |y_{\sim m}(t-1)|}$$

$$= \frac{|\hat{c}(t)|}{\delta^{-1} + |y_{\sim m}(t-1)|/|y_m(t)|} > \frac{|\hat{c}(t)|}{\delta^{-1} + |\hat{c}(t-1)|\,\delta}.$$

Therefore,

$$|\hat{c}(t)| < L(\delta^{-1} + |\hat{c}(t-1)|\,\delta) \leqslant L(\delta^{-1} + b\delta),$$

and for all t,

$$|c^i(t)| \leqslant |\hat{c}(t)| \leqslant \max(K, b, L(\delta^{-1} + b\delta)).$$

It has been seen that under certain conditions trade efficiency or Pareto optimality implies competitive behavior (Chapters 2 and 4). The results following apply to these cases and hence to a wide range of socio-economic situations. In particular, the competitive price system is a highly useful tool of analysis.

Preferences are *weakly τ-time separable* on $x = (l, c)$ if for all times $j \in \mathscr{J}$ and $k \in \mathscr{K}$, $| j - k | > \tau$,

$$(x_{\mathscr{J}}, x_{\mathscr{K}}, \bar{x}_{\sim \mathscr{J} \cup \mathscr{K}}) \, \mathscr{P} \, \bar{x} \qquad \text{implies} \qquad x \, \mathscr{R} \, (\bar{x}_{\mathscr{J}}, \bar{x}_{\mathscr{K}}, x_{\sim \mathscr{J} \cup \mathscr{K}}).$$

Preferences are τ-*stationary* if there is a $y = (y^1, ..., y^{t-1})$ such that $(z, y, x) \, \mathscr{R}(z, y, \bar{x})$ if and only if $x \, \mathscr{R} \, \bar{x}$. Not only the (generalized) Koopmans function but also the intertemporal efficiency preference relation are weakly τ-time separable (for $\tau = 0$). The following shows the existence of a rate of interest (equal to $l_i / \alpha_i - 1$).

6 Lemma *Suppose consumers with a separation of production and consumption have τ-stationary, weakly τ-time separable, weakly convex, and locally unsaturated preferences, and $\sum_i \mathscr{R}_i(x^i) \, n_i$ is directional dense with competitive prices $p(t)$. If for $t_n = j_n \tau + k$, $n = 1, 2, ...,$*

$$z(t_0) = z(t_n) \equiv (x^{t_n - \tau + 1}, ..., x^{t_n + \tau - 1}),$$

then for each consumer i there exists α_i such that

$$p(t_n) = p(t_0) \left(\frac{\alpha_i}{l^i(t_0)} \right)^{t_n - t_0}.$$

Note that directional density allows certain kinds of partial orderings where preferences over nearby time periods can be analyzed only by the detailed study of the partial ordering. It is unknown whether the other conditions cited are compatible with so complex a partial ordering.

Proof The consumption of only one consumer is considered. For him, as others, the path $z = (w, z(t_0), z(t_0), ...)$ has the same values as $x = (x^0, x^1, ...)$ in the time periods $t_n \pm s$, $| s | \leqslant \tau - 1$. In view of weak τ-time separability, changes in $x(t_n)$ that improve x do not reduce the desirability of z. Therefore, the prices associated with z are the same as those associated with x in times t_n. By τ-stationarity, preferences on $(w, z(t), z(t_0), ...)$ are the same as on $(x(t_0), z(t_0), z(t_0), ...)$. Directional density implies $p(t_n) = \beta(p(t_n - \tau))$ or $p(t_n) = (\beta)^{j_n} p(t_0)$, $n = 1, 2, ...$.

Therefore

$$p(t_n) = (\beta)^{(t_n - t_0)/\tau}\, p(t_0)$$

for both z and x. Setting $\alpha = l(t_0)\,\beta^{1/\tau}$ gives

$$p(t_n) = \left(\frac{\alpha}{l(t_0)}\right)^{t_n - t_0} p(t_0). \qquad \text{q.e.d.}$$

The term $\alpha/l(t_0)$ may be interpreted as $1/(1 + \rho)$, where for some family, it happens that ρ is the asymptotic rate of interest.

7 Remark The α in Lemma 6 applies to the generalized Koopmans utility function $v = \sum u\alpha^i$. If u is quasi concave and differentiable, then profit maximization and the conditions in Lemma 6 are sufficient for competitive choice. If v is concave or there is the law of nonincreasing marginal utility and no line segments over which utility is linear, then $c(t) \to 0$ for the consumer with $\alpha/l(t_0)$ less than that of the economy and $c(t) \to \infty$ for the consumer with $\alpha/l(t_0)$ greater than that of the community. Otherwise, consumption is nonzero.

Proof Maximizing v subject to

$$\sum (p(t)\,\bar{c}(t)\,y_m(t)) \leqslant \sum p(t)\,c(t)\,y_m(t)$$

(assuming no market for the mth good) leads in the "$c(t) = c(t_0)$, $l(t) = l(t_0)$" case to maximization of v subject to

$$\sum \bar{p}(t)\,\bar{c}(t)\,\bar{y}(t) \leqslant \sum p(t)\,c(t_0)^{t - t_0}\, y_m(t_0).$$

The first-order condition is

$$\sum_{s=-\tau+1}^{\tau-1} \alpha_i^{t-s}\, \frac{\partial u}{\partial c_j(t)} = \alpha_i^{t_0 - t}\left(\frac{p_j(t)}{p_j(t_0)}\right)(l(t_0))^{t - t_0}$$

$$\times \sum_{s=\tau+1}^{\tau-1} \alpha_i^{t_0 - s}\, \frac{\partial u}{\partial c_j(t_0 - \bar{s})}$$

or, letting $v_j(t) = \sum_{s=\tau+1}^{\tau-1} \alpha_i^{-s}\, \partial u / \partial c_j(t)$,

$$\left(\frac{\alpha_i}{l_i(t_0)}\right)^{t - t_0} v_j(t) = \left(\frac{p_j(t)}{p_j(t_0)}\right) v_j(t_0).$$

If $p_j(t) = p_j(t_0)(\alpha/l(t_0))^{t-t_0}$,

$$\left| v_j(t) = \left(\frac{\alpha/l(t_0)}{\alpha_i/l_i(t_0)}\right)^{t-t_0} v_j(t_0) \right| \to 0.$$

For u nondifferentiable, we can approximate by u^n differentiable and let $p^n(t)$ be the normal to the manifold, $u^n(c(t)) = u^n(c(t))$. In the limit, $p^n(t) \to p(t)$.

On the other hand, if u is quasi concave and if the first-order conditions hold, then there is cost minimization subject to a constant utility constraint. In view of Lemma 14 of Chapter 2 and the separation of production and consumption, profit maximization of production is sufficient with the second-order conditions to ensure utility maximization. In particular,

$$v_j(t) \left(\frac{\alpha}{l(t_0)}\right)^t = \beta^{-t_0} v_j(t_0)$$

or

$$v_j(t) \to \infty \qquad \text{if} \quad \beta > \frac{\alpha}{l(t_0)}$$

contrary to boundedness, and

$$v_j(t) \to 0 \qquad \text{if} \quad \beta < \frac{\alpha}{l(t_0)}.$$

In case of the law of strictly diminishing marginal utility, or of nonincreasing utility and no line segments along which utility is linear,

$$c_i(t) \to 0 \qquad \text{if} \quad v_i(t) \to \infty$$

and

$$c_i(t) \to \infty \qquad \text{if} \quad v_i(t) \to 0. \qquad \text{q.e.d.}$$

In many cases we obtain an asymptotic interest rate, uniform over time, even though consumptions are not stationary.

8 Lemma *If consumers with a separation of production and consumption have locally unsaturated, weakly convex, τ-stationary, and weakly τ-time separable preferences, $\sum_i \mathcal{R}_i(x^i)$ is directional dense, and competitive trades and per capita capital stock and reproduction rates at time $t_i = j_i\tau + k$ tend to the level at t_0, $t_i \to \infty$, then for the competitive price system p,*

$$\left| p(t_n) \left(\frac{\alpha}{l(t_0)}\right)^{t_n-t_0} - p(t_0) \right| \to 0.$$

Proof If necessary, renumber t_n so that $t_n > t_m$ for $n > m$. Letting $c(t) = c(t_0)$ for $t \neq t_n$, $n = 1, 2, \ldots$, we have a price system $\bar{p}$. By directional density the prices (of norm one) are continuous functions of consumption. Since $\bar{p}(t) = (\alpha/l(t_0))^{t_n-t_0} p(t_0)$ for the case in which $c(t) = c(t_0)$ for all t, for $c(t_n)$ sufficiently near $c(t_0)$, $p(t_n)$ is near $p(t_0)(\alpha/l(t_0))^{t_i-t_0}$. Indeed, this fact is independent of the magnitude of t since, whatever t, for $\varepsilon > 0$ there is a $\delta > 0$ such that

$$\left| p(t_n) - p(t_0) \left(\frac{\alpha}{l(t_0)} \right)^{t_n-t_0} \right| < \varepsilon \qquad \text{whenever} \quad |c(t_n) - c(t_0)| < \delta.$$

This follows from the fact that choice at time t is exactly as if it had taken place earlier, given that always before, $c(t) = c(t_0)$ (t-stationarity). q.e.d.

An application of Lemma 8 occurs whenever consumers are maximizing $v = \sum u\alpha^t$. Most consumers either moderate their reproduction, or else their per capita consumptions tend to zero.

9 Theorem *Let the respective conditions on consumers and producers of Lemma 4 and 8 hold, or more generally, let there be bounded per capita consumptions, competitive behavior, a unique price system, τ-stationary preferences, and τ-time separability.*

Among consumers with separation of production and consumption, and preferences represented by $v = \sum u\alpha^t$, u concave or quasi concave and continuously differentiable, only those with largest α (eventually) will outweigh all the others in total wealth. Otherwise, a positive ultimate level of consumption will accrue only to consumers who prefer to adjust down their reproduction rates; that is, only for which the following is true:

$$1 > \delta > 0, \qquad s > T, \qquad l^i(s) = \delta, \qquad c^i(s) = c^i(s) \frac{l^i(s)}{l^i(s)},$$

implies there is a b such that $(ul^i, \bar{c}^i)$ is preferred to $(l^i(t), c(t), t = s, s + 1, \ldots)$ whenever $l^i(s) > \delta$, $|c^i(t)| < b$.

These conclusions are remarkable. When reproduction is fixed, all consumers except possibly the least myopic are reduced to the subsistence or slave level. Even if the poor have numerical superiority due to a faster reproduction rate, they ultimately agree to put themselves in a very bad state of affairs. To make matters worse, if we suddenly introduce a new consumer with a still higher α, the former high α's now agree to enslave themselves.

Varying reproduction along Malthusian lines leads to the numerical dominance by the most myopic- (and least self-sacrificing) type of consumer, who may nonetheless be at a level near serfdom, depending on how severe the myopia is. All these results are independent of the productivity of the consumers. In effect, high productivity will allow myopic consumers to consume large amounts at early periods, but they will ultimately indebt themselves to the least myopic. One is reminded of the frequent experience of many societies where interest rates are high and wealth is ultimately concentrated in the hands of the few, whereas debt and obligations are concentrated in the hands of the many.

Theorem 9 illustrates the general principle that the competitive system is exactly as good as its members—no better. It also calls into question the justice of the use of the Koopmans utility function and thereby of the justice of complete, continuous orderings. Results such as the foregoing could be avoided by the Protestant ethic, according to which sustainable consumption paths were preferred. (In this way, the analysis supports the mother's view in *Look Homeward, Angel*.) We should not interpret too quickly the maxim "the purpose of production is consumption." Alternatively, in the absence of a Protestant ethic, it may be necessary to institute consumption-preserving programs such as public education and social security.

Proof Let $t_n \to \infty$, $x^i(t_n) \to x^i$, for all i. Then there is some subsequence

$$t_{n_m} = j_m \tau + k$$

and for all but a finite number of t_n, t_n can be broken up into such subsequences. For each such subsequence, Lemma 8 applies, except that α depends on k. The first conclusion of the theorem follows from Remark 7.

For a single change to $l(t_0) = \delta$, $y_m(t_0)(\delta/l(t))$ is the new population for $t > t_0$, and the following computation shows that a lower $l(t_0)$ can be chosen,

$$\sum p(t)\, c(t)\, y_{im}(t) = \sum_{t \leqslant t_0} p(t)\, c(t)\, y_{im}(t) + \sum_{t > t_0} p(t) \left(\frac{l(t_0)}{\delta} \right) c(t) \frac{\delta}{l(t_0)}\, y_{im}(t).$$

Therefore, for $|c^i(t)| \to 0$, there must be a choice $l^i(t) \to 0$ and $\alpha_i/l^i(t)$ is eventually equal to that for the community. Hence, the consumers who prefer to reduce $l^i(t)$ survive at $|c(t)| > b$ (Remark 7).

q.e.d.

10 Remark If in Theorem 9 total per capita consumption of j tends to nonzero values and a generalized Koopmans-type consumer with the largest $\alpha^i/l_i(t_0)$ has the property that for some good j, $v_j(t) \to \infty^1$ as $x_i(t) \to 0$, then that consumer has a positive limiting consumption.

Proof Since quantities are not eventually zero, there is a price for j. For whatever t_0,

$$| v_j(t_n) - v_j(t_0)| \quad \text{small contradicts} \quad v_j(t_n) \to \infty.$$

Hence, $x_j(t_n) \to 0$ cannot be.   q.e.d.

A still more detailed picture can be obtained from an observation of Bergstrom:

11 Remark If a family's per capita wealth is decreasing over time fast enough so that reproduction does not decrease per capita wealth, the family necessarily reproduces at either the biological maximum or the point of maximum preference with respect to reproduction. For example, if all non labor assets are consumed by the father, so that the sons are left at best with no assets, then it is better for the father and no worse for the sons to enjoy reproduction at the level of highest preferences.

By Theorem 9, if wages rise as capital accumulates, then the families with low α's will eventually indebt the wages of the future generations. At this point we have a contradiction if the labor supply outgrows the stock of capital.

12 Corollary *Let there be at least two families with different α's. Eventually wages must fall below levels of both the natural maximum and the rate of highest preference whenever these exceed the rate of growth of capital.*

The corollary is Malthus' iron law of wages.

In the limit, those with the largest $\alpha^i/l_i(t_0)$ dominate in terms of labor and capital. Let them have total consumptions equal to

$$\sum n_i y_i(t) = y(t).$$

13 Remark If the surviving and dominating Koopmans-type consumers (0-time separable) have concave utility, then it is as though they were maximizing a single utility function.

Proof Since u^i is concave, efficient points can be attained by maxim-

---

[1] $v_j(t)$ is defined in the proof of Remark 7.

izing $\sum a_i u^i$, $a_i > 0$ (apply Minkowski's theorem to the space of attainable utilities). Then

$$\sum_i a_i u^i = \sum_i a_i \sum_t u^i \alpha^t = \sum_i a_i \sum_t u^i \alpha^t = \sum_t \left(\sum_i a_i u^i \right) \alpha^t.$$

Hence, one period utility is $U = \sum_i a_i u^i$ defined on distributions y^i. Clearly, max $\sum_i a_i u^i$ defined on distributions y^i. Clearly, max $\sum_i a_i u^i$ is a concave function of $y(t)$ alone and max $U = \sum_t (\max \sum_i a_i u^i) \alpha^t$. q.e.d.

For asymptotic properties, Remark 13 gives a rationale for looking at the one consumer economies. In view of Theorem 16 of Chapter 5 of the companion volume, if $\alpha > \frac{1}{2}$, then quasi concave utility implies concave utility; hence, concave utility would seem likely.

PROBLEMS

A. *One-Sector Growth Models*

Let output result from current capital stock and labor supply. Let capital stock deteriorate at rate d and let labor supply equals population growth be at the rate n.

(i)   Formulate the foregoing technology.
(ii)   Under what conditions can we apply the theorems of Sections 2–4?
(iii) What are the conditions of equilibrium for a consumer with the Koopmans-type utility function?
(iv)   Does the stationary state depend on the concavity of single-period utility?

This problem was solved by Samuelson [1967].

B. *Optimal Development V*

Let $u(x) = x^\beta$. Let $\sum x(t) = c$. Is there an intertemporally efficient path? A maximizer of the von Weizsäcker criterion? Of the Koopmans utility function?

This is referred to as the cake-eating example (Gale [1967]).

3. Stationary States

In the economics of Ricardo [1817], there is a stationary state toward which the economy is moving. This state is characterized by the fact that no changes in prices or quantities take place; the future is known with certainty to be identical with the present. The stationary state results because

(1) there is a fixed resource, land or labor, that constrains the indefinite expansion of output,

(2) other factors have been accumulated to the point of zero marginal productivity,

(3) tastes and technology are constant over time.

This has been generalized by von Neumann [1937], Solow [1956], and Robinson [1956] to include the case of a constantly growing labor force, due to either population increase or increases in labor productivity. There results the balanced growth path in which there is a stationary per capita consumption even though there is no need for marginal products to fall to zero. The marginal product of capital ordinarily equals the rate of growth of population, since at any lower value capital is not productive enough to reproduce as fast as labor.

The general question whether the economy tends to a stationary state is unsolved. There are, however, some known cases where stationary states of one kind or another result.

We present two here. First, we consider the case of two factors of production. Second, for many factors, we show stationarity if there is a consumer with preference for I.E. paths of outputs and consumptions.

If there are but two variable factors of production, capital and labor, stationarity can be established as the limiting state. This can be done with reference to very general properties on production and preferences, and we obtain discrete time versions of results of several economists (for example Uzawa [1964], Beales and Koopmans [1969], and Samuelson [1967]). See also Problem D.

14 Theorem *If*

(i) *there is one consumer whose preferences are stationary, continuous, and strictly convex,*

(ii) *attainable consumptions are a continuous correspondence of capital stocks,*

(iii) *production is convex and stationary and there are constant returns to scale,*

(iv) *per capita capital stock is one dimensional,*

(v) *nonzero stationary per capita capital stocks are bounded and convex and are never attained from nonstationary points,*

(vi) *sufficiently small capital stocks are not stationary, and lead to small capital stocks in the next period,*

(vii) *for sufficiently large capital stocks, next period capital is less than current,*

then the limiting state is a single stationary point (oftentimes zero) to which capital stocks tend monotonically.

Proof   By (i), (ii), and (iii), reproduction, consumption over time, and future capital stocks are continuous functions of current value. By (i) and (iii), given $\mathscr{Y}$ alone, all consumptions and capital stocks at or beyond t are determined. Hence, $x^t \to x^{t+1}$ is a quasi-dynamical system with a continuous law of change f.

Let

$$\bar{\mathscr{Y}} = \{y \mid y = f(y)\}, \qquad \hat{\mathscr{Y}} = \{y \mid y > \bar{\mathscr{Y}}\}, \qquad \underset{\smile}{\mathscr{Y}} = \{y \mid y < \bar{\mathscr{Y}}\}.$$

Then f maps only points of $\bar{\mathscr{Y}}$ into $\bar{\mathscr{Y}}$. Also, $f(\hat{\mathscr{Y}}) \cap \bar{\mathscr{Y}} = \varnothing = f(\underset{\smile}{\mathscr{Y}}) \cap \bar{\mathscr{Y}}(v)$.

Now $f(\hat{\mathscr{Y}})$ is connected, as is $f(\underset{\smile}{\mathscr{Y}})$. Also, there are points of $\underset{\smile}{\mathscr{Y}}$ that stay in $\underset{\smile}{\mathscr{Y}}$, namely, very small capital stocks (vi). Hence $\underset{\smile}{\mathscr{Y}}$ maps into $\underset{\smile}{\mathscr{Y}}$. Also, $\hat{\mathscr{Y}}$ must map either into $\hat{\mathscr{Y}}$ or into $\underset{\smile}{\mathscr{Y}}$ (but not both). In the latter case, after time zero, we need only consider $\hat{\mathscr{Y}}$ and $\underset{\smile}{\mathscr{Y}}$ separately and mapping into themselves.

Let

$$\hat{\mathscr{X}} = [y \mid f(y) > y], \qquad \underset{\smile}{\mathscr{X}} = [y \mid f(y) < y].$$

Clearly $\hat{\mathscr{X}}$ and $\underset{\smile}{\mathscr{X}}$ are disjoint open subsets containing $\underset{\smile}{\mathscr{Y}} \cup \hat{\mathscr{Y}}$ (continuity). Also, $\underset{\smile}{\mathscr{X}}$ is not empty and intersects with $\hat{\mathscr{Y}}$ (iii). Therefore $\hat{\mathscr{Y}} \subset \underset{\smile}{\mathscr{X}}$, for otherwise $\hat{\mathscr{Y}}$ would be disconnected into $\hat{\mathscr{Y}} \cap \hat{\mathscr{X}}$ and $\hat{\mathscr{Y}} \cap \underset{\smile}{\mathscr{X}}$. Hence, if y^t is in $\hat{\mathscr{Y}}$, $f(y^t) \neq y^t$, $f(y^t) - y^t \to 0$ since y^t is bounded from below, $\lim f(y^t) = f(\lim y^t)$, and $\lim y^t$ is in the closure of $\hat{\mathscr{Y}}$. Hence, $\lim y^t = \sup \bar{\mathscr{Y}}$.

If $\underset{\smile}{\mathscr{Y}} \subset \hat{\mathscr{X}}$, all nonzero capital stocks tend to $\bar{\mathscr{Y}}$. Those in $\underset{\smile}{\mathscr{Y}}$ tend to $\inf \bar{\mathscr{Y}}$ since $f(y^t) > y^t$, $f(y^t) - y^t \to 0$ (y^t bounded from above), $f(\lim y^t) = \lim y^t$ (continuity of f), and $\lim y^t$ is in the closure of $\underset{\smile}{\mathscr{Y}}$, Otherwise, $\underset{\smile}{\mathscr{Y}} \subset \underset{\smile}{\mathscr{X}}$ and y^t tends to zero, which is a stationary state.   q.e.d.

As an application, consider a one-good economy, where c^t is the amount devoted to per capita consumption and y^t the per capita stock.

Then let

$$c^t + y^{t+1} = f(y^t) \qquad \text{and} \qquad g(y^t) = f(y^t) - y^t.$$

Substitution gives

$$\sum_{t=0}^{\infty} u(c^t)\, \alpha^t = \sum_{t=0}^{\infty} u(f(y^t) - y^{t+1})\, \alpha^t,$$

Let $\alpha = 1/(1 + c)$. The first-order condition is

$$u'_t = \frac{1+\rho}{1+g'_t}\, u'_{t-1} = \left(\frac{1}{\alpha f'_t}\, u'_{t-1}\right) \qquad \text{where} \quad u'_t = \frac{du(y^t)}{dy^t}.$$

Now for concave, $c_t \gtreqless c_{t-1}$ according as $u'_t \lesseqgtr u'_{t-1}$ according as $\rho \gtreqless g'_t$.

In Figure 1, if the marginal product of capital exceeds ρ, consumption is increasing, whereas if the marginal product of capital is less than ρ, consumption is decreasing. Clearly, the stationary points are $\mathscr{Y}$, which is convex and which yields consumption $c = f(\bar{y}) - \bar{y}$ for $\bar{y} \, \varepsilon \, \mathscr{Y}$.

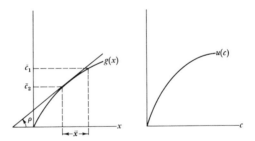

Figure 1

15 Remark   In the one-good economy, with strictly concave utility, $\mathscr{Y}$ is convex and if $y_t \, \varepsilon \, \mathscr{Y}$, then $y_{t-1} = y_t$.

Proof

$$u'_t = \frac{1+\rho}{1+g'_t}\, u'_{t-1} = \frac{1+\rho}{1+\rho}\, u'_{t-1} = u'_{t-1} \qquad \text{or} \qquad \bar{c} = c_t = c_{t-1};$$

that is,

$$f(y_{t+1}) = \bar{c} + x_t = \bar{c} + \bar{x} = f(\bar{y}) \qquad \text{or} \qquad y_{t-1} = \bar{y}$$

by the fact that f is monotonic increasing.   q.e.d.

16 Remark   In the one-good economy with concave utility and production, monotonic convergence occurs from time zero.

Proof The only exception in the proof of Theorem 4 was that where f mapped $\mathscr{Y}$ into $\mathscr{Y}$. As $y \to \infty$, $f(y) < \mathscr{Y}$ implies $c_0 \to \infty$. Since $c_1 \geqslant \mathscr{Y}$, $u_1' > u_0'$. Hence

$$\frac{1+\rho}{1+g_i} > 1 \quad \text{or} \quad \rho > g_1', \quad \text{or} \quad y_1 > \mathscr{Y},$$

a contradiction. q.e.d.

In Section 2, if consumers have variable $\alpha/l(t_0)$, there is a less paradoxical theory. For example, the intertemporal efficiency preference relation falls into this class.

It is possible for consumers to show preference for sustainable consumptions, which is the so-called Protestant ethic. For example, the consumer might seek to maximize lim inf $U(x^t)$, or possibly use the von Weizsäcker overtaking criterion. It was seen in Section 7 of Chapter 1 that a stationary state is approached under these relations.

Unfortunately, neither have the nice properties of $\mathscr{P}^{-1}(x)$ open or $\mathscr{R}(x)$ closed in the product topology. Hence it is hard to see how there can be consumer choice with respect to a price system. Indeed, the von Weizsäcker criterion is incompatible with the separation of production and consumption and stationarity. To see this, let x eventually overtake any other feasible path. Maximize $\sum_{t=0}^{T} u(y^t)$ subject to $\sum p^t y^t = \sum p^t x$ showing

$$\frac{\partial u}{\partial y_k^t} p_k^0 = \frac{\partial u}{\partial y^{t_0}} p_k^t.$$

Since additional income could be turned into a sustainable positive consumption, $y^t = x$ must be a maximizer and

$$\frac{\partial u}{\partial x_k} p_k^0 = \frac{\partial u}{\partial x_k} p_k^t \quad \text{or} \quad p^t = p^0.$$

However, the budget constraint is violated:

$$\sum_k \sum_{t=0}^{\infty} x_k p_k^t = \sum_k x_k \sum_{t=0}^{\infty} p_k^0 = \infty.$$

An extreme, Stalinist, form of the Protestant ethic is to obtain a certain per capita stock in minimum time, subject to given labor supply. Again it is hard to see how competitive choice can be reconciled with this kind of value judgment. One case seems to be straightforward, namely, where preference for intertemporally efficient paths is displayed. It can be shown that the intertemporally efficient individual eventually dominates. Again, there is a limiting price system yielding a time-uniform interest rate.

17 Theorem *If*

(i)   *one or more consumers with positive wealth have preference for intertemporally efficient consumptions,*

(ii)   *commodities are not negatively productive, the community production is primitive, strongly convex, upper semicontinuous, indecomposable, satisfies constant returns to scale, and has every commodity either substitutable in production or a universal capital good,*

(iii)   *preferences are similar and locally unsaturated, and $\mathscr{P}_i(x)$ is connected for all x, then competitive equilibrium leads to*

$$\sum(l^i(t),\, c^i(t),\, n^i(t)) \to (\lambda,\, \bar{y})$$

where λ is the von Neumann growth factor and $\bar{y}$ is the von Neumann vector of commodities. If production is directional dense at y, then

$$\frac{p(t)}{\mid p(t)\mid} \to p \quad and \quad \left| \frac{p(t)}{\mid p(t)\mid} - \frac{p(t-1)}{\mid p(t-1)\mid}\lambda \right| \to 0.$$

Proof   The assumption of constant returns to scale assures that each consumer can use the community production set (consumer efficiency of competitive equilibrium). Therefore, the consumer can attain at least the I.E. path from his initial wealth. In view of Lemma 14 of Chapter 1, any path of outputs containing at least the quantities of such an I.E. path must tend to the von Neumann vector, since for p in the lemma,

$$p\left(\sum_i y^i(t)\right) \geqslant py^i(t) \geqslant py^i(0)\,\lambda(\bar{y})^t$$

is possible only if $\sum_i y^i(t)$ tends to the von Neumann path. Evidently,

$$\frac{\sum_i y_n^i(t+1)}{\sum_i y_n^i(t)} \to \lambda\bar{y} \quad or \quad \sum n^i(t)\,l^i(t) \to \lambda$$

and

$$\frac{\sum_i y_m^i(t)}{\sum y_m^i(t)} \to \bar{y}, \quad \sum c^i(t)\,n^i(t) \to \bar{y}.$$

Evidently, the production price system p is continuous in outputs. q.e.d.

Theorem 17 gives the consequence of one kind of consumer following a Protestant ethic. In effect, the whole economy is eventually dominated by his kind.

More generally, it might be that the consumer would show preference for sustainable consumption at less than the biological maximum. Such a preference is characterized as *golden rule* behavior. A golden age results whenever there is in the stationary state the most desired sustainable per capita stock.

18 Remark If there are more than one attainable stationary states, the golden age may not be chosen by Koopmans-type consumers. A simple example where the golden age is not chosen appears in Fig. 7, where the limiting consumption c is not the maximum possible. (See Samuelson [1967] for other examples.) We have still another reason for questioning the ethical goodness of discounted utility. Even those who avert the disaster of ultimate poverty fall short of society's potential.

Exercise 1 Let $\alpha_1 = \frac{3}{4}$, $\alpha_2 = \frac{1}{4}$, $u(x) = x^{1/2}$ for two consumers. Let $x(t) = x_1(t) + x_2(t)$ be fixed. Derive the efficient distribution of consumptions.

PROBLEMS

C. *Optimal Development VI*

For the case in Problem A, suppose that there is an optimum under the von Weizsäcker criterion. When will there result a limiting stationary state ?

D. *Stationary States*

Let there be a continuum of time and two factors, capital and labor, only one consumer, who has strictly convex, continuous, and stationary preferences, and production convex and subject to constant returns to scale, where for large capital–labor ratios, per capita output is less than per capita capital.

(i) Show that if per capita capital stock at an intial period is known, there is a unique and continuous determination of future per capita capital stock.

(ii) Show that any path tends monotonically to a unique stationary point. (Hint: Use the fact that on the real line, connected paths are intervals.)

This generalizes results of Uzawa [1964].

4. Limiting States

However desirable as a basis for Ricardian analysis, stationarity seems impossible to obtain for n-good models. Nevertheless, weaker asymptotic properties might provide useful substitutions to stationarity. For this reason, we devote some effort to study of limiting states from a highly abstract viewpoint. Once we know $(l(t), c(t))$ for each family and the family size $y_{n,t}^i$, total capital stock for each family is given. Suppose an economic system such as competitive equilibrium with constant returns to scale and constancy of production technology and consumer preferences. The time-t state of per capita capital stocks, per capita population expansion, and relative family size are uniquely determined by their time-s values and numerical value of the intervening time, $t - s$. In this way, we can define a system quite analogous to that studied in mathematical dynamics and with similar properties.

There results a weak form of stationarity, as shown in Lemma 19. The property is sometimes called recurrence, but a recurrent point is not even necessarily cyclic. All that follows is that starting from a given per capita capital stock, as time tends to infinity there are limit capital stocks.

19 Lemma *If a general equilibrium has demands forming either a lower or an upper semicontinuous correspondence in capital stocks, there are constant returns to scale, production is stationary and preferences are τ-stationary, and per capita reproduction and capital stocks remain bounded by a number b, for at least some t_i, $t_i \to \infty$, then $(l(t), c(t))$ tends frequently to $(\bar{l}, \bar{c}, \bar{h},)$, such that starting from $(\bar{l}, \bar{c}, \bar{h})$, $(\bar{l}, (s), \bar{c}(s)\, \bar{c}(s), \bar{h}(s))$ tends frequently to $(\bar{l}, \bar{c}, \bar{n})$.*

Proof   Let

$$(l^i(t + 1 - s), c^i(t + 1 - s), n^i(t + 1 - s), \quad i = 1, 2,..., n, \quad s = 1,..., t - 1)$$

$$\in \mathscr{G}(l^i(t - s), c^i(t - s), n^i(t - s), \quad i = 1, 2,..., m, \quad s = 1,..., t - 1)$$

be the resulting "social solution"; then the hypothesis of Lemma 17 ensures that $\mathscr{G}$ is a (upper, lower) semicontinuous correspondence. It is said that $\mathscr{G}$ defines a *quasi-dynamical system* $\mathscr{G}^n(x)$. $\bigcup_{i=1}^{\infty} \mathscr{G}^n$ is called the *orbit.* There are dual theories—one for upper semicontinuous corre-spondences and one for lower semicontinuous correspondences.

A set $\mathcal{S}$ is *invariant* under $\mathcal{G}$ if $x \in \mathcal{S}$ implies $\mathcal{G}(x) \subset \mathcal{S}$. $\mathcal{S}$ is *quasi invariant* if for $x \in \mathcal{S}$, $\mathcal{G}(x) \cap \mathcal{S} \neq \varnothing$. Evidently, the intersection of (quasi-) invariant sets is (quasi) invariant. Also, the lower semicontinuity of $\mathcal{G}$ gives that the closure of an invariant set is invariant, while for upper semi continuous $\mathcal{G}$ and for a compact set $\mathcal{X}$, $\mathcal{X} \cap \mathcal{G}(x) \neq \varnothing$ for every x in a quasi-invariant set gives that its closure is quasi invariant.

Note that $\bigcup_{n-1} \mathcal{G}^n(x)$ contains points of a compact set $\mathcal{X}$ by virtue of the boundedness assumption.

A minimal (quasi-) invariant set is one that does not contain a proper closed (quasi-) invariant set. Evidently, every orbit closure contains a minimal set, denoted $\mathcal{O}$, since the intersection of a maximal monotone (in $\supset$) net of (quasi-) invariant sets in the orbit closure containing at least one point in a compact set $\mathcal{X}$ is nonempty and has compact intersection with $\mathcal{X}$. The intersection is the maximal net since it is (quasi) invariant.

A smaller (quasi-) invariant set would also contain points of $\mathcal{X}$ and hence be in the maximal net. Therefore, the intersection is minimal.

For every $x \in \mathcal{O}$, $\bigcup_{n=1}^{\infty} \mathcal{O}^n(x)$ has closure equal to $\mathcal{O}$ by minimality of $\mathcal{O}$. Choose $x^0 = x$, $x^i \in \mathcal{G}^{m_i}(x)^{i-1}$ such that x^i is within $\frac{1}{2}\varepsilon$ of y. Clearly, $x^i \to y$, $x^i \in \mathcal{G}^{\Sigma_i m_i}(x)$.   q.e.d.

In order to apply Lemma 19, we must verify the continuity and boundedness hypotheses. Recalling that excess demand correspondences and consequent capital stock correspondences are only upper semi-continuous, we encounter a definite problem with the lower semi-continuity property. Nothing more will be said to assure the condition of lower semicontinuity, and the reader is referred to Problems C and D of Chapter 4. For boundedness, see Lemma 4.

It is possible to apply Lemma 19 to obtain an asymptotic approach to recurrent points in a competitive economy.

20 Theorem *Suppose a competitive economy with compact price space such that*

(i) *either equilibrium is locally unique and excess demand is a contin-uous correspondence of prices, or*

(i)' *$l(t) > \delta > 0$ and excess demand is upper semicontinuous in prices,*

(ii) *production satisfies constant returns to scale and given capital bounded per unit labor and expanding labor inputs, production possibilities per unit labor are bounded,*

(iii) *there is either free disposal or costless transferral to unproductive consumer goods,*

(iv) *every commodity is either substitutable in production or a universal capital good,*

(v) *production and preferences are τ-stationary, and either*

(vi) $l^i(t) = \varepsilon + 1, \varepsilon > 0,$ *or*

(vi)′ $y(t)$ *is bounded and* $l(t) > 0,$ *or*

(vi)″ *for* $l(t) < 1, t > T,$ *there is an* $\varepsilon > 0$ *and* $ab > 0$ *such that for any* $s > T,$

$$\left(l^i(s) = \varepsilon + 1, \quad l^i(t) = l^i(t), \quad t \neq s, \quad \bar{c}^i(s) \equiv c^i(s)\, \frac{l^i(s)}{l^i(s)} \right)$$

is preferred to $(l^i(t), c^i(t), t = s, s + 1, ...),$ *and no commodities are undesirable to hold (or there is free disposal).*

Then $(l^i(t), c^i(t), c^i(t), n^i(t), i = 1, 2, ..., n)$ *tends frequently to* $(\bar{l}^i, \bar{c}^i, \bar{n}_i, i = 1, 2, ..., n),$ *and starting from* $(\bar{l}^i, \bar{c}^i, \bar{n}^i, i = 1, 2, ..., n),$ *the system tends frequently to the starting point.*

Hypothesis (vi)′ appears to be the limited resource case. Hypothesis (vi)″ can be interpreted as a preference for net reproduction at high levels of wealth.

Proof Equilibrium prices form an upper semicontinuous correspondence in initial wealth. Compositions of upper semicontinuous correspondences are upper semicontinuous whenever the intermediate space is compact (Exercise 2). Since the price appears in a compact set of prices, whenever they are locally unique, they are continuous. Excess demands, individual by individual, are upper semicontinuous correspondences on continuous functions of initial wealth and are upper semicontinuous whenever the intermediate price space is compact—as it is by hypothesis.

In view of Lemmata 4 and 17 it remains to show

$$| c^i(t) | > b, \quad t > T \qquad \text{implies} \quad l^i(t) > \varepsilon + 1, \quad t > T.$$

Otherwise, in case (vi)″, the only case at issue, $(l^i(t), c^i(t), t > T)$ is inferior to a choice possible for $i,$ namely

$$l^i(s) = \varepsilon + 1, \qquad l^i(t) = l^i(t), \quad t \neq s,$$

$$\bar{c}^i(s) \geqslant c^i(s)\, \frac{l^i(s)}{l^i(s)}$$

(commodities are not negatively productive, (iii) and (iv)).   q.e.d.

Exercise 2 Let $\phi: \mathscr{X} \to \mathscr{Y}$, $\psi. \mathscr{Y} \to \mathscr{Z}$. Show that $\phi\psi$ is upper semicontinuous whenever both ϕ and ψ are and $\mathscr{Y}$ is compact. Why does the result fail for $\mathscr{Y}$ not compact?

5. Extensions and Generalizations

Certain kinds of capital-augmenting technical change operate simply as though capital stock were increasing more rapidly than it would otherwise. They are easily worked into the production technology as extra fast reproduction of capital. Also, labor-augmenting changes can be worked into the analysis by modifying both the growth of population and the (homothetic) preferences defined thereon. Then, exponential growth of per capita capital stock becomes possible.

All such technical changes are exogenous and beyond the power of the producer. On the other hand, the endogenous technical change may be effected by means of applications of certain combinations of the factors. Therefore they are simply accumulative-type production processes not differing from more direct methods of capitalist production.

Should $\mathscr{G}$ be *cyclic* (*seasonal*) instead of invariant, so that for its period $\mathscr{G}_{ma} = (\mathscr{G}_a)^m$, the analysis in the three previous sections can be applied to the quasi-dynamical system $\mathscr{G}_a(x)$. We must verify the upper semicontinuity of $\mathscr{G}_a$, which would follow if $\mathscr{G}$ maps into a compact set. The resulting stationary states will be part of a cycle: $x \in \mathscr{G}_a(x)$ but generally not $x \in \mathscr{G}_s(x)$, $0 < s < a$.

The incorporation of uncertainty is not so satisfactory. We can imagine commodities in time t being produced conditional on natural events regarded as random. In such cases they can be used a new to produce goods in the next time period. However, the production techniques from period to period should not change, given the surviving capital stock. Choice takes place with knowledge of the possibilities that capital constructed may not survive natural disasters. In such a technology, we would have a stationary production–consumption system (or a cyclic one) provided the natural events are actually identical (or cyclic from period to period). This seems a farfetched case. After a while, people would cease to believe the future to be uncertain.

More generally, there is the Markov law for a finite number of possible events, whereby the natural events tend to a normal state. Let a_{ij} be the probability of j given the occurrence of i in the last period. Then there is a Markov matrix

$$A = (a_{ij})$$

such that

$$Av = \left(\sum_j a_{ij}v_j\right) = v \qquad (\text{for} \quad v = (1,\dots 1)).$$

It is easy to show that A has characteristic vectors associated with the root one and that all other roots are less than one in real part. On the other hand, the state in time t occurs with probability e_iA^t where i is the state occurring in time zero and $e_i = (0,\dots, 1,\dots, 0)$. With probability one, e_iA^t tends to a characteristic vector x, for which $xA = x$. In the particular case where events are independent over time, $a_{ij} = b_j$. Nevertheless, among them, the most likely one (for which b_j is greatest) is not approached with probability one, since $e_jA \neq e_j$.

Only in conditions incompatible with independence between events and time can we obtain a limiting state. If the expected outcome is the same as the immediately preceding outcome, as in a *martingale*, Doob's theorem applies (Doob [1953] or Kemeny, Snell, and Knapp [1966, Chapter 3]): except for a set of events over time zero of probability zero there is a limiting natural state. However, even in such a case, $_t\mathscr{G}_{t+1} \to \mathscr{G}$ does not assure that the limiting (quasi-) dynamical behavior of $\mathscr{G}(x)$ and $_t\mathscr{G}_{t+1}(x)$ are similar. Unfortunately, limiting states are not generally continuous in the laws of motion.

7

Adjustment Dynamics

When demand and supply are in stable equilibrium, if any accident should move the scale of production from its equilibrium position, there will be instantly brought into play force tending to push it back to that position; just as, if a stone hanging by a string is displaced —, the force of gravity will at once tend to bring it back. But in real life such oscillations are seldom as rhythmical as those of a stone hanging freely from a string; the comparison would be more exact if the string were supposed to hang in the troubled waters of a mill-race, whose stream was at one time allowed to run freely, and at another partially cut off.

Alfred Marshall
in PRINCIPLES OF ECONOMICS, 1890, 8th ed., p. 346

1. Price Adjustment

Equilibrium, optimal but unattainable, would be a will-o'-the-wisp. In this chapter, the economy is considered to be out of equilibrium. Conditions are given for price and quantities to tend to an equilibrium state. In the next chapter, we consider the speed with which the system approaches equilibrium.

A powerful theory of disequilibrium economics would be of great importance in two ways. First, if it shows the stability of equilibrium, then we have a method of finding equilibrium: Simply set up the disequilibrium system and trace its path to equilibrium. Second, most economic variables are likely to be in at least slight disequilibrium; therefore a more realistic theory would be forthcoming relative to the macrostatics ordinarily used by applied economists.

Through this chapter, several different price adjustment systems appear. First, we study systems independent of asset accumulation, both Walrasian (Section 1) and Keynesian (Section 2). The analysis is appropriate to the very short run—say, a month. Then we consider asset accumulation but without growth in productive capital (Sections 3–6). This would apply to intermediate-run adjustments—perhaps over six months. Only superficial attention is paid to long-run disequilibrium dynamics (Section 7).

In this section, the Walrasian system is set forth. Then the Lyapunov stability theory is applied to show stability of equilibrium. Application is to the conditions in Sections 5–7 of Chapter 5.

The neoclassical economists Walras, Marshall, and Edgeworth first emphasized disequilibrium economics. Especially Walras envisaged the economic system along lines analogous to classical mechanics, whereby an approach was made to equilibrium by means of a dynamical adjustment system. He thereby supplanted the classical idea of economic method applied to political problems with that of *the* economy.

Walras [1877] saw the markets as under the control of boards who adjust price in the direction of excess demand. Contracts signed under current prices were binding for the future only if they turned out to be equilibrium prices for all markets. Otherwise, new prices were set and new demands and supplies were compiled. This process was called *tâtonnement*, and it is often viewed more as a process for computing equilibrium prices than as a description of everyday markets.

Alternatively, we could imagine a marketplace in a peasant economy, to which the farmer-merchants bring grains, fruits, vegetables, and meat, every day. They trade their own produce for that of others at prices fixed at the beginning of the day. If before the end of the day they have sold out a good, then the next day they raise their price slightly. If they have an oversupply on one day, it rots and is unfit for sale the next day. They price the new produce that they bring to market at a slightly lower level in order to avoid so much rotting. From day to day, this system would operate just like *tâtonnement*. Each day would be a repetition of the previous day except that prices would be changed in the direction of excess demand. Hence, new demands and supplies would be compiled at new prices. There results a dynamical system in prices.

Beginning with Walras' *Eléments*, the modern approach to general equilibrium theory has been to view the economy as an interconnected dynamical system in n variables. It is usually described by differential equations

$$\frac{dp_i(t)}{dt} = h_i(p_1(t),...,p_n(t)), \qquad i = 1,..., n, \tag{1}$$

or as a difference equation system

$$p_i(t+1) - p_i(t) = h_i(p_1(t),..., p_n(t)), \qquad i = 1,..., N. \tag{2}$$

Here attention is given to differential equations or to difference equations that are derived from differential equations. In effect, h_i may be chosen to be very small. Given

$$p(0) = (p_1(0),..., p_n(0),...),$$

it is then possible to deduce the time path of

$$p(t) = (p_1(t),..., p_n(t))$$

by solving either Equations (1) or Equations (2). For example, (1) or (2) may refer to a price system that is propelled through time by laws of supply and demand. Therefore, an economic system is a feedback mechanism that operates according to certain economic laws. The differential equation system is usually preferred since it has "nicer" properties.

The reader will recall from Chapter 5, Section 1, that local stability is assured whenever the real part of the roots of the matrix, $\partial h / \partial \bar{p}$, are negative. In the case of $\bar{p}$ *globally stable* on $\mathscr{P}$, $p(t)$ tends to $\bar{p}$, for any $p(0) \in \mathscr{P}$. Hence global stability involves both convergence and existence of paths of solution. With regard to convergence alone, there is a result due to the Russian mathematician, Lyapunov.

1 Lemma *If there is a function $v(p)$ bounded from below for which*

(i) $dv(p(t))/dt < 0$,
(ii) $dv/dt_i \to 0$, $p(t_i) \to p$, *only if* $dv/dt = 0$ at p *for all t*,
(iii) *for ε sufficiently small, $\mathscr{P}(\varepsilon) = \{p \mid v(p) \leqslant \varepsilon\}$ is compact*,

then the distance between $p(t)$ and $\mathscr{P}(0)$ tends to zero. (The proof is left to the reader as an exercise.)

Virtually all stability results are consequences of Lyapunov's lemma. For example, if $\partial h/\partial \bar{p}$ has roots with negative real parts,

$$\frac{\partial h}{\partial \bar{p}} = SA$$

where S is positive definite and A is negative quasi definite (Lemma 3 of Chapter 5).

2 Corollary *If h is differentiable at $\bar{p}$, $\partial h/\partial \bar{p}$ has roots with negative real parts, and $h(p) = 0$, then $p(t)$ is locally stable at $\bar{p}$.*

Proof For $v(p) = (p - \bar{p}) S(p - \bar{p})$, S symmetric,

$$\frac{dv}{dt} = 2h(p) S(p - \bar{p}).$$

For $\varepsilon > 0$, there is a $\delta > 0$ such that

$$\left| \frac{1}{(p - \bar{p})^2} \frac{dv}{dt} - \frac{2(p - \bar{p})}{|p - \bar{p}|} \frac{\partial h}{\partial \bar{p}} S \frac{(p - \bar{p})}{|p - \bar{p}|} \right| < \varepsilon$$

whenever $|p - \bar{p}| < \delta$. Since

$$\frac{(p - \bar{p})}{|p - \bar{p}|} \frac{\partial h}{\partial \bar{p}} S \frac{(p - \bar{p})}{|p - \bar{p}|} = \frac{(p - \bar{p})}{|p - \bar{p}|} SAS \frac{(p - \bar{p})}{|p - \bar{p}|}$$

$$< -\sigma \qquad \text{for some} \quad \sigma > 0,$$

for ε small and $|p - \bar{p}| < \delta$,

$$0 > \varepsilon - \sigma > \frac{1}{|p - \bar{p}|} \frac{dv}{dt} = \frac{(p - \bar{p})}{|p - \bar{p}|} SAS \frac{(p - \bar{p})}{|p - \bar{p}|}$$

or, for all p in $\{p \mid v(p) < k\}$, k small

$$0 > \frac{dv}{dt}$$

unless $|p - \bar{p}| = 0$. q.e.d.

In the *Walrasian system,*

$$h_i(p) = d_i(p) e_i(p)$$

where the rate of market response is given by

$$d_i(p) > 0.$$

In the *normalized* Walrasian system, for $i = 0$,

$$h_i(p) = 0,$$

so that 0 is the *numéraire*.

Section 6 of Chapter 5 contains conditions $\Delta e(p) \Delta p < 0$ for $e(p) \neq 0$. In this context, we recall the analysis in Chapter 11 of the companion volume whereby an increase in the price of money is equivalent to an increase in its supply, which is equivalent to lowering all prices or increasing purchasing power. Normally, this increases demands for other goods, just as required in theorems of Chapter 5. In view of the large number of applications with $\Delta e \Delta p < 0$, Theorem 3 is the main result for Walrasian *tâtonnement*. The basic idea is due to Wald [1936].

In Theorem 3, we show how a comparative statics theorem $\Delta e \Delta p$ implies dynamic stability in the sense that prices tend to the set of equilibria.

3 Theorem *Let*

$$\frac{d(p - \bar{p})}{dt} = D(p, t)\, e(p, t), \qquad e(p, t) \in \mathscr{E}(p, t),$$

except $h_0(p) = 0$, $\mathscr{E}$ *with closed domain* $\mathscr{P}$.
If

    (i) $\bar{p}(t) \to \bar{p} \gg 0$,
    (ii) $D(p, t) \to D(p)$ *uniformly as* $t \to \infty$, $D(p)$ *continuous at* $\bar{p}$, $D(\bar{p})$
positive definite,
    (iii) $\Delta e(p) \Delta p < 0$ *unless* $\Delta e(p) = 0$ *on an open set containing* $\bar{p}$,
    (iv) $e(p_i, t_i) \to 0$, $p_i \to p$, *implies* $e(p, t) = 0$ *for all* t,
then for some $\mathscr{P}(\varepsilon) = \{p \mid (p - \bar{p})\, D(\bar{p})^{-1}(p - \bar{p}) < \varepsilon\} \subset \mathscr{P}$, *and* $\varepsilon > 0$,
$p(s) \in \mathscr{P}(\varepsilon)$ *and* s *large imply* $p(t)$ *tends to* $\mathscr{P}(0)$. *If* $D(p, t) = D(p)$,
then for $p(s) \in \mathscr{P}(\varepsilon)\, \mathscr{P}$, $p(t)$ *tends to* $\mathscr{P}(0)$.

The difficulty with extending Theorem 3 to the whole of the price space can be seen from Figure 1, where the path moves inside the ellipses even closer to $\bar{p}$ and yet tends to the boundary of the price space where $e_i(p)$ tends to infinity, even though $p_i e_i(p)$ remains finite. Finally, at time t, the differential equation solution has "reached the boundary."

Since $d\bar{p}/dt = 0$ is not assumed, we allow seasonal cases where changes in equilibrium prices are foreseen. Alternatively, if $(dp_i/dt)/p_i$ is known, the adjustment equation

$$\frac{dp_i/dt}{p_i} - \frac{d\bar{p}_i/dt}{\bar{p}_i} = f_i(p) = d_i(p)\, e_i(p)$$

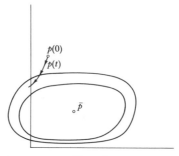

Figure 1

can be transformed to

$$\frac{d}{dt}(q_i - \bar{q}_i) = f_i(e^{q_1}, e^{q_2},...) = \left(d_i(p)\,\frac{q_i}{p_i}\right)\left(e_i(p)\,\frac{p_i}{q_i}\right), \qquad q_i = \ln p_i.$$

Clearly the diagonal matrix with elements $d_i(p)(q_i/p_i)$ is positive definite and $\Delta\, q\Delta((p_i/q_i)\, e_i(p)) = \Delta p\, \Delta e < 0$. Hence, cases of proportional price changes are included as well.

Proof   For $v(p) = (p - \bar{p}(t))\, D(\bar{p})^{-1}(p - \bar{p}(t))$,

$$\frac{dv}{dt} = 2(p - \bar{p}(t))\, D(\bar{p})\, h(p, t).$$

For p near $\bar{p}$, t large, dv/dt is nearly

$$2(p - \bar{p}(t))\, D(\bar{p})^{-1}\, D(\bar{p})\, e(p, t) = 2(p - \bar{p}(t))(e(p, t)) - e(\bar{p}(t), t)) < 0$$

unless $e(p) = e(\bar{p}(t)) = 0$. Therefore until reaching equilibrium, $dv/dt < 0$. Clearly, $dv/dt = 0$ at p if $h(p_i t_i) \to 0$, $p_i \to p$. Also, the set of normalized equilibrium prices is compact and hence so is $\mathscr{P}(\varepsilon)$. Apply Lemma 1: If $p(t)$ is within ε of $\bar{p}(t)$, $\bar{p}(t)$ within δ of $\bar{p}$, then $p(t)$ is within $\varepsilon + \delta$ of $\bar{p}$. Hence, choose δ small enough (t large enough) that $dv/dt < 0$ for $p(\varepsilon) \in \mathscr{P}(\varepsilon + \delta)$.   q.e.d.

The following corollaries give conditions under which *tâtonnement* leads the price system to a single equilibrium state.

4 Corollary   *If in Theorem 3 normalized equilibria are discrete, they are locally stable.*

5 Corollary   *If in Theorem 3 the normalized equilibrium is unique,*

$$\frac{dp_i}{dt} = d_i e_i(p, t) \qquad or \qquad \frac{dp_i/dt}{p_i} = d_i e_i(p, t),$$

and $\mathscr{P}(k)$ is a hyperellipse of prices with finite excess demands, then equilibrium is always globally stable on $\mathscr{P}(k)$.

In the absence of the particular comparative statics result, $\Delta p \, \Delta d < 0$, it is possible to obtain stability under the assumption of gross substitution. The rest of this subsection is concerned with gross substitution. Again, a Lyapunov function is used. However, another version of Lyapunov's results is required.

6 Lemma *If $dp/dt = h(p, t)$, h continuous and of period a (that is, $h(p, t + a) = h(p, t)$), and $v(p) > 0$ (unless $h(p) = 0$) is continuous and everywhere decreasing over time except at t, where $h(p(t), t)$ is zero, then all limit points p of $p(t)$ satisfy $h(p) = 0$.*

Proof Let

$$\pi_t(p) = p + \int_0^t h(p, \pi_s) \, ds$$

(fundamental theorem of differential equations; Birkhoff and Rota [1962, pp. 124–126]). $\pi_t(p)$ has period a and $\pi_{t+na} = \pi_t$.
  For $p(t_i) \to p$,

$$v(\pi_{na}(p)) = v(\pi_{na} \lim p(t_i))$$
$$= v(\lim \pi_{na} p(t_i)) \qquad \text{(continuity of } \pi\text{)}$$
$$= \lim v(p(t_i + na)) \qquad \text{(continuity of } v\text{)}$$
$$= \lim v(p(t)) \qquad \text{(monotone convergence).}$$

Therefore for n sufficiently large

$$\lim v(p(t)) = v(\pi_0 p) \geqslant v(\pi_t p) \geqslant v(\pi_{na} p)$$
$$= \lim v(p(t)),$$

or $\lim v(p(t)) = v(\pi_t(p))$ and $h(t) = 0$ for all t. q.e.d.

Dynamic stability is shown for gross substitution.

7 Theorem *Let the adjustment be*

$$\frac{d(p - \bar{p})}{dt} = D(p, t) \, e(p, t), \qquad e(p, t) \in \mathscr{E}(p, t),$$

except possibly $h_0(p) = 0$.

If

(i) $e(\bar{p}, t)$ *is cyclic in* t *of period* a *and* $\bar{p}(t) \gg 0$ *and* $e(\bar{p}(t), t) = 0$ *for all* t,

(ii) $D(p, t) \rightarrow D(p)$ *uniformly as* $t \rightarrow \infty$, $D(p)$ *continuous at* $\bar{p}$, $D(\bar{p})$ *positive diagonal,* $D(p, t)$ *of period* a *in* t,

(iii)   *there is weak gross substitution and for every increase from* $p_{\mathscr{I}}$ *to* $kp_{\mathscr{I}}$, $k > 1$, *at least one* e_j *is increased,* $j \in \sim\mathscr{I}$,

(iv) $e(p)$ *is continuous on a set,* $\mathscr{P}\{p \mid K \geqslant p_i - \bar{p}_i \geqslant k\}$,

then on $\mathscr{P}$ *(possibly equal to* Int Ω*) the normalized adjustment* $(h_0(p) = 0)$ *is globally stable in a market system and the nonnormalized adjustment system is globally stable in a market–exchange system.*

The theorem is an extension of results of Metzler [1945], Negishi [1958], Hahn [1958], Arrow and Hurwicz [1958, 1962], Arrow, Block, and Hurwicz [1959], and McKenzie [1960b].

Proof   1.   First, max $p_i/\bar{p}_i$ is nonincreasing, min $p_i/\bar{p}_i$ is nonincreasing over time, and at least one is changing, unless p is proportional to $\bar{p}$.

Arrange prices in order of $p_i/\bar{p}_i$. Then, starting from equilibrium prices for i for which $p_i/\bar{p}_i \leqslant 1$, decrease prices so that ratios fall to the level of the largest $p_i/\bar{p}_i \leqslant 1$. The remaining prices with still smaller ratios $p_i/\bar{p}_i$ are decreased to the next largest, etc. At each stage, the excess demands are nonincreasing for j for which $p_j/\bar{p}_j > 1$, whereas that of the (remaining) i whose prices are being decreased is not decreased (Theorem 34 of Chapter 5). At the last stage, the changes are not zero for some i with minimum $p_i/\bar{p}_i$ (iii). Next, increase the prices of the j for which $p_j/\bar{p}_j > 1$ so that the level of each ratio rises to that of the least $p_j/\bar{p}_j > 1$. The prices with still larger $p_i/\bar{p}_i > 1$ are further increased to the next smallest level, etc. At each stage, the excess demand for commodities with ratios $p_i/\bar{p}_i \leqslant 1$ does not decrease, whereas that for the commodities for which $p_i/\bar{p}_i > 1$ is not increased. At the last stage, for one of the $p_i/\bar{p}_i$ increased, e_i actually decreases. To conclude, either one of the least $p_i/\bar{p}_i$ has an excess demand greater than zero or one of the greatest $p_j/\bar{p}_j$ has excess demand less than zero. All of the i with least $p_i/\bar{p}_i$ have nonnegative excess demand and all of the i with largest $p_i/\bar{p}_i$ have nonpositive excess demand.

For any $p(t)$, continuity of the path implies that for nearby $p(s)$, the set of ratio maximizers does not increase, nor does the set of ratio minimizers. Hence, for a neighborhood of t, the maximum ratio is nonincreasing and the minimum is nondecreasing. Indeed, if over an interval of time there is no change in, say, the maximizing ratio, which happens to not be the *numéraire* only, then one of the maximizing coordinates i falls out of the set of maximizing coordinates. Continuity of the derivative implies that the maximum ratio is strictly decreasing for a nearby t. Therefore, for any μ between t and s, still another has fallen out, etc. Clearly, there are an uncountably infinite number of such occurrences, contrary to the fact that each i is equal to the maximum on a closed set of time periods. In sum, even though $dp_i/dt = 0$ is possible for some i maximizing $p_i/\bar{p}_i$, it is still necessary that all such p_i be strictly decreasing over a small interval. Hence, $p_i/\bar{p}_i$ is strictly decreasing. In the event that only the *numéraire* maximizes $p_i/\bar{p}_i$, then by the same reasoning as above, $\min p_i/\bar{p}_i$ must be decreasing.

Now a function v that is locally increasing (nondecreasing) is globally so by virtue of the fact that of the small neighborhoods of $u \in [s, t]$ covering $[s, t]$, a finite cover can be extracted (finite cover property of compact sets). Induction can be employed to show that $f(a) \leqslant f(t)$.

2. Next, it is shown that the solution of $p(t)$ exists and stays within $\mathscr{P} = \{p \mid K > p_i/\bar{p}_i > k\}$ (possibly $K = \infty$ and $k = 0$).

So long as defined, $p(t)$ remains away from Bnd $\mathscr{P}$ and in a compact set upon which $h_i(p, t)$ is defined (since $\max p_i/\bar{p}_i$ and $\min p_i/\bar{p}_i$ are nondecreasing). Also, by hypothesis, $h_i(p, t)$ is bounded as $t \to \infty$. Hence, the Peano theorem of ordinary differential equations applies to give an $\eta > 0$ such that $p(t)$ can be extended to $t \leqslant s \leqslant \eta$, whatever its value (Birkhoff and Rota [1962, pp. 124–126]). Therefore, the solution can be extended indefinitely simply by extending by η ever and again.

3. Clearly, the Lyapunov lemma (Lemma 6) applies to

$$v(p) = \max p_i/\bar{p}_i - \min p_i/\bar{p}_i \geqslant 0.$$

Evidently v is continuous in p.

4. The equilibrium is unique up to a multiplicative constant since the process in 1 can be applied to $p \neq k\bar{p}$ for any $k > 0$ to obtain non-zero excess demands.

5. Finally, in the nonnormalized case, $(d/dt)(pD^{-1}p) = 2pe(p) = 0$, so that at most one equilibrium proportion is approached

$$(k\bar{p}D^{-1}\bar{p} = \bar{p}D^{-1}\bar{p} \text{ implies } k = 1). \qquad \text{q.e.d.}$$

PROBLEMS

A. *Stability of Tâtonnement I*

Let there be a finite number of commodities in an exchange system, weak gross substitution, continuously differentiable demand, and a *numéraire* whose excess demand strictly increases with increases in the price of other goods.

Show that equilibrium is always locally stable.

B. *Stability of Tâtonnement II*

Let $e^i(p_{\sim 0}) = A^i p_{\sim 0} + b^i$ for all (competitive) consumers i.
Show that equilibrium is always globally stable.

C. *Stability of Tâtonnement III*

Let demand for three consumers and three goods be given by

$$x_i^i = 0, \qquad x_j^i = \frac{p_j}{p_j + p_k} \qquad \text{if } j = i + 1,$$

such that $x_j^i \neq x_j^k$ for $i \neq k$, and $3 + 1 \equiv 1$. Also let

$$x_j^i = -\frac{p_j}{p_j + p_k} \qquad \text{if } j = i + 2.$$

Show that the solution of $dp_i/dt = \sum x_j^i$ is not stable and that equilibrium is given by $p_1 = p_2 = p_3$.

This problem was first solved by Scarf [1960].

D. *Stability of Tâtonnement IV*

Suppose there are so-called *dominant diagonals*:

$$\sum_{j \neq i} \left| \frac{\partial e_i}{\partial p_j} \right| p_j < \left| \frac{\partial e_i}{\partial p_i} \right| \qquad \left(\text{or } \sum_{i \neq j} \left| \frac{\partial e_i}{\partial p_j} \right| p_i < \left| \frac{\partial e_j}{\partial p_j} \right| \right).$$

Show that $\partial e / \partial p$ has roots with negative real parts. How would the answer change if $\partial e / \partial p$ were multiplied by a positive definite matrix?

This problem was solved by McKenzie [1960a].

E. *Stability of Tâtonnement V*

Suppose computations lead to an expected price change

$$q = f(p, e), \qquad f(\bar{p}, 0) = 0.$$

Suppose also that excess demands are influenced by expected price changes.

(i)   What assumptions on $\partial f/\partial p$ and $\partial f/\partial e$ could ensure that sums of (quasi-) definite matrices are (quasi) definite and the product of a quasi-definite matrix and a definite matrix has roots with negative real parts?

(ii)   Let $q = B(dp/dt)$. What conditions ensure stability?

(iii)   Let $dq/dt = C(dp/dt - q)$, so that past disappointment figures in expectations. What conditions ensure stability?

The problem is solved, in related forms, by Enthoven and Arrow [1956], Arrow and McManus [1958], Arrow and Nerlove [1958], and Karlin [1959].

2. Marshallian and Keynesian Price Quantity Adjustment

In this section, we show how Marshallian- and Keynesian-type systems incorporate constraints on the Walrasian-type system. The rather peculiar Keynesian approach to interest rates is outlined. The Keynesian system is perhaps superseded by the asset system developed in Sections 4–6, but the system suggests a method of pasting together several dynamical systems (Remark 9) that possibly has further application. In any case, the Keynesian system plays such an important role in current economic thinking that a comparison with Walrasian economics is of at least doctrinal interest.

Marshall [1890] suggested that prices adjust to demand, fixing supply, but supply adjusts to price. In a general equilibrium framework, it is not easy to see what distinction Marshall had in mind. Perhaps he believed the supply side was relatively slow in response and approved of an adjustment system such as

$$\frac{dp}{dt} = d(p) - q, \qquad \frac{dq}{dt} = s(p) - q. \tag{3}$$

8 Remark   The matrix of partial derivatives

$$H = \begin{pmatrix} \dfrac{\partial d}{\partial p} - I \\[2mm] \dfrac{\partial s}{\partial p} - I \end{pmatrix}$$

has characteristic roots equal to one less than, and characteristic vectors equal to, those of $\partial d/\partial p$ and $\partial s/\partial p$.

Proof   For example,

$$H(x, 0) = \frac{\partial d}{\partial p} x - x = \lambda x - x, \qquad H(0, y) = \frac{\partial s}{\partial p} y - y = \mu y - y,$$

so that the roots of H are those of $\partial d/\partial p$ minus 1 and those of $\partial s/\partial p$ minus 1.   q.e.d.

Normally, $\partial s/\partial p$ is negative semidefinite. Hence, so long as $\partial d/\partial p$ has roots less than one real part, the Marshallian system is stable, as is Walrasian *tâtonnement*. The reader is directed to Theorem 41 of Chapter 5 for the relevant analysis of (3).

If closer correspondence with actual market operations is desired, the model described by equation system (3) would be a half measure. Especially, we should distinguish between actual supply, as represented by output from factors available, and potential supply, which would represent output if factors were available at going prices. This would give a reason for the delayed response of supply and would be an extension of the common differentiation between long-run and short-run adjustments.

Presuming factor supplies at a level y, firms would maximize $px - w\bar{y}$, where x is output, subject to $\bar{y} \leqslant y$. On the other hand, given factor inputs $\bar{y}$, the firms might still be seeking factors in quantities in excess of y. In sum, factor demands may well exceed but production is limited by available factor supplies. This leads to the notion of effective supply (and demand) as opposed to the potential supply of the Walrasian system. The distinction is that effective supply is that which is actually recorded in the market, whereas potential supply is that which would have been recorded had it been possible. Elaboration of this principle would lead to the exclusion of demand for labor contingent upon obtaining capital whenever the capital was not forthcoming, or demand for capital contingent upon unavailable labor. Still $\partial s/\partial(p, w)$ will be negative semidefinite and the analysis of Section 6 of Chapter 5 will apply to this case.

The signs of the elements of $\partial s/\partial(p, w)$ can be determined. First, we note that so long as all of a factor is demanded, changes in its price do not change output. Otherwise, an increase in factor j's price decreases output of i, so that in effect we add a positive number to the element ij of $\partial e/\partial p$. Similarly, the demand for other factors k will respond less rapidly, since hiring the one will enhance the demand for others. In this case, the kj elements will be increased from otherwise negative elements. Finally, increases in the price of output will have a weaker effect on the supply of goods, tending to reduce in absolute value the positive ij terms and the negative ii term.

Once the causes of the delay in supply response are ascertained, it would seem natural to define effective consumer demand to be demand from income acquired by factors actually hired. In this way, the chapters of Keynes [1936] on effective demand appear as a natural extension of the effective supply dynamics of Marshall.

The Keynesian system is not a recontract system. Contracts made in separate industries are not subject to recontract. Therefore actual purchases must be covered with actual income. Excess demand can be conveniently broken down into three components:

d_j^1 = effective demand,

s_j^1 = purchased supply,

s_j^2 = unpurchased supply,   where $s_j = s_j^1 + s_j^2$ = total supply.

(Of course $s_j \leqslant s_j^i$, $i = 1, 2$). These quantities are illustrated in Figure 2.

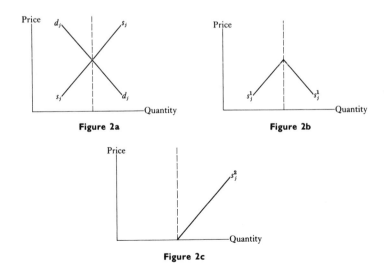

Figure 2a   **Figure 2b**

Figure 2c

The particular theory of Keynes says that for y equal to income,

$$y = \sum_{\text{goods } i} p_i s_i^1 = \sum_{\text{goods } i} p_i \min(d_i, s_i)$$

$$= \sum_{\text{factors } i} p s_i^1 = \sum_{\text{factors } i} p_i \min(d_i, s_i)$$

(assuming constant returns to scale). This could be characterized as the *Keynes law* of effective demand. In addition, under the assumption of no distribution effects on demand,

$$\frac{1}{\bar{p}} \sum_{\text{goods } i} p_i d_i = c(y)$$

where $\bar{p}$ is an index of prices used to deflate money income to obtain real income y, and c is the consumption function plus investment plus exogenous demand.

Finally, in analogy to the classical stationary state, there is a rate of interest to link current to future transactions. Indeed, given relative prices of goods, c is a function of the rate of interest via investment demand and the marginal propensity to consume out of real income. Hence,

$$\frac{1}{\bar{p}} \sum_{\text{goods } i} p_i d_i = c(y, \rho)$$

where ρ is the interest rate. From the foregoing, $c(y, \rho) \geqslant y$. In deflation in the goods markets, where $s_i > d_i$, $y = c(y, \rho)$ which determines y by an implicit function. The y so derived is often misnamed "the equilibrium income."

The difference between y and consumption contributes to demand in the futures for various assets. In the short run, however, these are assumed to be insignificant compared with demands from the stock of assets in existence. Hence, there is a dichotomy between current commodities and financial assets. The rate of interest is determined in the assets market where, again, the demand for one asset is influenced by and contingent on sales of others.

$$\sum_{\text{assets } i} d_i p_i = \sum_{\text{assets } i} p_i \min(d_i, s_i).$$

For example, if $i =$ consols, $p_i = 1/\rho$. (Friedman [1957] and Modigliani and Brumberg [1954] objected to the dichotomy upon both the empirical and the theoretical grounds that, under utility maximization, changes in income lead to an effect on consumption as weak as the effect on asset holding (see Problems B–D of Chapter 8 of the companion volume).) Generally, the asset market adjusts instantaneously, so that the rate of interest is given by equating the present value of the prospective earnings of the capital stock with its market value in terms of the prices of the goods of which it is composed (see Chapter 11 of the companion volume).

As in the normalized Walrasian system, there is a money good in terms of which other commodities are stated. This good is denoted 0, so that there are now $n + 1$ commodities. This good has no formal market and therefore it is not subject to the same constraints. Unpurchased, nonmoney commodities cannot be the basis of effective demand (since only money is generally acceptable). This is in contrast to the case of potential demand, where the individual assumes that he can sell his commodities. For each individual, and therefore the community, the sum of the value of effective demand of nonmoney goods must equal the sum of the value of his actual income plus the change in money balances he expects to make. For the whole community, the sum of the value of income is simply the sum of the value of purchased supply,

$$\sum_{j=1}^{n} p_j d_j = \sum_{j=1}^{n} p_j s_j + m$$

where m is the excess of the actual over the desired rate of increase (or decrease) of holdings of the money commodity. From another viewpoint, the fact of unsatisfied demands is simply reflected in an increase in the money good beyond that which the consumer planned. Since

$$d_j \geqslant s_j, \qquad m \geqslant 0.$$

Also,

$$\sum_{j=1}^{n} p_j e_j = m - \sum_{j=1}^{n} p_j s_j^2 \equiv \mu,$$

which is a generalized form of the Keynes law that substitutes for Walras' law in effective demand systems (Clower [1965]). In particular, if all markets are in equilibrium

$$m = s_j^2 = 0 \qquad \text{for all } j.$$

In this instance there is also the Walras law.

If there is at least as much unwanted money available as unsold output, then

$$\mu = m - \sum_{j=1}^{n} p_j s_j^2 \geqslant 0;$$

otherwise,

$$\mu = m - \sum_{j=1}^{n} p_j s_j^2 < 0,$$

which represents the normal situation of insufficient demand. We can think of μ as the Keynesian analog of the Walrasian excess demand for money. It does not represent excess demand from the viewpoint of actual income, but rather from the viewpoint of income if all goods could be sold. Whenever $\mu = 0$, potential demand for money is zero. Therefore, the form of Walras' law is quite general; the value of that offered must equal the value of that demanded. Nevertheless, μ is not exactly the same as the Walrasian money good, since there will be changes in the composition of expenditures for nonmoney goods whenever all desired sales are made.

Normally, the quantities m, s_j^2 are not differentiable at their zero values, but the difference

$$\mu = m - \sum_{j=1}^{n} p_j s_j^2$$

may be. In Problem F, it is seen that the derivative form of Keynes' law is analogous to the derivative form of Walras' law and leads to the same kind of restrictions on the matrix, $\partial e / \partial p$, where μ plays the role of the *numéraire*.

In passing, it should be mentioned that Keynes, like David Hume [1741], Marshall [1923], and Cassel [1932] before him, had in mind a transactions notion of the (planned) demand for money, where another constraint appeared in addition to the budget constraint. This was written as a function of the rate of interest. Given the rate of interest, the value of all other assets was determined. Hence, the asset market was characterized by a single equation:

$$d_0(\rho, y) = s_0$$

where s_0 was determined by the structure of the banking system and the government monetary policy. This resolution of the rate of interest precipitated a lively debate, part of which is summarized by Klein [1947]. One possible viewpoint would be that (present value of capital) equals (value of capital) determines the rate of interest; the rate of interest and the supply of money determine money income; the rate of interest and the consumption function determine real income; and therefore, the price of goods and the value of capital is determined. The system is circular but perhaps solvable. Only adjustments in the wage rate are possible. Since the foregoing approach to money was rejected in Chapter 11 of the companion volume, it seems pointless to pursue the matter.

We have seen that effective demand and supply systems are put together from taking extremum of differing systems (Figure 2). These can be analyzed so long as there is a decreasing v common to all the systems, in which case it can be shown that v is decreasing in the hybrid system. Any price path $p(t)$ passes through the regions of dominance $\mathscr{D}_i$ of each of the systems,

$$i = 1,\dots, \eta, \qquad \text{where} \quad \frac{dp}{dt} = f^i(p)$$

for $p(t) \in \mathscr{D}_i$. On the boundaries of the $\mathscr{D}_i$'s, the functions f^i agree, but not their derivatives.

9 Remark Let the excess demand function reflect effective demand and supply. If with respect to each domain $\mathscr{D}_i$, v is continuously differentiable and $dv/dt < 0$, then v is decreasing.

Proof   For t, there is an $\varepsilon(t)$ such that

$$v(s) > v(t) > v(u) \qquad \text{for} \quad s > t > u,$$

$$|s - t| < \varepsilon(t), \qquad |t - u| < \varepsilon(u).$$

(If, for example, $t_n \to t$, $t_n \to t$, $v(t_n) > v(t)$, then there is some $\mathscr{D}_i$ such that $p(t_{n_k}) \in \mathscr{D}_i$, $t_{n_k} \to t$. In such a case,

$$\frac{[v(t_{n_k}) - v(t)]}{t_{n_k} \ t} > 0,$$

or taking limits, we get $dv/dt \geqslant 0$ on $\mathscr{D}_i$, contrary to hypothesis.) The finite cover property of compact sets gives that v is decreasing over its whole range.   q.e.d.

An application appears in Problem F.

PROBLEMS

F. *The Keynesian System II*

Let there be (in addition to bonds) goods, labor, and money, with excess demand equations reflecting effective demand.

(i)   What is the form of the excess demand for goods, given the

Keynes law and the Keynes consumption function, as well as a production function on labor and goods?

(ii)   What is the effective excess demand for labor, assuming supply fixed?

(iii)   Let the banking system expand the money supply at a rate increasing with the rate of interest. What are the determinants of the excess demand of money—without the inclusion of balances due to unsatisfied demand for goods?

(iv)   What are the signs of $\partial e/\partial p$, when defined? Does equilibrium exist?

(v)   Assuming the money "market" always in equilibrium, observe that in full employment,

$$\frac{\partial e}{\partial p} = \begin{pmatrix} \dfrac{\partial d_G}{\partial p_G} & \dfrac{\partial d_L}{\partial p_G} \\ 0 & \dfrac{\partial d_L}{\partial p_L} \end{pmatrix}$$

and in unemployment,

$$\frac{\partial e}{\partial p} = \begin{pmatrix} \dfrac{\partial d_G - s_G}{\partial p_G} & \dfrac{\partial d_L}{\partial p_G} \\ \dfrac{\partial d_G - s_G}{\partial p_L} & \dfrac{\partial d_L}{\partial p_L} \end{pmatrix}$$

whenever the derivatives are defined. Show that until reaching equilibrium, the economy passes through the stages full employment–deflation, unemployment–inflation, full employment–inflation, and back again.

(vi)   In (v), show that equilibrium is locally stable whenever

(a)   Under full employment, $\partial d_G/\partial p_L < 0$, which could be as long as investment decreases in response to increases in interest rates, and

(b) $\partial d_G/\partial p_L > 0$ under unemployment. (Hint: Break down the cases. Show that (s_G, d_L) is profit maximizing under unemployment; that d_L and s_G are zero homogeneous in p_L and p_G under unemployment; that under unemployment,

$$\det \frac{\partial E}{\partial p} = \left(\frac{\partial d_L}{\partial p_L} \frac{\partial d_G}{\partial p_G} + \frac{\partial d_G}{\partial p_L} \frac{p_L}{p_G} \right);$$

that dependence of d_G on p_L is indirect through dependence of d_G on s_G; that a negative semiquasi-definite matrix that has roots with negative real parts is quasi definite; and finally, that $\partial e/\partial p$ is negative quasi definite.)

(vii) What can be said about global stability? (Recall that a system $dx/dt = f(x)$ is globally stable if the roots $\partial f/\partial x$ are negative in real parts and if there are two constants ε and δ such that $|f(x)| \geqslant \varepsilon > 0$ for $|x| \geqslant \delta > 0$ (Olech [1963]).)

(viii) Why should $\partial d_G - s_G/\partial p_L > 0$ under unemployment?

(ix) What will follow increases in money supply, goods demanded, or labor supplied in the adjustment process? In ultimate prices?

A simplified form of this problem was solved by Samuelson [1947, pp. 276–283] and Marshak [1951] among many others. Another version was analyzed by Patinkin [1956], who emphasized the role of money balances by a source of demand goods as the stabilizing factor, although it should be clear from the foregoing that no such "real balance effect" need be invoked.

Reference to Keynes [1936] will reveal the importance of expectations in investment. This can be incorporated in the foregoing analysis by taking the real rate of interest to be the nominal rate minus the expected relative change in the price of goods. This real rate is determined by equilibrium in the money "market" and is the one that is "fed back" into the demand for goods.

G. *The Keynesian System III*

In the effective demand system, the demand for money for transactions purposes is increasing in prices. What of m? (Hint: Account for income changes as well as the substitution among commodities.)

H. *Almost Equilibria in Dynamics*

Suppose $dp_i/dt = d_i(p)\, e_i(p)$ for all i, $d_i(p) > 0$. Let $p(t)$ be bounded, $d_i(p)\, e_i(p)$ continuously differentiable.

(i) Show that if $e_{i_0}(p) < 0$ and if $d_{i_0}(p)$ is sufficiently large relative to $d_i(p)$, $i \neq i_0$, and if $\varepsilon > 0$, there is a $\delta > 0$ such that $|E_i(p)| < \varepsilon$ for all $t > \delta$.

(ii) Let all $d_i(p) > 0$ and let the $d_{i}(p) > d_{i_{j+1}}(p)$. Show that if $d_i(p)/d_{i_{j+1}}(p)$ are sufficiently large, for $\varepsilon > 0$, there is a $\delta > 0$ such that $|E_i(p)| < \varepsilon$ for all $t > \delta$ except for $i = i_n$. Show that $|e(p)| \to 0$.

This problem rationalizes the approach in Problem F, according to which the interest rate is assumed to equilibrate immediately. What does it say about the Keynesian assumption that the labor market equilibrates very slowly relative to goods and goods slowly relative to interest rates?

I. *Expectations I*

Keynes [1937] stated that on the average, people expect the future prices to be like the present. Only the variances change over time. This is the notion of a martingale.

(i) If expectations are lagged from present and past experience, as in Markov processes, can we have a martingale? (Hint: Let $e_i A$ be expected probabilities for differing events, given i occurred today. Let prices be expected p^j, given an event j. Then expectation is $e_i A p$, $p = \binom{p^1}{p^2}$. Hence, find out conditions for

$$e_i A p = e_i p \qquad \text{for all} \quad e_i A v = v, \quad v = (1,...,1), \, e_i = (0,...,1,...,0).)$$

(ii) Suppose instead that expectations are fixed over time. What condition on the structure of probabilities is implied?

J. *Unemployment Equilibrium*

Prove that there is an "unemployment equilibrium" where all excess demands except labor's are zero. (Hint: Let labor be reduced in quantity. Show that the resulting equilibrium is an unemployment equilibrium under an effective demand system.)

3. Utility Adjustment

Edgeworth [1881] envisaged an adjustment process whereby mutually beneficial contracts were made and then recontracting was allowed to take advantage of any residual benefits. These contracts could be between pairs or between groups of individuals. The trades were then supposed to converge to the core. In unpublished papers, J. Green and W. Neuefeind have recently shown that a stochastic version of this process converges to the core. (Hahn and Negishi [1962] obtained convergence to a Pareto optimal choice by a recontract system, and their theorem is deduced simply as a consequence of nondecreasing consumer preference levels.) Since the market processes are not always stable (Problem C), there is also a need for a general method to compute the competitive price system. This is offered by Scarf [1967].

4. Asset–Price Adjustment

Here we add asset accumulations or decumulations to the Walrasian system. Then stability is proved by showing connections between the asset system and *tâtonnement*. An important role is played by the influence of both prices and assets on excess demand. By moving to assets, we move beyond produce markets with merchant-peasants to markets for consumer durables, capital goods, and the like. We are still short of a model of disequilibrium behavior with growth in productive capital since the production possibilities of the economy are not allowed to change.

So long as the economy receives a small "shock," so that prices are slightly different from equilibrium, *tâtonnement* would seem to be an adequate representation of market processes. This could be argued by noting that most of an individual's demand for current goods derives from his asset position, and the fact that he could not find work or sell commodities today will not affect his purchases tomorrow. Only after his asset position had deteriorated by sustained unemployment would the restriction in demand occur (Friedman [1957] and Modigliani and Brumberg [1954]; also Problem B of Chapter 8 of the companion volume). In the meantime the system would have moved closer to equilibrium. However, with a larger shock or with prolonged disequilibrium, *tâtonnement* seems a totally inadequate description. In particular, as asset positions deteriorate, as unwanted stocks accumulate, the excess demands change. One way to capture this is to assume (real economic) limitations on the rate at which assets may be bought or sold, like those discussed in Chapter 11 of the companion volume. Since large quantities of unwanted assets cannot be disposed of immediately, traders may participate in otherwise inferior transactions. Hence, construction of an adjustment theory appropriate for classical economics entails short-run changes in asset positions.

Clower [1965] calls for the inclusion of changes in demand due to the disequilibrium accumulation of assets. A vestigial form of this appears in Patinkin [1956], where the accumulation of money assets plays a role. In particular, Patinkin has in mind the accumulation of money balances by unsatisfied demanders who thereafter demand more commodities from this balance. Evidently, the accumulation of bonds should play a role, as in the model of Tobin [1955]. Symmetrically, we should include the increased supply from past unsold inventories, as in Metzler [1941]. It is shown that assets can be introduced without greatly altering the traditional method of analysis, and indeed that doing so allows us to retain Walras' law.

That which follows was prompted by Keynes' [1936] famous attempt. Keynes took into consideration a number of longer-term phenomena, including the changes in asset holdings. In particular, involuntary savings played a significant role in the construction of the nature of his demand curves, as already discussed in Section 2. Similarly, he regarded expectation as important in the construction of demand curves. Nevertheless, his formal analysis proceeded on the basis of stationary excess demand functions that had been disturbed by once and for all changes in expectations. In none of his discussions of the comparative statics or dynamics did endogenous changes in stocks have a significant role. It was only in modification of his theory that he took account of the time change in stock. So far as the dynamic processes were concerned, he regarded them as relatively minor compared with such stationary relationships as the consumption function, the supply of labor, the production function, and the demand for financial assets (Problem F). At least, this is one view of the Keynesian approach. Nevertheless, in deference to contrary views and because it is a useful extension of the neoclassical system, it is well to incorporate assets into a stationary system amenable to modern techniques of general equilibrium theory. A fairly simple version of asset accumulation is considered, to uncover what modifications if any must be made to analyze the case where the distribution of assets changes.

It should be noted that there already exist some general equilibrium asset models due to Hahn and Negishi [1962] and Uzawa [1963]. One objection to these models is quite simply that their analysis proceeds on the basis of utility changes due to trading. The main property is that trading leads to no utility decrease and for some, to utility increase. (1) Consumer utility is assumed to accrue to stocks, which over the trading period are indestructible. As a result, the kind of equilibrium reached is of a trivial sort in that no trading takes place by anyone. Hence, it does not represent a competitive situation from the initial wealth position, and applied repeatedly, it implies noncompetitive trading over time. (2) Many price equilibria may be totally unstable, so that the equilibrium may not be neutral vis-à-vis asset holdings. In this case, starting from a particular asset position, the route to equilibrium may be very long indeed. (3) What is more, it is not easy to see how to judge the speed of adjustment of the process, which will be the point of Chapter 8.

We now construct a model of asset–price adjustment and discuss its equilibrium states. Recall that there are n goods plus the *numéraire*. Therefore, there are $n + 1$ relevant stocks. Let the stock of the ith commodity held by the jth individual be denoted F_i^j. Then the planned accumulation is equal to E_i^j, the excess demand of the jth individual for the ith good, whereas the unplanned accumulation is equal to E_i^j minus the unfilled demand (or plus the unsold supply), which is denoted by $\bar{E}_i^j$:

$$\frac{dF_i^j}{dt} = E_i^j - \bar{E}_i^j, \qquad i = 1,\dots, n.$$

(Evidently, it is assumed that decaying assets are replaced, so that F. is defined as a sustained asset.) For the money commodity,

$$\frac{dF^j_{n+1}}{dt} = - \sum_{i=1}^{n} p_i \frac{dF^j_i}{dt} = - \sum_{i=1}^{n} p_i E^j_i + \sum_{i=1}^{n} p_i \bar{E}^j_i .$$

Also,

$$\sum_{i=1}^{n+1} p_i \frac{dF^j_i}{dt} = 0,$$

so that the value of assets, $\sum p_i F_i$, is variable over time only if price is variable over time.

The preservation of value of assets requires some explanation. As an asset decumulates, it can have negative quantities. There can be negative bonds, negative money, etc., which represent obligations to pay money on demand, dividends in the case of bonds and the full equity in the case of money. Therefore negative assets represent liabilities. For example, consider the process by which individuals place money in the bank, which is then lent out to firms. The balance sheet reads:

Deposit Holder

    Assets   *Liabilities*

    Money in the form of
    demand deposits

Bank

    Assets   *Liabilities*

    A "bond" payable by the   Demand deposits
    firm and a possible cash
    reserve

Firm

    Money in the form of cash   A bond payable to the bank

The net value of these assets, whenever liabilities are counted as negative assets, is equal to the original money deposited in the bank. Money is created only in the sense that the non bank investors have more money, but also more liabilities. If the firm's cash is deposited in the banking system for one reason or another, the process continues, but again with no net creation of value. Of course, rotting or growth will ultimately change asset values, but in the short run, the only way value can be created for the community as a whole is for prices to change, or for some outsider, such as the government, to print money and spend it directly or give it as subsidies to private individuals. In this sense, only time, the state, and the price system create asset values, whereas financial institutions, such as banks, merely alter the distribution of assets between individuals. In the case where banking is a state monopoly, banks have a unique position insofar as only they are allowed to hold negative money on demand, but in an economy where everyone could operate as a bank, they would have no such distinction among financial institutions.

Financial institutions are intermediaries between three groups: their owners, who desire to hold certain negative financial assets and other positive financial assets; firms, who wish to hold negative financial assets corresponding to the financial intermediaries' positive assets and certain positive capital assets; and other individuals, who wish to hold positive financial assets. As such, they play a role of bringing together these several investors. There is no sense in which they are producing money for the community. Of course, they alter the asset distribution and may thereby impair financial solvency. In this way they may represent a threat to competitive market organization. They are the object of analysis only from the viewpoint of their effect on expectations and the distribution of assets (if bankruptcy actually results).

The definition of $\bar{E}_i^j$ requires some method of determining the distribution of community excess demand,

$$e_i = \sum_{j=1}^{m} E_i^j = \sum_{j=1}^{m} \bar{E}_i^j \,,$$

among the m individuals. For example, this might be done by allocated excess demand to buyers in accordance to their shares of demand and excess supplies to sellers in accordance to their shares of supply. Or it might be allocated equally to individuals or perhaps according to one's status or physical location, etc.

At any particular time period, given the first n assets, the $(n + 1)$st asset is immediately known from the equation

$$F_{n+1}^j = W^j - \sum_{i=1}^{n} p_i F_i^j$$

where W^j represents the value of j's wealth. Therefore, analysis can proceed with respect to the first n commodities, provided we always keep in mind that changing one or more of these commodities requires a change in money balances.

The *flow equilibrium price system* $\bar{p}$ for any distribution of assets

$$(F_i^j, \quad i = 1,..., m, \quad j = 1,..., n)$$

is that for which community excess demand is zero,

$$e_i(\bar{p}, F^1,..., F^n) = 0.$$

Therefore, to each distribution of assets, there is an equilibrium price system. Of course, the equilibrium pair, asset distribution and price system, is not unique, but has a dimension equal to that of the asset distribution, namely, mn. This is illustrated in Figure 3 for $m = 1$,

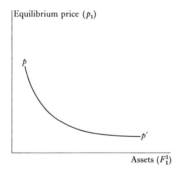

Figure 3

$n = 1$. As F_1^1 increases, money holdings decrease. In order to ensure that the individual does not wish to switch out of asset 1, we must decrease its price, and make it more attractive to hold. The path of price is pp', which corresponds to Tobin's *portfolio balance*. Note that the curve is drawn such that for each quantity of asset, there exists an equilibrium price. This is the Arrow–Debreu theorem of classical general equilibrium theory (Chapter 4).

In the m-person economy, some constraints appear in addition to the requirements that community excess demands be zero. Even if excess demands are presently zero, but the asset composition of some individual is such that his excess demand is temporary, then in the next period, as it were, the excess demand will no longer be zero. Assets that influence excess demands, of which there are q, are *nontrivial assets*. Otherwise, the asset is *trivial*. Factors for current use are trivial, whereas claims on their future use are nontrivial. Ordinarily, accumulations of goods appear as firm inventories, which are nontrivial. It is required that the asset distribution be such that

$$e_i^k = 0$$

for any nontrivial asset i.[1]

The added requirement corresponds to the notion of *stock equilibrium* as opposed to the weak notion of flow equilibrium. Incidentally, as long as n of the commodities are in stock equilibrium, also the $n + 1$ is, by virtue of

$$0 = \sum_{k=1}^{n} p_i e_k^i = -e_{n+1}^i,$$

so that

$$e_{n+1}^i = 0$$

whenever there is stock equilibrium.

If there is stock equilibrium for all nontrivial assets and flow equilibrium for the others, then there is *stock–flow equilibrium*. There are n restrictions in order to obtain flow equilibrium. For stock–flow equilibrium, there must be an additional $(m - 1)q$ restriction, corresponding to the q nontrivial assets. Therefore, the stable asset–price combination is of dimension

$$n(m + 1) - (n + (m - 1)q) = nm - (m - 1)q = m(n - q) + q.$$

For example, if all assets are nontrivial, $q = n$, then the dimension of the stable asset–price combination is n. For each price, there corresponds one stable asset configuration.

Since equilibrium is highly indeterminate, we must amplify our stability theory from Section 1. In the application following, the difficulties occur because the redistribution of assets normally leads to a new equilibrium. It is necessary to have another lemma. An *m-dimensional differentiable manifold* $\mathcal{M} \subset \mathcal{E}^n$ is a space such that there are diffeomorphisms from open disks in $\mathcal{E}^n$ into $\mathcal{E}^n$ that take neighborhoods of $\mathcal{M}$ onto neighborhoods of $\mathcal{E}^m$.

10 Lemma *If $dx/dt = f(x)$, $x \in \mathcal{E}^n$, and if on an m-dimensional differentiable manifold $\mathcal{M}$, $f(x) = 0$ for $x \in \mathcal{M}$, and $\partial f / \partial x$ is continuous and has m zero roots and $n - m$ roots with negative real parts, for $x \in \mathcal{M}$, then for every path $p(t)$ for which $p(0)$ is sufficiently near $\mathcal{M}$, there exists a $\bar{p} \in \mathcal{M}$ such that $p(t) \rightarrow \bar{p}$.*

---

[1] The notation has been altered slightly so that now E^k is excess demand instead of e^k or $\mathcal{E}^k$. This emphasizes that hereafter excess demand is the primitive notion rather than production or preferences.

Whenever the conclusion of the lemma holds, the equilibrium is *weakly locally stable*.

Proof   According to Coddington and Levinson [1955, Chapter 13], there is a 1–1 continuously differentiable function g such that for the first $m - n$ components of $g(x)$, the solution of

$$\frac{dy}{dt} = \frac{\partial g}{\partial x}\frac{dx}{dt} = \frac{\partial g}{\partial x}f(g^{-1}(y))$$

tends to equilibrium, where $f(g^{-1}(y)) = 0$ and $g_{m+1,...,n}(x(t)) = 0$ for all t. Changes in the manifold $\mathcal{M}$ lead to no change in the fact that $dy/dt = 0$, whereupon these must include changes in the first m components only. Since $\mathcal{M}$ is of dimension m, it is identical with the space in which there are changes in those m components, fixing the others. Euclidean subspaces of a Euclidean paces of the same dimension have open sets in common, which is the Brouwer invariance of domain theorem; hence, near x, there is an identity of open sets in $g(\mathcal{M})$ with those obtained by projecting the first m components of $\mathcal{E}^n$. Therefore, near x for which $f(x) = 0$, $g(x(t))$ tends to its first m components, the others tending to zero. Hence, $x(t)$ tends to $g^{-1}(x_1,..., x_m(0), 0,..., 0)$, which is the equilibrium (since g is a homeomorphism).   q.e.d.

Consider the all-important matrix of partial derivatives:

$$B = \begin{bmatrix} \dfrac{\partial\{dp/dt\}}{\partial \bar{p}} & \dfrac{\partial\{dp/dt\}}{\partial F^1} & \cdots & \dfrac{\partial\{dp/dt\}}{\partial F^m} \\[2ex] \dfrac{\partial\{dF^1/dt\}}{\partial \bar{p}} & \dfrac{\partial\{dF^1/dt\}}{\partial F^1} & \cdots & \dfrac{\partial\{dF^m/dt\}}{\partial F^1} \\ \vdots & \vdots & & \\ \dfrac{\partial\{dF^m/dt\}}{\partial \bar{p}} & \dfrac{\partial\{dF^m/dt\}}{\partial F^1} & \cdots & \dfrac{\partial\{dF^m/dt\}}{\partial F^m} \end{bmatrix}$$

$$= \begin{bmatrix} \sum\limits_{j=1}^{n} D\,\dfrac{\partial E^j}{\partial \bar{p}} & D\,\dfrac{\partial E^1}{\partial F^1} & \cdots & D\,\dfrac{\partial E^m}{\partial F^m} \\[2ex] -\dfrac{\partial E^1 - \bar{E}^1}{\partial \bar{p}} & -\dfrac{\partial E^1 - \bar{E}^1}{\partial F^1} & \cdots & -\dfrac{\partial \bar{E}^1}{\partial F^m} \\ \vdots & \vdots & & \vdots \\ -\dfrac{\partial E^1 - \bar{E}^m}{\partial \bar{p}} & \dfrac{\partial \bar{E}^m}{\partial F^1} & \cdots & \dfrac{\partial E^m - \bar{E}^m}{\partial F^m} \end{bmatrix}.$$

Of course, this matrix has $nm + (m - 1)q$ zero roots, which correspond to the fact that a variation in the mn directions to a new equilibrium pair of asset distributions and price systems does not lead to any adjustment back to the old pair. Referring to Figure 4, which is an extension of Figure 3, we see that only movement along the curve pp' leads to no change. Off pp', the dynamical system pushes toward equilibrium, as will be seen. Therefore, curves are drawn with arrows indicating the

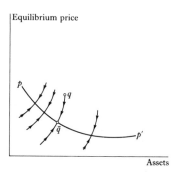

Figure 4

direction in which the system moves over time. If the matrix had all negative roots, then it would have to be locally stable. This is not the case, since it is not true that from any starting position (say, q) in figure 4 the system necessarily tends to $\bar{q}$; some do, some do not. What is true is that the system is only *weakly locally stable* in the sense that starting near the locus pp', one tends to *some* equilibrium price–asset combination. Therefore, one of the roots of B must be zero. Note that one is the dimension of possible variation in assets. In general, there will be $nm + (m-1)q$ zero roots, corresponding to movements in the subspace of stable asset–price combinations.

As a first application, consider the case in which

$$q = 0, \qquad \frac{\partial E^j}{\partial F^j} = 0$$

so that the number of zero roots of B is nm.

11 Remark   If $\partial E^j/\partial F^j = 0$, then the matrix

$$B_1 = \begin{bmatrix} D\,\dfrac{\partial e}{\partial \bar{p}} & 0 \\[2mm] -\dfrac{\partial E^1 - \bar{E}^1}{\partial \bar{p}} & 0 \\[2mm] \vdots & \vdots \\[2mm] -\dfrac{\partial E^m - \bar{E}^m}{\partial \bar{p}} & 0 \end{bmatrix}$$

has n nonzero roots corresponding to the n nonzero roots of $D(\partial e/\partial p)$. This is the case of *tâtonnement*, already analyzed.

Proof

$$(x, 0, ..., 0)\, B_1 = \lambda(x, 0, ..., 0), \qquad \lambda \neq 0,$$

implies that

$$\lambda D\, \frac{\partial e}{\partial p} = \lambda x. \qquad \text{q.e.d.}$$

A second application occurs whenever prices and wages are inflexible.

12 Remark Whenever $dp/dt \equiv 0$, the matrix B is equal to

$$B_2 = \begin{bmatrix} 0 & 0 & \cdots & 0 \\ -\dfrac{\partial E^1 - \bar{E}^1}{\partial \bar{p}} & \dfrac{\partial E^1 - \bar{E}^1}{\partial q^1} & \cdots & \dfrac{\partial \bar{E}^1}{\partial F^m} \\ \vdots & & \ddots & \\ -\dfrac{\partial E^m - \bar{E}^m}{\partial \bar{p}} & -\dfrac{\varepsilon \partial \bar{E}^m}{\partial F^1} & & \dfrac{\partial F^m - \bar{E}^m}{\partial F^m} \end{bmatrix}$$

which has exactly the nonzero roots of the matrix

$$\begin{bmatrix} \dfrac{\partial E^1 - \bar{E}^1}{\partial F^i} & \cdots & -\dfrac{\partial \bar{E}^1}{\partial F^m} \\ \vdots & & \vdots \\ -\dfrac{\partial E^m}{\partial F^1} & \cdots & \dfrac{\partial E^m - \bar{E}^1}{\partial F^m} \end{bmatrix}$$

$$= \begin{bmatrix} \dfrac{\partial E^m}{\partial F^1} & & 0 \\ & \ddots & \\ 0 & & \dfrac{\partial E^m}{\partial F^1} \end{bmatrix} - \begin{bmatrix} \dfrac{\partial \bar{E}^1}{F^1} & & \dfrac{\partial \bar{E}^1}{F^m} \\ \vdots & & \vdots \\ \dfrac{E^m}{F^1} & \cdots & \dfrac{\partial E^m}{F^m} \end{bmatrix}.$$

Of course, stability cannot be expected.

Proof

$$B_2 = \begin{bmatrix} 0 \\ y^1 \\ \vdots \\ y^m \end{bmatrix} = \lambda \begin{bmatrix} 0 \\ y^1 \\ \vdots \\ y^m \end{bmatrix} \neq \lambda$$

implies

$$\begin{bmatrix} \dfrac{\partial E^1 - \bar{E}^1}{\partial F^1} & \cdots & -\dfrac{\partial \bar{E}^1}{\partial F^m} \\ \vdots & & \vdots \\ \dfrac{\partial \bar{E}^m}{\partial F^1} & \cdots & \dfrac{\partial E^m - \bar{E}^m}{\partial F^m} \end{bmatrix} \begin{pmatrix} y^1 \\ \vdots \\ y^n \end{pmatrix} = \lambda \begin{pmatrix} y^1 \\ \vdots \\ y^n \end{pmatrix}. \qquad \text{q.e.d.}$$

In this case, also, stability is not ensured, due to an insufficient number of negative roots.

A third application occurs whenever there are no distribution effects from changes in asset holdings, presuming asset values constant. It is further assumed that each individual bears the excess demand equally. Therefore:

13 Theorem *If*

$$\frac{\partial E^i}{\partial F^i} = \frac{\partial e}{\partial F}, \qquad \frac{\partial E^i}{\partial p^j} = \frac{\partial e}{\partial F^j} = \frac{1}{m}\frac{\partial e}{\partial F},$$

the nonzero roots of the matrix $B = B_3$ *are the roots of*

$$D\frac{\partial e}{\partial \bar{p}} \qquad and \qquad \frac{1}{m}\frac{\partial e}{\partial F}.$$

Hence, if these roots have negative real parts, the equilibria are weakly locally stable.

Difficulties in proof arise whenever $\partial e/\partial F$ or $\partial e/\partial p$ have multiple solutions of $\det | \partial e/\partial F - \lambda I |$ or $\det | \partial e/\partial p - \lambda I | = 0$ for the same λ. To analyze this case, the Jordan canonical form is of great help.

14 Lemma *If A is a matrix, there exists a matrix B such that*

$$\text{(i)} \quad A = BJB^{-1} \qquad and \qquad J = \begin{pmatrix} J_0 & & & 0 \\ & J_1 & & \\ & & \ddots & \\ 0 & & & J_n \end{pmatrix}$$

where J_0 is a diagonal matrix, and

$$J_k = \begin{pmatrix} \lambda_k & 1 & 0 & & & \\ 0 & \lambda_k & 1 & & & \\ 0 & 0 & \lambda_k & & & \\ & & & \ddots & & \\ & & & & \lambda_k & 1 \\ & & & & 0 & \lambda_k \end{pmatrix}, \quad k > 0,$$

(ii) *the roots of A are the roots of J and the characteristic vectors of A are all of the form $e_i B^{-1}$.*

The diagonals of J_0 are called *simple roots*. Evidently, whenever there is a block J_k, $k \geqslant 1$, there is but one characteristic vector associated with the multiplicity of λ_k. Also, in such cases, if the multiplicity is n_k, there are vectors $x_1, x_2, ..., x_{n_{k-1}}$, such that $x_i A = \lambda_k x_i + x_{i+1}$ except for x_{n_k} ($x_{n_k} A = \lambda_k x_{n_k} A$). These are called *quasi-characteristic vectors*. All vectors and quasi vectors are of the form $e_i B^{-1}$.

Proof of Theorem 13 n roots are given by

$$(0, y, ..., y)B = 0,$$

another n by

$$(x, y, ..., y)B = \left(xD\, \frac{\partial e}{\partial p}, \; \frac{1}{m} xD\, \frac{\partial e}{\partial F}, ..., \frac{1}{m} xD\, \frac{\partial e}{\partial F} \right),$$

$$= \lambda(x, y, ..., y) \quad \text{for} \quad \lambda x = xD\, \frac{\partial e}{\partial p} \quad \text{and}$$

$$y = (\lambda m)^{-1} xD\, \frac{\partial e}{\partial F}.$$

In the case of quasi-characteristic vectors, solving

$$\lambda y^i + y^j = \frac{1}{m} xD\, \frac{\partial e}{\partial p}, \qquad \lambda y^m = \frac{1}{m} xD\, \frac{\partial e}{\partial p}$$

gives

$$(x_i, y, ..., y)B = \lambda(x_i, y, ..., y) + (x_{i+1}, y, ..., y).$$

The remaining $m(n-1)$ roots are given by

$$
B_3 \begin{bmatrix} 0 \\ y \\ -y \\ \vdots \\ 0 \end{bmatrix} = \begin{bmatrix} 0 \\ \dfrac{1}{m}\dfrac{\partial e}{\partial F}\,y \\ -\dfrac{1}{m}\dfrac{\partial e}{\partial F}\,y \\ \vdots \\ 0 \end{bmatrix} = \lambda(0,\, y,\, -y,\, 0,\dots,\, 0).
$$

$$
B_3 \begin{bmatrix} \vdots \\ 0 \\ \vdots \\ 0 \\ y \\ -y \end{bmatrix} = \lambda \begin{bmatrix} 0 \\ y \\ -y \\ 0 \\ \vdots \\ 0 \end{bmatrix} \quad \text{for} \quad \lambda y = \frac{\partial e}{\partial F}\,y.
$$

(The argument modified applies to the quasi vectors.) Apply Lemma 14
to show that all roots have been considered.   q.e.d.

Returning to application two, we see that there are n zero roots besides
those due to the number of equilibrium conditions, so that stability is
not ensured whenever $D = 0$.

5. Assets in Price Dynamics

As studied in Section 1, the roots of $\partial e/\partial p$ were seen to be important to
the model in the last section. Here we study the other important determinant of stability, namely, the influence of assets on excess demands.
In this way, a list of conditions ensuring local stability is completed.

The asset model here is purely Walrasian in any given time period.
This is because expenditure plans in the present period are not influenced
by unexpected asset accumulation until enough time has passed for
them to significantly influence the level of assets. Therefore, the standard
analysis of $\partial e/\partial p$ performed in general equilibrium theory applies
(Chapter 5). Of course, asset accumulations do influence the operation of
the whole system, as is illustrated in application three, where the roots
of $(1/m)(\partial e/\partial F)$ are roots of the matrix of partial derivatives B_3 .

Even though the unexpected accumulation of excess supplies of a
commodity, say, labor, does not directly influence demands, nevertheless
there must have been an unexpected decumulation of money balances
which will decrease the demand for other goods. In the case of a nontrivial asset, the normal reaction is for the trader to try to establish his

desired position. Having made the commitments and discovered that his money balances were unexpectedly low, he would try again to maximize utility by offering the asset for sale. Then

$$\frac{\partial E_i^k}{\partial F_i^k} = -1 \quad \text{and} \quad \frac{\partial E_i^k}{\partial F_j^k} = 0 \quad \text{if } i \neq j.$$

More generally, he may assume for the time being that the immediate sale of assets is not possible, whereupon he would increase his demand for other assets. Then

$$\frac{\partial E_i^k}{\partial F_j^k} > 0.$$

In no case would he offer to make transactions that he could not cover with his wealth, so that

$$\sum_j \frac{\partial E_i^k}{\partial F_j^k} p_j = -p_i .$$

Hence, $\partial E_i^k / \partial F_j^k$ is Metzler–Mosak. In general,

$$\frac{\partial E_i^k}{\partial F_j^k} = \frac{\partial E_i^k}{\partial F_k^k}\bigg|_{F_0^k \text{constant}} + \frac{\partial E_i^k}{\partial F_0^k}\bigg|_{F_j^k \text{constant}} \frac{\partial F_0^k}{\partial F_j^k}$$

$$= \frac{\partial E_i^k}{\partial F_j^k}\bigg|_{F_0^k \text{constant}} - \frac{\partial E_i^k}{\partial F_0^k}\bigg|_{F_j^k \text{constant}} p_j .$$

The second term on the right is a *real balance effect*. For a trivial asset, such as labor or other current factors, the main effect of an excess supply is to reduce money balances below their expected value. Then,

$$\frac{\partial E_i^k}{\partial F_j^k} < 0 \quad \text{for all } j.$$

For nontrivial assets, such as futures claims and inventories of goods, wealth (and hence demand) remains virtually unchanged, so that the main effect is to simply increase sales of the asset. There may be secondary effects, due to reduced money balances at the moment.

15 Theorem *If*

$$\frac{\partial E_i^k}{\partial F_j^k} = -a_i^k \, \delta_{ij} - b_i^k \frac{\partial E_i^k}{\partial F_0^k}\bigg|_{F_j^k \text{constant}} p_j ,$$

$$a_i^k \leqslant 0, \quad b_i^k \leqslant 0, \quad \delta_{ij} = 0 \quad \text{if } i \neq j, \quad \delta_{ii} = 1,$$

if each person responds in the same way to changes in money balances (Keynesian consumption) and if all assets are normal, then

$$\frac{\partial e}{\partial F} = A + Bq'p, \qquad \left(q_i = -b_i \left.\frac{\partial E_i}{\partial F_0}\right|_{F_j \text{constant}}\right),$$

A and B nonpositive diagonal matrices, has either all negative roots (no trivial assets) or one more negative root than the number of trivial assets. All other roots are zero.

Proof   Let

$$A = \begin{pmatrix} A_1 & & 0 \\ & A_2 & \\ 0 & & A_3 \end{pmatrix}, \qquad A_3 = 0, \quad A_i \text{ negative diagonals for } i \neq 3,$$

$$B = \begin{pmatrix} B_1 & & 0 \\ & B_2 & \\ 0 & & B_3 \end{pmatrix}, \qquad B_1 = 0, \quad B_i \text{ negative diagonals.}$$

Then $\partial e/\partial F$ has roots of A_1 and of

$$G = \begin{pmatrix} A_2 & 0 \\ 0 & 0 \end{pmatrix}\begin{pmatrix} B_2 & 0 \\ 0 & B_3 \end{pmatrix} q'p.$$

Now consider a positive diagonal,

$$C = \begin{pmatrix} C_2 & 0 \\ 0 & C_3 \end{pmatrix} \quad \text{such that} \quad C\begin{pmatrix} B_2 & 0 \\ 0 & B_3 \end{pmatrix} q' = -p'.$$

Evidently,

$$CG = \begin{pmatrix} C_2 A_2 & 0 \\ 0 & 0 \end{pmatrix} - p'p$$

is negative semidefinite (since only vectors tangent to p and $C_2 A_2$ have zero quadratic form). The dimension of the space of x over which CG has strictly negative quadratic form is equal to one plus the number of rows of $C_2 A_2$. Because x is a weighted sum of the matrix's (orthogonal) characteristic vectors, as is its quadratic form a positive weighted sum of the quadratic form for the characteristic vectors, its negative roots are of the same number. Lyapunov's Lemma 3 of Chapter 5 applies to show that C has the same number of roots with negative real parts; the other roots are zero.   q.e.d.

To assume that all individuals respond to such changes in money balances in the same way is to assume that they spend effective increases in their wealth in the same way. This assumption ignores a number of distribution effects and is therefore an objection against the assumptions on which application three is made. An exception to this strict interpretation occurs if there is only one trivial asset. The matrix $\partial e/\partial F$ is triangularized and its roots are negative except for the one corresponding to the trivial asset, which is negative or zero, depending on the influences of the accumulation of the trivial asset on its own excess demand. Furthermore, $\partial e/\partial F$ itself may be triangularized, and again in this case, all the roots are nonnegative.

Exercise 1 For a symmetric matrix A, show that the roots are simple and the characteristic vectors are orthogonal (for any two different vectors, a and y, $xy' \equiv 0$). Show that $xAx = \sum x_i^2\lambda_i$, where λ_i are the characteristic roots.

PROBLEMS

K. *The Keynesian System IV*

The four-commodity Keynesian model viewed as a stock–flow model has three nontrivial assets (goods, money, and bonds) and one (short-run) trivial asset (labor). Excluding money, these are only bonds and goods. Supply of goods and demand for factors is effective rather than potential.

(i) What is the sign pattern matrix of partial derivatives for excess demands and assets? (Hint: Suppose firms are pure competitors.) What signs have the real values of the characteristic roots?

(ii) How would the introduction of monopoly in the goods market alter the answer in (i)? (Hint: Would monopolists change their demand for labor in response to changes in inventories?)

(iii) How would the answers in (i) and (ii) be altered by increasing the number of sectors in the economy?

L. *Expectations II*

In Section 5, how can expectations be worked into the stock–flow model? (Hint: See Problem E.) How can stability be ensured?

M. *Seasonal Price Changes*

Suppose the market foresees equilibrium price changes not due to changes in asset holdings. What conditions ensure stability? (Hint: Note that $\partial e/\partial F$ is negative definite for some positive diagonal.)

6. Applications: Relative and Absolute Prices

In this section, we show that the Hicksian statical laws (Sections 5 and 7 of Chapter 5) apply in the dynamical setting.

In the applications of the asset model there is emphasis on the roots of

$$D\,\frac{\partial e}{\partial p} \quad \text{and} \quad \frac{1}{m}\,\frac{\partial e}{\partial F}.$$

The roots of both the matrices have negative real parts. After multiplication by appropriate diagonal matrices, not only

$$\frac{1}{m}\,\frac{\partial e}{\partial F}$$

but also the matrix

$$D\,\frac{\partial e}{\partial p}$$

has negative-definite quadratic form whenever there is no money illusion. Therefore, the system is weakly locally stable.

The inverse of

$$D\,\frac{\partial e}{\partial F}$$

is nonpositive, so that the comparative statics results of Chapter 5 apply to obtain that an increase in the excess demand of one or more (non-money) commodities (say, due to the operations of the state) leads to no decrease in the equilibrium price of the others, given the asset distributions. Suppose the interrelations between the different sectors are such that all sectors are connected, directly or indirectly. This is the case where $\partial e/\partial p$ is *indecomposable*, that is, it cannot be triangularized in

$$\frac{\partial e}{\partial p} = \begin{pmatrix} A & 0 \\ C & B \end{pmatrix}$$

even with reordering the commodities. Then the equilibrium price of the other commodities increases. Starting from a particular price system and asset redistribution, the adjustment system would carry it to the new (higher) equilibrium price system, were it not for consequent changes in asset distributions and equilibrium prices. It can be shown, however, that for initial prices near equilibrium, the redistribution of assets is a relatively insignificant factor in determining the final price.

16 Theorem *Eventually as the price–asset system tends to equilibrium, an increase in excess demands leads to a higher price system than would have been the case at the old distribution of assets, provided this were the case without asset redistribution.*

Application occurs in the gross substitution cases covered in Chapter 5, where increases in excess demand increase prices. Even though the distribution of assets will be different from that under the old regime, the price system will be higher in the new situation. The theorem is an immediate consequence of the following lemma.

17 Lemma *If*

$$\frac{dp}{dt} = H(p, F) + \varepsilon h(p, F),$$

$$\frac{dF}{dt} = e(p, F) - \bar{E}(p, F) + \varepsilon h(p, F), \qquad e(\bar{p}, \bar{F}) = 0, \qquad H = De,$$

D a positive diagonal, then

$$\frac{d\bar{p}}{d\varepsilon} = \left(\frac{H + \varepsilon h}{\partial p} \right)^{-1} h(\bar{p}, \bar{F}).$$

Proof   The dynamic price adjustment equations are

$$p(t) = \int_0^t \{H(p(s), F(s)) + \varepsilon h(p(s), F(s))\} \, ds + p(0)$$

where $\varepsilon h(p(s), F(s))$ is the added demand. It is necessary to determine $dp/d\varepsilon$, for t very large, as p nears equilibrium. Differentiating with respect to ε gives

$$\frac{dp}{d\varepsilon} = \int_0^t \left(\frac{\partial H + \varepsilon h}{\partial p} \frac{dp}{d\varepsilon} \right) ds + \int_0^t h(p(s), F(s)) \, ds.$$

Letting

$$\frac{dp}{d\varepsilon} = g(t), \qquad h(p(t), F(t)) = h(t),$$

and differentiating with respect to t, we have

$$\frac{dg}{dt} = \frac{\partial H + \varepsilon h}{\partial p} g(t) + h(t),$$

which is a linear differential equation with coefficients variable in t. The equilibrium value is

$$g = -\left(\frac{\partial H + \varepsilon h}{\partial p}\right)^{-1} h(t),$$

where

$$-\left(\frac{\partial H + \varepsilon h}{\partial p}\right)^{-1}$$

is nonnegative. Since

$$h(t) \to h(\bar{p}, \bar{F}), \qquad t \to \infty,$$

it can be shown that for $p(0)$ and $F(0)$ near $\bar{p}$ and $\bar{F}$, and therefore for $g(0)$ near

$$-\left(\frac{\partial h + \varepsilon h}{\partial p}\right)^{-1} h(\bar{p}, \bar{F}),$$

$$\frac{dp}{d\varepsilon} = g(t) \to -\left(\frac{\partial H + \varepsilon h}{\partial p}\right)^{-1} h(\bar{p}, \bar{F}), \qquad t \to \infty$$

(Coddington and Levinson [1955, pp. 327–329]).   q.e.d.

Proof of Theorem 16   The quantity $dp/d\varepsilon$ is positive and is the rate of change of equilibrium price with respect to ε, where the asset distribution is fixed at F. To obtain the total change for $\varepsilon = 1$, integrate:

$$\Delta p = \int_0^1 \frac{dp}{d\varepsilon}\, d\varepsilon.$$

Since, as ε changes, $p(t)$ changes, the matrix

$$\left(\frac{\partial H + \varepsilon h}{\partial p}\right)$$

and the vector $h(t)$ change. Nevertheless, these changes are continuous by virtue of the continuity of the solution of a differential equation in its derivative (Birkhoff and Rota [1962, pp. 105–107]). Therefore, the fundamental theorem of differential equations applies to obtain that Δp exists, equals the integral, and tends to a positive quantity for t tending to infinity whenever $h(\bar{p}, \bar{F}) > 0$.   q.e.d.

A first application of Theorem 16 would be the case of a technological change in the ith industry that would increase the supply of the ith good at all possible prices. There would be a decrease in excess demand, which would cause a decrease in the ultimate price of that good and all other goods for which it was a substitute. It is apparent that the result is a formal verification of the intuition of many economists.

As a second application, in the case of zero homogeneity (or the no-money illusion), a dynamical version of the laws of comparative statics of Hicks can be derived. These concern the effect on relative prices of a decrease in the demand for one good and an increase in the demand for the other. Consider the $(n + 1)$st good as the *numéraire*. A decrease in its demand leads to an increase in its (excess) supply and hence to an increase in some other prices. If $\partial e / \partial p$ is indecomposable, there is actually an increase in all other prices. An increase in the demand of another good also leads to an increase in the price of the own good and possibly other prices. In the indecomposable case, there is an increase in all other prices. Whatever the *numéraire*, the relative prices obey the Hicksian laws: From a dynamic viewpoint, an increase in the demand for one good at the expense of another leads ultimately to an increase in the price of the one good relative to all others.

The analysis relates mainly to the intermediate run, when the equilibration of the economy has been nearly accomplished. (It is not the long run, since nowhere in this section has adequate account been taken of capital accumulation.) For the Keynesian approach it often happens that full employment is the aim of equilibration. Policies are advocated that permanently distort the private economy, in order to equilibrate the labor market. Therefore, a third application is the possibility of evaluating the effects of such policies in terms of their price effects, and by further analysis, their effects on supplies of various goods.

Consider the case of the state making purchases in order to increase the demand for commodities. Suppose the state chooses deficit financing to do this. Initially, the sale of bonds tends to lower prices, whereas the purchase of goods increases prices. The net effect depends on the actual magnitude of $D(\partial e / \partial p)$. Gradually, the economy is propelled toward equilibrium in the commodity and labor markets. But in financing the deficit, the state has sold bonds to the public. At equilibrium, while the state ceases its purchases of commodities, the bonds are still outstanding. These bonds are a potential source of flows into the bond market, and therefore the equilibrium price of bonds will be increased. Hence, the intermediate-run effect has been to increase the supply of bonds and to raise the rate of interest, as well as to lower the prices of all other commodities that are influenced by bonds. Since investment funds are more expensive and prices are below what they would have been in equilibrium, firms can be expected to reduce their production of investment goods. The real outcome is a slowing of the rate of accumulation of capital compared to what it would have been under equilibrium when the private economy finally attained it.

Said differently, the debt gives rise to the expectation of future taxes. At any nominal interest rate, the real interest rate is lowered. Hence, people shift out of capital (Chapter 8, Problem D of the companion volume) and into consumption. The rise in interest rates is necessary to restore equilibrium at the lower real income to the given capital stock. Hence, new investment projects are judged by more stringent criteria than before. In other words, the expected tax can be avoided through current consumption, and this is reflected to the degree that the new rate of interest is different from the old one. (In contrast, a tax to be paid now would not affect the value of capital.) The bond places the burden directly on the future. In the long run, there will be a reduction in the wage rate to less than what it would have otherwise been, due to the relative shortage of capital (by Wicksell's law). Especially if the ratio of public debt to national wealth is maintained over time, we would expect the existence of the public debt to have a depressing effect in the investment market for all time. This gives some validity to the notion of a burden of the public debt on future generations (especially future workers) whenever that debt is steadily accumulated. Of course, there are also the benefits of the debt derived from the purposes for which the funds so raised were spent, including possibly the attainment of full employment and a high marginal efficiency of capital.

7. On Reconciliation with Classical Economics

In classical economics, equilibrium prices and excess demands tend to stationary levels. According to Coddington and Levinson [1955, Chapter 13], if the limiting dynamic laws have matrices of partial derivatives with roots with negative real parts, then prices tend to equilibrium. The problem is to assure the stationary state when there is disequilibrium. As time passes, the involuntary accumulation of assets may prevent the attainment of the desired path of consumption goods and the desired limiting state. Also, the resulting change in equilibrium prices may outrun actual changes (Arrow [1960]).

One case occurs when at least one consumer has preference for intertemporally efficient paths and has the community production set. That consumer can choose, on the basis of his own resources, a path dominating any other not tending to the von Neumann path. Therefore, the proof of Theorem 15 of Chapter 6 can be repeated without reference to competitive equilibrium (or efficiency).

A more traditional approach has been to assume that secular forces change prices and assets slowly relative to the rate of equilibration. Let

$$\frac{dp}{dt} = De(p, F), \qquad \frac{dF}{dt} = H(p, F).$$

18 Remark   Let v be the metric

$$(p - \bar{p}) A^{-1}(p - \bar{p}),$$

A a positive diagonal matrix, and

$$A^{-1} \frac{\partial De}{\partial p}$$

negative quasi definite. If $p(0)$ is within δ of $\bar{p}(0)$ and if over the period $[0, t_0]$,

$$2(p - \bar{p}) A^{-1}De \leqslant -\varepsilon,$$

whenever $v(p, \bar{p}) = \delta$, then there are ε_1, ε_2 such that

$$\left| \frac{d\bar{p}}{dt} \right| < \varepsilon_2 \qquad \left| \frac{d}{dt} A^{-1} \right| < \varepsilon_1, \qquad \text{for all} \quad t \in [0, t_0]$$

imply $p(t)$ is within δ of $\bar{p}(t)$ for all $t \in [0, t_0]$.

Proof   At a point where $v(p) = \delta$,

$$\begin{aligned}
\frac{dv}{dt} &= 2(p - \bar{p}) \frac{d}{dt} (A^{-1})(p - \bar{p}) \\
&= 2(p - \bar{p}) A^{-1}De - 2(p - \bar{p}) A^{-1} \frac{d\bar{p}}{dt} \\
&\quad + 2(p - \bar{p}) \frac{d(A^{-1})}{dt} (p - \bar{p}) \\
&\leqslant 2(p - \bar{p})^2 \varepsilon_1 + 2 \mid p - \bar{p} \mid \max a_{ii}\varepsilon_2 - \varepsilon.
\end{aligned}$$

To assure $dv/dt \leqslant 0$, choose

$$(p - \bar{p})^2 \varepsilon_1 \leqslant \tfrac{1}{2}\varepsilon \qquad \text{and} \qquad 2 \mid p - \bar{p} \mid \max a_{ii}\varepsilon_2 \leqslant \tfrac{1}{2}\varepsilon.$$

or

$$\varepsilon_1 \leqslant \frac{1}{2} \varepsilon \frac{1}{(p - \bar{p})^2} \qquad \text{and} \qquad \varepsilon_2 \leqslant \frac{1}{4} \varepsilon \frac{1}{\mid p - \bar{p} \mid \max a_{ii}}.$$

In such a case,

$$\frac{dv}{dt} \leqslant 0 \qquad \text{whenever} \quad v(p) = \delta$$

so that $v(p)$ cannot exceed δ.   q.e.d.

In words, small changes in market conditions do not overturn almost equilibrium prices.

From Remark 18, it is possible to derive a cycle whereby as capital accumulates, its rate of return falls and hence its value as an asset falls (Theorems 22 and 41 of Chapter 5). At a critical point, negative bonds are no longer covered by other assets. Falling capital values may not be offset by new investments, since relatively insolvent firms are not desirable instruments for investing new capital; old debt is too likely to draw upon returns from new equity.

Under pure competition, with no indivisibilities, paucity of investment might not result, since entrepreneurs could merely organize a new firm. Of course we could imagine a decrease in the demand for bonds. However, with large indivisibilities in production and consequent monopolies, new investments in many industries must be placed in already existing firms if they are to be profitable. Multiple bankruptcies cause a discrete failure in expectations and a restriction in investment demand (Keynes [1937]). After equilibrium with a new asset distribution, expectations recover and growth continues to new and lower rates of return on capital. Again a new crisis develops. Perhaps the most successful stabilization policies are those which restrict the growth of negative bonds and put off the cycle, and those which moderate the effects of widespread insolvency.

8

Stabilization

I see no reason to suppose that the existing system seriously misemploys the factors of production which are in use—It is in determining the volume, not the direction, of actual employment that the existing system has broken down. For if effective demand is deficient, not only is the public scandal of wasted resources intolerable, but the individual enterprise who seeks to bring these resources into action is operating with the odds loaded against him.

John Maynard Keynes
THE GENERAL THEORY, 1936, pp. 379–381

1. Initial Price Dynamics

As mentioned in chapter 2, an economic system can be regarded as a mechanism by which certain goals are attained. This chapter considers the question of the speed with which the system attains its equilibrium state, which is assumed to be stationary. It is presumed that the purpose of any government policy is to attain an equilibrium state. The theory obtained seems especially rich in policy conclusions. Possibly at some future date, they can be generalized to a long-run disequilibrium economic system.

In this chapter, projects of value other than stabilization are not considered. In equilibrium, changes in excess demands are assumed to be zero. What is more, it is assumed that the policy is *equilibrium price neutral*; that is it does not affect the equilibrium price. Since the path of equilibration affects the equilibrium, this is no mean requirement. (In Chapter 5, there is a detailed analysis of the effect of changes in excess demands on equilibrium price.) Nevertheless, there will be an adequate number of such policies, even though they may be difficult to distinguish. The context of application is to the price–asset adjustment model of Section 4 of Chapter 7.

In this section we present a simple characterization of market behavior in the very near future. In succeeding sections, the rate of adjustment to equilibrium is considered for the short run (Section 2) and the intermediate run (Section 3). Applications are to sluggish markets and government policy (Sections 4–7).

Given an increase in demand for i, we would expect in the near future that the price of i will rise more rapidly (or fall less rapidly) than otherwise. The indirect effect on other commodities is slightly harder to ascertain.

Let

$$\frac{dp - \bar{p}}{dt} = H + h \qquad (H = De)$$

and

$$\frac{d(p - \bar{p}, F)}{dt} = G + g, \qquad (G_1, ..., G_n = H, g_1, ..., g_n = h)$$

where h and g give the *state policy*. If $(h(\bar{p}), g((\bar{p}))) = 0$, there is a *stabilization policy*.

Our first theorem states that changes in excess demand have the obvious influence on the markets immediately affected. Prices increase more rapidly where excess demand increases. Prices increase less rapidly where excess demand decreases. If there is no change in excess demand in a given market, it is shortly influenced by changes in prices elsewhere. Prices of goods rise as the prices of substitutes rise and fall as prices of complements rise. Prices fall for inferior goods and rise for superior goods as individual wealth increases.

1 Theorem   *Let there be a continuous stabilization policy.*

(i) *For every positive (negative) component of h, the differential of actual over equilibrium price increases (decreases) in the sufficiently close future.*

Let $\partial H + \varepsilon h/\partial p$, $\partial H + \varepsilon h/\partial F$ *exist and be continuous at* $p(0)$.

(ii) *If changes in* h_i *are sustained* $(dh_i/dt \geqslant 0)$ *i is gross substitutable with all j for which* $h_j(p) > 0$ *and gross complementary with all j for which* $h_j(p) < 0$, *i is superior (inferior) and all individual wealths are increased (decreased), then for* $h_i = 0$, $p_i - \bar{p}_i$ *increases relative to what it would have been in the near future.*

(iii) *If changes in* h_i *are not enhanced* $(dh_i/dt < 0)$, *i is gross substitutable with all j for which* $h_j(p) < 0$ *and gross complementary with all j for which* $h_j(p) < 0$), *i is superior (inferior) and individual wealths are decreased (increased), then for* $h_i = 0$, $p_i - \bar{p}_i$ *decreases relative to what it would have been in the near future.*

Theorem 1 applies to cases where seasonal price changes are foreseen by the market. It gives the kind of initial dynamical rules that we would expect. Buying a good raises its price as well as the prices of other substitutable goods, while selling it lowers its price and that of other substitutable goods—even in the general economic framework. Such dynamical properties are often used by economists.

To prove the theorem in full generality, a lemma is needed.

2 Lemma *If* $g(t)$ *and* $f(t)$ *are continuous,* $g(0) = 0$, g *differentiable at* $t = 0$, *then*

$$\frac{dg(t)f(t)}{dt} = \frac{dg}{dt}f(0).$$

Proof

$$\frac{g(t)f(t) - g(0)f(0)}{t} = \frac{g(t)f(t)}{t} = \frac{(g(t) - g(0))f(t)}{t}$$

$$\rightarrow \frac{dg}{dt}f(0). \quad \text{q.e.d.}$$

Proof of Theorem 1   Consider $Q = (p - \bar{p}, F)$, $dQ/dt = G + g\varepsilon$. By virtue of continuity of $G + \varepsilon g$, dQ/dt is greater or smaller in the near future according as g is greater or smaller.

In the case where $g_i = 0$, the analysis is more involved. Now

$$\frac{d}{dt}\frac{\partial Q}{\partial \varepsilon} = \frac{\partial}{\partial \varepsilon}\frac{dQ}{dt} = g + \frac{\partial G + g}{\partial Q}\frac{\partial Q}{\partial \varepsilon}.$$

Since $\partial Q/\partial \varepsilon = 0$ at time zero, we can apply Lemma 2. At time zero,

$$\frac{d^2}{dt^2}\frac{dQ}{\partial \varepsilon} = \frac{\partial g}{\partial t} + \frac{\partial G + \varepsilon g}{\partial Q}\frac{d}{dt}\frac{\partial Q}{\partial \varepsilon} = \frac{\partial g}{\partial t} + \frac{\partial G + \varepsilon g}{\partial Q}g.$$

In terms of $p - \bar{p}$,

$$\frac{d^2}{dt^2} \frac{\partial p - \bar{p}}{\partial \varepsilon} = \frac{\partial h}{\partial t} + \frac{\partial H + \varepsilon h}{\partial p} + \frac{\partial H + \partial h}{\partial F} (e - \bar{E}).$$

If at time $t = 0$,

$$\frac{d^2}{dt^2} \frac{\partial p_i - p_i}{\partial \varepsilon} > 0 \quad \text{and} \quad \frac{d}{dt} \frac{\partial p_i - \bar{p}_i}{\partial \varepsilon} = 0,$$

then $p_i - \bar{p}_i$ will be greater than otherwise. The reader can verify this by computing $\Delta^2(p_i - \bar{p}_i)/t^2$ for small t.   q.e.d.

In many instances, such as in cases of unemployment of resources, we are mainly concerned with de/dt. It can be evaluated as

$$\frac{de}{dt} = \frac{\partial e}{\partial p} \frac{dp}{dt} + \frac{\partial e}{\partial F} \frac{dF}{dt}$$

$$= \frac{\partial e}{\partial p} De(p) + \frac{\partial e}{\partial F} (e - \bar{E}). \tag{2}$$

Since factors are mutually complementary and gross substitutable with final goods, sales of other factors and purchase of goods contribute to higher demand for factors in the near future. If the own factor is purchased, Theorem 1 shows that there will be compensating effects in the near future. The demand for other factors will rise as the price of the other factor increases, and this will decrease the demand for the other factor. Also, the supply of goods and their price will fall, which will offset the demand for all factors.

PROBLEMS

A. *Expenditure Multipliers*

Let the government increase its demand for goods.

(i)   In the price–asset adjustment system, what are the short-run changes in demand for goods, assuming full employment of all factors? Assuming unemployment of some factors?

(ii)   Will the accumulation of assets in the interim magnify the effect? How does this differ from the multiplier in the Keynesian income and effective demand model?

(iii)   In a multigood Keynesian model, what is the multiplier in time of inflation in all goods markets?

Versions of (iii) appear in Metzler [1950], Mosak [1944], Chipman [1950], and Gale [1960, Chapter 8]. Part (ii) has been of interest to Friedman [1957] and Modigliani and Brumberg [1954], among others.

B. *Taxation Multipliers*

Let the government increase the tax on individual income.

(i) Presuming wealth to be related to return by present value calculations, what is the influence on demand for goods in the price–asset adjustment model?

(ii) In the Keynesian model, how do the multipliers depend on the losses of inflation or deflation?

(iii) In both cases above, how does the analysis proceed for the case of increases in a balanced budget?

C. *Monetary Policy*

In addition to the budgetary transactions, let the government participate in monetary policy, selling and buying governments bonds.

What is the net impact on the bond market? How does the answer differ between the price–asset model and the Keynesian model? How does the answer depend on the nature of the demand for money?

2. Initial Speed of Adjustment

In the near future, there are market changes that leave equilibrium prices unchanged but that speed the process of equilibration. The cases cited in this section apply mainly near equilibrium. The main results are commonplace: when heading toward equilibrium, it is best to magnify the response upward of underpriced goods and downward of overpriced goods.

The *initial speed of adjustment* is defined as

$$\frac{d(p - \bar{p}) D^{-1}(p - \bar{p})}{dt}$$

for prices and

$$\frac{deBe}{dt}$$

for quantities, for any positive diagonal B. As before, it is assumed that policies leave the path of assets $F(t)$ unaffected.

3 Lemma   *The initial speed of adjustment from p to $\bar{p}$ is decreased (increased) if the change in H_i, h_i, has opposite (same) sign of $\{(p - \bar{p}) D^{-1}H(p)\}(p_i - \bar{p}_i)$.*

Let H and h be differentiable at $\bar{p}$. The speed of adjustment from p to $\bar{p}$ is decreased (increased) if $\partial h_i/\partial \bar{p}_i$ has the opposite (same) sign as $\{(p - \bar{p}) D^{-1}H(p)\}(p_i - \bar{p}_i)$, for p sufficiently close to $\bar{p}$. The quantity speed of adjustment is decreased (increased) if $\partial h_i/\partial p_j$ has the opposite (same) sign as

$$\frac{deDe}{dt} \, e_i \, \frac{\partial e_i}{\partial p_j} \, .$$

The theory is radically different according to whether the system is (momentarily) heading toward or from equilibrium. The preceding results apply to all points in the price–asset space. A result applying near equilibrium is Theorem 4. If the system is heading toward equilibrium, then increasing the excess demand in a market where price is too low has the effect of moving the system faster toward equilibrium.

4 Theorem   *Suppose $(\partial H/\partial \bar{p})$ is negative quasi definite. Then near equilibrium $\bar{p}$, $(p - \bar{p}) D^{-1}H(p)$ is negative and the initial speed of adjustment from p to $\bar{p}$ is decreased (increased) if the change in H_i has the same (opposite) sign as $(p_i - \bar{p}_i) D^{-1} \partial h_i/\partial \bar{p}_j (p_j - \bar{p}_j)$. For those diagonals of $\partial H/\partial p$ which are negative and for those off-diagonals which are positive, the immediate price (quantity) speed of adjustment is increased whenever $\partial h_i/\partial p_i < 0$ and $\partial h_i/\partial p_j$ has the same sign as $(p_i - \bar{p}_i)(p_j - \bar{p}_j)(e_i e_j)$ for $i \neq j$.*

Proof   According to the mean value theorem of differential calculus,

$$\frac{(p - \bar{p})D}{(p - \bar{p})^2} \, H(p)$$

is approximately

$$\frac{(p - \bar{p})}{|p - \bar{p}|} \, D \, \frac{\partial H}{\partial p} \, \frac{(p - \bar{p})}{|p - \bar{p}|} < 0.$$

$$\left(\frac{\partial H_i}{\partial \bar{p}_j} = \frac{\partial d_i}{\partial \bar{p}_j} \, H_i + d_i \, \frac{\partial H_i}{\partial \bar{p}_j} = d_i \, \frac{\partial H_i}{\partial \bar{p}_j} \right).$$

Therefore, the speed of adjustment is negative near $\bar{p}$. The quantity case follows from

$$\frac{deBe}{dt} = 2eB \, \frac{de}{dt} = 2eB \, \frac{\partial e}{\partial p} \, De + 2eB \, \frac{\partial e}{\partial F} \, (e - \bar{e}). \qquad \text{q.e.d.}$$

According to the last sentence of Theorem 4, complicated changes in H_i speed the adjustment mechanism provided the influence of the ith price on the jth commodity has the opposite direction as the product of the ith and jth margin of their respective prices over equilibrium prices. In effect, this condition assures that changes in one or more prices toward equilibrium do not cause other prices to diverge from equilibrium, provided that the equilibrium price system itself is not disturbed by the change in H.

The metric

$$\| q \| = \left(\sum \frac{1}{a_i} q_i^2 \right)^{1/2}$$

is used to measure speed of adjustment in the immediate future. This implies that excess supplies in slow-moving markets have special social significance. This may be true for labor but not for other slow-moving sectors, such as heavy industry.

Decreasing $d \| p - \bar{p} \| / dt$ increases the speed of adjustment, $| d \| p - \bar{p} \| / dt |$. Hence, whenever the change in H is such that equilibrium b_{ii} is decreased, b_{ij} is decreased for $(p - \bar{p})_i$ and $(p - \bar{p})_j$ having different signs, there is an increase in the speed of adjustment. Because of this, close to $\bar{p}$ the components of p can be divided into two classes, depending on whether they are greater than or less than those corresponding components of $\bar{p}$. Coefficients b_{ij} within each class should be decreased to speed the adjustment mechanism.

Proof of Lemma 3   Two cases appear:

$$(p - \bar{p}) H(p) < 0 \quad \text{and} \quad (p - \bar{p}) H(p) > 0.$$

In the former case, the immediate speed of adjustment from p can be increased by decreasing components of H for which the corresponding components of p are above those of $\bar{p}$ and increasing components of H for which the corresponding components of p are below those of $\bar{p}$. The opposite relationship holds whenever $(p - \bar{p}) H(p) > 0$.

A somewhat more detailed picture can be obtained for p near $\bar{p}$. Only the case $(p - \bar{p}) H(p) < 0$ is considered. The other case follows in opposite fashion:

$$\lim_{p \to \bar{p}} \frac{d}{dt} (p - \bar{p})^2 = \lim 2(p - \bar{p}) \frac{d}{dt} (p - \bar{p})$$

$$= 2(p - \bar{p}) \frac{\partial H}{\partial \bar{p}} (p - \bar{p}).$$

Therefore, if $\partial H_i/\partial \bar{p}_j$ is increased, then for p sufficiently near $\bar{p}$, $(d/dt)(p - \bar{p})^2$ must also be increased. Therefore, it is sufficient to speak of changes in $\partial H_i/\partial \bar{p}_j$ alone. The quantity case follows from

$$\frac{deBe}{dt} = 2eB\,\frac{de}{dt} = 2eB\,\frac{\partial e}{\partial \bar{p}}\,Ae \qquad \text{q.e.d.}$$

3. Ultimate Rate of Adjustment

Here, we show how in the intermediate run the approach to the equilibrium state can be quickened. The asymptotic, exponential rate of adjustment is defined, and its determinants are listed for application. Later in Sections 4–6 we consider the efficacy of increasing the response of prices to demand conditions and/or of decreasing the interconnectedness between different economic sectors. Also, in Section 6, light is thrown on the role of the real balance effect and the liquidity trap as impediments to stabilization.

Let $\| p - \bar{p} \| = (p - \bar{p})\,D(p - \bar{p})$, D a positive diagonal. The *dominant root* of a matrix is the characteristic roots with largest real part. The real part is denoted λ and the roots: $\rho = \lambda + i\mu$. An $n - 1$ *manifold* is a topological space with neighborhoods homeomorphic to $\mathscr{E}^{n-1}$. Lemma 5 follows from the analysis of Coddington and Levinson [1955, Chapter 13]. It shows that the dominant root determines the asymptotic, exponential rate of adjustment.

5 Lemma   *Let $d\bar{x}/dt = f(\bar{x}) = 0$, f satisfy Lipschitz conditions, f be differentiable at $\bar{x}$, and λ be the dominant root of $\partial f/\partial \bar{x}$. Except for initial conditions on an $n - 1$ manifold,*

$$\lim \frac{1}{t} \log \| x(t) - \bar{x} \| = \lambda$$

(whatever D). Hence $|\lambda|$ is called the *ultimate speed of adjustment.*

Proof   Coddington and Levinson prove the case for $D = I$. In the general case,

$$\max d_{ii}\,|\,x(t) - \bar{x}\,| \geqslant \| x(t) - \bar{x} \| \geqslant \min d_{ii}\,|\,x(t) - \bar{x}\,|.$$

Hence

$$\lim \frac{1}{t} \log |\,x(t) - \bar{x}\,| + \lim \frac{1}{t} \log \max d_{ii} = \lim \frac{1}{t} \log |\,x(t) - \bar{x}\,| \geqslant \lambda \geqslant \lim \frac{1}{t}$$

$$\log |\,x(t) - \bar{x}\,| = \lim \frac{1}{t} \log |\,x(t) - \bar{x}\,| + \lim \frac{1}{t} \log \min d_{ii}\,. \qquad \text{q.e.d.}$$

Therefore, the theory of ultimate stabilization reduces to the study of the roots of certain matrices. Here, the price–asset adjustment system is of particular concern.

6 Corollary *If g is a function of x in Lemma 5, satisfying a Lipschitz condition in x, then*

$$\lim \frac{1}{t} \log | g(x(t)) - g(\bar{x})| \leqslant \lambda.$$

The corollary applies to e as a function of e and p so that we need only analyze the price–asset speed of adjustment to limit the excess demand speed of adjustment.

Proof

$$| g(x(t)) - g(\bar{x})| \leqslant k \,|\, x(t) - \bar{x} \,|$$

so that

$$\lim \frac{1}{t} \log |\, g - \bar{g} \,| \leqslant \lim \frac{1}{t} \log K + \lim \frac{1}{t} \log |\, x(t) - \bar{x} \,| = \lambda. \qquad \text{q.e.d.}$$

The results following apply only to matrices whose roots with largest real part are simple. Included are matrices with Jordan form $A = BDB^{-1}$, D a positive diagonal. Such matrices form an open and arc wise connected set dense in the space of matrices. It is the purpose here to analyze the effect of changes in the matrix of partial derivatives on the real part of the dominant root.

7 Lemma *Let ρ be the root of $A = C + \varepsilon B$ with maximum real part ρ. If ρ is continuous in ε, then*

$$\frac{d\rho}{d\varepsilon} = \frac{xBy}{xy} \tag{3}$$

for $xA = \rho x$ and $Ay = \rho y$ if and only if ρ is simple.

Proof Since ρ is continuous, it is the continuous solution of $xA = \rho x$. Referring to Lemma 13 of Chapter 7, we see that there is a vector y, $Ay = \rho y$, not orthogonal to x, if and only if ρ is a simple root. Therefore, if ρ is a simple root,

$$xB + \frac{dx}{d\varepsilon} A = \frac{\rho dx}{d\varepsilon} + \frac{d\rho}{d\varepsilon} x$$

or

$$xBy + \frac{dx}{d\varepsilon} Ay = \frac{\rho dx}{d\varepsilon} y + \frac{d\rho}{d\varepsilon} xy$$

or

$$xBy = \frac{d\rho}{d\varepsilon} xy$$

or

$$\frac{d\rho}{d\varepsilon} = \frac{xBy}{xy}.$$

If ρ is not simple, then $xy = 0$ and $xBy = 0$ and their ratio is undefined.

8 Corollary *If the dominant root ρ of A, is continuous in a_{ij}, then $d\rho/da_{ij} = x_i y_j$ for $xA = \rho x$, $Ay = \rho y$ if and only if ρ is simple.*

A particular case occurs whenever we multiply a matrix by a diagonal greater than the identity.

9 Corollary *If*

$$A = B + \varepsilon \begin{bmatrix} 0 & \cdots & 0 \\ \vdots & & \vdots \\ b_i & \cdots & b_n \\ \vdots & & \vdots \\ 0 & \cdots & 0 \end{bmatrix}$$

and ρ is continuous in ε, then

$$\frac{d\rho}{d\varepsilon} = \frac{\rho x_i y_i}{xy}$$

for $xA = \rho x$ and $Ay = \rho y$, if and only if ρ is simple.

Proof

$$\frac{d\rho}{d\varepsilon} = x \begin{bmatrix} 0 & \cdots & 0 \\ \vdots & & \vdots \\ b_i & \cdots & b_n \\ \vdots & & \vdots \\ 0 & \cdots & 0 \end{bmatrix} y \frac{1}{xy} = \frac{x_i \sum b_j y_j}{xy} = \frac{\rho x_i y_i}{xy}. \qquad \text{q.e.d.}$$

Beyond these exact calculations, we should mention, as in Chapter 5, Section 1, that the sum of the roots equals the sum of the diagonals and the product of the roots equals the determinant of the matrix.

4. Distributive Speeds of Response

Recall that $a_i(p)$ gives the speed of response of the ith price to excess demands in the ith market. Keynes [1936] asked whether increasing $a_i(p)$ would increase the speed of adjustment or, more generally, whether $a_i(p)$ limits the speed of adjustment, particularly for $i = $ labor. Evidently the speed of adjustment in the own market is increased in the short run. On the other hand, equilibration in complementary markets is effected by a decrease in $\partial H_j/\partial p_i = b_{ji} < 0$. It was seen in Section 1 that if $(p - \bar{p})_i(p - \bar{p})_j > 0$, the initial speed of adjustment may actually be decreased. On the other hand, if $\partial H/\partial p_i > 0$ and $(p - \bar{p})(p - \bar{p})_j < 0$, the initial speed of adjustment may decrease. Hence, in the short run, there is no clear-cut answer.

In the intermediate run, there is an unambiguous result. Increasing the rate of response of market prices to demand conditions increases the asymptotic exponential speed of adjustment. A matrix is *Metzler–Mosak* if it has all nonnegative off-diagonals.

10 Theorem   (i) *Let A be negative quasi definite, D a diagonal. The real part of the roots of DA lie between*

$$0 > \bar{\lambda} = (\max_{x^2=1} xAx)\ \min d_{ii}$$

and

$$\underline{\lambda} = (\max_i d_{ii}) \min_{x^2=1} xAx$$

which decrease as $\min d_{ii}$ *and* $\max d_{ii}$ *increases, respectively.*

(ii) *If A is symmetric or else indecomposable and Metzler–Mosak, the dominant root decreases as one or more components of D increase.*

(iii) *If A is Metzler–Mosak and decomposable, increases in d_{ii} for i in the indecomposable block of A with the dominant roots decrease that root.*

The interpretation for stabilization is immediate from Lemma 5. Applications are as follows. With competitive producers and consumer gross substitution, there is negative quasi definite $\partial e/\partial p$. With homothetic preferences, $\partial e/\partial p$ is symmetric. With consumer and producer gross substitution, $\partial e/\partial p$ is Metzler–Mosak. In the case where A is the sum of a Metzler–Mosak and a symmetric matrix, all that can be said is that there is an upper bound on the ultimate speed of adjustment that decreases as D increases. Without improving response in the most languid market, it cannot be said that the upper bound decreases.

Referring to Corollary 8, $d\rho/de = \rho x_i y_i$ and there is in general no way of knowing whether $x_i y_i \geqslant 0$, whereupon the actual direction of change of ρ is unknown. Otherwise, for the Metzler–Mosak or symmetric case, improving response in one market improves overall stability, although to a degree limited by the improvement of response in the least active market.

Proof   For a characteristic vector $x + iy$,

$$DA(x + iy) = (\lambda + i\mu)(x + iy)$$

or

$$Ax = \lambda D^{-1}x - \mu D^{-1}y \quad \text{and} \quad Ay = \lambda D^{-1}y + \mu D^{-1}x$$

or

$$xAx = \lambda x D^{-1}x - \mu D^{-1}y \quad \text{and} \quad xAy = \lambda y D^{-1}y + \mu y D^{-1}x,$$

or

$$xAx + yAy = \lambda(xD^{-1}x + yD^{-1}y),$$

whereupon

$$\max \frac{xAx}{x^2} \geqslant \left(\min \frac{xAx}{x^2} \leqslant \right) \frac{xAx}{x^2} \left(\frac{x^2}{x^2 + y^2} \right) + \frac{yAy}{y^2} \left(\frac{y^2}{x^2 + y^2} \right)$$

$$\geqslant \lambda \max \frac{xD^{-1}x}{x^2} \left(\leqslant \lambda \min \frac{xD^{-1}x}{x^2} \right)$$

and

$$\bar{\lambda} = \frac{\max \dfrac{xAx}{x^2}}{\max d_{ii}^{-1}} \geqslant \lambda$$

$$\geqslant \underline{\lambda} = \frac{\min_{x^2 = 1} xAx}{\min_i d_{ii}^{-1}} .$$

In the case of a symmetric matrix, all roots of DA are real since $xAD = \lambda x$ implies $xA\bar{x} = xD^{-1}\bar{x}$, or $\lambda = xA\bar{x}/xD^{-1}\bar{x}$ is real (where $\bar{x} = x^1 - ix^2$ whenever $x = x^1 + ix^2$). Also, if $xDA = \lambda x$, then $(xD)\,AD = \lambda(xD)$, or $\lambda Dx = (AD)\,Dx$ and

$$\frac{d\rho}{d\varepsilon} = \frac{d_{ii} x_i x_i}{xDx} \lambda < 0$$

for a change in d_{ii}, εd_{ii} (Corollary 9).

In the case of a Metzler–Mosak matrix A, DA is Metzler–Mosak. The characteristic root with largest real part is unique for an indecomposable matrix and has a strictly positive characteristic vector for each of DA and AD. These vectors are x and y, for which

$$\frac{d\rho}{d\varepsilon} = \frac{x_i y_i}{xy} \lambda < 0 \qquad \text{(Corollary 9).}$$

For the decomposable case, small changes in d_{ii} increase the largest root only if i is in the set of components giving DA its largest root. Then

$$B = DA = \begin{pmatrix} B_{11} & 0 \\ B_{21} & B_{21} \end{pmatrix} = \begin{pmatrix} D_{11} & 0 \\ 0 & D_{22} \end{pmatrix}\begin{pmatrix} A_{11} & 0 \\ A_{21} & A_{22} \end{pmatrix}$$

and characteristic vectors are $(x, 0)$, $x \gg 0$, for DA and (x, y) for $A'D$, where y solves $B_{21}x + B_{22}y = \rho y$. Clearly, increasing components of D_{11} increases ρ (since $d\rho/d\varepsilon = x_i y_i/\rho y$ for a change εd_{ii}).

All of the foregoing derivatives may be integrated over their range to give a solution for large changes in the d_{ii}'s. Since the solutions λ remain bounded by $\bar{\lambda}$ and z, the solutions can be extended for indefinitely large values. q.e.d.

PROBLEMS

D. *Unemployment I*

In the Keynesian income–effective demand model, assume that the labor market becomes perfected so that real wages fall in time of unemployment. What will be the effect on labor real income? (Hint: How is investment affected by a wage decrease and how does it affect unemployment?) Is the answer different in the price–asset model?

E. *Keynesian System V*

Hurewicz [1958] shows that in two dimensions, if the dominant root of $\partial H/\partial p$ is negative and unique, and $\bar{x}$ is the associated characteristic vector, then except for initial conditions on a one-dimensional manifold,

$$\frac{x(t) - \bar{x}}{|x(t) - \bar{x}|} \to 0.$$

(i) Use the Hurewicz result to show that the Keynesian system as analyzed in Problem F of Chapter 7 does not spiral toward, but directly approaches, equilibrium.

(ii) If there is a bankruptcy shock as described in Section 8 of Chapter 7, what would the path to equilibrium be? How might we observe the "cycle" over time?

F. *Unemployment II*

(i)   During recovery from a bankrupcy shock on the Keynesian system, what is the relationship between inflation and unemployment, given a rigid money wage?

(ii)   During growth of capital stock, assuming relatively slow adjustment of wages, what is the relationship between changes in price of goods and wages?

(iii)   How would the answer differ in a multicommodity Keynesian or price–asset model?

This problem was considered by Phillips [1958] and Lipsey [1960] among others.

5. Market Stabilization

In this section, we seek to show how intermediate-run stabilization is speeded (or impeded) by state action.

State policies for stabilization are often of a very simple nature. Monetary policy consists of selling bonds, fiscal policy of buying goods. These policies increase the diagonal elements of $\partial H/\partial p$ by $\partial h/\partial p$. Should bonds and goods constitute the only markets, and should the operations be such that at the equilibrium price,

$$\frac{\partial h \text{ bonds}}{\partial p \text{ bonds}} = \frac{\partial h \text{ goods}}{\partial p \text{ goods}},$$

then there is an addition of a matrix of the form $-\mu I$, where $-\mu = \partial h_i/\partial p_i$. Evidently for a large μ, the system will be stable, and a larger μ improves ultimately stability as compared with a smaller μ. In the case of the more complicated policies, or where

$$\frac{\partial h \text{ goods}}{\partial p \text{ goods}} \neq \frac{\partial h \text{ bonds}}{\partial p \text{ bonds}},$$

the conditions under which adjustment is speeded depend on the characteristic vector associated with the characteristic root with maximum real part (Corollary 6). Some methods of improving adjustment are listed below.

11 Theorem   (i)   *If A is negative quasi definite, the bounds on the real part of the real part of the characteristic roots, of DA, $\bar{\lambda}$ and $\underline{\lambda}$ are not* *increased wherever a diagonal element of A is decreased and are decreased whenever a negative quasi-definite matrix is added.*

(ii) *If A is symmetric, the dominant root does not increase whenever a diagonal element of A decreases and the dominant root decreases if there is an addition to A of a negative definite matrix.*

(iii) *If A is Metzler–Mosak, a decrease in the components of DA in each of the indecomposable blocks with dominant root equal to that of DA leads to a decrease in the dominant root of DA.*

Proof Decreasing A decreases $\max_{x^2=1} xAx$ and $\min_{x^2=1} xAx$. Let E_{ij} be the matrix with zeros except in the ij element. If A is symmetric, for $DA + \varepsilon E_{ii}$, we have

$$\frac{d\rho}{d\varepsilon} = \frac{-x_i^2}{xDx}$$

for x the vector of the dominant root. If B is negative definite, ρ is the dominant root of $D(A + \varepsilon B)$,

$$\frac{d\rho}{d\varepsilon} = \frac{-xDB\,Dx}{xDx} < 0.$$

If A is Metzler–Mosak, for $DA - \varepsilon E_{ij}$,

$$\frac{d\rho}{d\varepsilon} = \frac{-x_i y_i}{xy} > 0, \qquad x_i > 0, \;\; y_i > 0$$

for i in the block with dominant characteristic vector. As usual, the bounds on the roots allow us to solve the foregoing differential equations for arbitrarily large changes (provided the appropriate Metzler–Mosak properties are not violated by a large change).   q.e.d.

In the case of complex policies, say, purchases in the goods market, a sector of markets rather than a particular market may be the object of control. Hence, the changes are such that for

$$B = \begin{pmatrix} B_{11} & B_{12} \\ B_{21} & B_{22} \end{pmatrix}$$

B_{11} is multiplied by constant.

12 Corollary *Let a block B_{ii} in A be multiplied by k.*

(i) *If A is negative quasi definite, the bounds, $\bar{\lambda}$ and $\underline{\lambda}$, are not increased.*

(ii) *If A is negative definite, the dominant root is not increased.*

(iii) *If A is Metzler–Mosak and if the block contains components in the indecomposable block of DA with dominant root, the dominant root is decreased.*

Proof In the quasi-definite (or definite) case, one is adding a semiquasi-definite (or semidefinite) matrix.

If A is Metzler–Mosak, we are multiplying by a diagonal matrix

$$\begin{pmatrix} kI & 0 \\ 0 & I \end{pmatrix}$$

that is greater than or equal to the identity matrix and then decreasing the off-diagonals a_{ij}, i in the first set and j in the second set, to obtain A_{12} as before. This leads to no impairment of the stability of the system (that is, to no increase in the largest characteristic root of $\partial H/\partial \bar{p}$).   q.e.d.

The following theorem, though a simple consequence of the fact that an increase in elements does not decrease roots, gives an important limitation to the extent to which stability can be improved in the case of gross substitution.

13 Theorem *Let*

$$\frac{\partial H}{\partial p} = \begin{pmatrix} B_{11} & B_{12} \\ B_{21} & B_{22} \end{pmatrix} = DA$$

and let A be Metzler–Mosak or symmetric. Then the ultimate speed of adjustment $|\lambda|$, is not greater than the absolute value of the largest real part of roots of B_{ii}, $i = 1, 2$, denoted $|\lambda_i|$. Consequently, if for some i, B_{ii} is unchanged, increases in $|\lambda|$ become arbitrarily small as one or more of the elements of $\partial H/\partial p$ are decreased.

Operating in one sector alone, we run into diminishing returns. For example, if

$$B_{11} \to \infty, \qquad B_{12} \to 0, \qquad \text{or} \qquad B_{21} \to 0,$$

all of which improve stabilization, nevertheless

$$|\lambda| < |\lambda_2|,$$

or if

$$B_{22} \to \infty, \qquad B_{12} \to 0, \qquad \text{or} \qquad B_{21} \to 0,$$

still

$$|\lambda| < |\lambda_1|.$$

Proof of Theorem 13   In the symmetric case,

$$\lambda = \max xAx \geqslant \max xA_{ii}x = \lambda_i$$

where λ_i is the largest root of A_{ii} .

In the Metzler–Mosak case Corollary 12 applies, so that λ is less than or equal to the maximum real part of the root of

$$\begin{pmatrix} B_{11} & 0 \\ 0 & B_{22} \end{pmatrix}.$$

This has at least two real roots, namely, the maximum for B_{11}, λ_1, and the maximum for B_{22}, λ_2 . Clearly,

$$\lambda \geqslant \lambda_1, \qquad \lambda \geqslant \lambda_2 .$$

Therefore,

$$|\lambda| = -\lambda \leqslant -\lambda_1, \qquad |\lambda| = -\lambda \leqslant -\lambda_2. \qquad \text{q.e.d.}$$

An immediate corollary of Theorem 13 is the following.

14 Corollary   *Let A be Metzler–Mosak or symmetric $\partial H/\partial p = DA$, D positive diagonal. If there is no way to change $\partial H_i/\partial \bar{p}_i < 0$, then the ultimate speed of adjustment of the system is limited by*

$$|\lambda| \leqslant \left| \frac{\partial H_i}{\partial \bar{p}_i} \right|.$$

In the case where A is only negative quasi definite, analogous results apply to $\bar{\lambda}$, but the significance of $\bar{\lambda}$ being minimal is not clear.

6. Limitations on Stability in the Price–Asset Adjustment System

Here we consider the limitation on the ultimate speed of adjustment due to the effect of assets on excess demand.

Returning to Section 6 of Chapter 7, we find that stabilization is limited by the largest real value of the roots of

$$\frac{\partial e}{\partial F} = A + B \left(\frac{\partial e}{\partial F_0} \right) p$$

where A and B are diagonal matrices. One influence of the *real balance effect* $\partial e/\partial F_0$ on stability is listed below.

15 Theorem   *In the price–asset adjustment system where*

$$\frac{\partial e}{\partial F} = A + B\left(\frac{\partial e}{\partial F_0}\right)p,$$

A and B are negative diagonals; if all commodities are normal, then the dominant root of $\partial e/\partial F$ is nonincreasing in components of the real balance effect $\partial e/\partial F_0$. If all components of $\partial e/\partial F_0$ increase, then the dominant root decreases.

Evidently, a weak real balance effect limits stabilization.

Proof   Since $\partial e/\partial F$ is nonpositive, its dominant characteristic vector is nonnegative. Also, as the product of a positive diagonal and a symmetric matrix, its roots are simple with the paired characteristic vectors, x and Dx', D a positive diagonal. Therefore, Corollary 9 applies: multiplying $\partial e_i/\partial F_0$ by $1 + \varepsilon$, we obtain

$$\frac{d\rho}{d\varepsilon} = \frac{x_i d_{ii}}{xDx}\,\rho < 0. \qquad \text{q.e.d.}$$

There are also influences of the real balance effect upon $\partial H/\partial p$. Symmetrically, the *liquidity trap*, as reflected in a small value of $\partial e_0/\partial p_i$ limits stabilization.

16 Theorem   (i) *If $\partial e/\partial p$ is negative quasi definite for $\partial H/\partial p = D(\partial e/\partial p)$, then in a market system*

$$\bar{\lambda} \geqslant -\frac{p}{p^2}\frac{\partial e}{\partial F_0}\min d_{ii} \geqslant \underline{\lambda}$$

and in an exchange system

$$\bar{\lambda} \geqslant -\frac{\partial e_0/\partial p}{p^2}\,p \min d_{ii} \geqslant \underline{\lambda}.$$

(If $\partial e/\partial p$ is also symmetric, $\bar{\lambda}$ is the dominant root.)
   (ii) *If $\partial e/\partial p$ is Metzler–Mosak, the dominant root ρ is bounded by the equilibrium value of*

$$\frac{-\max d_{ii}\,\partial e_i/\partial F_0}{\max_i p_i} \leqslant \rho \leqslant \frac{-\min d_{ii}\,\partial e_i/\partial F_0}{\min p_i}$$

(*in a market system*) *and*

$$\frac{-\max_i \partial e_0/\partial p_i \, d_{ii}}{\max_i p_i} \leqslant \rho \leqslant \frac{-\min_i \partial e_0/\partial p_i \, d_{ii}}{\min_i p_i}$$

(*in an exchange system*).

In summary, a weak real balance effect or a liquidity trap puts bounds upon the ultimate speed of adjustment.

Proof   Clearly,

$$\max_{x^2=1} x \, \frac{\partial e}{\partial p} \, x \geqslant \frac{p}{|p|} \frac{\partial e}{\partial p} \frac{p}{|p|} = -\frac{p}{|p^2|} \frac{\partial e}{\partial F_0} = -\frac{\partial e_0}{\partial p} \frac{p}{|p^2|}.$$

In the Metzler–Mosak case the dominant root of $\partial H/\partial p$ is related to a strictly positive characteristic vector x. Hence, at equilibrium p,

$$xD \, \frac{\partial e}{\partial p} \, p = \lambda x p$$

or

$$\lambda = \frac{xD \, \partial e/\partial p \, p}{xp} = \frac{-xD}{xp} \frac{\partial e}{\partial F_0}.$$

or

$$\frac{-\max_i d_{ii} \, \partial e_i/\partial F_0}{\max_i p_i} = \frac{\min_{x \geqslant 0, |x|=1} - xD \, \partial e/\partial F_0}{\max_{x \geqslant 0, |x|=1} xp}$$

$$\leqslant \lambda = \rho \leqslant \frac{\max_{x \geq 0, |x|=1} - xD \, \partial e/\partial F_0}{\min_{x \geq 0, |x|=1} xp}$$

$$= \frac{-\min d_{ii} \, \partial e_i/\partial F_0}{\min_i p_i}.$$

The case for an exchange system follows in like fashion.   q.e.d.

Occasionally, stability results are dismissed whenever the relationship from which stability was derived is quantitatively small. For example, if the real balance effect is small, it is said that stabilization will be slow (Patinkin [1956]). Similarly, if there is a liquidity trap, we might conclude that adjustment will be slow. To some extent, this reasoning confuses the proof with the conclusion. ($\partial e_i/\partial F_0$) and $\partial F_0/\partial p_i$ set lower bounds on the ultimate speed of adjustment, but that speed may be greater. Suppose the impediment to stabilization, the large dominant root, appears in the market adjustment matrix $\partial H/\partial p$. Consider the vectors $(\partial e/\partial p)p$ and $p(\partial e/\partial p)$, which are equal, respectively, to minus the response of the demand for goods to money holding and to minus the slope of the demand for money vis-à-vis other commodities. To increase these vectors is to require some increase in $\partial e_i/\partial p_j$, which is stabilizing, by virtue of Theorem 11. However, there may be a decrease in some of the $\partial e_i/\partial p_j$ compensated by increases in others. We can thereby obtain an increase in the speed of adjustment. To do this, simply find the $\partial e_i/\partial p_j$ whose changes have large influence upon λ and decrease these, while increasing others enough to compensate for the changes in the real balance effect and/or liquidity trap. Hence, there appears to be no clear-cut connection between the speed of adjustment and the real balance effect or the liquidity trap. As another example, a small real balance effect or liquidity trap can always be offset by a large response rate, as represented by the elements of D.

PROBLEMS

G. *International Finance*

Suppose there are four markets: bonds, goods, labor, and foreign exchange. In the latter market, the ratio of the home price system to the foreign one is determined, and this influences mainly the goods market by affecting exports and imports. Let the bond market equilibrate automatically, the labor market very slowly. Let the foreign exchange market equilibrate according to the trade balance equal to the difference between exports and imports plus capital movements (into the bond market). Let fiscal policy be used to speed the adjustment of the goods market, monetary policy to increase the rate of adjustment of the foreign exchange.

(i) What impact does the sale of bonds have on the foreign exchange market? (Hint: Fix p_{goods}, p_{labor}, $p_{foreign\ exchange}$, and consider only equilibrium p_{bonds}.)

(ii) In time of a negative trade balance, what is the appropriate monetary policy?

(iii) What is the connection between monetary policy and the goods market?

(iv) What is the government policy vector $\partial h/\partial p$? Show that $\partial h/\partial p$ is decomposable Metzler–Mosak. Are such polices as described above short-run stabilizing? Intermediate-run stabilizing? How would symmetry or magnitude of policies affect the answer?

(v)   How do the answers to questions (i)–(iv) differ in the price–asset and the Keynesian models?

The problem has been analyzed by Mundell [1960, 1962] and Quirk and Zarley [1968].

H. *Structural Stabilization*

Keynes [1936, pp. 250–251] gave four conditions for improving stability.

1.   The expenditure multiplier should be greater than one, but not very much so.
2.   The marginal efficiency of capital should be such that the demand for capital goods does not respond greatly to changes in bond prices.
3.   The wage rate should be rigid with respect to excess demand for labor.
4.   Investment goods should deteriorate rapidly.

Analyze these four policies in both the Keynesian and the price–asset model. Which are stabilizing? Which of them moderate the amplitude of the "cycle?"

7. Stationarity versus Stabilization

Stationarity of prices and quantities implies only lack of change. If it is only stationarity that is desirable, then the state might as well just purchase or sell whatever is necessary to accomplish equilibrium at current prices. Apart from physical difficulties in doing so, it is apparent that such a policy is not sound from a welfare viewpoint. It is the (competitive) equilibrium prices and quantities that are desired.

From Section 7 of Chapter 7, we recall that changes in prices from bankruptcies and a failure in confidence will be more severe, the greater the effect of changes in excess demand upon prices. This leads us back to the comparative statics analysis of Chapter 5, where it was seen that the magnitude of $-(\partial H/\partial p)^{-1}$ is at issue. The rule

$$\frac{d}{d\varepsilon}\left(\frac{\partial H}{\partial p}\right)^{-1} = -\left(\frac{\partial H}{\partial p}\right)^{-1}\frac{d}{d\varepsilon}\left(\frac{\partial H}{\partial p}\right)\left(\frac{\partial H}{\partial p}\right)^{-1}$$

relates changes in $(\partial H/\partial p)^{-1}$ to those in $(\partial H/\partial p)$. For example, if $\partial H/\partial p$ increases and is Metzler–Mosak, $(\partial H/\partial p)^{-1}$ decreases. Before adopting a policy that reduces $(\partial H/\partial p)^{-1}$, it should be recognized that no matter what the price changes, equilibration will be faster ultimately for that situation in which the dominant root of $\partial H/\partial p$ is smallest. Hence, increases in $\partial H/\partial p$ that decrease $(\partial H/\partial p)^{-1}$ will also increase the dominant root of $\partial H/\partial p$ and slow ultimate equilibration. The time path of price may be more nearly stationary, but ultimate stabilization will be impeded.

For quantities, the matrix $C = -(\partial e/\partial p)(\partial H/\partial p)^{-1}$ determines the response to shocks, and

$$
\frac{dB}{d\varepsilon} = -\frac{\partial e}{\partial p}\left(\frac{\partial H}{\partial p}\right)^{-1}\frac{d}{d\varepsilon}\left(\frac{\partial H}{\partial p}\right)\left(\frac{\partial H}{\partial p}\right)^{-1} - \frac{d}{d\varepsilon}\frac{\partial e}{\partial p}\left(\frac{\partial H}{\partial p}\right)^{-1}
$$

$$
= -D^{-1}\frac{d}{d\varepsilon}\left(\frac{\partial H}{\partial p}\right)\left(\frac{\partial H}{\partial p}\right)^{-1} - \frac{d}{d\varepsilon}\frac{\partial e}{\partial p}\left(\frac{\partial H}{\partial p}\right)^{-1},
$$

D^{-1} a positive diagonal, where it is assumed that $(d/d\varepsilon)(\partial e/\partial F) = 0$. Hence, analogous remarks apply to quantities as well as prices. Increasing $\partial H/\partial p$ decreases the amplitude of variation but also increases the time periods in which excess demands are far from equilibrium. To obtain stationarity is to sacrifice stability. Stationarity of excess demands would reduce occasional unemployment, but only at the cost of the economy's ultimately operating farther from the level of consumer efficiency.

References

Alexandroff, A. D.
   [1939] "Almost Everywhere Existence of Second Differentials of Convex Functions and Some Related Properties of Convex Surfaces," (in Russian) *Leningrad State University Annals* [*Uchenye Zapiski*] **37**, *Mathematical Series* **6**, 3–35.

Arrow, K.
   [1951] *Social Choice and Individual Value*. Wiley, New York.
   [1951a] "An Extension of the Basic Theorems of Classical Welfare Economics," in *Proceedings of the Second Berkeley Symposium on Mathematical Statistics and Probability* (J. Neyman, ed.), pp. 507–532. University of California Press, Berkeley, California.
   [1960] "Price Quantity Adjustment in Multiple Markets with Rising Demands," in *Mathematical Methods of the Social Sciences* (K. Arrow, S. Karlin, and P. Suppes, eds.), pp. 3–15. Stanford University Press, Stanford, California.

Arrow, K. J., and Debreu, G.
   [1954] "Existence of an Equilibrium for a Competitive Economy," *Econometrica* **22**, 265–290.

Arrow, K. J., and Hurwicz, L.
   [1958] "On the Stability of the Competitive Equilibrium, I," *Econometrica* **26**, 522–552.
   [1962] "Competitive Stability under Weak Gross Substitutability," *International Economic Review* **3**, 233–255.

Arrow, K. J., and McManus, M.
   [1958] "A Note on Dynamic Stability," *Econometrica* **26**, 448–454.

Arrow, K. J., and Nerlove, M.
   [1958] "A Note on Expectations and Stability," *Econometrica* **26**, 297–305.

Arrow, K. J., Block, H., and Hurwicz, L.
   [1959] "The Stability of the Competitive Equilibrium, II," *Econometrica* **27**, 82–109.

Atsumi, H.
  [1965] "Neoclassical Growth and the Efficient Program of Capital Accumulation,"
          Review of Economic Studies **32**, 127–136.
Aumann, R. J.
  [1965] "Markets with a Continuum of Trade," *Econometrica* **32**, 39–50.
  [1966] "Existence of Competitive Equilibrium in Markets with a Continuum of
          Traders," *Econometrica* **34**, 1–17.
  [1967] "Survey of Cooperative Games without Side Payments," in *Essays in Mathe-
          matical Economics* (M. Shubik, ed.), pp. 3–27. Princeton University Press,
          Princeton, New Jersey.
Barone, E.
  [1908] *Principi di Economia Politica.* Rome.
Bator, F.
  [1958] "The Anatomy of Market Failure," *Quarterly Journal of Economics* **72**, 351–379.
Beals, R., and Koopmans, T. C.
  [1969] "Maximizing Stationary Utility in a Constant Technology," *SIAM J. Appl.
          Math.* **17**, 1001–1015.
Bentham, J.
  [1789] *Principles of Morals and Legislation.*
Bergson, A.
  [1938] "A Reformulation of Certain Aspects of Welfare Economics," *Quarterly
          Journal of Economics* **52**, 310–334.
Bergstrom, T.
  [1971] "Interrelated Consumer Preference and Voluntary Exchange," in *Papers in
          Quantitative Economics* (A. Zarley, ed.), Vol. II, pp. 79–94. University of
          Kansas Press, Lawrence, Kansas.
Bewley, T.
  [1969] "Equilibrium Theory with an Infinite Dimensional Commodity Space,"
          mimeographed, CORE, University of Louvain, Belgium.
Birkhoff, G., and Rota, G.-C.
  [1962] *Ordinary Differential Equations.* Ginn, Boston, Massachusetts.
Buchanan, J.
  [1966] "Joint Supply, Externality, and Optimality," *Economica* (N.S.) **33**, 414–415.
Cass, D., and Yaari, M.
  [1966] "Re-examination of the Pure Consumption Loans Model," *Journal of Political
          Economy* **74**, 353–367.
Cassel, G.
  [1932] *The Theory of Social Economy* (new rev. ed.; J. McCabe, trans.). Barron,
          New York.
Chipman, J.
  [1950] "The Multisector Multiplier," *Econometrica* **18**, 355–374.
  [1966] "A Survey of the Theory of International Trade, III," *Econometrica* **34**,
          18–76.
  [1970] "Economies of Scale and Competitive Equilibrium," *Quarterly Journal of
          Economics* **84**, 347.
Clark, J. B.
  [1890] *The Philosophy of Wealth.*
Clower, R.
  [1965] "The Keynesian Counter Revolution," in *The Theory of Interest Rates* (F. Hahn
          and F. Brechling, eds.), pp. 103–125. St. Martin's Press, New York.

Coase, R. H.

[1960] "The Problem of Social Cost," *Journal of Law and Economics* **3**, 1–44.

Coddington, E. A., and Levinson, N.

[1955] *Theory of Ordinary Differential Equations*. McGraw-Hill, New York.

Coleman, J. S.

[1966] "The Possibility of a Social Welfare Function," *American Economic Review* **56**, 1105–1122.

Davis, O. A., and Whinston, A. B.

[1965] "Welfare Economics and the Theory of Second Best," *Review of Economic Studies* **32**, 1–14.

Debreu, G.

[1952] "A Social Equilibrium Theorem," *Proceedings of the National Academy of Sciences of the U.S.A.* **38**, 886–893.

[1954] "Valuation of Equilibrium and Pareto Optimum," *Proceedings of the National Academy of Sciences of the U.S.A.* **40**, 588–592.

[1959] *Theory of Value*. Wiley, New York.

[1970] "Economies with a Finite Set of Equilibria," *Econometrica* **38**, 387–392.

Debreu, G., and Scarf, H.

[1963] "A Limit Theorem on the Core of an Economy," *International Economic Review* **4**, 235–246.

Doob, J. L.

[1953] *Stochastic Processes*. Wiley, New York.

Dorfman, R., Samuelson, P., and Solow, R.

[1958] *Linear Programming and Economic Analysis*. McGraw-Hill, New York.

Edgeworth, F. Y.

[1881] *Mathematical Psychics*. Kegan Paul, London.

Eilenberg, S., and Montgomery, D.

[1946] "Fixed Point Theorems for Multivalued Transformations," *American Journal of Mathematics* **68**, 214–222.

Enthoven, A., and Arrow, K. J.

[1956] "A Theorem on Expectations and the Stability of Equilibrium," *Econometrica* **24**, 288–293.

Federer, H.

[1969] *Geometric Measure Theory*. Springer, New York.

Foley, D.

[1967] "Resource Allocation and the Public Sector," *Yale Economic Essays* **7**, 45–102.

Foster, E., and Sonnenschein, H.

[1970] "Price Distortion and Economic Welfare," *Econometrica* **38**, 281–297.

Friedman, M.

[1957] *A Theory of the Consumption Function*. Princeton University Press, Princeton, New Jersey.

Furuya, H., and Inada, K.

[1962] "Balanced Growth and Intertemporal Efficiency," *International Economic Review* **3**, 97–107.

Gale, D.

[1955] "On the Laws of Supply and Demand," *Mathematica Scandinavica* **3**, 155–160.

[1956] "The Closed Linear Model of Production," in *Linear Inequalities and Related Systems* (H. Kuhn and A. Tucker, eds.), Annals of Mathematics No. 38, pp. 285–303. Princeton University Press, Princeton, New Jersey.

[1960]   *The Theory of Linear Economic Models.* McGraw-Hill, New York.
[1967]   "On Optimal Development in a Multi-Sector Economy," *Review of Economic Studies* **34**, 1–18.

Gale, D., and Nikaido, H.
[1965]   "The Jacobean Matrix and Global Univalence of Mappings," *Mathematische Annalen* **159**, 81–93.

Gantmacher, F. R.
[1959]   *The Theory of Matrices.* Chelsea, New York.

Georgescu-Roegen, N.
[1951]   "Some Properties of a Generalized Leontief Systems," in *Activity Analysis of Production and Allocation* (T. C. Koopmans, ed.), pp. 165–176. Wiley, New York.

Gorman, W. M.
[1953]   "Community Preference Fields," *Econometrica* **21**, 63–80.
[1964]   "More Scope for Qualitative Economics," *Review of Economic Studies* **31**, 99–123.

Gregoire, H.
[1966]   "The Amorians and Macedonians," in *The Cambridge Medieval History* (J. M. Hussey, ed.), Vol. IV, Part I. Cambridge University Press, London and New York.

Hahn, F. H.
[1958]   "Gross Substitutes and the Dynamic Stability of General Equilibrium," *Econometrica* **26**, 169–170.

Hahn, F. H., and Negishi, T.
[1962]   "A Theorem on Non-Tâtonnement Stability," *Econometrica* **30**, 403–409.

Hansen, T.
[1968]   "On the Approximation of a Competitive Equilibrium," unpublished Ph.D. dissertation, Yale University, New Haven, Connecticut.

Harsanyi, J.
[1955]   "Cardinal Welfare, Individualistic Ethics, and Interpersonal Comparisons of Utility," *Journal of Political Economy* **63**, 309–321.
[1963]   "A Simplified Bargaining Model for the n-Person Cooperative Game," *International Economic Review* **4**, 194–220.

Hicks, J. R.
[1938]   *Value and Capital*, Oxford University Press, London and New York.

Hildenbrand, W.
[1968]   "The Core of an Economy with a Measure Space of Economic Agents," *Review of Economic Studies* **35**, 443–452.

Hildreth, C.
[1953]   "Alternative Conditions for Social Orderings," *Econometrica* **21**, 81–94.

Hocking, J., and Young, G.
[1961]   *Topology.* Addison-Wesley, Reading, Massachusetts.

Hotelling, H.
[1938]   "The General Welfare in Relation to Problems of Taxation and Railway and Utility Rates," *Econometrica* **6**, 242–269.

Hume, D.
[1741]   *Essays, Moral, Political, and Literary*, Vol. I, Part II, Chapter 1. [1963 Ed. (T. H. Green and T. H. Grose, eds.). Oxford University Press, London and New York.]

Hurewicz, W.
[1958]   *Lecture in Ordinary Differential Equations.* M.I.T. Press, Cambridge, Massachusetts.

Hurwicz, L.
[1960] "Optimality and Informational Efficiency in Resource Allocation Processes,"
in *Mathematical Methods in the Social Sciences* (K. Arrow, S. Karlin, and
P. Suppes, eds.), pp. 27–46. Stanford University Press, Stanford, California.

Inada, K.
[1964] "Some Structural Characteristics of Turnpike Theorems," *Review of Economic
Studies* **31**, 43–58.

Joseph, M. F. W.
[1939] "The Excess Burden of Indirect Taxation," *Review of Economic Studies* **6**,
226–231.

Kaldor, N.
[1957] "A Model of Economic Growth," *Economic Journal* **67**, 591–624.

Kant, I.
[1788] *Critique of Practical Reason.*
[1797] *The Metaphysics of Morals.*

Karlin, S.
[1959] *Mathematical Methods and Theory in Games, Programming, and Economics,*
Vol. I. Addison-Wesley, Reading, Massachusetts.

Kelley, J.
[1955] *General Topology.* Van Nostrand-Reinhold, Princeton, New Jersey.

Kelley, J., and Namioka, I.
[1963] *Linear Topological Spaces.* Van Nostrand-Reinhold, Princeton, New Jersey.

Kemeny, J. G., Morgenstern, O., and Thompson, G. L.
[1956] "A Generalization of the von Neumann Model of an Expanding Economy,"
Econometrica **24**, 115–135.

Kemeny, J. G., Snell, J. L., and Knapp, A. W.
[1966] *Denumerable Markov Chains.* Van Nostrand-Reinhold, Princeton, New Jersey.

Kemp, M.
[1962] "The Gain from International Trade," *Economic Journal* **72**, 803–819.

Keynes, J. M.
[1936] *General Theory of Employment, Interest and Money.* Harcourt, New York.
[1937] "The General Theory of Employment," *Quarterly Journal of Economics* **51**,
209–223.

Klein, L. R.
[1947] *The Keynesian Revolution.* New York.

Koopmans, T. C.
[1957] *Three Essays on the State of the Economic Science.* McGraw-Hill, New York.
[1965] *On the Concept of Optimal Growth,* pp. 225–288. Pontifica Academia Scientiarum,
Scripta Varia, Vol. 28. Vatican City, Italy.

Koopmans, T. C., and Bausch, A.
[1959] "Selected Topics in Economics Involving Mathematical Reasoning," *SIAM
Review* **1**, 79–148.

Kreuger, A., and Sonnenschein, H.
[1967] "The Terms of Trade, the Gains from Trade, and Price Divergence,"
International Economic Review **8**, 121–127.

Kuhn, H. W.
[1959] "Factor Endowments and Factor Prices: Mathematical Appendix," *Economica*
(N.S.) **26**, 142–144.

Lancaster, K.
[1962] "The Scope of Qualitative Economics," *Review of Economic Studies* **29**, 99–123.

Lange, O.

[1938] *On the Economic Theory of Socialism.* Minneapolis, Minnesota.

Lerner, A.

[1946] *The Economics of Control.* Macmillan, New York.

Lipsey, R.

[1960] "The Relation between Unemployment and the Rate of Change of Money Wages: A Further Analysis," *Economica* (N.S.) **27**, 1–31.

Lipsey, R. G., and Lancaster, K.

[1956] "The General Theory of the Second Best," *Review of Economic Studies* **24**, 11–32.

Little, I. M. D.

[1951] "Direct versus Indirect Taxes," *Economic Journal* **61**, 511–584.

Loomis, L. H.

[1948] "On a Theorem of von Neumann," *Proceedings of the National Academy of Science of the U.S.A.* **36**, 213–215.

McFadden, D.

[1967] "The Evaluation of Development Programs," *Review of Economic Studies* **34**, 25–50.

McKenzie, L.

[1955] "Equality of Factor Price in World Trade," *Econometrica* **23**, 239–257.

[1957] "Demand Theory without a Utility Index," *Review of Economic Studies* **24**, 185–189.

[1959] "On the Existence of General Equilibrium for a Competitive Market," *Econometrica* **27**, 54–71.

[1960] "Matrices with Dominant Diagonals and Economic Theory," in *Mathematical Methods in the Social Sciences* (K. Arrow, S. Karlin, and P. Suppes, eds.), pp. 47–62. Stanford University Press, Stanford, California.

[1960] "Stability of Equilibrium and the Value of Positive Excess Demand," *Econometrica* **28**, 606–617.

[1963] "Turnpike Theorems for a Generalized Leontief Model," *Econometrica* **31**, 165–180.

[1963a] "The Dorfman–Samuelson–Solow Turnpike Theorem," *International Economic Review* **4**, 29–43.

[1968] "Accumulation Programs of Maximum Utility and the von Neumann Facet," in *Value, Capital and Growth*; *Essays in Honor of Sir John Hicks* (J. N. Wolfe, ed.), pp. 353–384. Edinburgh University Press, Edinburgh.

Malinvaud, E.

[1953] "Capital Accumulation and Efficient Allocation of Resources," *Econometrica* **21**, 233–265; "Efficient Capital Accumulation: A Corrigendum," *Econometrica* **30** (1962), 570–573.

Mantel, R.

[1968] "Toward a Constructive Proof of the Existence of Equilibrium in a Competitive Economy," *Yale Economic Essays* **8**, 152–196.

Marshak, J.

[1951] *Income Employment and the Price Level.* Augustin M. Kelly, New York.

Marshall, A.

[1890] *Principles of Economics*, 8th ed. Macmillan, New York.

[1923] *Money Credit and Commerce*, London.

Metzler, L.

[1941] "The Nature and Stability of Inventory Cycles," *Review of Economic Statistics* **25**, 49–57.

[1945] "The Stability of Multiple Markets: The Hicks Conditions," *Econometrica* **13**, 277–292.

[1950] "A Mulitple-Region Theory of Income and Trade," *Econometrica* **18**, 329–354.

Modigliani, F., and Brumberg, R.

[1954] "Utility Analysis and the Consumption Function," in *Post-Keynesian Economics* (K. Kurihara, ed.), pp. 388–436.

Moore, J.

[1968] "A Note on Point-Set Mappings," in *Papers in Quantitative Economics I*, (J. Quirk and A. Zarley, eds.), pp. 129–142. University of Kansas Press, Lawrence, Kansas.

Morishima, M.

[1961] "Proof of a Turnpike Theorem: The 'No Joint Production Case'," *Review of Economic Studies* **28**, 89–97.

[1964] *Equilibrium Stability and Growth.* Oxford University Press, London and New York.

Mosak, J.

[1944] *General Equilibrium Theory in International Trade.* The Principia Press, Bloomington, Indiana.

Mundell, R. A.

[1960] "The Monetary Dynamics of International Adjustment under Fixed and Flexible Exchange Rates," *Quarterly Journal of Economics* **74**, 277–257.

[1962] "The Appropriate Use of Monetary and Fiscal Policy for Internal and External Stability," *IMF Staff Papers* **9**, 70–79.

[1968] *International Economics.* Macmillan, New York.

Muth, J.

[1961] "Rational Expectations and the Theory of Price Movements," *Econometrica* **30**, 315–335.

Negishi, T.

[1958] "A Note on the Stability of an Economy Where All Goods Are Gross Substitutes," *Econometrica* **26**, 445–447.

[1960] "Welfare Economics and the Existence of an Equilibrium for a Competitive Economy," *Metroeconomica* **12**, 92–97.

[1961] "Monopolistic Competition and General Equilibrium," *Review of Economic Studies* **3**, 196–202.

Nikaido, H.

[1956] "On the Classical Multilateral Exchange Problem," *Metroeconomica* **8**, 135–146.

[1957] "A Supplementary Note," *Metroeconomica* **9**, 209–210.

[1964] "Persistence of Continual Growth near the Von Neumann Ray: A Strong Version of the Radner Turnpike Theorem," *Econometrica* **32**, 151–162.

Olech, C.

[1963] "On the Global Stability of an Autonomous System on the Plane," in *Contributions to Differential Equations* **1**, 289–400.

Patinkin, D.

[1956] *Money, Interest, and Prices.* Harper, New York.

Pearce, I.

[1967] "More about Factor Price Equalization," "Rejoinder to Professor McKenzie," and "Rejoinder to Professor Samuelson's Summary," *International Economic Review* **8**, 255–270; 296–306.

Peleg, B., and Yaari, M.
  [1970] "Markets with Countably Many Commodities," *International Economic Review* **11**, 369–377.
Phelps, E.
  [1961] "The Golden Rule of Accumulation: A Fable for Growthmen," *American Economic Review* **51**, 638–343.
  [1965] "Second Essay on the Golden Rule of Accumulation," *American Economic Review* **55**, 793–814.
Phillips, A. S.
  [1958] "The Relation between Unemployment and the Rate of Money Wages in the United Kingdom, 1861–1957," *Economica* (N.S.) **25**, 283–299.
Pigou, E. C.
  [1920] *The Economics of Welfare.* Macmillan, New York.
Quirk, J., and Ruppert, R.
  [1965] "Qualitative Economics and the Stability of Equilibrium," *Review of Economic Studies* **32**, 311–326.
Quirk, J., and Zarley, A.
  [1968] "Policies to Attain External and Internal Balance: A Reappraisal," in *Papers in Quantitative Economics I*, pp. 73–100. University of Kansas Press, Lawrence, Kansas.
Rader, T.
  [1964] "Edgeworth Exchange and General Economic Equilibrium," unpublished dissertation, Yale University, New Haven, Connecticut.
  [1965] "On Intertemporal Efficiency," *Metroeconomica* **17**, 152–170.
  [1968] "Pairwise Optimality and Non-Competitive Behavior," in *Papers in Quantitative Economics I* (J. Quirk and A. Zarley, eds.), pp. 101–128. University of Kansas Press, Lawrence, Kansas.
  [1968a] "International Trade and Development in a Small Country, II," in *Papers in Quantitative Economics I* (J. Quirk and A. Zarley, eds.), pp. 399–431. University of Kansas Press, Lawrence, Kanasas.
  [1971] "International Trade and Development in a Small Country, II," in *Papers in Quantitative Economics II* (A. Zarley, ed.), pp. 177–209. University of Kansas Press, Lawrence, Kansas.
Radner, R.
  [1961] "Paths of Economic Growth that Are Optimal Only with Regard to Final States: A Turnpike Theorem," *Review of Economic Studies* **28**, 98–104.
Rado, T., and Reichelderfer, P. V.
  [1955] *Continuous Transformations in Analysis.* Springer-Verlag, Berlin.
Ramsey, F. P.
  [1928] "A Mathematical Theory of Savings," *Economic Journal* **38**, 543–559.
Ricardo, D.
  [1817] *The Principles of Political Economy and Taxation.*
Riesz, F. and Sz-Nagy, B.
  [1955] *Functional Analysis.* Ungar, New York.
Robinson, J.
  [1956] *The Accumulation of Capital.* Irwin, Homewood, Illinois.
Samuelson, P.
  [1938] "The Gain from International Trade," *Canadian Journal of Economics and Political Science* **5**, 195–205. Reprinted in *Readings in the Theory of Inter-*

national Trade (H. Ellis and L. Metzler, eds.), pp. 239–252. Allen & Irwin, London, 1950.

[1947] *Foundations of Economic Analysis.* Harvard University Press, Cambridge, Massachusetts.

[1949] "International Factor Price Equalization Once Again," *Economic Journal* **59**, 181–197.

[1958] "An Exact Consumption Loan Model of Interest with or without the Contrivance of Money," *Journal of Political Economy* **66**, 467–482.

[1962] "The Gains from International Trade Once Again," *Economic Journal* **72**, 820–829.

[1965] "A Catenary Turnpike Theorem," *American Economic Review* **55**, 486–495.

[1967] "A Turnpike Refutation of the Golden Rule in a Welfare-Maximizing Many-Year Plan," in *Essays on the Theory of Optimal Economic Growth* (K. Shell, ed.) pp. 269–280. MIT Press, Cambridge, Massachusetts.

Sard, A.
[1958] "Images of Critical Sets," *Annals of Mathematics* **68**, 158–174.

Scarf, H.
[1960] "Some Examples of Global Instability of the Competitive Equilibrium," *International Economic Review* **1**, 157–172.

[1962] "An Analysis of Markets with a Large Number of Participants," in *Recent Advances in Game Theory* (mimeograph), Princeton University Conference, Princeton, New Jersey.

[1967] "The Core of an *N*-Person Game," *Econometrica* **35**, 50–70.

Schumpeter, J.
[1934] *Theory of Economic Development.* Harvard University Press, Cambridge, Massachusetts.

Schwartz, J. T.
[1961] *Lectures on the Mathematical Method in Analytical Economics.* Gordon & Breach, New York.

Scitovsky, T.
[1942] "A Reconsideration of the Theory of Tariffs," *Review of Economic Studies* **9**, 89–100.

Shapley, L.
[1965] "Cores of Convex Games," RAND Corporation Memorandum. RM-4571-PR, Santa Monica, California.

Shapley, L., and Shubik, M.
[1967] "Ownership and the Production Function," *Quarterly Journal of Economics* **81**, 88–111.

Shubik, M.
[1959] "Edgeworth Market Games," in *Contributions to the Theory of Games* (A. W. Tucker and A. D. Lace, eds.), Vol. IV, pp. 267–278. Princeton University Press, Princeton, New Jersey.

Solow, R.
[1956] "A Contribution to the Theory of Economic Growth," *Quarterly Journal of Economics* **32**, 65–94.

Starr, R. M.
[1969] "Quasi-Equilibria in Markets with Non-Convex Preferences," *Econometrica* **37**, 25–38

Stolper, W. and Samuelson, P.
[1941] "Protection and Real Wages," *Review of Economic Studies* **9**, 58–73.

Tobin, J.
  [1955] "A Dynamic Aggregative Model," *Journal of Political Economy* **63**, 103–115.
Uzawa, H.
  [1960] "Preference and Rational Choice in the Theory of Consumption," in *Mathematical Methods in the Social Sciences* (K. Arrow, S. Karlin, and P. Suppes, eds.), pp. 129–148. Stanford University Press, Stanford, California.
  [1963] "On the Stability of Edgeworth's Barter Process," *International Economic Review* **3**, 218–232.
  [1964] "Optimal Growth in a Two-Sector Model of Capital Accumulation," *Review of Economic Studies* **31**, 1–24.
Vind, K.
  [1964] "Edgeworth Allocations in an Exchange Economy with Many Traders," *International Economic Review* **5**, 165–177.
  [1965] "A Theorem on the Core of an Economy," *Review of Economic Studies* **32**, 47–48.
von Neumann, J.
  [1937] "Über ein Ökonomisches Gleichungs-Systeme und eine Verallgemeinerung der Browershen Fixpunktsatzes," in *Ergebnisse eines Mathematisches Kolloquiums* (K. Menger, ed.), 8, pp. 73–83. Translated as "A Model of General Economics Equilibrium," *Review of Economic Studies* **13**, 1–9.
von Neumann, J., and Morgenstern, O.
  [1944] *Theory of Games and Economic Behavior*. Princeton University Press, Princeton, New Jersey.
von Weizsäcker, C. C.
  [1965] "Existence of Optimal Programs of Accumulation for an Infinite Time Horizon," *Review of Economic Studies* **32**, 85–104.
Wald, A.
  [1936] "Über einige Gleichungssysteme der mathematischen Ökonomie," *Zeitschrift für Nationalökonomie* **7**, 637–670. Translated and published in *Econometrica* **19**, 368–403 (1951) as "On Some Equations in Mathematical Economics."
Walras, L.
  [1877] *Éléments d'économie politique pure*, 1st ed. (2nd ed., 1889; 3rd ed., 1896; 4th ed., 1900; definitive ed., 1926).
Winter, S.
  [1967] "The Norm of a Closed Technology and the Straight 'Down the Turnpike' Theorem," *Review of Economic Studies* **34**, 67–84.

Author Index

Numbers in italics refer to the pages on which the complete references are listed.

A

Alexandroff, 189, *343*
Arrow, K. J., 61, 74, 95, 100, 102, 155, 156, 163, 179, 209, 235, 249, 286, 289, 318, *343, 345*
Atsumi, H., 36, *344*
Aumann, R. J., 92, 108, 132, *344*

B

Barone, E., 106, *344*
Bator, F., 104, *344*
Bausch, A., 100, *347*
Beals, R., 268, *344*
Bentham, J., 67, *344*
Bergson, A., 64, 65, *344*
Bergstrom, T., 107, *344*
Bewley, T., 152, *344*
Birkhoff, G., 285, 287, 316, *344*
Block, H., 286, *343*

B

Brumberg, R., 292, 299, 325, *349*
Buchanan, J., 73, *344*

C

Cass, D., 89, 107, *344*
Cassel, G., 294, *344*
Chipman, J., 106, 225, 230, 232, 325, *344*
Clark, J. B., 108, *344*
Clower, R., 293, 299, *344*
Coase, R. H., 73, *345*
Coddington, E. A., 204, 305, 316, 318, 328, *345*
Coleman, J. S., 60, *345*

D

Davis, O. A., 66, 102, *345*
Debreu, G., 95, 100, 102, 108, 109, 153, 155, 156, 163, 172, 179, 182, 183, *345*

353

Subject Index

A

Absolutely continuous, 182
Absolutely equitable, 68, 109
Acyclic, 160
Additive utility, 64
Additivity theorem, 46
Adjustment
  initial speed of, 325
  untimate rate of, 328
Almost equilibria, 297, 319
Appropriability, 104
Assets, nontrivial, 303
Asset–price adjustment system, 298–310
Attainable, 36, 101
Axiom of choice, 153

B

Balanced game, 112, 119
Balanced growth path, 14, 22, 33
Banking system, 301
Base, Hamel, 44, 153

B (cont.)

Benevolent, 84
Bergson welfare theory, 65
Blocking, 71, 134
Bolzano–Weierstrass theorem, 9

C

Capital good, universal, 18
Catenary, 20
Characteristic root, 309
Characteristic vector, 309
Cluster point, 8
Coalition, 132
Coalitions, majority, 147
Compact set, 8, 9, 22
Comparative statics, 203, 204, 244, 245
Compensated demand, 186
Compensated income, 186
Compensation, 120
Competitive
  ϵ-choice, 158
  equilibria, existence, 151–154, 162–171,
    179